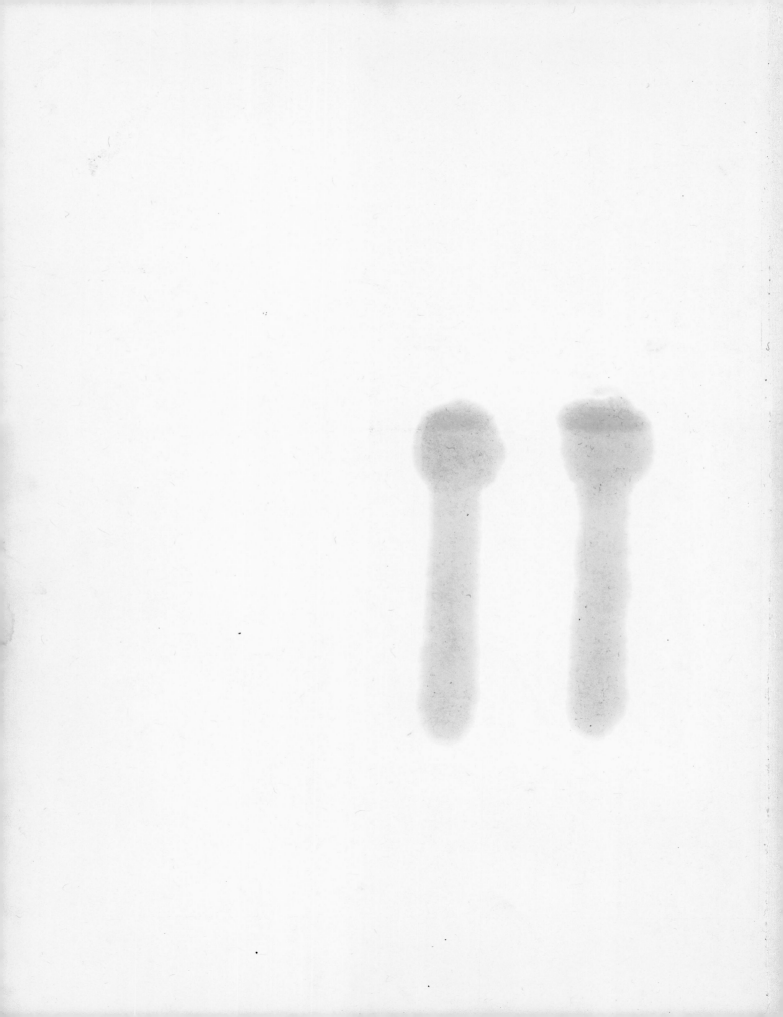

Skippy
and
Percy Crosby

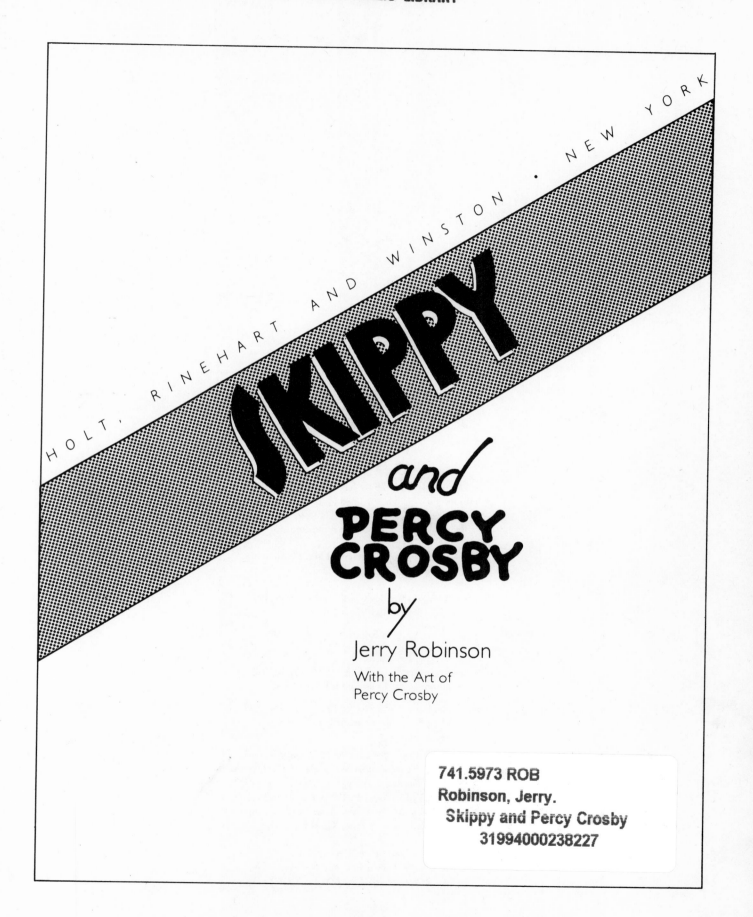

HOLT, RINEHART AND WINSTON · NEW YORK

SKIPPY

and

PERCY CROSBY

by

Jerry Robinson

With the Art of
Percy Crosby

For Gro

———————————————

Published simultaneously in Canada by Holt, Rinehart and
Winston of Canada, Limited.

Library of Congress Catalog Card Number: 78-53777
ISBN: 0-03-018491-6

First Edition

Designer: Robert Reed
Printed in the United States of America
2 4 6 8 10 9 7 5 3 1

Contents

My first acknowledgment must be for the encouragement and assistance of a talented and courageous woman, Joan Crosby Tibbetts. She made available to me the collection of her father's art, correspondence, and unpublished manuscripts that came into her possession as administrator of the Percy Crosby estate. Any first-person quotations used in this book, unless otherwise noted, are from these manuscripts. In our interviews and correspondence, she graciously contributed other data and personal reminiscences of her father from the tragically few years of her childhood when she knew him. Her dedication to her father and the preservation of his art have been an inspiration.

I am grateful to Gladys Petterson and Mrs. Dale Crosby, Percy Crosby's sister and former wife, respectively, for their hospitality, the time they made available for interviews, and the precious memorabilia they provided.

Particular appreciation is due to the late Woody Gelman, David Kaler, and Joseph Parente for the generous loans of original Crosby material from their extensive collections of cartoon art, particularly the color reproductions in this book.

This project met with unanimous enthusiasm from Percy Crosby's friends and associates. They were unfailingly patient during many, often lengthy interviews, searching for remote reminiscences, background information, and leads for further research: Marc Connelly, Frank Fogarty, Leona Hoff, Dick Hyman, Miriam Storm Long, S. J. Perelman, Richard Reddy, and Jack Shuttleworth. Many others, Crosby's professional contemporaries, were equally enthusiastic and generous in contributing to a book about an artist they consider to be one of the finest and most influential the cartoon medium has produced: Ernie Bushmiller, Milton Caniff, Bill Kavanagh, Bob Dunn, Bill Gallo, Herblock, Clark Kinnaird, Edward Kuekes, Jack Markow, the late McGowan Miller, Walt Partymiller, the late Joseph Musial, the late Russell Patterson, and George Wolfe.

I am especially indebted to Arthur Gwirztman for his encouragement and expert advice. He was unstinting with his time and professional knowledge, and his many contributions, particularly to the understanding of Percy Crosby's medical and psychological history, were invaluable.

I am grateful, too, for the cooperation given by numerous institutions and individuals: Stuart Klunis and Emily Smith of the Arts Students League; Jack Tippit and the Cartoon Museum of Art; Reginald Townsend and Richard Harrison of the Coffee House Club; Theresa Parker and the Jacques Seligmann Gallery; Sylvan Byck and Frank Chillino of King Features Syndicate; Lewis Rachow and Susan Neher of the Players Club; Clifford Young of the Salmagundi Club; Dan Poole of the *Washington Star*; Lillian Owens and Diana Franklin of Time-Life, Inc.; and Robert Lesser and Charles Roberts. My appreciation to Jackie Coogan and Jackie Cooper for background information on the Skippy movie.

My thanks, also, to Steve Stedd and Anthony Tolin for their able research, and to Marjorie Wheaton, who contributed more than just her expert typing.

Several talents deserve credit for the handsome production of this volume. Robert Reed, art director of Holt, created the basic design; George DiSabato was responsible for the layout; Camillo LoGiudice for production management; and Jill Gutelle for the production editing. My thanks to all.

Finally, I wish to express some measure of my appreciation to two whose efforts were so essential to the book: Frances Collin, my literary agent, for her consistent support and direction; and Donald Hutter, my editor at Holt, Rinehart and Winston, who not only shared my enthusiasm for and vision of the Crosby book, but also demonstrated how a creative editor can assist a writer in bringing his vision into focus and form.

Percy Crosby caught lightning in a bottle and learned how to draw with it. His line radiated raw energy, the sheer pleasure of sketching figures in flight. His pen tore across a page, an expanding wad of line, swallowing little boys inside it: funny hats, droopy socks, muddy shoes, passionate propagandists for the glory of childhood. In them reposited the dream: How good it was, this America, this nation of small towns, roguish boys, seldom-seen parents, and virtually no girls whatever. (One of the few females Crosby's art tolerated was "Mother," a maturing Gibson Girl.)

As Jerry Robinson describes Crosby's career, a second dream comes to mind. The twenties, the Jazz Age, its highs and its horrors; Crosby behaving like Scott and Zelda Fitzgerald rolled into one.

The small-town roots, the exploding career, fame, celebrities, booze, ocean voyages, European tours, dandyism, a mansion in Virginia, horses, servants, elegance—all earned out of sketching mythology. And part two: patriotism turning into crackpotism, booze turning into alcoholism, domesticity into desertion, genius into madness, freedom into confinement. The American Dream ending in a nuthouse. If Crosby's life was not a twentieth-century American metaphor, it was not for lack of trying.

Rereading *Skippy* forty years later is a disturbing experience. The effortless brilliance of Crosby's line stands undiminished. The problem is Skippy himself; one of the most successful characters in the history of comics, but who in hell is he?

Skippy is not a kid; he is a little man living inside a kid. Sometimes the little man is philosophical, sometimes he is political, sometimes he is prayerful, sometimes violent.

The little man disguised as Skippy lives in Small Town, U.S.A., which is not really a small town, but a disguised small town. In truth, it is a desert; more empty than the desert Herriman designed for Krazy Kat. The decor of Skippy's desert is flat, sketchy, barely present: sparse fences, single trees, empty houses. Skippy's environment is all horizon. Indoors, too, he seems to be surrounded by horizon. Parents appear as distant as houses.

In a 1938 cartoon Skippy approaches his friend Sooky, lounging barefoot against the ever-present fence. Next to Sooky is a stick drawing of a man in top hat and monocle. "Who drew the picture?" asks Skippy. "I did," says Sooky. "I don't like to be alone."

Situation and punch line might have come directly out of the yet-to-be-born life of Charlie Brown. But had this been Schulz's cartoon, not Crosby's, we would have been taken with Sooky. In Crosby, we are taken with Sooky's oversized cap and bare legs; we are dazzled by graphics, not life. We relate to a punch line.

Crosby, brilliant though he was, lacked resonance. He distanced himself from his characters, drew a space that separated himself from his art; often where there should be echoes there are merely hollows. Far more lonely than the world of Charlie Brown, which we are accustomed to perceive as lonely.

Skippy often appears to be written in code. A rough and tough kid who, as Robinson points out, dresses almost foppishly: fancy cap, high collar, string tie, and jacket. Only his collapsed socks hinted at the rowdy in him. Literate, he spends hours in libraries, reads Kant, and yet will use words like "disgustful" or sentences like "I ain't gettin' the support like I oughta."

No character consistency, no hard and fast rules can be applied to Skippy because half the time he existed as a kid-suit Crosby put on and took off. When Crosby climbed into the suit we found a philosopher, a loner, a dreamer, sometimes an intellectual. When the kid-Skippy occupied the suit we found an assertive, self-confident, good-hearted American boy-boy talking urchin English to his friends.

What friends? Skippy associated with an assortment of oversized pants and sweaters and hats and caps and bonnets with unidentifiable dirty faces poking out of them. Slum kids in hand-me-downs playing with Skippy, the middle-class loner. There are no second bananas in Skippy's life, no characters outside the lead one; no pals with the traits found in other comic-strip gangs of the day: the *Reglar Fellers* gang, the *Just Kids* gang, Perry Winkle's Rinkeydinks gang.

Yet *Skippy* enjoyed a popularity far beyond these other strips—and while only archivists, die-hard fans, and nostalgia buffs remember the previously mentioned cartoons, an entire generation recalls *Skippy*.

Obviously Crosby struck a nerve. Maybe it was the loneliness behind the busyness, the unhappiness that passed for fun and games. A wistful longing in Skippy that reflected a nation's wistfulness.

Our yearning to reclaim a nonexistent past: a society more homey, more congenial, free of cutthroat values and offensive change. The change of big cities, boom and bust, strikes, poverty, depersonalization, noise. Free of growing up and growing old.

In Crosby's pre-*Skippy* political cartoons Uncle Sam appears as a victim: to be locked in a pillory or stabbed in the back. Crosby's self-pity reflected our own.

As a people, we have always been ambivalent about change; desperately demanding it, desperately resisting it; looking back on the good old rural days, while eating up books and films on the computerized future.

Skippy's surface energy and inner gloom connect well to our own national ambivalence, reason enough for its hold on us. Crowded with incident, haunted with solitude: solid stuff for a generation stumbling out of the Roaring Twenties through the Depression thirties into the uncertainty of World War II.

Skippy was a kid for grown-ups to read because it was the Crosby in Skippy with whom grown-ups identified—and it was the Skippy in Skippy whom grown-ups still longed to be.

Skippy
and
Percy Crosby

1 / "THE CHILD OF MY SOUL"

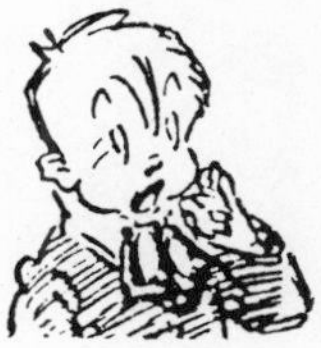

He made an indelible impression on first encounter. An amorphous checked hat perched at a rakish angle, an odd touch of faded elegance in his dress—white Eton collar with a huge dotted bow tie, an oversized jacket, short pants, eternally drooping socks. An image of indefinable charm. He was often seen sauntering, or more precisely swaggering, along the street, hands thrust in pockets or swishing a stick, lolling on a doorstep engaged in profound discourse, or just sitting on a curb, chin in hand, deep in reverie. He was Skippy. A pen-and-ink creation. A character who lived only a few moments every day when you picked up the newspaper and turned to the comic pages. A two-dimensional graphic image on cheap pulp paper, quickly etched in a form of visual shorthand. But he was much more. For those of us who knew him for any part of his comic-strip existence from 1925 to 1945, he was part of our own reality.

Nothing like *Skippy* had been seen before in the comic strips. It was not just *Skippy*'s expert draftsmanship or remarkable flair, although that artistry earned its creator a reputation as "the cartoonist's cartoonist." And *Skippy* certainly was not the first kid strip. Children and their antics had been one of the most enduring themes in the comics since the first strip, Richard Outcault's *Down in Hogan's Alley* (later popularly known as *The Yellow Kid*), appeared in 1895. The brilliance of *Skippy* was that here was fantasy with a realistic base, the first kid cartoon with a definable and complex personality grounded in daily life. *Skippy* was the first strip to attempt to fathom the wonder of a boy. Charles Dana Gibson described its hero as "one of the truest and most thoroughly sympathetic characters that I have ever known. He deserves to be placed with Kim, Huck Finn, and Penrod in the gallery of real boys." As Gibson recognized, Skippy was more than just a comic-strip character, he was a contribution to American literature, and it was that literary quality in his characterization and dialogue that was new to the art form. That, as well as a degree of sophistication not found in his predecessors. Skippy was at once maturely philosophic and boyishly mischievous. One time in class, after hitting the kid at the desk ahead with a slingshot, he rationalized, "School ain't so hard if ya balance it with a little pleasure now an' then." Skippy could be cocky, exuberant, bored, inquisitive—sometimes endearing, other times exasperating. In short, he was one of us, and we loved him for it. We recognized our own search for identity in Skippy's growing self-awareness. Looking in the mirror one day, Skippy cried, "Gee, who'd thought it! Hey, Ma! . . . Why didn't ya tell me I had blue eyes?"

Comic-strip dogma had dictated that characters must act in a narrowly drawn idiosyncratic manner. To preserve a strip's identity, variations of the same themes were endlessly replayed, and the characters remained stereotyped. Skippy, however, was unpredictable—he was alternately cautious and impulsive, outgoing and introspective, optimistic and pessimistic, belligerent and pacific. Yet all these traits somehow fitted into the mosaic of his personality. If his actions seemed contradictory,

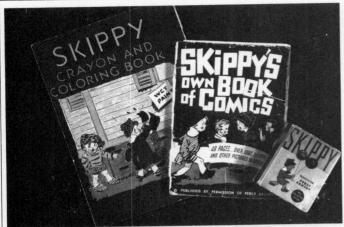

SKIPPY CRAYON AND COLORING BOOK
WET PAINT
SKIPPY'S OWN BOOK of COMICS
48 PAGES... OVER 1000 SKIPPY AND OTHER PICTURES
PUBLISHED BY PERMISSION OF PERCY CROSBY
SKIPPY
PERMISSION PERCY CROSBY
OUR BELOVED SKIPPY in JIG-SAW
Skippy
A CARD GAME
SKIPPY
A few of the many Skippy products

they never seemed false. And that was perhaps the key to Skippy's wide appeal: its creator understood boys. As Isaac Anderson observed in *The New York Times*: "He knows all their moods, their thoughts, their desires and ambitions, and he knows their reactions to the sometimes unreasonable demands of their elders. And knowing all these things, he draws boys as they are."

Skippy had a greater influence on later cartoonists than any other comic strip of its genre. It was the prototype for Hank Ketchum's *Dennis the Menace*, as well as the precursor of today's sophisticated kid strips as exemplified by Charles Schulz's modern-day classic, *Peanuts*. In fact, *Skippy* and *Peanuts* have a great deal in common. Much of the humor of both derives from disarmingly frank youngsters giving voice to mature philosophical and psychological observations. And in terms of commercial success, *Skippy* was the *Peanuts* of its day. It appeared in hundreds of papers, both here and abroad, and its readers numbered in the millions. In those pre-TV days, Skippy had enormous commercial appeal. There were Skippy dolls, toys, food, endorsements, novels, comic books, and Big Little Books. Five hundred thousand kids who bought Phillips' toothpaste received a premium Skippy comic book, the first four-color reprint of any comic strip. Skippy was also adapted to film, radio, and song.

Ev'ry little girl and boy's in love with Skippy,
Who's the one they're always dreaming of? It's Skippy!
You can always see him in the daily papers, you'll love
his capers,
You'll love him too: Isn't he the cutest little devil?
Skippy!
In his little heart he's on the level, Skippy!
When he gets in trouble we feel badly,
We would take his place and help him gladly,
Do you wonder why we love you madly, Skippy? Skippy?*

America fell in love with Skippy. Generations of kids and their dogs became his namesakes. He was just as avidly read by adults as by children, and Skippyisms were quoted by pundits. His creator became an international celebrity. But as meteoric as was *Skippy*'s rise, its life, in

*Words by Benny Davis; music by Con Conrad.

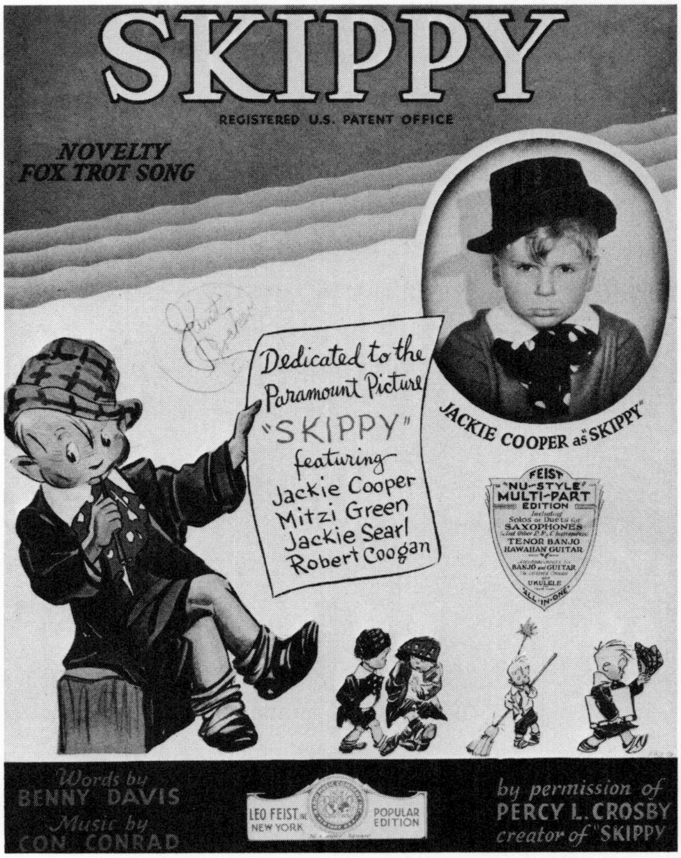
SKIPPY
REGISTERED U.S. PATENT OFFICE
NOVELTY
FOX TROT SONG
Dedicated to the Paramount Picture "SKIPPY" featuring Jackie Cooper Mitzi Green Jackie Searl Robert Coogan
JACKIE COOPER as SKIPPY
FEIST "NU-STYLE" MULTI-PART EDITION
Words by BENNY DAVIS
Music by CON CONRAD
LEO FEIST INC NEW YORK
POPULAR EDITION
by permission of PERCY L. CROSBY creator of "SKIPPY"

comparison with other strip successes, was short. *The Katzenjammer Kids* has appeared since 1897, *Mutt and Jeff* since 1907, and *Bringing Up Father* since 1913. Many others have run for over forty and fifty years. But after only twenty years, *Skippy*'s newspaper life ended abruptly. Skippy simply dropped out of the public consciousness—just as his creator dropped out of public life. Their beings seem to have been intertwined—as if one couldn't exist without the other.

If any comic-strip character can be said to have evolved from its author's person and experience, it is Skippy. Throughout his life, Percy Crosby remained to an exceptional degree the simple boy of his youth. Yet he was a complex man with a wide-ranging intellect who wrote extensively and with subtle distinctions on philosophy, politics, and art. Crosby's career was a continuous explosion of talent that sent shock waves in all directions. It was stormy and intense. He had many friends, romances, and travels. But his career was also punctuated by periods of loneliness, deep depression, and melancholia. His work, however, remained eternally optimistic, with only occasional hints of the turmoil that raged within the man.

Crosby was born in Brooklyn, New York, in 1891,* of parents of very modest means. As a boy he loved to ride the rounds of the neighborhood on the horse-drawn milk wagon. He adored animals and longed to live in the country where he could own his own horse. Eventually he acquired a palatial home far beyond his boyhood dreams—an estate of over two hundred acres of beautiful rolling Virginia hills—which he loved to roam on his favorite horse, Eagle. Then, almost overnight, all was gone, and for the last sixteen years of his life he was never again to step foot on a blade of grass.

Alcoholism caused much of his misery, but the final tragedy of his life was confinement to a mental institution. For those last years, he battled unceasingly and heroically for his freedom, as throughout his career he had fought over issues of censorship and personal liberty. His adversaries had included the President of the United States, the Internal Revenue Service, the FBI, the press, his own syndicate, and one of the most powerful publishers in the country. In the end, not only did he lose his own freedom, but in final ignominy he had to submit all his writings, even personal letters, to censorship.

Crosby was an artist of immense range: adept in oils and portraiture; an expert in watercolor, lithography, and drypoint; and a virtuoso in pen and ink. His exhibitions were acclaimed in the United States, London, Paris, and Rome, but he was finally reduced to sketching on scraps of paper, and even, in desperation, on napkins and the backs of the lined, yellow pages of his manuscripts.

Crosby was also a writer of inordinate talent. He published fourteen books—novels, philosophy, poetry, politics, as well as literary and art criticism. Yet he left far more unread manuscripts (written, out of necessity, in the dim quiet of the night in the mess hall of the mental institution) than he had published. While Crosby's audience once numbered in the millions, he ended his life

*This is the birth year cited in all published materials dealing with Percy Crosby and is the year he himself reported. According to surviving members of his family, however, his mother maintained he was born in 1890. Crosby's birth was not officially recorded in any New York archives; he may have been born at home, usually the reason for lack of public record at that time.

knowing that his epic work, an ambitious series on the arts on which he labored for more than a decade, would probably never have even one reader. So he invented one to provide the intellectual stimulation that was denied him in his isolation, a companion and critic whom he included in the work itself. The reader was Crosby, and the Socratic-like dialogue of ego and alter ego reflected the conflict of opposing forces within the author.

The creator of some of the most engaging child characters in literature was separated from four of his own children when they were mere youngsters, never to see or hear from them over the last twenty-five years of his life. The pen-and-ink Skippy became the child of Crosby's soul, more real to him than his own son, named Skippy. It was perhaps the most tragic of the many paradoxes of Percy Crosby's tortured career.

2 / THE LONE KNIGHT

Skippy's alter ego, nine-year-old Percy Crosby, was living in Richmond Hill, Long Island,* in the year 1900. Percy was captain of the Liberty Boys, many of whose epic battles were reenacted in *Skippy* a quarter of a century later. Its troops consisted of John Braham, Ray Moore, Willie Mormon, and other neighborhood friends, and (on occasion, when girls were tolerated in serious warfare) Elsie Marks, Percy's secret love, or his sister Ethel. One surviving photograph, probably taken with the ubiquitous Kodak Brownie camera, shows them in what must have been a victory parade. Percy is seen in a cap and a striped turtleneck, armed with sabre and rifle, leading his legion of warriors: four armed riflemen, two drummer boys in ornate caps performing a drum roll, and a petite Elsie as flag bearer in a polka-dot dress, looking quite pleased with the honor. Percy is of stern demeanor, befitting his station.

The Liberty Boys were not without moral blemish. A younger sister, Gladys, recalls that the boys, when tenting out in the backyard, would occasionally snitch rolls and milk left on the neighbor's doorstep—either a lapse of discipline, or a legitimate requisition of army supplies. Percy was also known to venture forth on somewhat less-than-heroic missions. His mother would see him on such occasions with a long stick with a nail in the end. She never knew its purpose until she saw the device in a *Skippy*

*Although the charter of 1898 had recently established the five boroughs of New York—including Queens, with Richmond Hill situated within it—the community was still regarded and referred to as part of Long Island (see Crosby's business card, p. 9).

cartoon. Skippy used it to hook oranges at the corner grocery.

Percy's favorite role, however, was as the Lone Knight. Knighthood always impressed young Percy: "They [knights] fought for the right, and defended the hapless from scheming barons and robbers. With sword and shield and a paper plume, I strode through the neighborhood in search of combat." Percy was once given a box of toy knights, and there was nothing he adored to play with more. Tales of heroism held his fascination. At an early age, Percy made copies of every drawing in his American history book. A favorite was of Mad Anthony Wayne with his bandaged head, waving a sword while taking Stony Point.

Percy's father, Thomas Francis Crosby, may have started it all by regaling his young son with grand, heroic stories of the fight for Irish freedom and insisting, with no one to refute him, that the first Crosby had been a tribal leader. A son of Catholic immigrants who had eloped at seventeen from County Lough, Ireland (a romantic story that fascinated young Percy), Thomas made his living from a small art-supply business he ran with his brother Ben. As a boy he had loved to draw cartoons on city fences, and he continued to draw and paint as a young man. One oil of rolling waves and sailing ships in the manner of Winslow Homer, painted at the time of the blizzard of 1888, still survives in the family. Thomas is remembered as a quiet gentleman, proud of being what he called "a one-hundred-percent American patriot," as was typical of many of the first- and second-generation immigrants. An engraved portrait of George Washington hung in the hallway, and Thomas would often recount stories of his hero to young Percy. While his father's aspirations for his son were West Point and a military career, his mother encouraged any evidence of artistic or literary talent. Percy's diverse careers as artist and author, political critic and patriot, may have expressed a subconscious need to fulfill both parents' expectations.

Percy's mother, Fanny, of English and Scottish descent, was a fine storyteller with an outgoing personality and a lively sense of humor. A frustrated singer and

Percy's mother, Frances Greene Crosby

actress, she doted on Percy. In fact, she was convinced that her son was a child of destiny. A favorite family story was of the time Fanny, while still in her teens, went to a fortune-teller. Her fortune was startling. "Young lady, you are going to give birth to a boy who will do something with his hands that will win fame on two continents. Your boy will be a genius, and the sign of it will become known at his birth." Percy was born on December 8, the day of

Percy on bicycle with unidentified friend

the Immaculate Conception. It was verification to Fanny of the prophecy, and she instilled in her son the belief that he was born with a divinely inspired mission. On one occasion, Fanny had a premonition that Percy should not go swimming in Jamaica Bay with his friend Tom Singer. Tom went alone that day and drowned. Percy and the rest of the choir of which Tom was a member sang at the funeral. The death of his friend made a deep impression on Percy and was probably the basis for the moving episode of the death of Sooky in his novel *Skippy*, written thirty years later.

Richmond Hill was typical of leisurely paced suburban America at the turn of the century: a horse-and-buggy village perched innocently at the fringe of the hustling inner city; beyond it the abrupt, sprawling countryside. Picnickers with their hampers of cold chicken took the trolley to the end of the line for outings in the fields and forest. Just three blocks in back of the Crosby home at 328 Beech

Street was farmland, and windmills could still be seen in the distance. Nearby was the Oberglock dairy farm, where the Crosby kids were often sent with pails to fetch milk. On the short walk, Percy and his younger sisters, Ethel and Gladys, could pick a bag of apples and even a bunch of carrots if they weren't spotted by the farmer, and they could rarely resist teasing the ducks and geese when passing the farm on the way to school. One of the most familiar sights was a horse-drawn milk wagon. The milkman, Jim, was Percy's special friend. Percy loved to ride on the step of the wagon, with one foot dangling and swinging—showing off before the other kids—all the while chattering away, mostly about horses. Back at the barn, Percy would help Jim feed the mare and rinse out the milk bottles.

Jim and the horses, the farm and the countryside, the nearby lake, the vacant lots, the trolley cars, the local bakery, candy store, grocery, and soda fountain—all were scenes from Percy's childhood that were to be revisited in *Skippy*. *Skippy*'s candy store, Mrs. Barkentine's, where the selection of two cents' worth of candy was a decision that took hours of exquisite agony, was based on Holt's, where Percy apparently had a small charge account. The prototype for Krausmeyer's Grocery, a standard set in the *Skippy* strip, was an old pickle-barrel general store run by a German family in Richmond Hill.

Percy started drawing in early boyhood and never stopped. Among his earliest memories was the trunkful of brushes, tubes of paint, palette knives, and other surplus art materials from his father's shop that was stored in the

The Crosby house on Beech Street, Richmond Hill, Long Island

Percy's father, Thomas (*right*), with his brother Ben in front of their shop

cellar. The myriad tubes of paint fascinated Percy, until one day when his father found dozens of colored "worms" dangling from the lid of the trunk. Thereafter it was kept locked, and Percy had to resort to drawing huge pictures on the cellar wall with lumps of coal.

For almost five years, Percy was a member of the Episcopal choir at the All Saints Church, where he apparently sang enthusiastically but was never confirmed. His mother loved to attend the services to hear Percy sing, particularly as he "looked so angelic in cotta and cassock." After sampling different services around the neighborhood, Percy found himself one Sunday in a Baptist church held spellbound by a sermon warning the damned to repent before final judgment. Crosby recalled, "I took heed and became baptized the ensuing Sunday. Thus protected, I am afraid I became careless and drifted away from the corrals of Christianity for all time, never to return." His formal worship may have ended, but Crosby remained deeply religious throughout his life. A boy once asked Skippy what church he went to, and Skippy replied he didn't go to any: "I go to God direct." Crosby's early religious training shaped his rigid moral, ethical, and puritanical attitudes. While he may have shunned institutional religious trappings, he was scornful of atheists and agnostics. He saw himself again as the Lone Knight in battle, for both God and country. But Skippy's faith, while just as absolute, was more practical. When asked by his mother if he'd said his prayers and asked the Lord for his daily bread, Skippy replied: "No, Mama, I just didn't want to overdo it. I'm cutting out the bread for a while until I get the express wagon I prayed for last week."

The world of nine-year-old Percy Crosby was undergoing radical change. That year alone almost half a million immigrants settled in New York (over twenty-five percent of the population was already foreign-born). From Russia, Italy, and Germany, mostly Catholics and Jews, they found little room in the teeming ghettos and began to move into the predominantly Irish-Protestant Richmond Hill. Despite the new languages and customs they brought with them, they were on the whole easily assimilated. They did, however, bring the first pains of urban growth to Richmond Hill—new houses and stores, paved roads, and the extension of trolley lines—which gradually eliminated the nearby farms. Percy's favorite swimming pond was drained, and the vacant lots and fields where the Lone Knight roamed at will disappeared. The new people, sounds, and sights brought both wonder and anxiety, and it was Crosby's genius to be able to retrieve such emotions from his boyhood and translate them into the inimitable *Skippy* idiom. Skippy once commented on the new construction in his neighborhood: "I never saw a bathtub without a house over it, before this year."

Percy grew up, but he never outgrew the role of the crusading knight. He always seemed to yearn for the world of his childhood "when I was Skippy," a time when decisions of right and wrong were easy to make, and good and evil could be clearly identified and battled—unlike the complex forces he so desperately contended with in later years.

3 / AGE OF INNOCENCE

On Saturday, March 25, 1911, a terrible fire destroyed the Triangle shirtwaist factory in New York City. One hundred forty-five lives were lost, most of them young women who were caught in the firetrap factory without any way to escape. An immediate cause cèlébre and rallying cry for the struggling labor-reform movement, the Triangle fire inspired a series of front-page editorial cartoons in the socialist paper, the *New York Daily Call*. One, captioned "The Result of the Combination," pictured the open door of a safe labeled GREED, out of which poured smoldering skulls representing CAPITAL and LABOR. Another, entitled "The Mark on the Pay Envelope," was a stark drawing of a skeleton being consumed by a snakelike flame, adroitly forming a dollar sign. The cartoonist was nineteen-year-old Percy Leo Crosby. It was his first newspaper job, and the cartoons made such a hit that the paper's editorials praised him as "the great crusader, Comrade Crosby." That the first published cartoons of the future pamphleteer against communism and socialism were attacks on capitalism was one of the more ironic paradoxes of Crosby's career.

Percy had begun that career three years earlier when he quit high school in his sophomore year and got a job as an office boy in the art department of *The Delineator* magazine during the editorship of Theodore Dreiser. The art director, seeing Percy's comic drawings, hired him to do all the decorations, and at sixteen Crosby became a professional artist, at five dollars per week. The job, unfortunately, ended after one issue. The aspiring cartoonist found himself selling magazines and delivering sandwiches and drinks for a delicatessen to earn his keep. In his spare time, he would draw batches of cartoons, take the trolley into New York, make the rounds of the newspapers, and often, with no return fare, walk the fifteen miles back to Richmond Hill. He even had a business card printed, boldly stating:

> **PERCY LEO CROSBY**
>
> *Illustration • Lettering*
> *Cartoons • Pictures of all Kinds*
> *Ideas a Specialty*
> *Richmond Hill,*
> *Long Island*

One day while peddling his cartoons among the East Side business lofts, he stumbled into the offices of the *Call* and entered the socialist paper's office not knowing where he was. A dusty haze hung over the zigzagging halls, there was a complete absence of windows, and ventilators sucked in the stale air of the crowded streets. He found no one anywhere, and then couldn't find his way out. As he later observed, "Like communism, it was easy to get into the place, but getting out was similar to running a race through a briared garden maze." When Percy found to his surprise that he was in the offices of a newspaper, he quickly whipped out samples of his work. The editor disappeared with the precious portfolio, and, after what seemed to be an interminable wait, he reappeared. Putting out his hand, he greeted Percy with a smile, saying, "Comrade Crosby, welcome to the staff of the *New York Call!*"

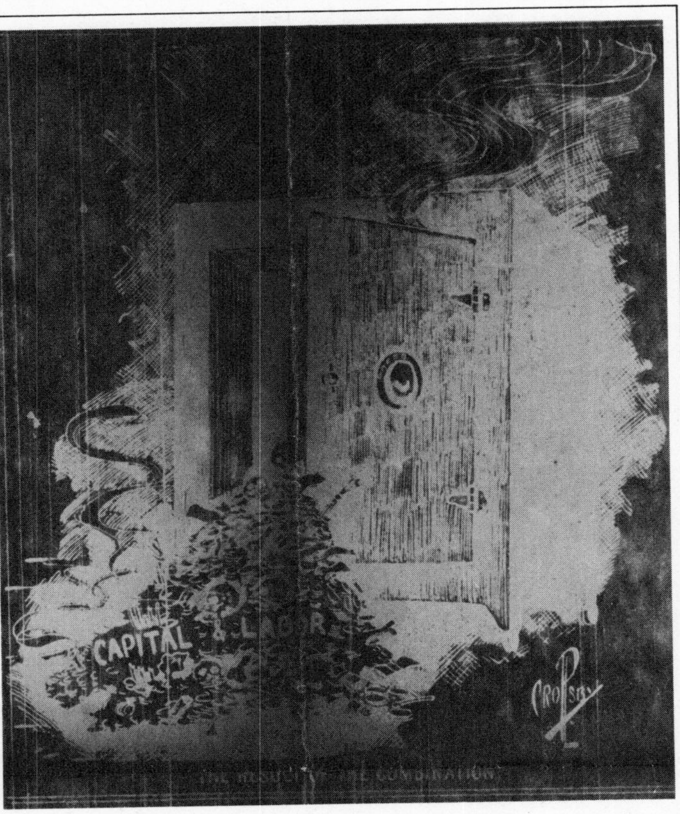
CAPITAL
CROSBY

One of Crosby's first editorial cartoons for the *New York Call*, in the aftermath of the Triangle fire

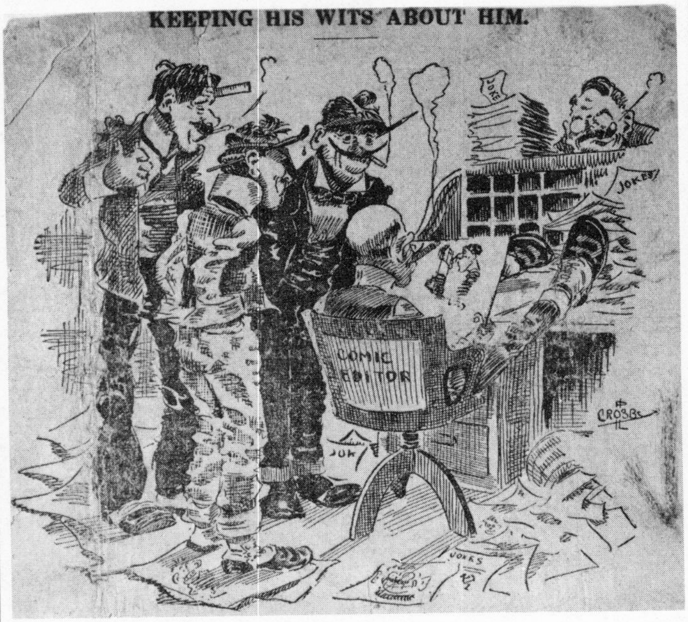
KEEPING HIS WITS ABOUT HIM.
JOKES
COMIC EDITOR
CROSBY

This may be Crosby's first published newspaper cartoon, drawn in 1909 when he was seventeen.

While the *Call* was popular enough among reformers, as was the new weekly socialist magazine, *The Masses*, such literature was unlikely to be found at the Crosby home in Richmond Hill. Thomas Crosby made no distinctions among anarchists, radicals, communists, and socialists—one was equated with the other, and all consorted with the Devil. Fortunately, Uncle Ben convinced Tom that Percy had a very keen mind and would see through "those radicals" in no time. The boy was really fighting their battle, the brothers rationalized. What better place to get experience than right in the enemy's camp!

Unknown to his father and uncle, however, Percy actually cherished the title "comrade," for it seemed to carry a deep significance, a sort of diploma which sanctioned his concern for the mass of downtrodden humanity. One of Crosby's most appealing qualities was his generous response to the poor and those in pain. As a youngster, he was once surrounded in a tough neighborhood by a gang of snarling boys. One was pushed to the center to fight him. Percy landed a few blows, and the boy began to bleed profusely. At the sight of the blood and tears streaming down the boy's face, Percy, to the amazement of the gang, impulsively threw his arms around his antagonist. They were soon pals. The incident seemed to make a lasting impression, for, as Crosby recalled in later years, "It might have been the birth of universal brotherhood in the breast of Skippy's creator."

While his editorial cartoons championing the weak and downtrodden against the powerful capitalists satisfied Crosby's crusading zeal, he wanted to publish as well something that would reveal "the rollicking side of my nature." Working frantically through the night, he conceived his first two comic strips. One was called *Biff*, and the other *The Extreme Brothers–Laff and Sy*. Percy inked them in through tears of laughter and spasms of giggling as he envisioned further sequences. He couldn't wait to get to the paper with his gems. His editor proclaimed them "Great stuff!" and ordered them published. But the roar that greeted them was not of laughter. The *Call*'s readers considered the comics bourgeois frivolity. Never had the paper received such a barrage of complaints—over three hundred letters and innumerable phone calls. As one outraged reader wrote, "With conditions the way they are, people starving and in rags, does the *Daily Call* think it is a laughing matter to have that man, Comrade Crosby, come out and poke fun at the readers?" Needless to say, Crosby's first, cherished comic strips were yanked from the paper. (The movement later came to a different conclusion when the communist *Daily Worker* carried a comic strip—its hero appropriately named Lefty Louie.) Crosby learned one thing from the experience: "Communists absolutely have no sense of humor, and they positively dread ridicule."

Further disillusionment with the *Call* was soon to come. Weeks went by without his promised ten-dollar-a-week salary. Percy was forced to pawn a ring as well as his treasured gold scarf pin for carfare. At the end of the second month, he finally mustered the courage to insist on being paid. Finding that Comrade Crosby was not working just for the cause, but considered himself one of the exploited workers that the party was seeking to release from bondage, the paper paid him in full and asked him to resign.

Shortly after his relations were severed at the *Call*, Crosby managed to obtain a position as sports cartoonist for the *New York Globe*. One of his first assignments was to cover a polo match. He knew nothing about the game, nor was he given the slightest indication of what the leading players looked like. In his eagerness to make good, Crosby got right out in the middle of the dashing melee of charging horses and was nearly killed trying to get his close-up likenesses. It was only later that he found there was such a thing as a "morgue" where he could have gotten portraits of the players from which to refine his on-the-spot drawings.

Crosby's work was attracting attention. His style was so original that many thought he had received his art training abroad. The action he instilled in his cartoons was admired by the staff—they noted especially his gift for making the figures move. But Crosby's mind was not on sports. He desperately yearned to make people laugh. He turned out comic after comic only to have them used in the Home Edition as fillers. Sometimes his desire to create laughter was so intense that he vowed that if he couldn't accomplish it in the newspapers, he would do it as a

vaudeville hoofer. A shuffle and a click, click, click often broke the stillness of the night at the paper. Even in the act of drawing his comics, Crosby would get up to do a soft shoe or a tap, accompanied by a routine of quips for his imagined audience in the vacant chairs. He thought his cartoons were getting funnier and funnier, but unfortunately the editor-in-chief did not agree. Despite his versatile talents, Percy was fired.

The bottom dropped out of Crosby's world. He was too dazed to think and had to fight off the impulse to jump in the river. Utterly forlorn, he wandered listlessly up Broadway. Something impelled him to look up from the pavement under the window of the Edison Company, and his eyes focused on three words in gold: LIGHT HEAT POWER, the Edison slogan. He remembered a contest had been announced for the best cartoon on the use of electric light. The first prize was seventy-five dollars. It had meant nothing to him at the time, but now he was out of work. He rushed back to the *Globe* and in a burst of inspiration finished a cartoon and sent it off to the Edison Company, enclosing his home address. It was the last picture he drew at the *Globe*.

Day after day Percy spent just looking out the window of his room. His dismissal plunged him into a state of depression that was impossible to shake. Even rereading his favorite classics failed to stir him from his lethargy. Again and again, he tried to think up new comic series, but his mind seemed to have gone dead. He had lost the ability to create. Home meals went by in silence, with surreptitious glances from his father that seemed to suggest he was a failure, a nonpaying boarder.

Percy was still in deep despair several weeks later when a letter arrived from the Edison Company. Eagerly he tore open the envelope. It was the list of winners in the cartoon contest, and the name on top was Percy Crosby. A seventy-five-dollar check fluttered to the floor. Percy's cartoon appeared in every morning and evening paper in New York. It proved to be a turning point in his career. The publicity brought an offer to rejoin the staff at the *Globe*, but Percy spurned it to accept a position at the prestigious *New York World*, at the time the promised land for aspiring cartoonists.

An intense and elegant Crosby, in his early twenties

Percy Crosby never forgot his high state of excitement that first day as he rode the trolley across the East River toward the gleaming, gold-domed World Building. We can imagine him as others were to recall him, a jaunty gait giving him the appearance of being more than his actual height of slightly over five and a half feet. Neatly dressed, although his budget did not permit the stylish attire he would later affect, he was someone you took notice of. His fair hair, blue eyes, and aquiline but faintly battered nose were in contrast with a jutting chin and a stocky build. His handsome, rugged looks were a curious blend of sensitive artist and street fighter. He was, in fact, both.

It was the golden age of journalism and of newspaper art in New York, with over a dozen competing papers in addition to the numerous foreign-language papers. Most were profusely adorned with editorial and sports cartoons; on-the-spot sketches of courtroom trials, fires, and other local news; fashion, society, and theater drawings; portraits and illustrations; and a plethora of cartoons and comic strips. They nurtured an astonishing range of artistic talent, attracted from all parts of the country.

The staff of the *World*, which Crosby was joining at the age of nineteen, included such luminaries as Carl Anderson (who later created *Henry*), Clifford McBride (who later created *Napoleon and Uncle Elby*), Charles Payne (*S'matter Pop?*), and Albert Freuh (whose brilliant caricatures later appeared in *The New Yorker* mag-

azine). At the *New York American* were Winsor McCay, creator of the classic *Little Nemo*; George McManus, one of the most prolific of the early masters, who would soon launch *Bringing Up Father*; and T. E. Powers, the great editorial and sports cartoonist. The *New York Journal* boasted Thomas "Tad" Dorgan, the versatile sports cartoonist who later created that burlesque of human foibles, *Indoor and Outdoor Sports*; Harry Hershfield, busy with *Desperate Desmond*, a satire on melodrama in the manner of Charles Kahles's *Hairbreadth Harry*; and Cliff Sterrett, just then developing *Polly and Her Pals*, the first strip to feature a heroine. Rube Goldberg—whose name was to become part of the American vocabulary—came from California to the *Evening Mail*, which also had young Gus Edson, who was to take over *The Gumps* at Sidney Smith's death. On the staff of the *American Press* was a rare comic genius of dialect humor, the sixteen-year-old Milt Gross; also twenty-year-old Frank Fogarty, who later drew *Clarence* for the *New York Herald Tribune* and then succeeded Clare Briggs on *Mr. and Mrs.* The great political cartoonist Caesar was at the *Sun*, and Palmer Cox, creator of *The Brownies*, could be found at the *Herald*.

Among cartoonists working in New York for syndication were Bud Fisher from San Francisco, who created the first daily comic strip, the intrepid pair of *Mutt and Jeff*; Richard Outcault, delineating the mischief of the memorable *Buster Brown*; and Frederick Burr Opper, whose notable fantasies included *Happy Hooligan*, *And Her Name Was Maude*, and *Alphonse and Gaston*. In 1911, George Herriman's *Krazy Kat* made its debut, to be called by Gilbert Seldes the most amusing, fantastic, and satisfactory work of art produced in America. The newspapers and journals of the day also abounded with the work of such brilliant artists as A. B. Frost, T. S. Sullivant, Walt McDougal, James Montgomery Flagg, and Charles Dana Gibson. They all contributed to an unprecedented era of American graphic and literary humor.

Crosby's experience at the *Globe*, where he had not only done sports cartoons and comic strips but also occasionally filled in as political cartoonist and sketch artist, led to his being assigned to the coveted Metropolitan

Section of the *Sunday World*. There he received some of the choicest assignments, and some of the worst—the city morgue, the municipal courthouse and the juvenile court, Hell's Kitchen, political outings, homicides, and murder trials. Crosby rapidly developed into an adept graphic reporter. Under the furious pace and pressure of deadlines, a characteristic style began to emerge, along with a personal philosophy. Crosby's work forced him to explore for the first time the seamy fringes of society, the cruelty of the criminal underworld, and the plight of those trapped in poverty and slums. "I've seen sorrow as few ever saw it," Crosby wrote of those years. "One thing all those newspaper assignments did, if nothing else, was to stir compassion in me for all humanity. . . . I learned never judge any human being by the events that brought about the effect in his life, but rather look to the cause . . . and no one creed or race is better than any other, for we are brothers all."

Crosby matured in other ways as well. New York was a cultural, political, and social stew that excited and nourished the mind, spirit, and eye of the young artist. Although the great surge of European immigration was over, the continuing experiment of the United Melting Pot of America was not. Many of the pioneer comic-strip cartoonists were themselves immigrants or first-generation Americans, and racial themes and dialect humor were as prevalent in the comics as they were in vaudeville. It was a time when ethnic humor was less self-conscious than it is today. In addition to the Irish (*Bringing Up Father*), the Germans (*Katzenjammer Kids*), the blacks (*Li'l Mose* and *The Blackberries*), and the Jews (*Abie the Agent*), even the Swedes (*Yanitor Yens Yenson*) and the Chinese (*Ah Sid, the Chinese Kid*) were represented.

The technological explosion—the electric light, the automobile, the telephone, the radio, the airplane—affected everyone's life-style. Motion-picture houses were springing up everywhere, replacing the nickelodeons. Sheet music brought the latest hits to everyone's living room. The sixty-story Woolworth Building, the world's tallest, topped the skyline, and mass production of the Model T was chasing the last horse from the streets. An exhibition of modern art was held at the Sixty-ninth Regiment Armory with such unfamiliar names as Picasso,

Matisse, and Rouault. There the New York art world, as well as the impressionable young Crosby, was thunderstruck by the cubists, impressionists, and fauvists, and such abstractions as Marcel Duchamp's *Nude Descending a Staircase*. And for the romantic Crosby, the city had beautiful women—models and actresses; dancers and singers; secretaries, debutantes, and telephone operators; chorus girls, college girls, salesgirls; girls from everywhere.

Frank Fogarty remembers Percy as a nice-looking lad "with his fair hair close cut, extremely talented, and with an eye for the girls, and apparently, they for him." On one occasion, Crosby was sent to cover a Hungarian wine-tasting party. In the romantic candlelight, he was smitten by a raven-haired beauty who exercised the alluring charms of Cleopatra, Salome, and Aspasia combined. As Crosby recalled, in addition to an overpowering sexual appeal "she had finesse and subtlety, as well as the fine, splendid mind of a woman of breeding." They discussed Rosa Ponselle's recent debut with Caruso, Geraldine Farrar's and Scotti's performances in *Tosca*, history, politics, and poetry. Crosby was not to be as passionately "in love" again for weeks.

Tall, willowy, and seemingly unattainable brunettes would always start Crosby on a romantic binge—limited only by his finances. Having little left from his salary for such unessentials as food, Percy would frequent the newspaper-row barrooms: "With a 5¢ beer as a decoy, my hand was employed plastering a sandwich and delving into the assortment of herrings, pickles, and cheese at the free lunch counter." Just as resourceful romantically, Crosby would frequently take his date for an evening stroll down lower Broadway to South Ferry for a five-cent ride across New York harbor, past the majestic Statue of Liberty to Staten Island and back toward the skyline silhouetted in the dusk. As a backdrop to Crosby's growing repertoire of newspaper adventures, the excursion was surefire romance. Another favorite trysting spot, when he could afford it, was Fraunces Tavern, the site of General George Washington's farewell to his officers. The restaurant maintained the atmosphere of the Revolution, and it provided the perfect setting for Crosby to impress his latest infatuation with his knowledge of American history.

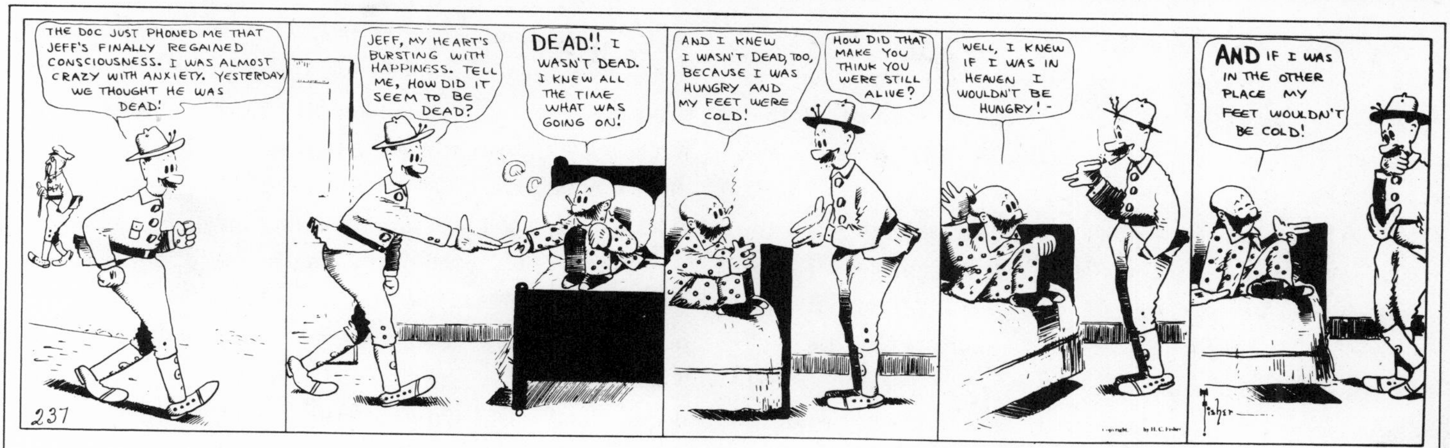
THE DOC JUST PHONED ME THAT JEFF'S FINALLY REGAINED CONSCIOUSNESS. I WAS ALMOST CRAZY WITH ANXIETY. YESTERDAY WE THOUGHT HE WAS DEAD!
JEFF, MY HEART'S BURSTING WITH HAPPINESS. TELL ME, HOW DID IT SEEM TO BE DEAD?
DEAD!! I WASN'T DEAD. I KNEW ALL THE TIME WHAT WAS GOING ON!
AND I KNEW I WASN'T DEAD, TOO, BECAUSE I WAS HUNGRY AND MY FEET WERE COLD!
HOW DID THAT MAKE YOU THINK YOU WERE STILL ALIVE?
WELL, I KNEW IF I WAS IN HEAVEN I WOULDN'T BE HUNGRY! -
AND IF I WAS IN THE OTHER PLACE MY FEET WOULDN'T BE COLD!
237
Fisher

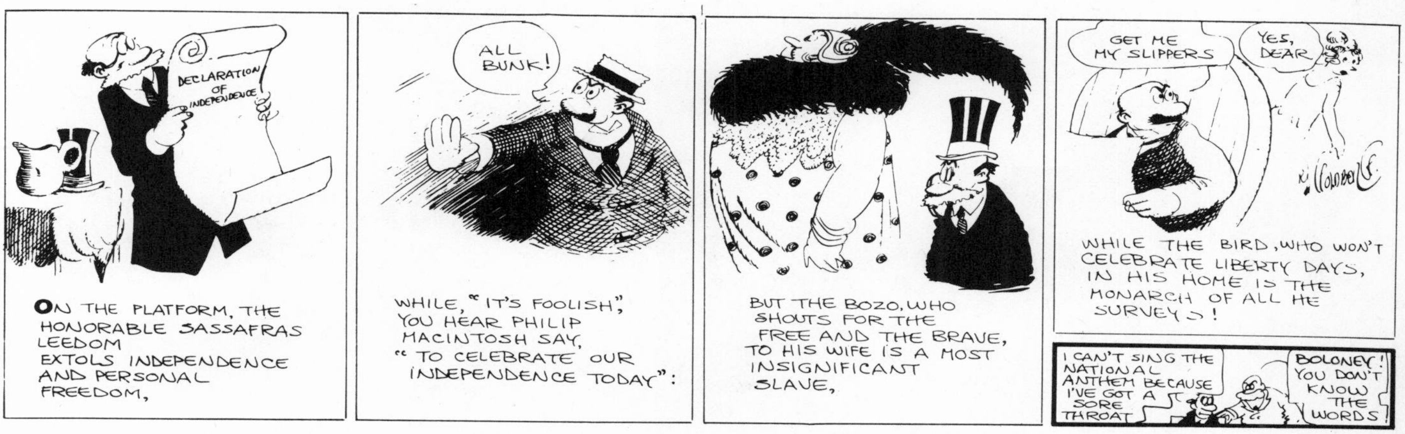
DECLARATION OF INDEPENDENCE
ON THE PLATFORM, THE HONORABLE SASSAFRAS LEEDOM EXTOLS INDEPENDENCE AND PERSONAL FREEDOM,
ALL BUNK!
WHILE, "IT'S FOOLISH", YOU HEAR PHILIP MACINTOSH SAY, "TO CELEBRATE OUR INDEPENDENCE TODAY":
BUT THE BOZO, WHO SHOUTS FOR THE FREE AND THE BRAVE, TO HIS WIFE IS A MOST INSIGNIFICANT SLAVE,
GET ME MY SLIPPERS
YES, DEAR
WHILE THE BIRD, WHO WON'T CELEBRATE LIBERTY DAYS, IN HIS HOME IS THE MONARCH OF ALL HE SURVEYS!
I CAN'T SING THE NATIONAL ANTHEM BECAUSE I'VE GOT A SORE THROAT
BOLONEY! YOU DON'T KNOW THE WORDS!

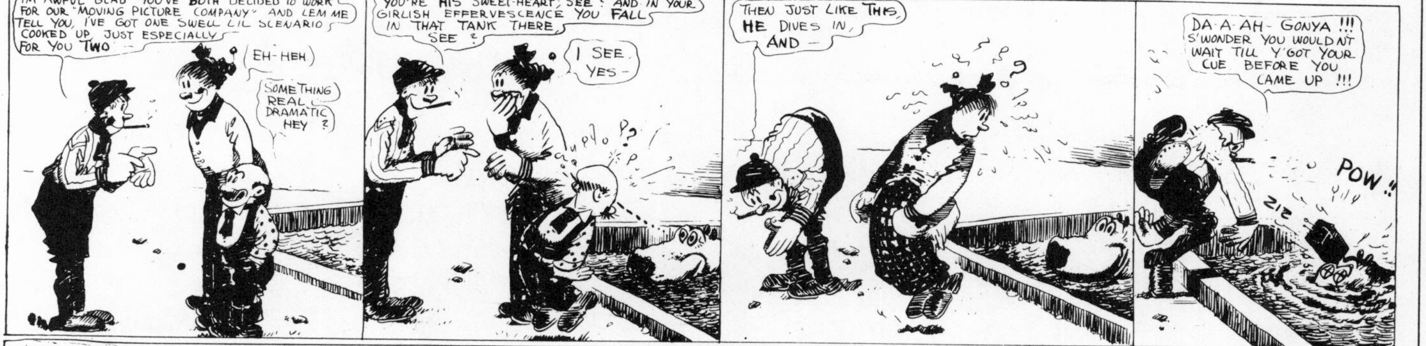
I'M AWFUL GLAD YOU'VE BOTH DECIDED TO WORK FOR OUR MOVING PICTURE COMPANY AND LEM ME TELL YOU, I'VE GOT ONE SWELL LIL SCENARIO COOKED UP, JUST ESPECIALLY FOR YOU TWO -
EH-HEH
SOMETHING REAL DRAMATIC HEY ?
YOU'RE HIS SWEET-HEART, SEE? AND IN YOUR GIRLISH EFFERVESCENCE YOU FALL IN THAT TANK THERE SEE ?
I SEE. YES -
THEN JUST LIKE THIS, HE DIVES IN, AND -
DA-A-AH-GONYA !!! S'WONDER YOU WOULDN'T WAIT TILL Y'GOT YOUR CUE BEFORE YOU CAME UP !!!
POW !!

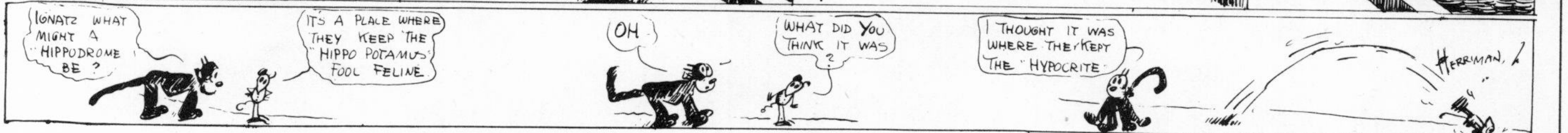
IGNATZ WHAT MIGHT A HIPPODROME BE ?
ITS A PLACE WHERE THEY KEEP THE HIPPO POTAMUS FOOL FELINE
OH
WHAT DID YOU THINK IT WAS ?
I THOUGHT IT WAS WHERE THE KEPT THE "HYPOCRITE"
HERRIMAN

Some of the strips of Crosby's contemporaries from his early days as a staff cartoonist on the *New York Globe* and the *New York World*: *Their Only Child* (George McManus), *Mutt and Jeff* (Bud Fisher), *Life's Little Jokes* (Rube Goldberg), and *The Family Upstairs* in tandem with *Krazy Kat* (George Herriman).

Despite its use as a romantic ploy, Crosby's love of history was real and intense. On at least one occasion when his date was suspected of merely feigning interest in the subject, Corsby's ardor cooled and the affair ended.

After a few years at the *World*, Crosby felt ready to assume the precarious life of a free-lance artist. One day he showed some cartoons of kids to John Tennant, the editor of the *World*. Impressed, Tennant bought them at space rates of two dollars a column. They were published about twice a week. Thus encouraged, Crosby began to focus his talents on the antics of kids. In 1916, the George

While continuing his career as a cartoonist, he enrolled in the Art Students League, determined to be an accomplished artist in other mediums as well. He studied under some of the most renowned instructors of the day, among them George Bridgman, Frank DuMond, Joseph Pennell, and Max Weber. Crosby didn't have to wait long for recognition—his technical brilliance saw to that. He soon came to the attention of Gifford Beal, a noted painter and president of the League. Beal invited Percy to his summer home in Provincetown, Massachusetts, where Percy became enthralled with the art colony of Edwin Dickinson, Edward Hopper, Eugene O'Neill, and many other

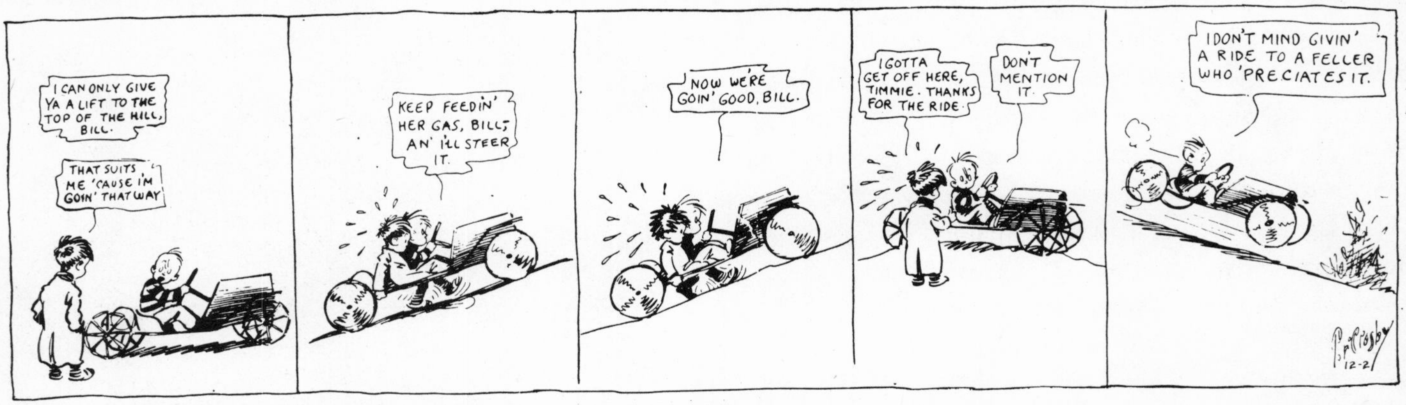
I CAN ONLY GIVE YA A LIFT TO THE TOP OF THE HILL, BILL.
THAT SUITS ME 'CAUSE I'M GOIN' THAT WAY
KEEP FEEDIN' HER GAS, BILL; AN' I'LL STEER IT.
NOW WE'RE GOIN' GOOD, BILL.
I GOTTA GET OFF HERE, TIMMIE. THANKS FOR THE RIDE.
DON'T MENTION IT.
I DON'T MIND GIVIN' A RIDE TO A FELLER WHO 'PRECIATES IT.
P. L. Crosby
12-2

The Clancy Kids (1916), Crosby's first syndicated newspaper strip, was not a great success, but it proved useful in sharpening his skills and in teaching him how to contend with the unrelenting demands of the genre.

Matthew Adams Service bought Crosby's first feature syndication, *The Clancy Kids*, a daily and Sunday comic strip. While not widely syndictated, it did provide an income of $135 a week, a not insignificant sum for Crosby. Best of all, it gave him the chance to experiment and develop, to shape his basic concepts and characters, and generally to gain the invaluable experience that can come only from the discipline of writing and drawing a daily comic strip. He mastered the balance of line with black areas of contrast, the use of white space in the design, and the timing of sequential narrative; he sharpened the graphic images and refined the pacing of the humor.

With his enormous energy, intensity, and ambition, Crosby was never content for long with just one challenge.

artists and writers attracted to that tiny fishing village at the tip of Cape Cod. He never forgot the spell of the nightly gatherings of painters in a fishing shack, "where a candle stuck into an empty wine bottle served to illuminate the faces listening to the critical symposiums against the mournful lap of waves slushing the barnacled poles of the dilapidated wharf."

The training at the League was rigorous. Crosby studied portraiture, anatomy, oils, lithography, drypoint, and one of his favorite mediums, watercolor. "Watercolor is to painting, in many ways, what a beautiful, lyrical poem is to a novel," he wrote, "so apparently effortless—however, while seeming so haphazard and full of dashing and splashing of brilliant color, every stroke must be carefully planned—for a miss is the kiss of death." He treated every painting like a romantic adventure. Percy was the only student at the League who could sketch a model in motion, helped undoubtedly by his training as a courtroom artist. Even Bridgman thought it a unique feat, and he borrowed the drawings to show his other classes. Percy knew every human bone and muscle, and was proud of the careful anatomical studies from Bridgman's lecture course that he kept in bound copybooks.

Percy also attracted the attention of a fellow student, Gertrude Volz, the daughter of a well-to-do New York realtor. As Crosby described her, "She was decidedly foreign in appearance. Hair parted in the middle, streaks of blue light on each side, exotic slanting eyes of grey-green." An attractive and popular woman (her credits included a full-page photograph in *Vogue*, and the honor of having been the mascot of the Yale crew), she was also a serious artist and an accomplished sculptor.

Percy Crosby had been commissioned a second lieutenant in the Officer Reserve Corps in 1916, and when the United States entered the war he was called to active duty. He served for a time as an instructor of jiujitsu, then prepared for service overseas as "an expendable lieutenant." Before leaving for France, he and Gertrude eloped and were married in a military ceremony at the training camp at Plattsburg, New York, on July 7, 1917.

Even a world war served only as diversion to the career of the fiercely ambitious cartoonist. While still in training, he created a new panel feature, *That Rookie from the Thirteenth Squad*, for McClure Syndicate, and he continued it after he was sent to France as a first lieutenant in the Seventy-seventh Division, AEF. "How I ever did it, I'll never know," Crosby later recalled. "I conceived humorous events from the Front and drew them up and sent them to my syndicate. Six a week." It was a remarkable accomplishment. While at the Argonne front, he was hit by shrapnel in the eye, which fortunately left no permanent damage and which earned him a Purple Heart. Crosby's wartime cartoons resulted in the publication of his first two books: *That Rookie of the Thirteenth Squad* in 1917, and, two years later, *Between Shots*, by Capt. P. L. Crosby "with the 77th Division in France."

After the war, Crosby resumed his free-lance career, and, for the next five years, his studies at the Art Students League as well. He soon developed several new features for syndication. One, a panel with various recurring themes in the manner of those by Clare Briggs and by H. T. Webster, was syndicated in 1921 and ran until

1925. Some of the most memorable titles were *When There's a Boy in the Family*, *The Supreme Moments of Life*, *When Young Love Dies*, and *Honeydale — 50 Minutes Out*, a parody on the burgeoning suburbia. The series sharpened Crosby's drawing and humor over a wide range of subjects, but still he would return to the world of children, particularly of the slums, in such series as *Who*

As a U.S. Army officer during World War I

Cares for the Feelings of a Small Boy, The Local Boy, Back o' the Flats, The Little Girl Who Moved Away, and *Send a Poor Child to a Farm.*

During this time, he also developed a small, one-column feature, *Always Belittlin'*. It consisted of a small drawing featuring a little tyke wearing a striped shawl and a bonnet with a black pom-pom. Below it, set in type, was the Crosby aphorism for the day. A typical one advised, "If you want to be known as a philosopher, use inch and a half words and write so that nobody knows what you're talking about. Look people in the eye, and be difficult on all occasions. And by all means, get yourself lots of furrows on the forehead. On any other place they don't count." *Always Belittlin'* later became the "top" for the *Skippy* Sunday page (the top was a convention of the Sunday page at that time, a small supplementary feature that ran above or below the artist's main strip, sometimes vying for interest with the star attraction), and the phrase itself became part of the American idiom. Crosby experi-

Always Belittlin'

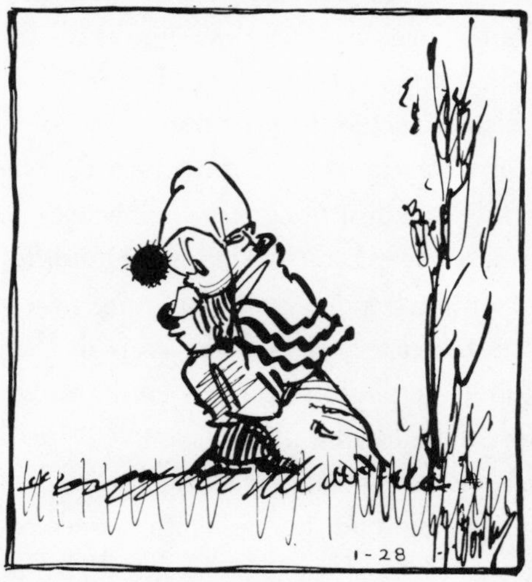
1-28

The wise man was once a fool, but got over it; the fool was once a wise man, but never got over it.
—Percy Crosby

Crosby Goes to War

Other artists recorded their graphic impressions of "the Great War"—men such as Bruce Bairnsfather, the Scottish creator of Ol' Bill, the classic portrayal of the veteran British Tommy; also Leroy Baldridge, A. A. Wallgren, and Wallace Morgan. Thomas Nast had performed similarly in the Civil War; but Percy Crosby was the first soldier on active duty to draw a daily cartoon for publication, often from the thick of the fighting. A number of brilliant cartoonists followed Crosby's example in World War II, and many of them returned from battle to continue their features created for *Stars and Stripes, Yank,* and other military publications—including Sgt. Bill Mauldin (*Up Front,* for which he won a Pulitzer Prize), Sgt. Leonard Sansone (*The Wolf*), Sgt. George Baker (*Sad Sack*), and Pvt. David Breger (*Private Breger* which became *Mr. Breger*).

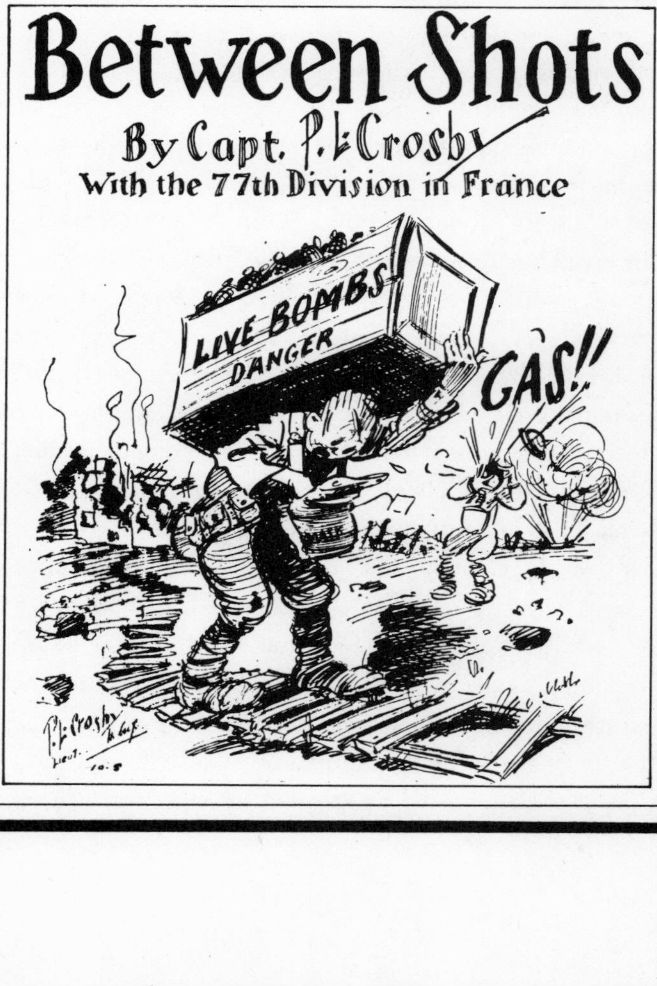
Between Shots
By Capt. P. L. Crosby
With the 77th Division in France
LIVE BOMBS
DANGER
GAS!!

mented with another feature, *Bugville*, a delightful fantasy tableau, and a panel on the same theme entitled *Bug Lugs*, which also was used as a top for *Skippy*. But continually he would return to the subject of children, his ambitions still unfulfilled.

More and more frequently, Crosby's cartoons began to appear in *Life* magazine. Founded in 1883, *Life* was America's leading humor magazine of the day. Together with its predecessors, *Puck* and *Judge*, it published the finest artists and writers of that genre and established the social cartoon as a feature in American literature, a tradition continued by *The New Yorker* after its founding in 1925. Crosby rapidly became one of *Life*'s most prolific and versatile contributors. His assignments soon progressed from a quarter page to a half page, and then to a full page in color. But what he really yearned for was a regular page every week (which would also pay $125 instead of the usual $100). He interested the art director,

(text continues on page 24)

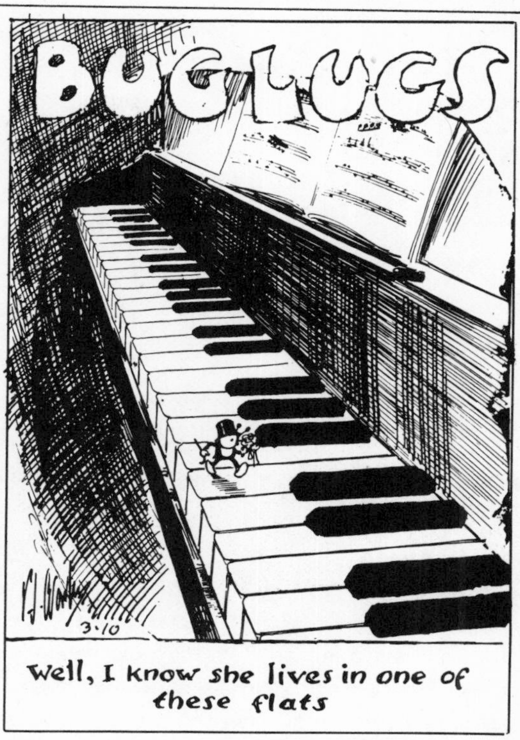
BUG LUGS
3-10
Well, I know she lives in one of these flats

That Rookie from the 13th Squad.

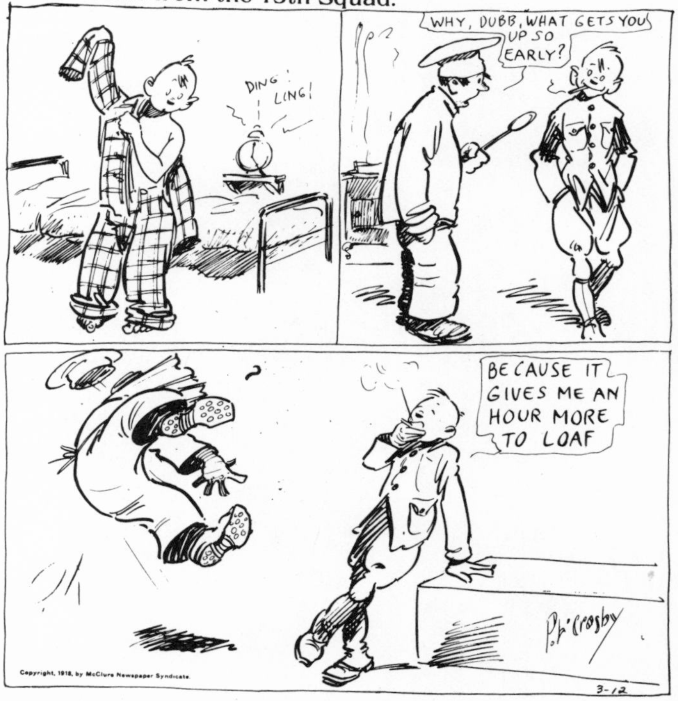
DING! LING!
WHY, DUBB, WHAT GETS YOU UP SO EARLY?
BECAUSE IT GIVES ME AN HOUR MORE TO LOAF
P.L. Crosby
Copyright, 1918, by McClure Newspaper Syndicate.
3-12

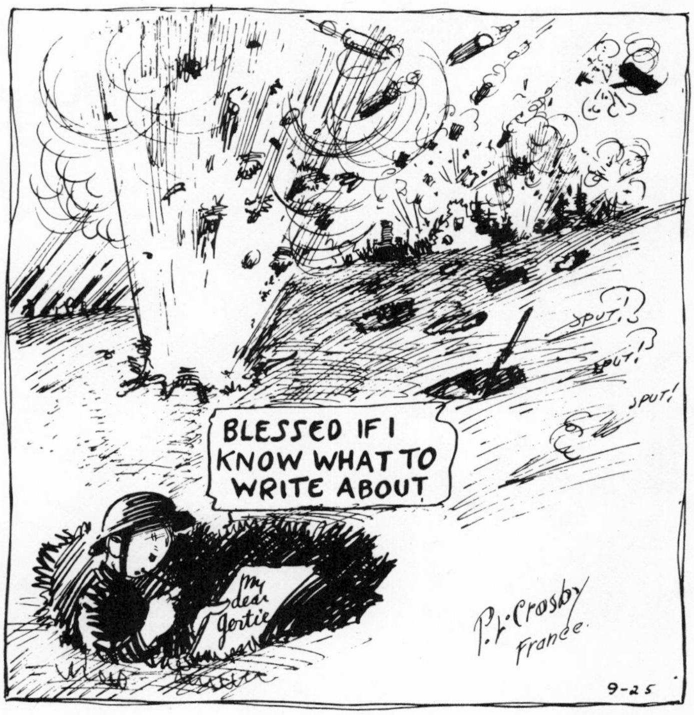
SPUT!
SPUT!
SPUT!
BLESSED IF I KNOW WHAT TO WRITE ABOUT
My dear Gertie
P.L. Crosby France.
9-25

Who Cares for the Feelings of a Small Boy.

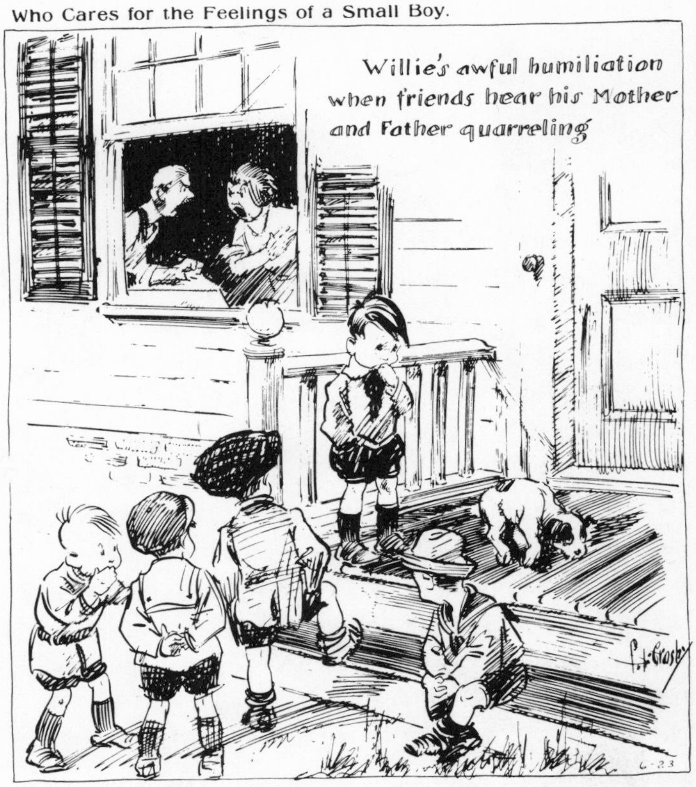
Willie's awful humiliation when friends hear his Mother and Father quarreling
6-23

Panel Cartoons

Crosby's syndicated panel of the early twenties focused on several themes that were partly autobiographical. Some were inspired by his observations of slum kids and memories of his own childhood experiences. Others were devoted to the tribulations of newlyweds; drawn around the time of Crosby's early marriage and the birth of his first child, they may have echoed his own domestic quarrels leading to his divorce.

Back o' the Flats

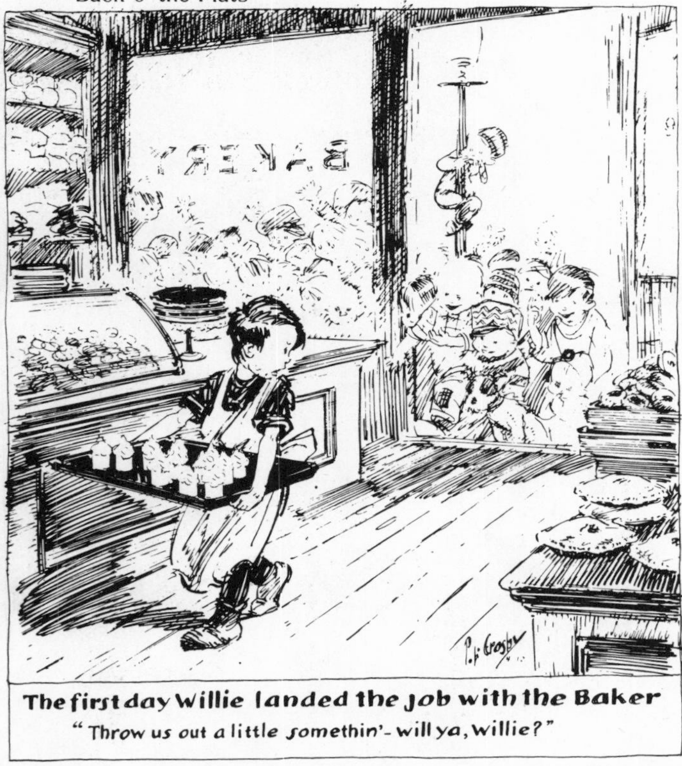
BAKERY

The first day Willie landed the job with the Baker

"Throw us out a little somethin'- will ya, Willie?"

Who Cares for the Feelings of a Small Boy.

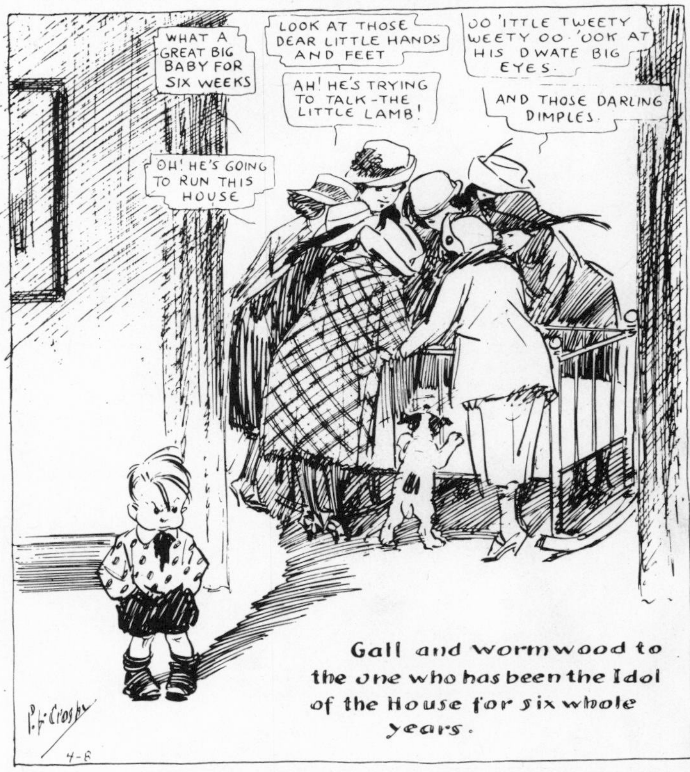
WHAT A GREAT BIG BABY FOR SIX WEEKS
LOOK AT THOSE DEAR LITTLE HANDS AND FEET
OO 'ITTLE TWEETY WEETY OO. 'OOK AT HIS DWATE BIG EYES.
AH! HE'S TRYING TO TALK - THE LITTLE LAMB!
AND THOSE DARLING DIMPLES.
OH! HE'S GOING TO RUN THIS HOUSE
Gall and wormwood to the one who has been the Idol of the House for six whole years.
4-8

The Little Girl Who Moved Away.

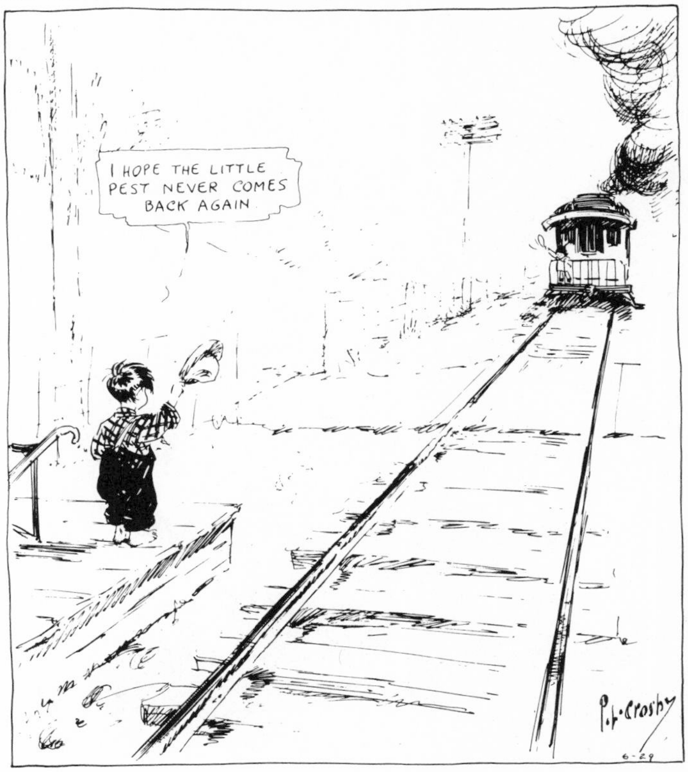
I HOPE THE LITTLE PEST NEVER COMES BACK AGAIN.

Three Rooms and Bath.

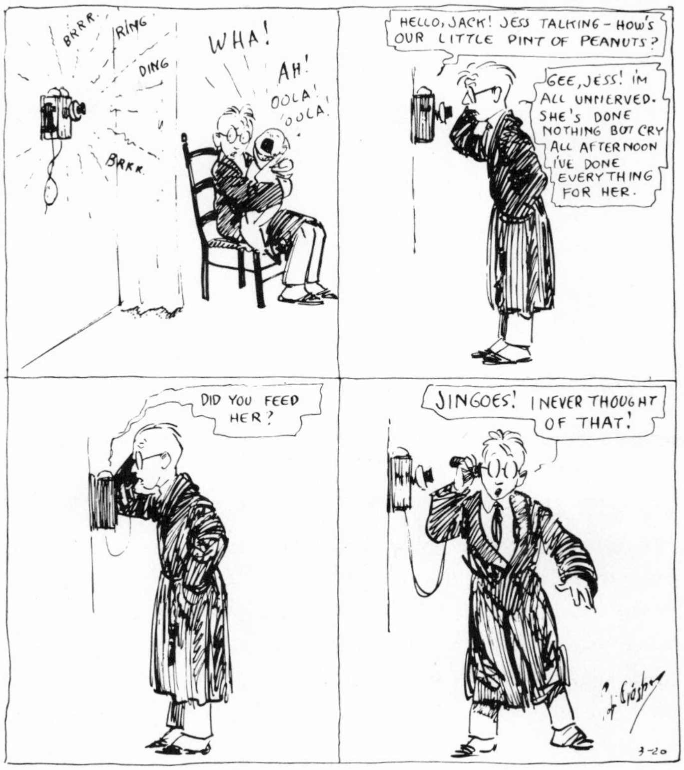
BRRR RING DING BRRR
WHA!
AH! OOLA! OOLA!
HELLO, JACK! JESS TALKING - HOW'S OUR LITTLE PINT OF PEANUTS?
GEE, JESS! I'M ALL UNNERVED. SHE'S DONE NOTHING BUT CRY ALL AFTERNOON I'VE DONE EVERYTHING FOR HER.
DID YOU FEED HER?
JINGOES! I NEVER THOUGHT OF THAT!

Honeydale—50 Minutes Out.

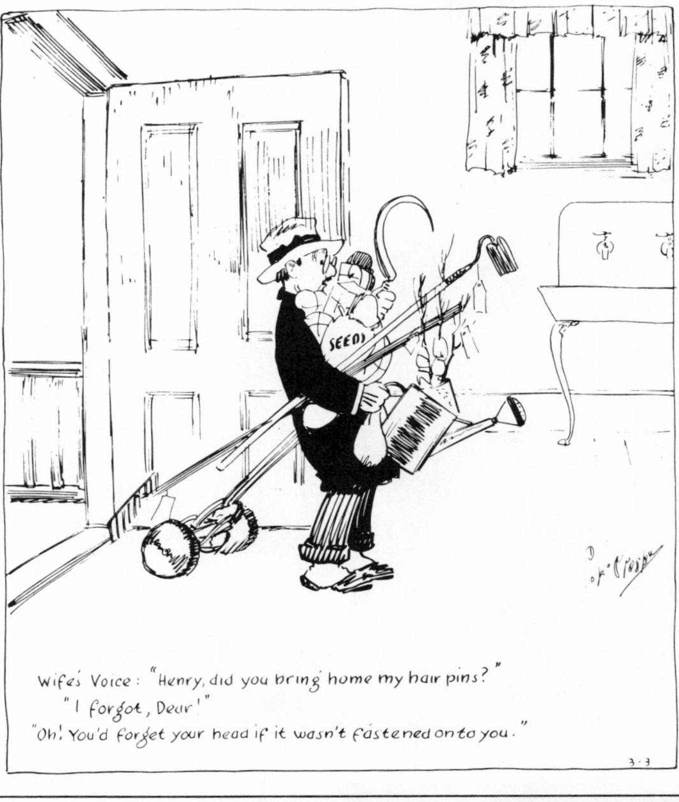
SEEDS
Wife's Voice: "Henry, did you bring home my hair pins?"
"I forgot, Dear!"
"Oh! You'd forget your head if it wasn't fastened on to you."

THE SECOND YEAR

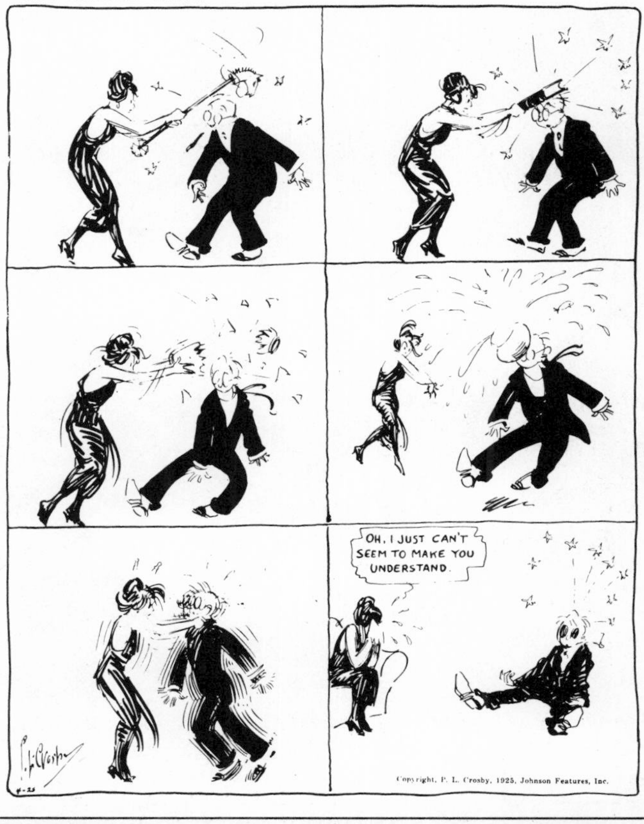
OH, I JUST CAN'T SEEM TO MAKE YOU UNDERSTAND.

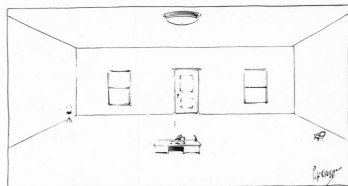

The President

The Workers

Crosby at <u>Life</u>

While Crosby's drawings for *Life* are best remembered for the *Skippy* series (see pp. 32–41), his other cartoons for the magazine comprise a notable body of work. They reveal his versatility in subject matter and a sure command of various mediums (wash, pen and ink, watercolor), together with expert draftmanship and a wide-ranging sense of satirical humor.

"Read the jokes offen 'em, will ya, Papa?"

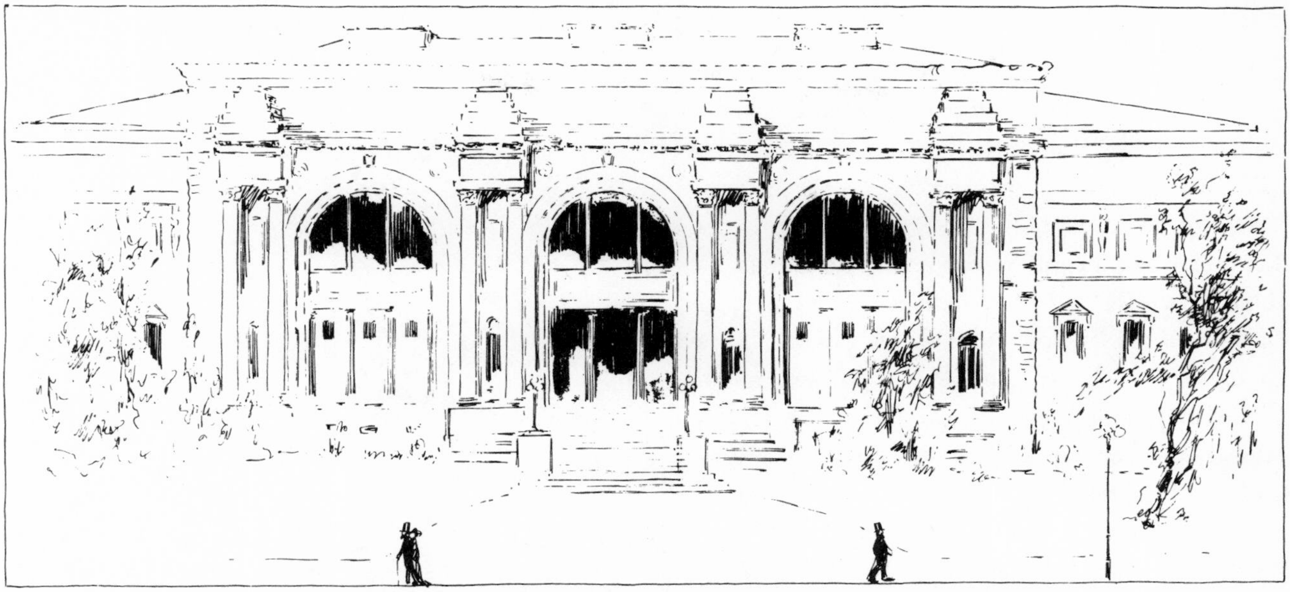

The Metropolitan Museum of Art under normal conditions.

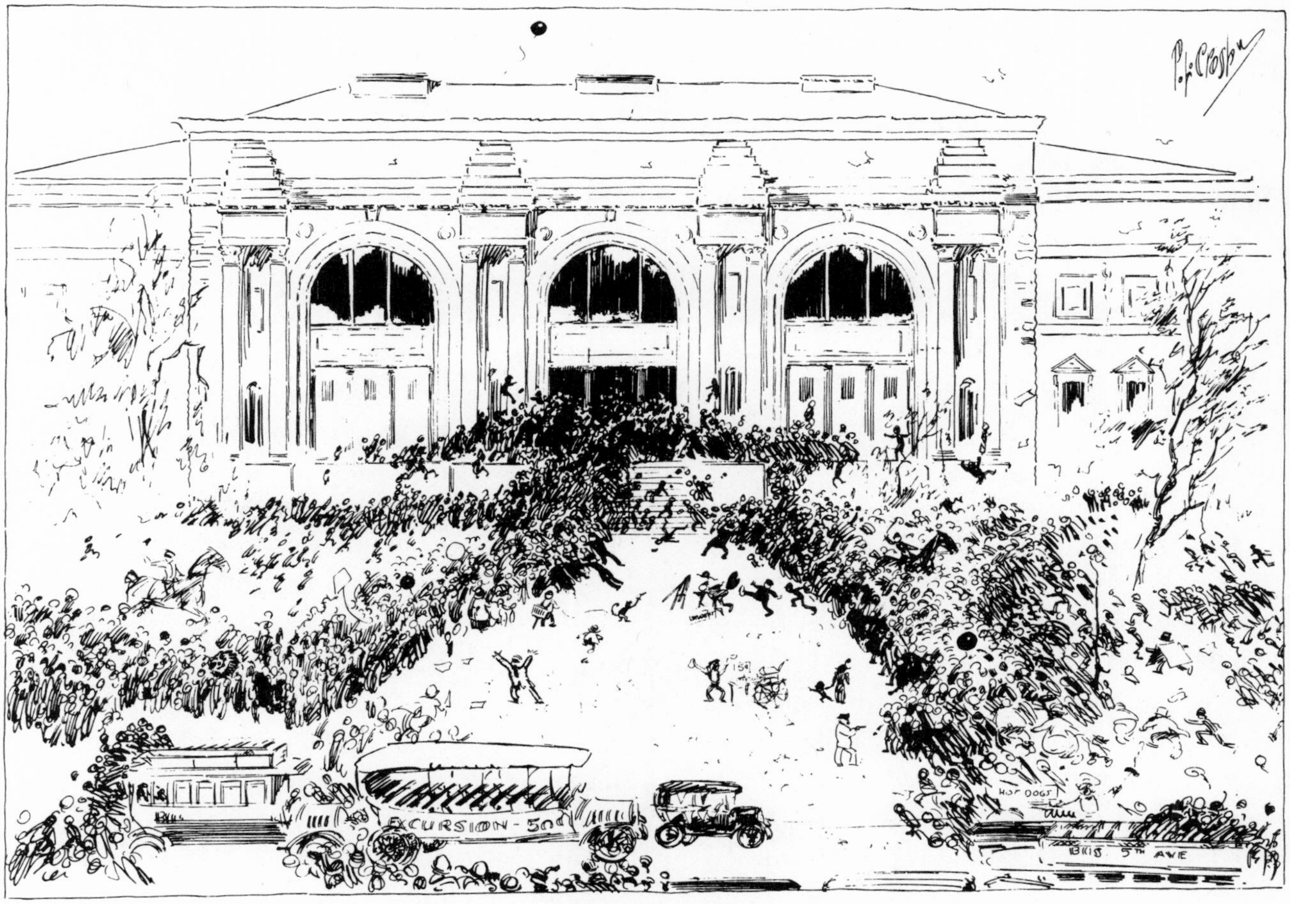
EXCURSION - 50¢
HOT DOGS

The museum after the announcement that its Rembrandts are fakes.

Frank Casey, in the idea of a feature based on a kid character. He had occasionally used a kid named Timmy in some of his *Life* cartoons, and the character became the prototype for Crosby's new creation. As he recorded the event, "I drew up three pages and thought of forty-four names (among them Beanie and Jumper)—Skippy last on the list. A minor editor put his oar in and suggested Tiny Tim. I bristled with such uncalled-for interference, and (like the sign on the Edison window) the thought flashed through my mind: 'It had to be *Skippy* and nothing else!' " Crosby worked furiously during the day and into the evening at the *Life* offices, from time to time conferring with Casey on his progress. Casey was pleased with the final results, but one more hurdle remained: "I'll show them to Mr. Gibson. He's the one who has the final say—and no one else!"

Gibson was the renowned Charles Dana Gibson, the illustrator, cartoonist, social satirist, and creator of that dazzling vision of and model for American womanhood, the Gibson girl. Himself a master draftsman and stylist, Gibson recognized Crosby's unique talents, and his final say on *Skippy* as publisher of *Life* was yes.

On March 15, 1923, a full-page house ad in *Life* announced Skippy's arrival:

> *Have you a little Demon in your home?* MEET SKIPPY SKINNER, the Latest Offspring of P. L. Crosby, Who Will Give Him His Start In Life on March 22nd, With Weekly Appearances Thereafter. What a Kid! And What a Kidder: You'll Love the Little Rascal As Your Own—More So, If Anything, For You Won't have to Pay For the Furniture He Breaks. "Mischief" Is His Favorite Alias, And Tricks Are Things He Is Always Up to. Nothing Else But.

Skippy was up to much more. The copywriter may be forgiven for thinking the new feature would be another cartoon stereotype of kids concerned with nothing but mischief and tricks, but that was not Crosby's métier. Skippy was a new kind of boy, the child of Crosby's soul, summoned forth to the pages of *Life* by way of Brooklyn, Richmond Hill, and the tenements of the Lower East Side.

Crosby worked harder on *Skippy* ideas and drawings during that first year than on almost any of his other

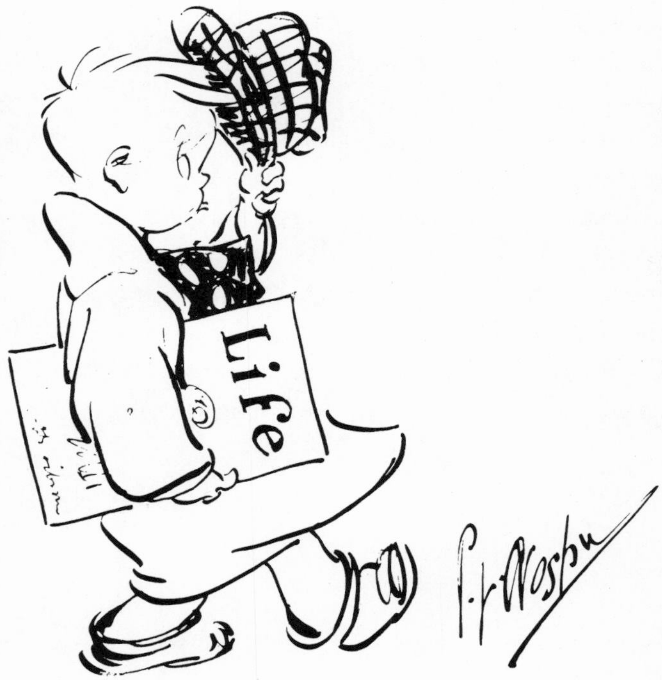
Life

work. The results were inventive and winsome, drawn with uncommon flair, and very quickly *Skippy* proved a great success. It became a regular *Life* feature. At last Crosby knew he had arrived.

But again, he found himself pulled in other directions. Newspaper syndicates immediately saw a greater potential for *Skippy* as a newspaper comic strip. Crosby had experimented with the genre on the *Globe* and the *World*, and with *The Clancy Kids*, all without notable success. He had to prove to himself that he could do it. A popular comic strip, after all, was the ultimate goal for many cartoonists, and a widely syndicated comic strip meant financial rewards far exceeding the top paid by any magazine. (Such comic-strip stars of the early twenties as Rube Goldberg earned $150,000 a year; and Sidney Smith signed the first million-dollar contract for *The Gumps*—$100,000 a year, guaranteed for ten years.)

The comic strip is a unique medium—the only living art form in constant change. The cartoonist, his creation, and the reader all grow and evolve together in continuous interaction. The comic strip is meant to be experienced for a few seconds or minutes at daily or weekly intervals, and this time element is its essential feature. The repetition and constant renewal provide accumulative force of great power, and a rhythm discernible only over many months or even years. Each episode is a part of a larger work, a continuum without end. The capacity to create time by chronological sequence of images provides the special power of the comic strip. It is a sequential narrative—one frame essential to the next; each frame truly growing out of the one before and impelling a further image as a result. Crosby had mastered the techniques. He knew that Skippy and the comic strip were made for each other.

Skippy began its newspaper life in 1925 and was syndicated at various times thereafter by Johnson Features, Central Press Association, and Editors Features Service.* Its rising success was noted by William Randolph Hearst, who had a deserved reputation for spotting cartooning genius. And Hearst was willing to pay for talent. He signed Crosby for his King Features Syndicate. Distribution of the Sunday page began on October 7, 1926, and of the daily strip on April 1, 1929. Crosby's original contract called for $1,150 a week against fifty percent of the gross receipts. A later seven-year contract raised his guarantee to $2,350 a week. Crosby was making more money than the President of the United States.

---

*Crosby astutely retained the *Skippy* copyright, one of the few cartoonists of that era to so protect his work. Perhaps he had been forewarned by his father's experience. Thomas Crosby once invented a process to make a type of academy (drawing) board, but failed to secure a patent. He never received any royalty for the invention, a bitter financial pill for the struggling art dealer.

4 / SKIPPY

Skippy shattered the concept of the idealized American childhood—that kids grow up in a sheltered cocoon of play and joyous mischief, free from the torment and worry of their elders. *Skippy* was based on the actual concerns of kids. Crosby knew that kids are often unhappy and lonely, and he could find humor in their unhappiness and loneliness. In one strip, Skippy comes across a solitary boy in a vacant lot and asks him why he drew the figure on the fence next to him. The boy replies, " 'Cause I don't like to be alone." Another time, Skippy muses "I ain't myself, I wonder if I'm goin' screwy. For no reason at all, I catch myself feelin' happy—an' it's all I can do to steer my mind back into things that worry me." The lines are not just Skippy, they are also Crosby, born out of his own psychology.

Crosby's kids are often quarrelsome. They engage in endless bickering over what might seem trifles to adults: who is to apologize to whom first, who is to get in the last word, who touched the other last, who is first up at bat, or who is first in anything. Crosby knew that these were important things. Like all flesh-and-blood youngsters, Crosby's kids find themselves constantly frustrated by little everyday matters—trying to get a kite into the air, hitting a ball, getting a dog to obey, losing things and forgetting errands, and just trying to understand the many perplexing incongruities and mysteries of life (like realizing that a doctor could get sick). Skippy wrestled with such mind-boggling thoughts as, "If God made the world and the stars and sun and everything, then who made God?" He was, of course, a firm believer, reflecting Crosby's

early religious training. Before *Skippy*, references to God and prayer in the comic strips had been considered sacrilegious and were almost as taboo as sex. Crosby's work, however, was energized by moral conviction, and it couldn't be repressed. Crosby once wrote, "My observations of children seem to bear out the belief which seeps through oriental literature and religious training, namely that children are endowed with spirituality." He was able to incorporate such themes in Skippy because he applied them with a humor that was at once gentle and universal.

Crosby's ear for the particular idiom of children was exceptionally acute. As in a comic-strip theater of the absurd, many conversations took place between two garbage cans inhabited by Skippy and his pals—a device Samuel Beckett used decades later in *Endgame*. Crosby's dialogue keenly reflected the child's struggle to articulate—as when Skippy asks his friend to name a "spaticular instanance"—and possessed an idiosyncratic ring of truth. A critic for the *New Republic* once questioned a line of Skippy's that was addressed to some small children hitching a ride on a milk wagon: "Geet off'en there youse kids—d'ya want to get hoited?" Crosby replied: "When I had Skippy suddenly talk in an exaggerated manner and go completely out of character, it was because any wholesome, dynamic boy is an exhibitionist. The very fact that this line was different from his usual talk suggested that I was not wholly unacquainted with boys' psychology. When I was Skippy's age, I occasionally used such language to put little children in their place. One of the greatest opportunities for a boy to 'show off' is, I

Mother and Father Skinner

There is a distant, almost formal relationship between Skippy and his parents. The two worlds are separate, with no episodes of common activity such as family outings. Usually portrayed reading the newspaper, listening to the radio, or lecturing Skippy in stilted precepts, Father Skinner is never seen playing ball or other games with his son. Quiet and reserved, as was Father Crosby, he usually displays great patience and understanding with his errant son. Mother Skinner, too, appears almost aloof and is limited to routine family roles, but is favored with a glamorous appearance: tall, willowy, often stylishly attired, more like Percy's wives than his mother. The Skinner parents seem to serve merely as props, when necessary to the episode, a role Crosby's parents seemed to have played in his own young life, and is a reflection of a time when children were supposed to be seen but not heard.

believe, from that platform of a milk wagon while one foot dangles in the air."

Some influence of Richard Outcault's *Buster Brown*, at its peak of popularity when Crosby was in his early teens, was apparent in *Skippy*. Both boys affected huge white collars and large bow ties. But Skippy's attire had a rumpled and battered gentility, almost as if he were wearing Buster's hand-me-downs. Buster was in the Little Lord Fauntleroy mold: sailor hat and belted jacket, above-the-knee knickers and button shoes. (Ironically, a family snapshot shows young Percy dressed for some special occasion in a Buster Brown outfit, complete with the skimmer hat, and looking none too happy about the honor.) Buster was the mischievous prankster in the tradition of Peck's *Bad Boy* and Wilhelm Busch's *Max und Moritz*. His world was affluent urban society: he lived in an elegant townhouse complete with maids, cooks, and chauffeurs; he rode in expensive limousines, had expensive toys; and he played with the children of the family's rich society friends. Skippy Skinner reflected rural, small-town America. His parents were of quite modest means, as were those of his friends. His toys, like his box car and swords, were homemade, and most of his time was spent on the streets in backyards.

So Crosby introduced a naturalism to the kid strip. It was, to be sure, a sentimental naturalism, an unabashed love of mother, country, and flag—at a time when people were less self-conscious about such emotions. But Crosby's strips did accurately reflect his personal sentiments. Of course, he expressed his patriotism in his own inimita-

Buster Brown and his dog, Tige

ble fashion, as in one cartoon that showed Skippy in profound dialogue with a worm: "Well, good morning, little worm; an' how are you today? What's the use o' rushin' someplace? Don't ya know that a thousand worms in China would give their eye teeth to be where you are?" In another cartoon, a typical Crosby tyke watches a magnificent naval flotilla passing upriver in review and remarks to a friend, "Gawd help anybody that spits on the flag today."

Crosby's puritanical attitudes were deeply rooted in the proper, middle-class, religious household of his adolescence, and he never tried to free himself of them. Indeed, he believed in them. His reformer's zeal to change things for the better was sincere, but his idea of "better"

was back to the way they were in his idealized boyhood. *Skippy* celebrated eternal youth and independence. Kids in Skippy's time weren't alienated, they just somehow grew up on their own—in vacant lots, backyards, and unpaved alleys, before bulldozers and developers turned them into asphalt playgounds and urban blight.

Skippy was typical of a time when kids made their own games and toys. All that was needed to play Kick the Can was a can. A box and roller skates made a dandy car. With sticks, paper, and string, kids constructed stilts and high-flying kites. They played mumblety-peg, marbles (with spiral agates), and Follow the Leader. Ponds were for skating and swimming, and vacant lots for exploring. They "drove" abandoned cars in junkyards. A bean-

Children of the City

Crosby's days at the *New York World* left him deeply touched by the plight of children. Life on the Bowery, just a step from the World Building, held a strange fascination for him: the Gary Society wagon rolling up the door of a tenement to take a child from its alcoholic parents; the haggard children wandering the streets, neglected and homeless, eyes swollen from crying; the slum-hardened kids in brutal gang rumbles under the Brooklyn Bridge; the indomitable breed who played stickball in the midst of swarms of people weaving in and out of the jumble of pushcarts and wagons. Poor children seemed to stir some deep, unconscious sense of abandonment in his psyche. In his early cartoons as well as in *Skippy*, Crosby would draw poignantly upon the memories of those Bowery days, mingled with others from his own childhood.

Impressed with Crosby's sensitive portraits of slum children, Mrs. Charles Dana Gibson, a dedicated social worker, asked Crosby to sit alongside a judge in juvenile court and observe some of the heartbreaking stories of mistreated children of broken homes or unfit parents. The experience led to the creation of a classic Crosby cartoon. Titled *Childhood Tragedies*, it first appeared as a full-page cover for the *American Weekly*. A youngster kneeling at bedside, head bowed,

clasps his hands in prayer: "Dear Lord, please make Mama and Papa stop fightin' 'cause it's hard to take sides when you love them both, an' besides I'm ashamed to face the kids." The magazine was swamped with requests for reprints, and the drawing was hung in divorce courts, judges' chambers, and lawyers' offices throughout the country. One divorce lawyer publicly credited the cartoon with his success in reconciling more than five hundred warring couples and saving their children from the emotionally scarring consequences of a broken home. Ironically, four years after drawing it, Crosby was divorced himself and lost the custody of his own children.

Percy Crosby's compassion for children increased, if anything, with the separation from his own. Learning that a twelve-year-old boy was sentenced to life for murder, he pleaded with the governor of Washington to have the boy paroled to the care of Father Flanagan's Boys Town. "Society . . . really brought about the tragic plight this child is in today," Crosby wrote. "According to my knowledge of boys, a sin of childhood can be erased by fine teaching and wholesome surroundings." For years Crosby also donated sensitively drawn portraits of neglected children that were featured in *The New York Times*'s Christmas fund solicitation, "The One Hundred Neediest Cases."

shooter, a top, a hoop from a barrel, or even an old tire was all that was needed for an afternoon's fun. But that world, that lazy suburban nowhereland, was slowly being extinguished by a new order, and Crosby fought against the change in *Skippy* as if it threatened to eradicate his own boyhood. In the novel *Skippy* Crosby had Skippy's friend Sooky die as an indirect result of their town's growth.* It was as if Crosby equated change with death and could survive only as long as Skippy's world survived.

Crosby was a voracious reader his entire life, with a remarkable range of literary tastes that had been nurtured in his youth. "I was a full-fledged member of the Public Library," Crosby wrote of himself at about Skippy's age. "The flipped pages gave me an instantaneous idea of the book. If there were ladders of dialogue racing up and down the pages, I knew it was the book for which I was in search. I walked out reading, and generally finished the story on my doorstep. Two books came in handy, for I read one going home from the library, and the other returning." Young Percy loved to visit his friend John Braham, whose house had a big library. The two boys would be content to spend the afternoon browsing through

*Sooky, a boy from a poor family, is accidentally killed one night while collecting wood at a building site. During the funeral service, Skippy sits outside on the curbstone as the sound of beating hammers at the nearby construction grows in intensity. His eyes fill with hatred and, with tears streaming down his face, he pounds his fists, sobbing: "It was all *your* fault! *You* did it! *You* did! Damn ya! Damn ya!"

THE AMERICAN WEEKLY
Greatest Circulation in the World
The Nation's Reading Habit
Childhood Tragedies by Percy Crosby The Distinguished Creator of "Skippy"
Be it ever so Humble, There's no place like Home

Nowadays.
By PERCY CROSBY
Copyright, 1921, by The McClure Newspaper Syndicate.
TO LET
THEIR ANNUAL OUTING.
10-5

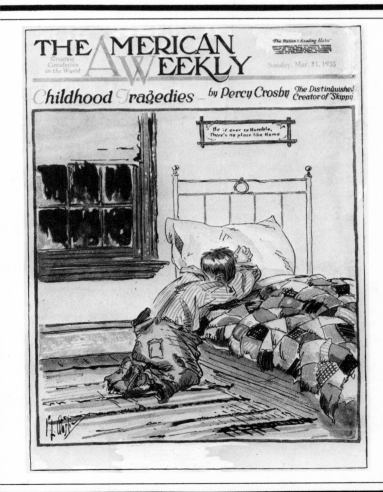

the books instead of in their usual play. Those visits undoubtedly inspired Skippy's recurring tussles with his friend before a huge wall of bookshelves or in the library that was such a frequent setting in *Skippy*.

Constantly on the move, jumping from one thing to another, inquisitive about everything, Skippy was practically a life-mask of his creator. The snub-nosed, tousle-haired philosopher loved nature and romance as did his creator. Skippy, relaxing against a tree on a high hill with a magnificent view below him, remarks, "They can say what they like—God certainly does bat out some elegant scenery." Another time, smitten by a girl in a pink dress, Skippy dreamily exclaims, "Oh, love's beautiful! Makes ya cry 'nside an' laugh outside, until ya think ya got a rainbow in ya."

Sports champions were Crosby's boyhood idols and, as with so much from his youth, he never outgrew his worship of them. He loved to hobnob with sports celebrities,* and his enthusiasm for athletics invested many *Skippy* sequences with a special vitality. Skippy, too, is an enthusiastic athlete, but often as inept and frustrated at

---

*One day Gene Tunney visited an exhibition of Crosby's art at the Anderson Gallery in New York, accompanied by Bradley Kelly, then general manager of King Features Syndicate. Kelly wrote of the meeting: "Crosby stood in the rear of the salon as we entered. I shall never forget his entranced expression as he focused on the heavyweight champion of the world. It was obvious he recognized him and seemed overwhelmed." Tunney soon became a special friend. His framed picture, inscribed with words of admiration, was found thirty-five years later in the trunk containing Crosby's last possessions.

Back O' the Flats

Willie! Mamma says never mind the stew meat — get chops! Papa's got a job.

Supreme Moments of Life.

HOOKING A LOST QUARTER

baseball or football as is Charlie Brown in *Peanuts* today. But while poor Charlie Brown freely admits he's a failure, Skippy never loses that feeling of a conqueror—even in defeat. When Skippy misses a fly ball, he assumes it was due not to his error but to an uncoordinated glove.

Esthetic pleasure is hard to define. Certainly much of *Skippy*'s appeal, in addition to the narrative, is in its visual expression. The comic-strip form is a blend of visual and verbal disciplines, brought into esthetic balance. It was eminently suited to Crosby's art. *Skippy* had an air of spontaneity, nothing belabored or forced. Its casual style was accomplished with great technical virtuosity: Crosby's dashing lines often were disconnected, and the backgrounds, when not eliminated entirely, were sketchily indicated, their details blurred—all of which served to focus attention on the characters and convey the action and vitality that were Crosby's forte. This "pen impressionism" and extraordinary draftsmanship made Crosby's *Skippy* a work of art as well as a classic comic strip.

On the Fresh Air Farm

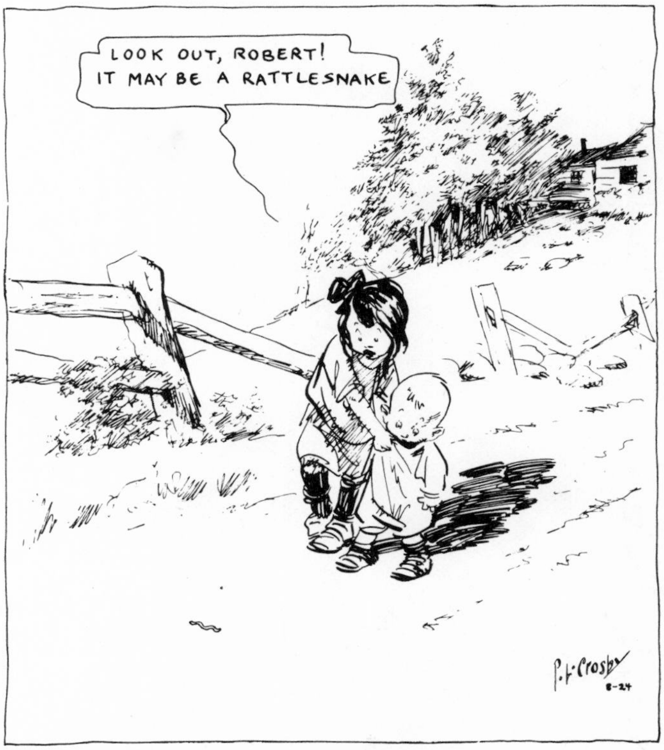
LOOK OUT, ROBERT!
IT MAY BE A RATTLESNAKE
P. L. Crosby
8-24

Send A Poor Child To A Farm.

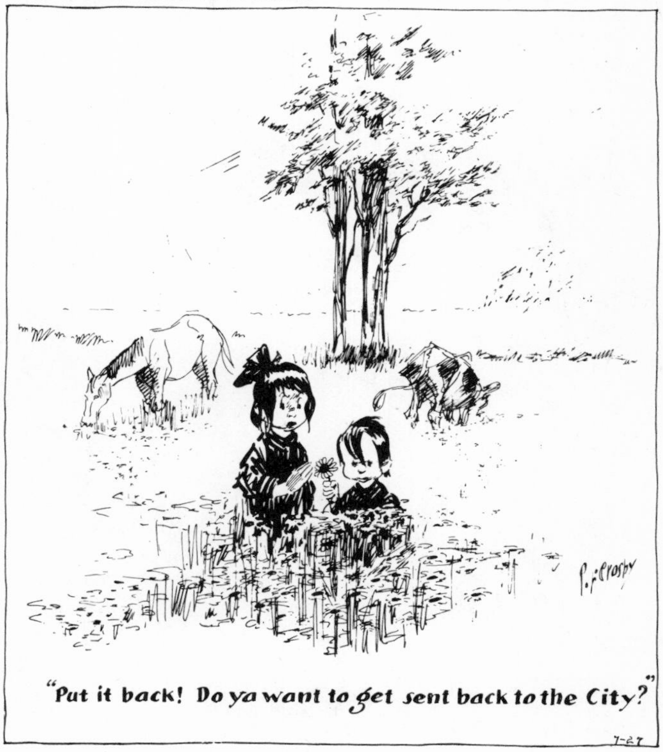
P. L. Crosby
"Put it back! Do ya want to get sent back to the City?"
7-27

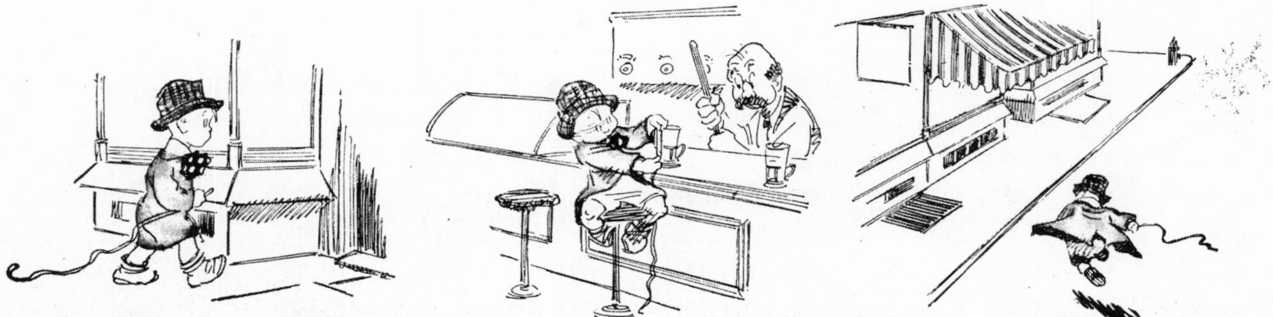

"At last, I got a tape measure."

"Five inches."

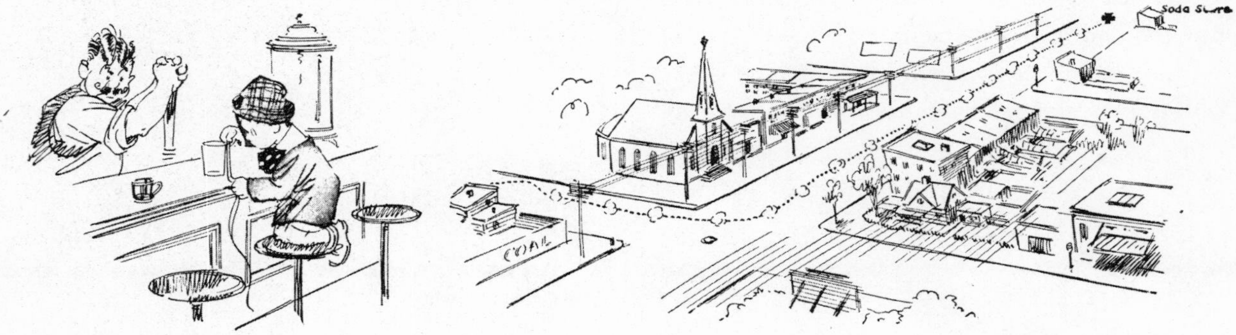
Soda Store
COAL

"Four and one-half inches."

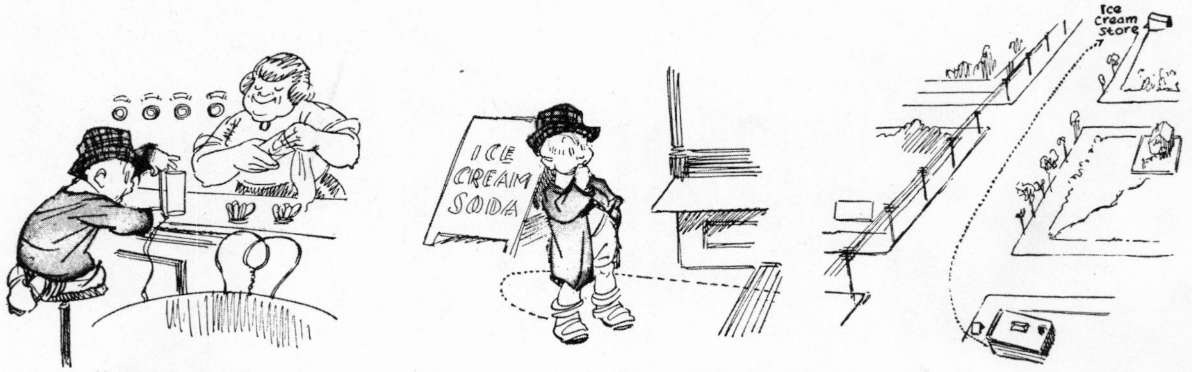
ICE
CREAM
SODA
Ice
Cream
Store

"Seven inches!"

? ? ?

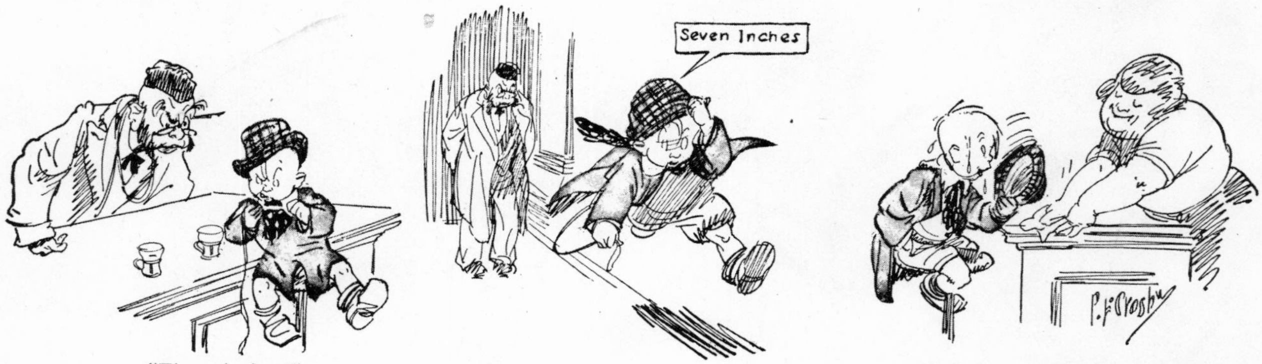
Seven Inches

"Three inches!"

"Choc'late soda—extra sweet!"

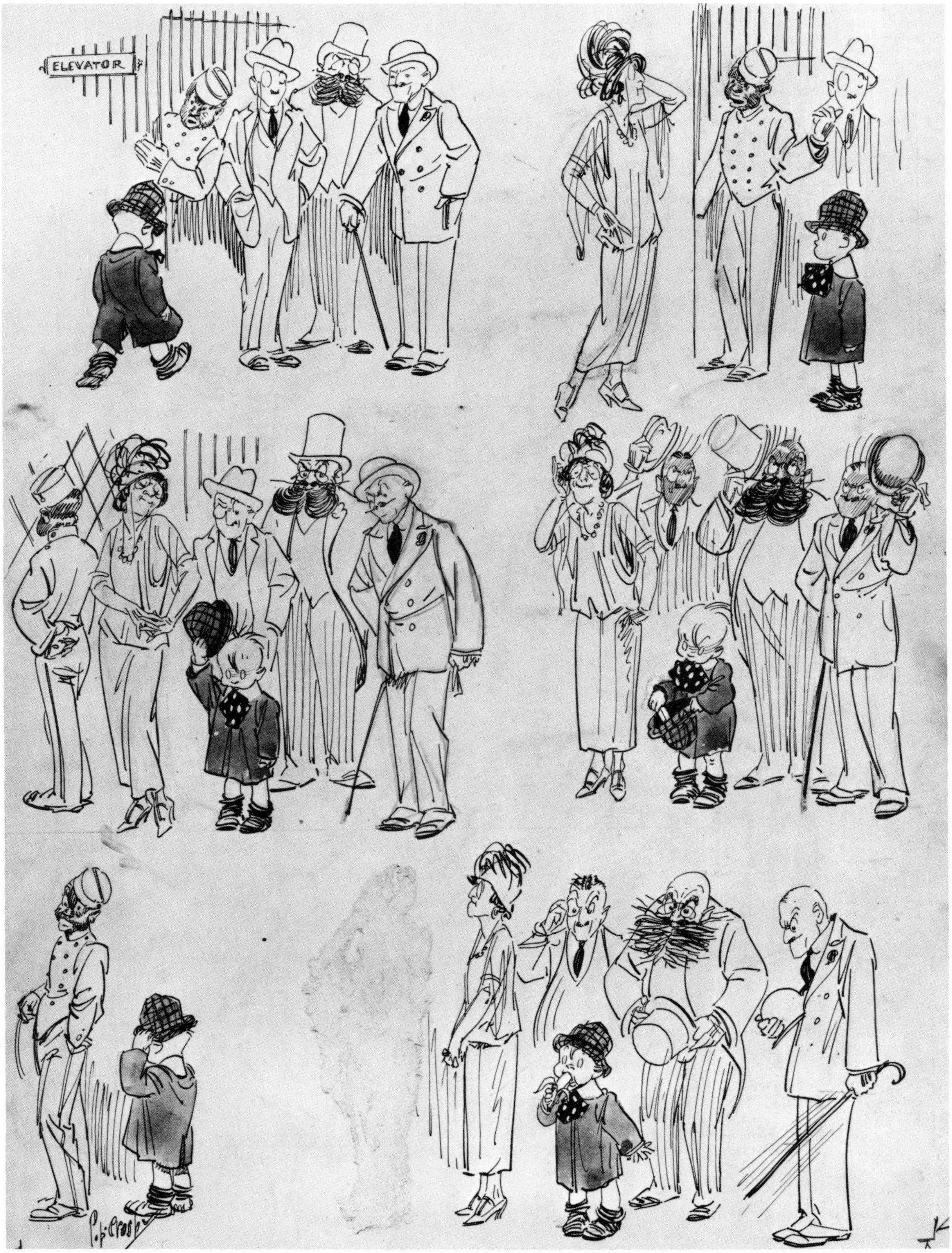
ELEVATOR

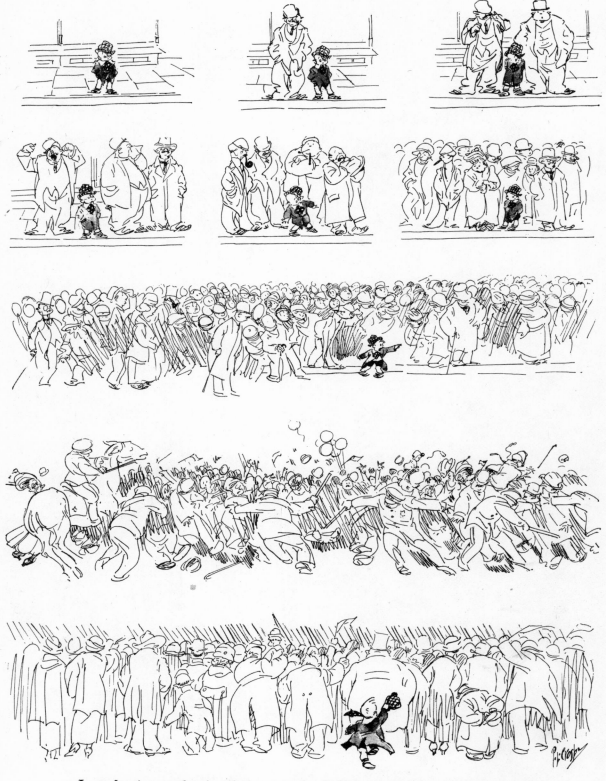

In order to see the Armistice parade, Skippy arrives two hours early.

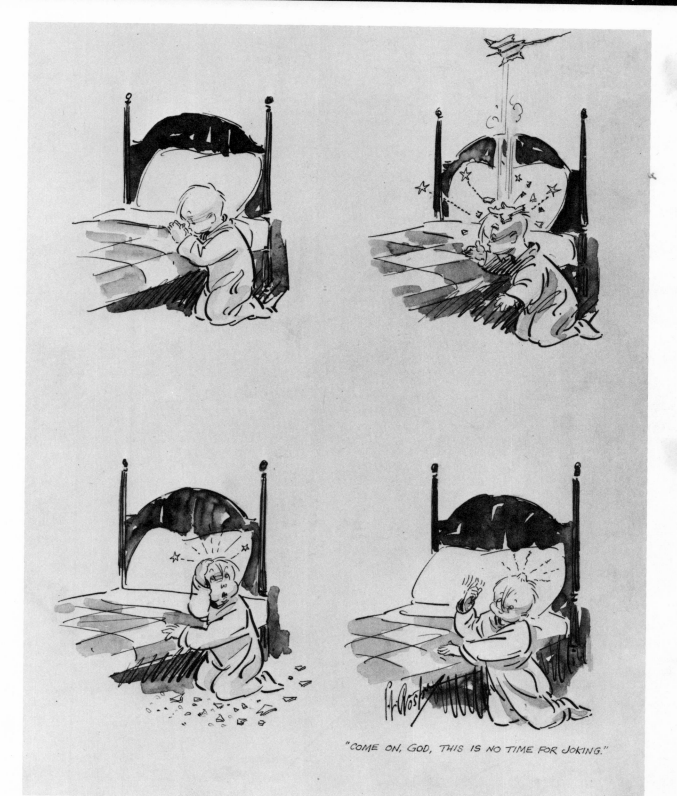

"COME ON, GOD, THIS IS NO TIME FOR JOKING."

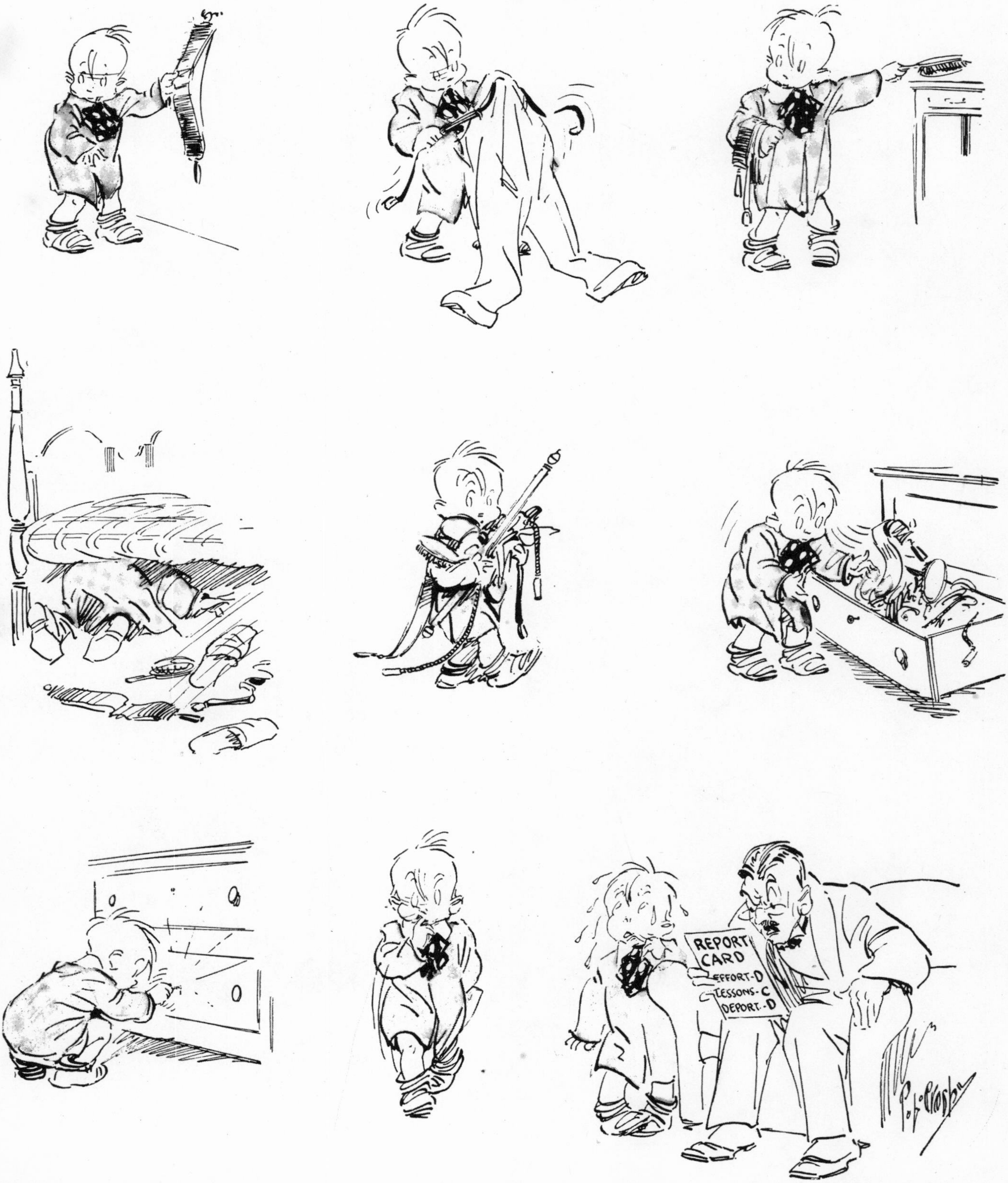
REPORT CARD
EFFORT-D
LESSONS-C
DEPORT.-D

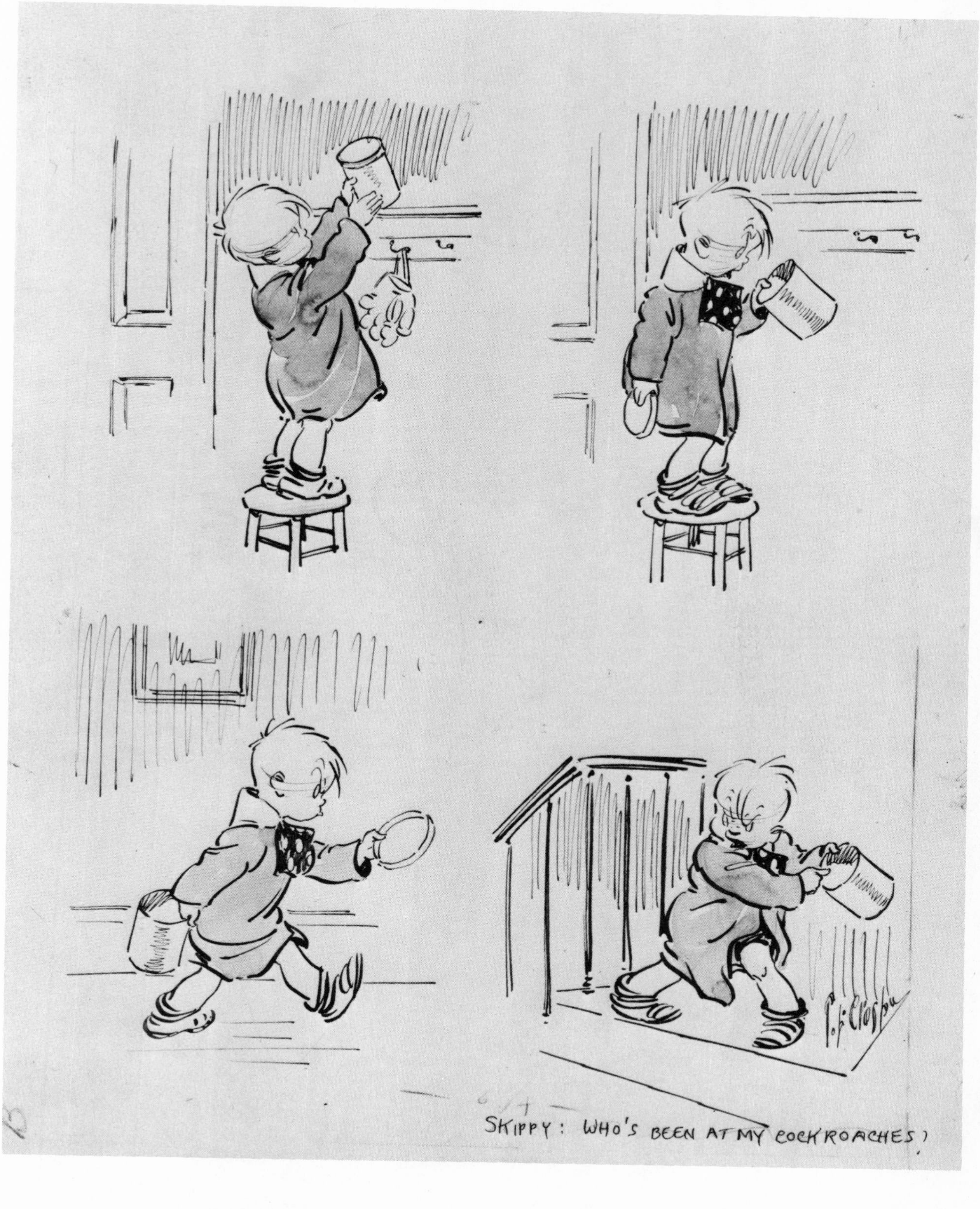
SKIPPY: WHO'S BEEN AT MY COCKROACHES?

"Ma!"

"Mama!"

"Muh-ma!"

"Mother!"

"Well, what is it?"

"Can I look at another corner?"

Father: NOW YOU KNOW WHEN I TELL YOU TO DO A THING I MEAN IT.

Skippy: AND—I—T-THOUGHT—Y-YOU—WERE—M-MY—P-PAL.

"W-WE'LL N-NEVER BE F-FRIENDS AGAIN, N-N-NO, SIR."

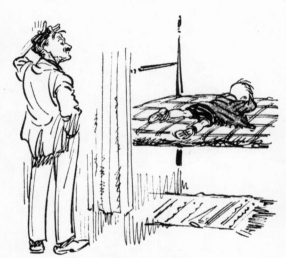

"N-NEVER—N-NO—M-MORE."

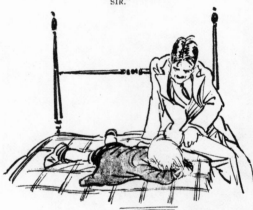

Father: COME ON, SON. LET'S FORGET ALL THIS. DADDY'S YOUR PAL. LISTEN, WHEN I COME HOME I'M GOING TO BRING YOU SOME NICE CHOCOLATE ICE CREAM.
"I-I-I—D-DON'T—WANT—ANY—C-CH-CHOCO-LATE ICE—C-CREAM

"G-GET—S-STRAWB—BERRY."

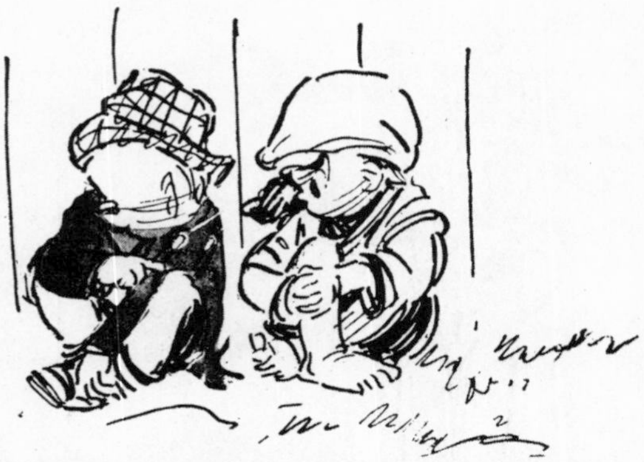

Skippy: If I had to go 'n' had one very, very last wish before I passed away—do ya know what I'd ask for?
Sooky: A chawklet aclair!

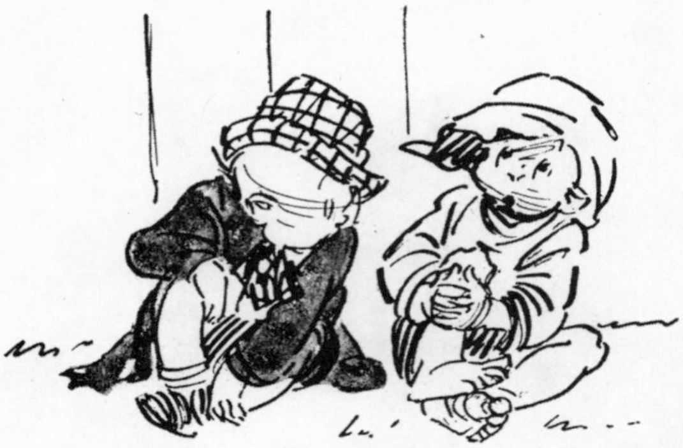

Skippy: No! Listen, I'm kickin' the bucket, see! 'N' I kin have one wish granted before I go. Now do ya know what I'd ask for?
Sooky: A vanilla aclair!

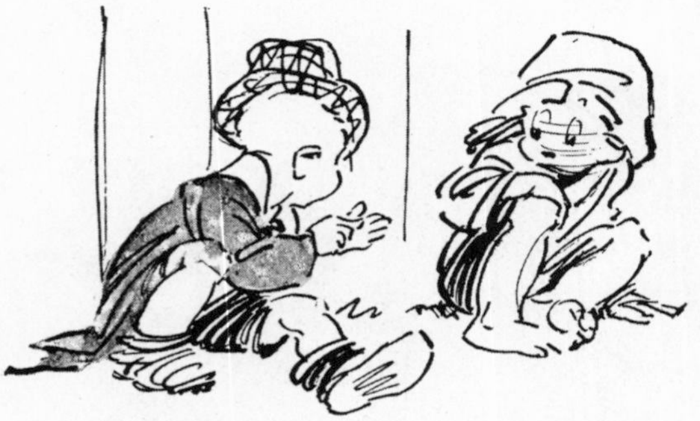

Skippy: No! Listen! I'm going to be hung, see! 'n' the hanger says to me, "What's on ya mind?" "Oh, nothin' but me hat!" I sez, 'n' he comes back 'n' sez, "You seem to talk like a reg'lar guy—is there anything we kin do to make ya happy before we croak ya?" Then he sez, "Ya kin have anything ya ask for." What do ya think I'd ask for?
Sooky: A chawklet and a vanilla aclair.

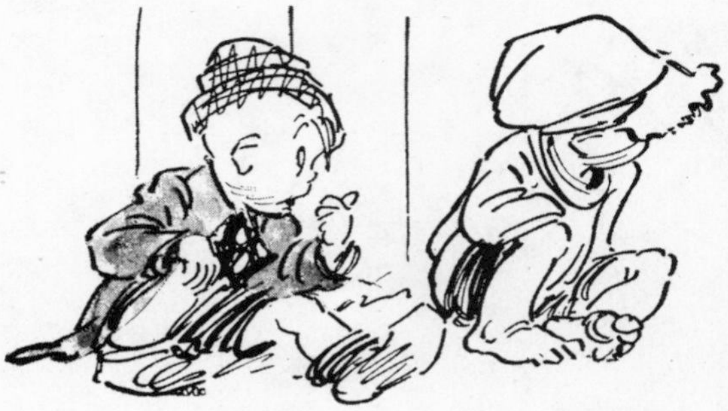

Skippy: There goes Danny Dowd, the cop! He's a reg'lar guy, don't ya think—for a cop, I mean?
Sooky: I hope to tell you, he's a reg'lar guy!

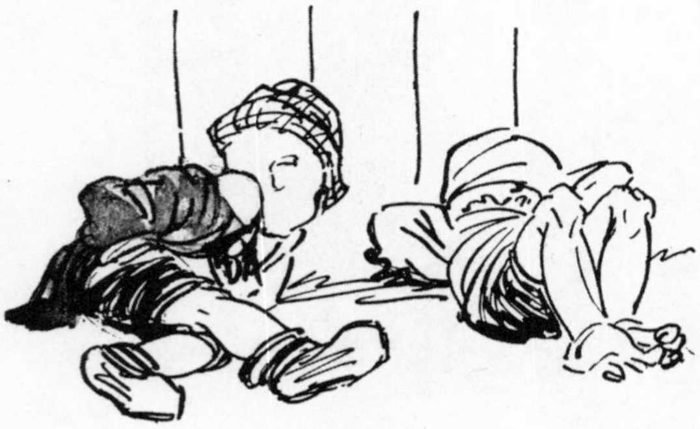

Skippy: What was we talkin' about?
Sooky: Huh! Darned if I kin think!

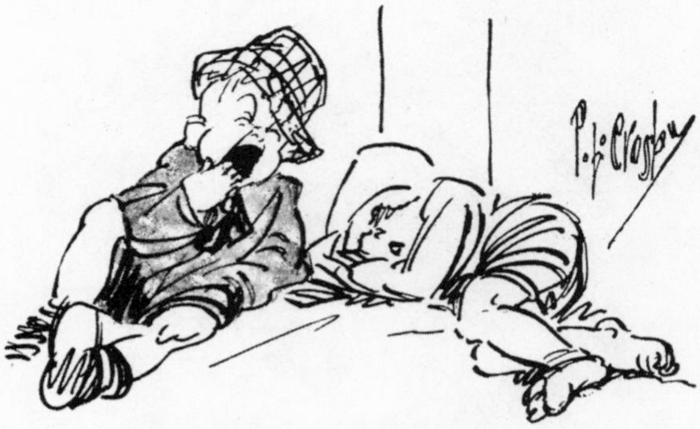
P.L. Crosby

Skippy: Oh, well! Maybe it'll come to me again.

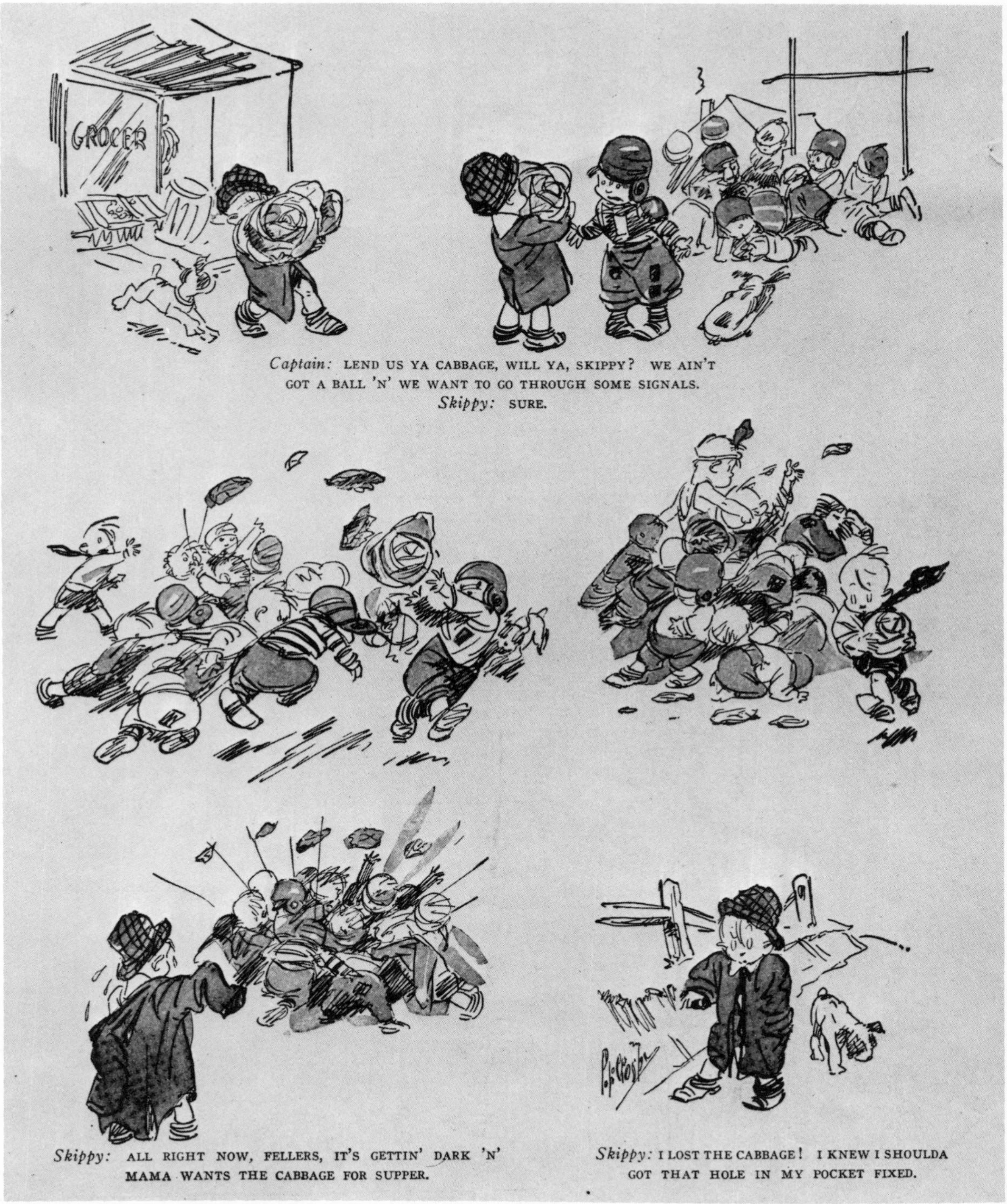
GROCER
Captain: LEND US YA CABBAGE, WILL YA, SKIPPY? WE AIN'T GOT A BALL 'N' WE WANT TO GO THROUGH SOME SIGNALS.
Skippy: SURE.
Skippy: ALL RIGHT NOW, FELLERS, IT'S GETTIN' DARK 'N' MAMA WANTS THE CABBAGE FOR SUPPER.
Skippy: I LOST THE CABBAGE! I KNEW I SHOULDA GOT THAT HOLE IN MY POCKET FIXED.

Skippy Themes

The Flying Boxcart

A prop frequently employed in *Skippy* was the homemade wagon. Pictured as a simple wooden box (or occasionally a dresser drawer) set rather unsturdily on thin-rimmed wheels, it became in Crosby's hands both a philosophic vehicle and a *tour de force* of sheer joy in motion—a conveyance of unsurpassed speed and grace that, no matter what obstacle it soared over, bounced off of, or crashed into, managed always and miraculously to hang together. . . . Well, almost always.

DO YOU BELIEVE IN SANTY CLAUS?
STORMS
YES - I BELIEVE IN SANTY CLAUS.
BUT WHAT GOOD'LL IT DO US IF THE SEWER'S OPEN.

I CARRY A POLICE WHISTLE AN' IT'S A GOOD THING, SO HELP ME.
WHY?
IN CASE SOMEBODY MIGHT START TO ROB ME, I'D BLOW FOR HELP
WHAT HAVE YA GOT THAT ANYBODY MIGHT ROB YA OF
ME POLICE WHISTLE.
© 1931 Perry L. Crosby, Great Britain rights reserved. King Features Syndicate, Inc.
5.5

I'M GLAD YA ASKED ME OVER THIS AFTERNOON.
OTHERWISE, I'D HAVE TO GO WITH MY MOTHER AN' FATHER.
WHERE ARE THEY GOIN'?
OUT FOR A RIDE.
11-8
Percy L. Crosby, Great Britain rights reserved.
© 1935, King Features Syndicate, Inc.

© 1929 Percy L. Crosby, Great Britain rights reserved.
King Features Syndicate, Inc.
TAKE IT EASY, EDDIE!
9-16

UNCLE LOUIE'S BEEN TALKIN' ALL DAY AN' WE DON'T KNOW WHAT IT'S ALL ABOUT.
WHY DON'T YA ASK HIM?
WE CAN'T.
WHY?
HE'S ASLEEP.
© 1933, King Features Syndicate, Inc.
4-27

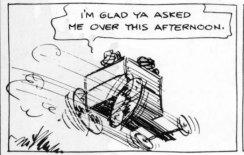

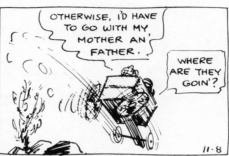

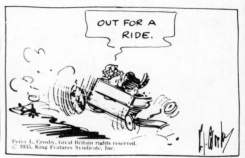

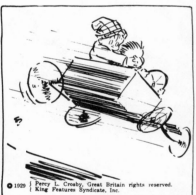

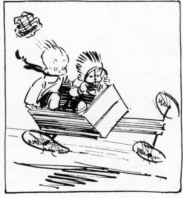

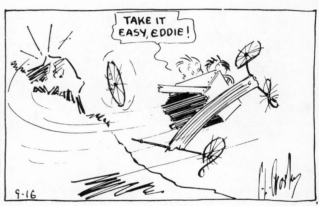

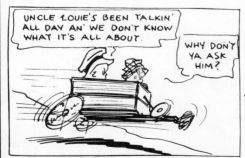

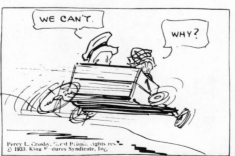

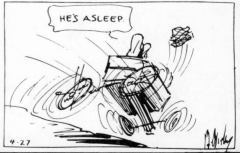

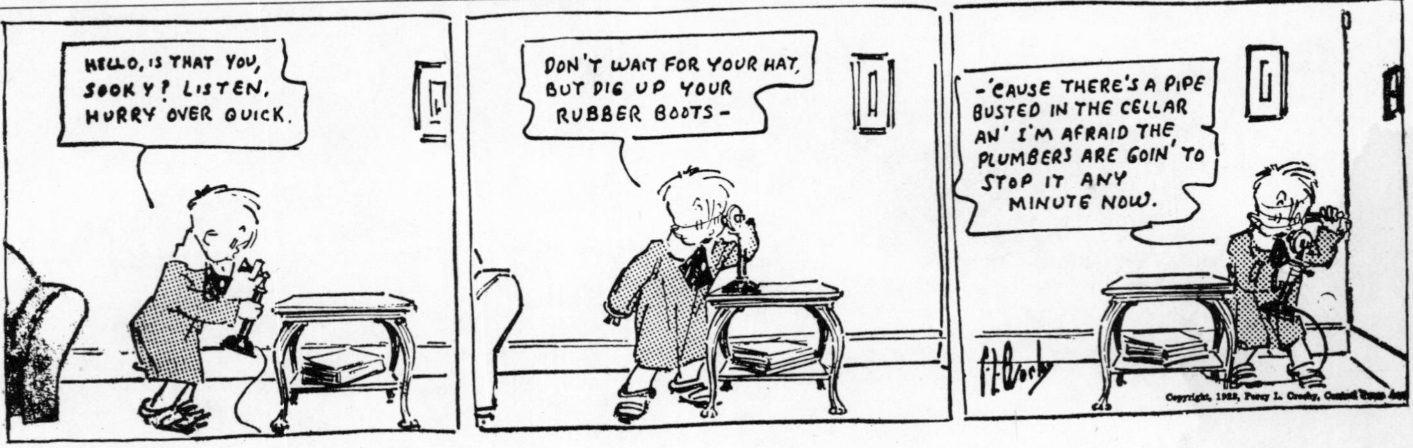
HELLO, IS THAT YOU, SOOKY? LISTEN, HURRY OVER QUICK.
DON'T WAIT FOR YOUR HAT, BUT DIG UP YOUR RUBBER BOOTS -
- 'CAUSE THERE'S A PIPE BUSTED IN THE CELLAR AN' I'M AFRAID THE PLUMBERS ARE GOIN' TO STOP IT ANY MINUTE NOW.

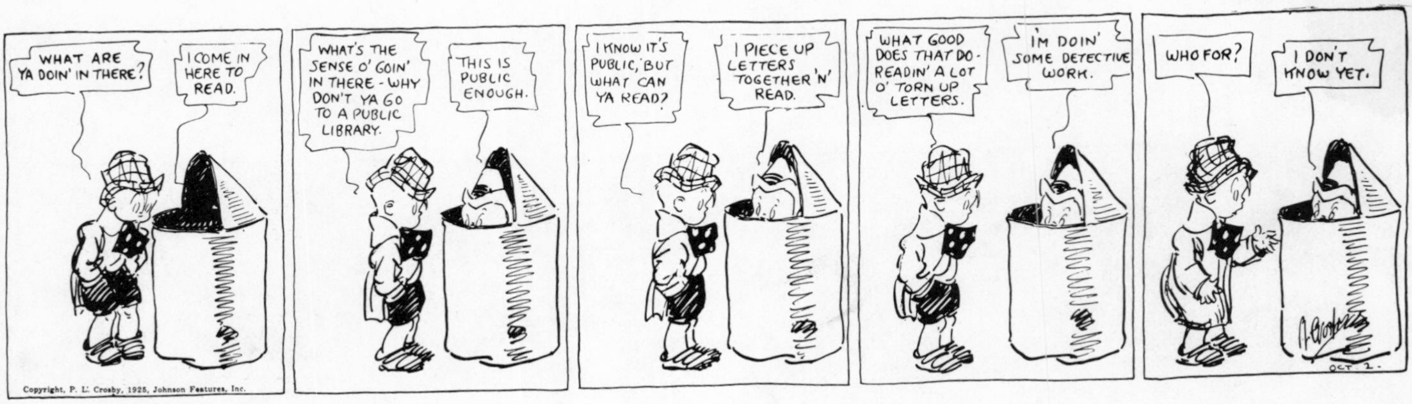
WHAT ARE YA DOIN' IN THERE?
I COME IN HERE TO READ.
WHAT'S THE SENSE O' GOIN' IN THERE - WHY DON'T YA GO TO A PUBLIC LIBRARY.
THIS IS PUBLIC ENOUGH.
I KNOW IT'S PUBLIC, BUT WHAT CAN YA READ?
I PIECE UP LETTERS TOGETHER 'N' READ.
WHAT GOOD DOES THAT DO - READIN' A LOT O' TORN UP LETTERS.
I'M DOIN' SOME DETECTIVE WORK.
WHO FOR?
I DON'T KNOW YET.
Copyright, P. L. Crosby, 1925, Johnson Features, Inc.

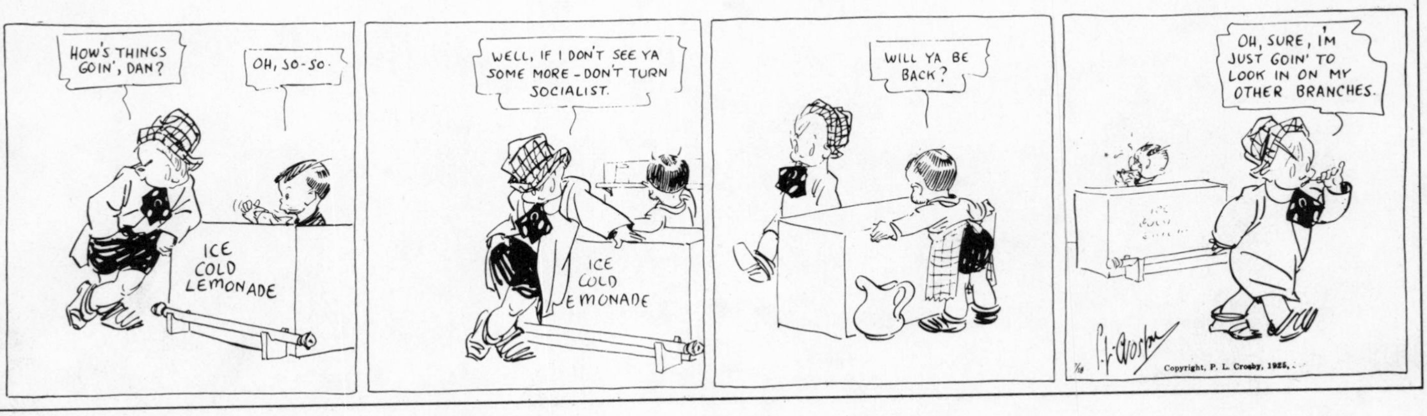
HOW'S THINGS GOIN', DAN?
OH, SO-SO.
ICE COLD LEMONADE
WELL, IF I DON'T SEE YA SOME MORE - DON'T TURN SOCIALIST.
ICE COLD LEMONADE
WILL YA BE BACK?
OH, SURE, I'M JUST GOIN' TO LOOK IN ON MY OTHER BRANCHES.

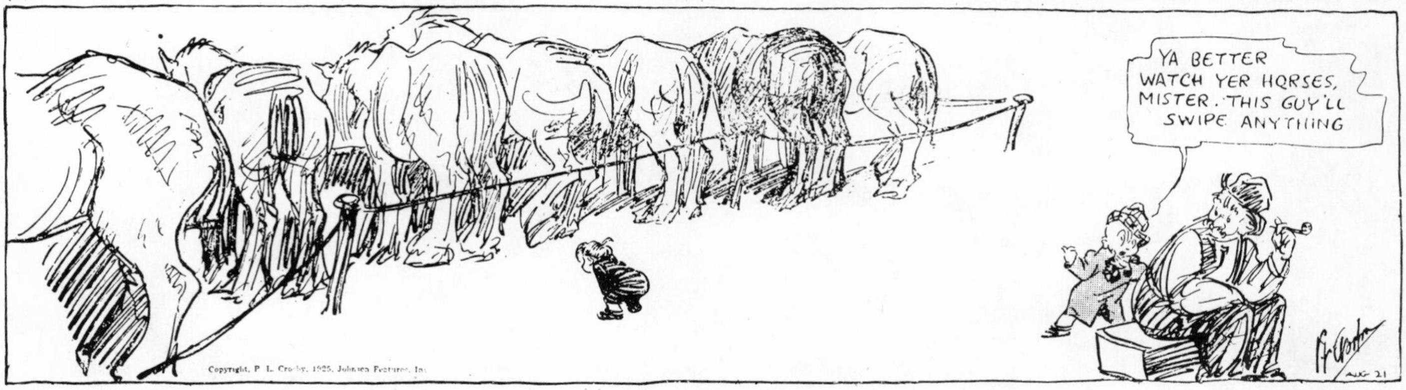
YA BETTER WATCH YER HORSES, MISTER. THIS GUY'LL SWIPE ANYTHING
Copyright, P. L. Crosby, 1925, Johnson Features, Inc.

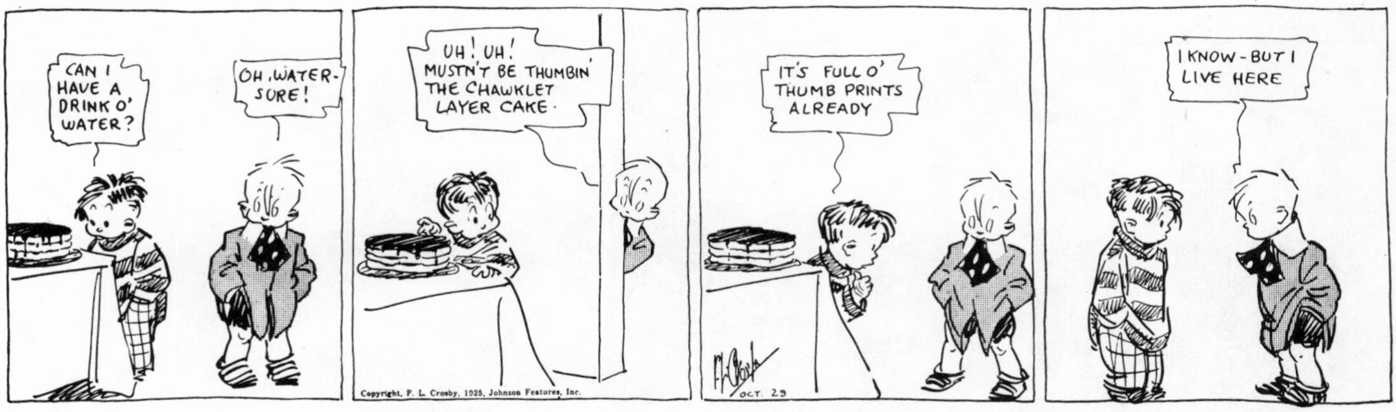
CAN I HAVE A DRINK O' WATER?
OH, WATER-SURE!
UH! UH! MUSTN'T BE THUMBIN' THE CHAWKLET LAYER CAKE.
IT'S FULL O' THUMB PRINTS ALREADY
I KNOW-BUT I LIVE HERE
Copyright, P. L. Crosby, 1925, Johnson Features, Inc.

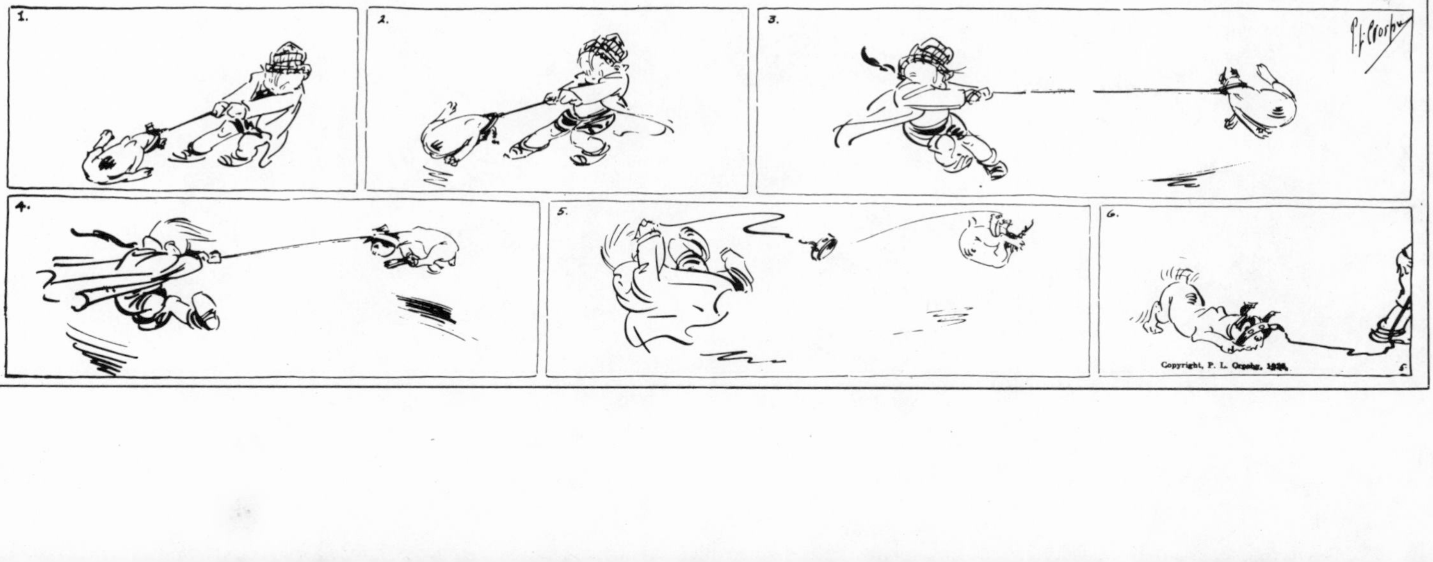
1.
2.
3.
4.
5.
6.
Copyright, P. L. Crosby,

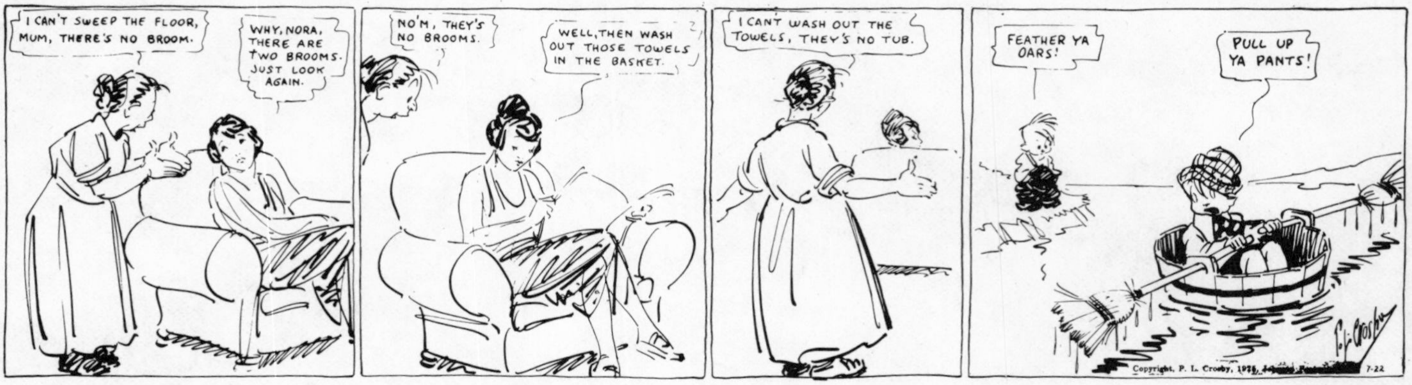
I CAN'T SWEEP THE FLOOR, MUM, THERE'S NO BROOM.
WHY, NORA, THERE ARE TWO BROOMS. JUST LOOK AGAIN.
NO'M, THEY'S NO BROOMS.
WELL, THEN WASH OUT THOSE TOWELS IN THE BASKET.
I CANT WASH OUT THE TOWELS, THEY'S NO TUB.
FEATHER YA OARS!
PULL UP YA PANTS!

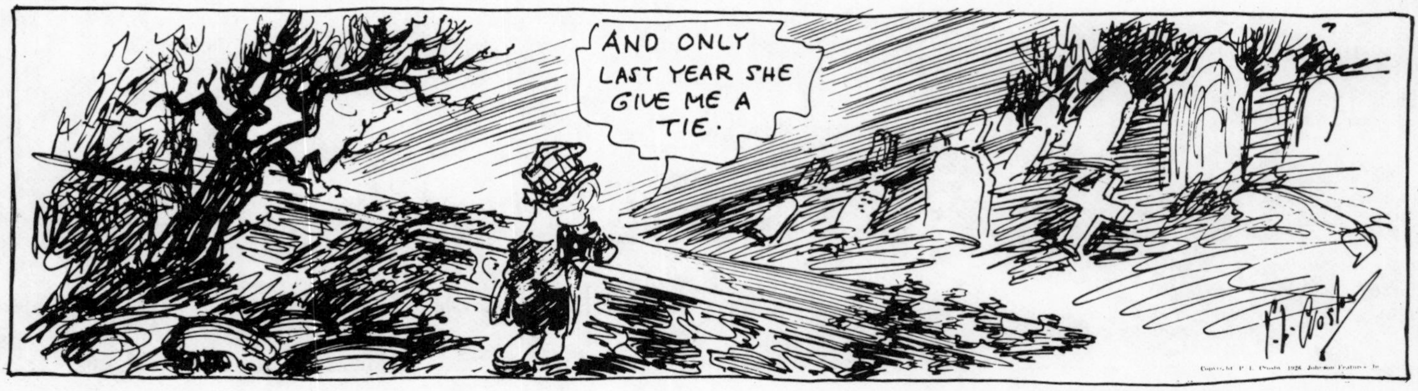
AND ONLY LAST YEAR SHE GIVE ME A TIE.

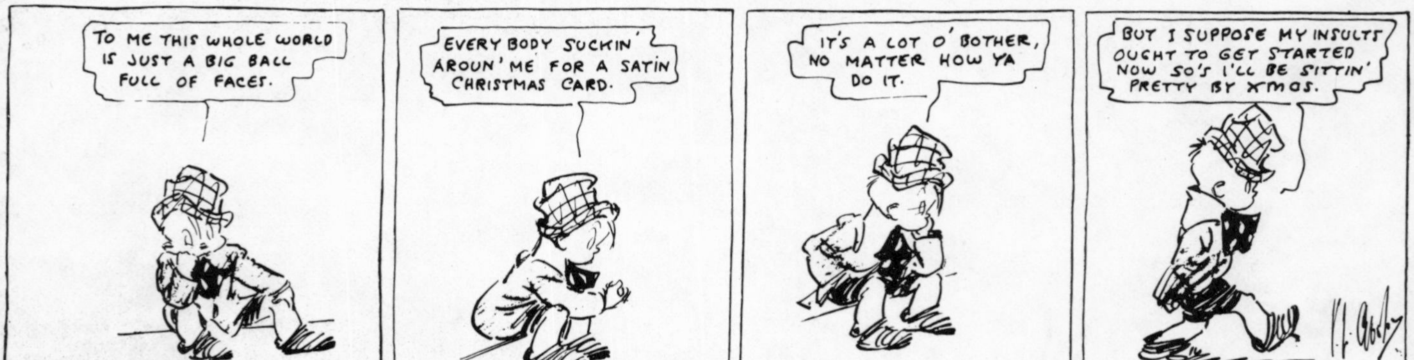
TO ME THIS WHOLE WORLD IS JUST A BIG BALL FULL OF FACES.
EVERY BODY SUCKIN' AROUN' ME FOR A SATIN CHRISTMAS CARD.
IT'S A LOT O' BOTHER, NO MATTER HOW YA DO IT.
BUT I SUPPOSE MY INSULTS OUGHT TO GET STARTED NOW SO'S I'LL BE SITTIN' PRETTY BY XMAS.

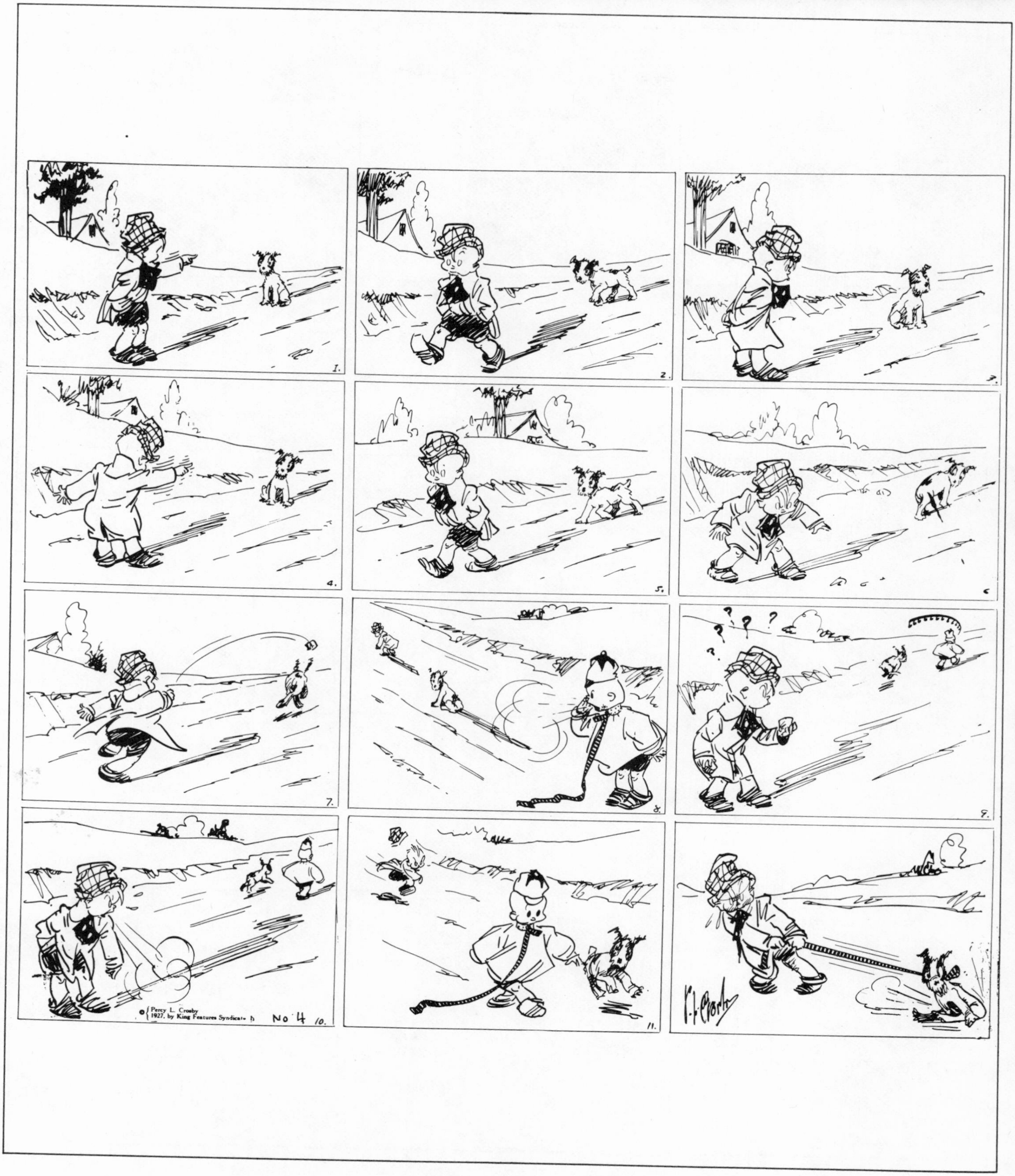
© Percy L. Crosby 1927, by King Features Syndicate
No 4

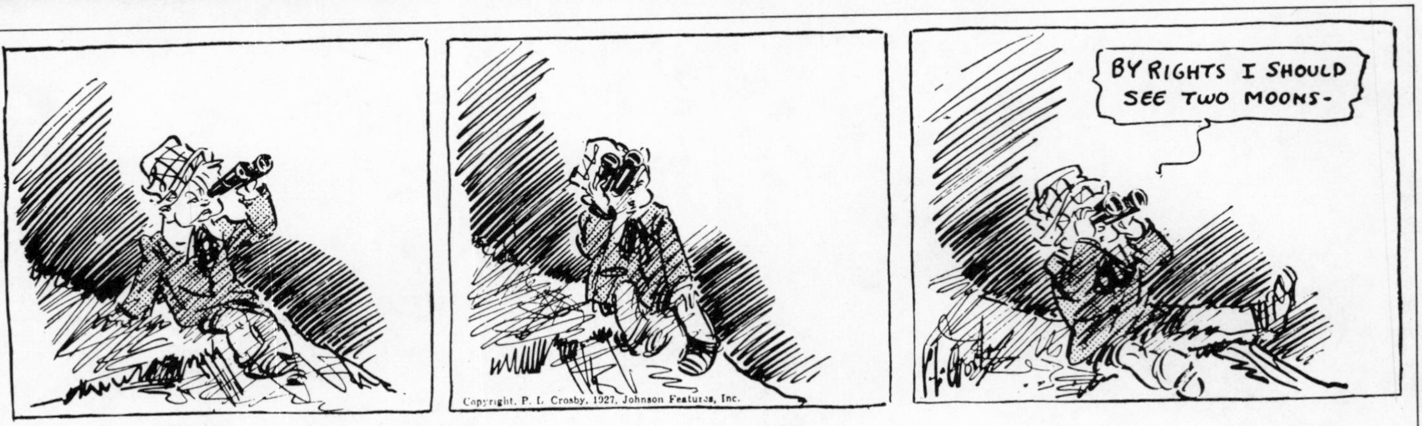
BY RIGHTS I SHOULD SEE TWO MOONS-
Copyright, P. L. Crosby, 1927, Johnson Features, Inc.

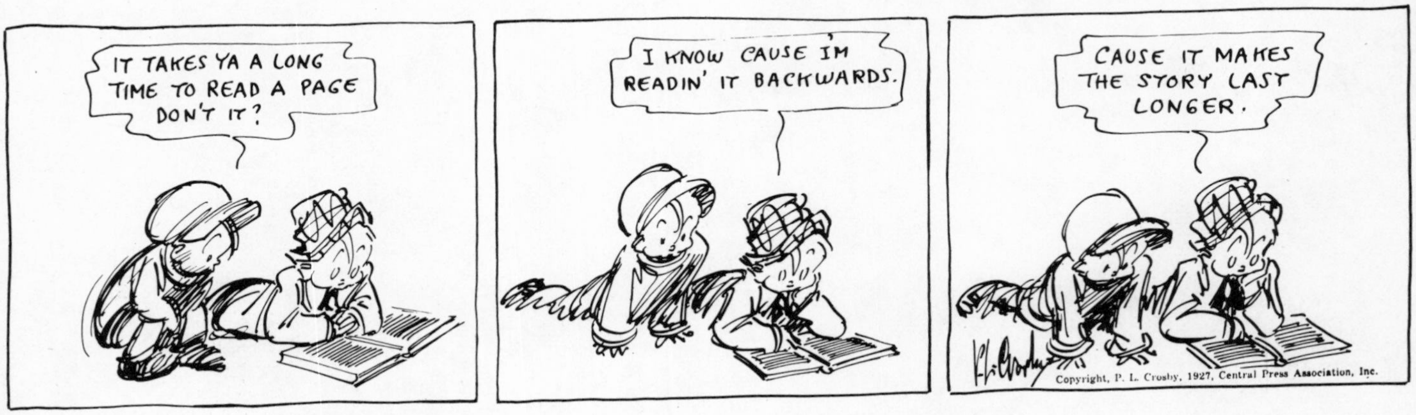
IT TAKES YA A LONG TIME TO READ A PAGE DON'T IT?
I KNOW CAUSE I'M READIN' IT BACKWARDS.
CAUSE IT MAKES THE STORY LAST LONGER.
Copyright, P. L. Crosby, 1927, Central Press Association, Inc.

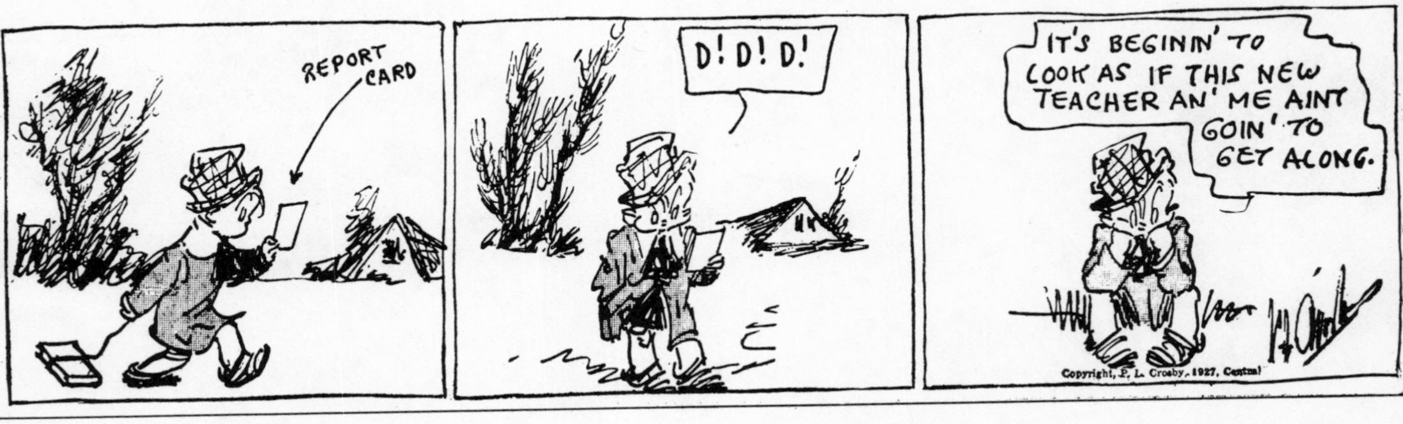
REPORT CARD
D! D! D!
IT'S BEGINNIN' TO LOOK AS IF THIS NEW TEACHER AN' ME AINT GOIN' TO GET ALONG.
Copyright, P. L. Crosby, 1927, Central

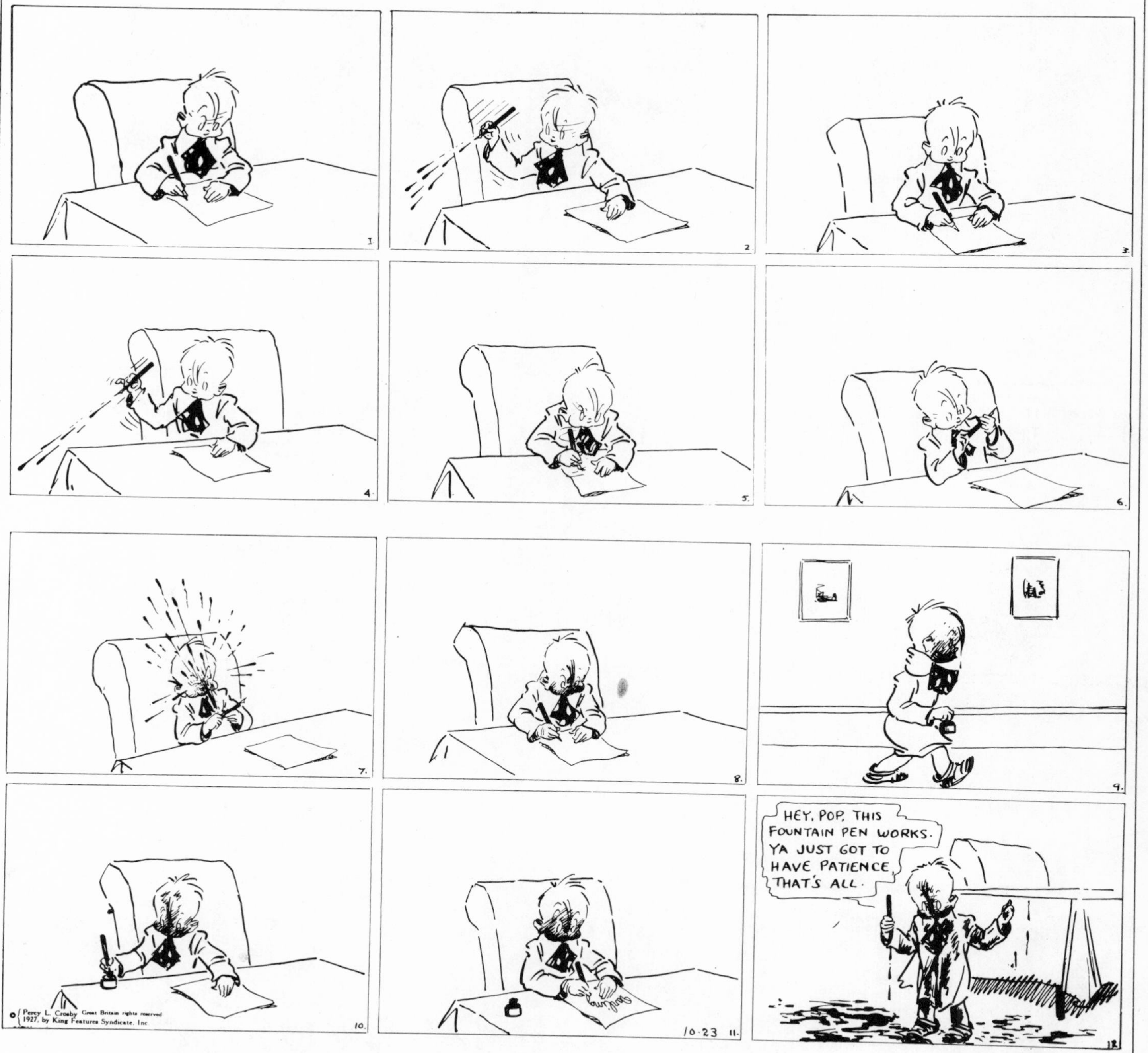
HEY, POP, THIS
FOUNTAIN PEN WORKS.
YA JUST GOT TO
HAVE PATIENCE,
THAT'S ALL.
© Percy L. Crosby Great Britain rights reserved
1927, by King Features Syndicate, Inc.
10-23

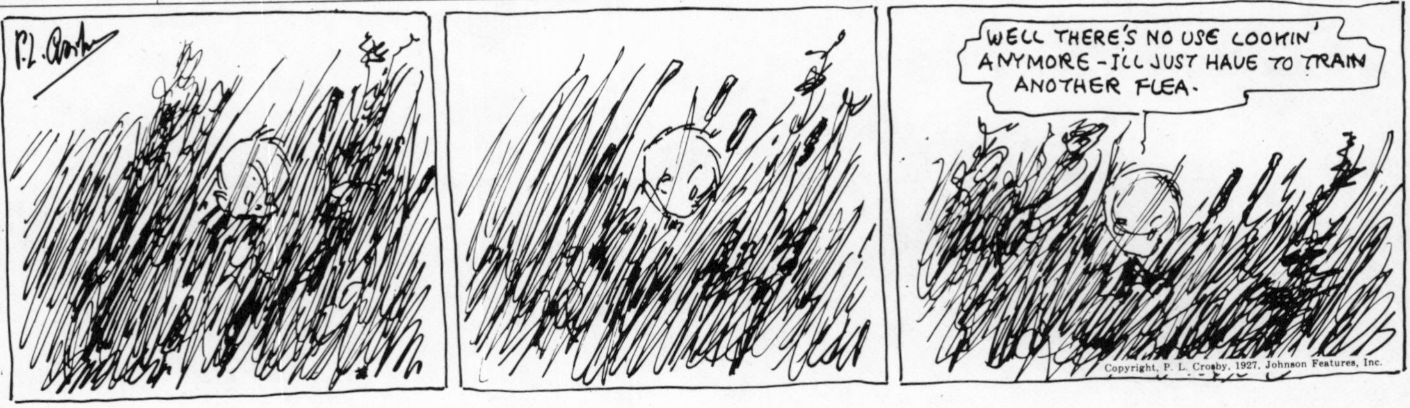
P. L. Crosby
WELL THERE'S NO USE LOOKIN' ANYMORE - I'LL JUST HAVE TO TRAIN ANOTHER FLEA.
Copyright, P. L. Crosby, 1927, Johnson Features, Inc.

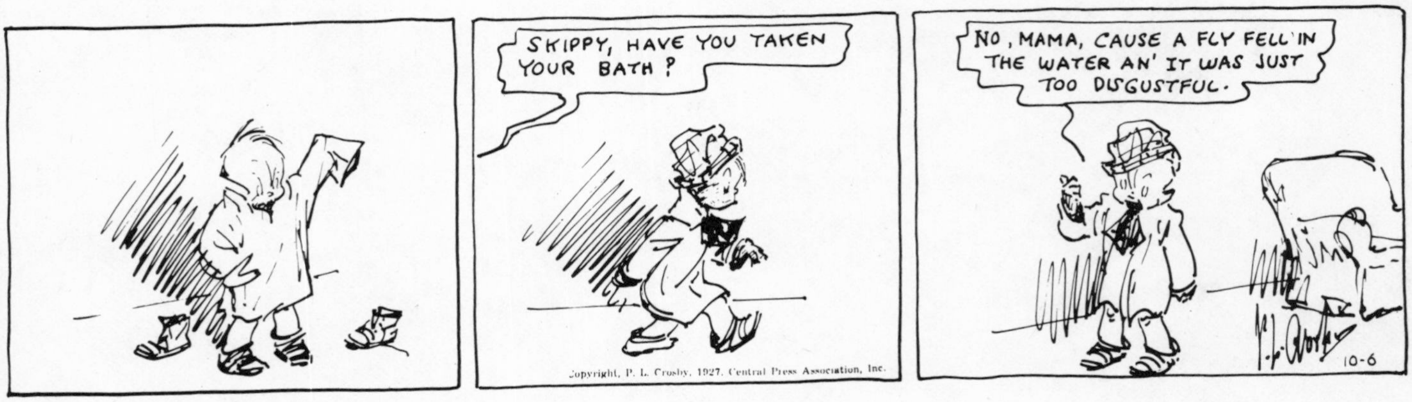
SKIPPY, HAVE YOU TAKEN YOUR BATH?
NO, MAMA, CAUSE A FLY FELL IN THE WATER AN' IT WAS JUST TOO DISGUSTFUL.
Copyright, P. L. Crosby, 1927, Central Press Association, Inc.
P. L. Crosby
10-6

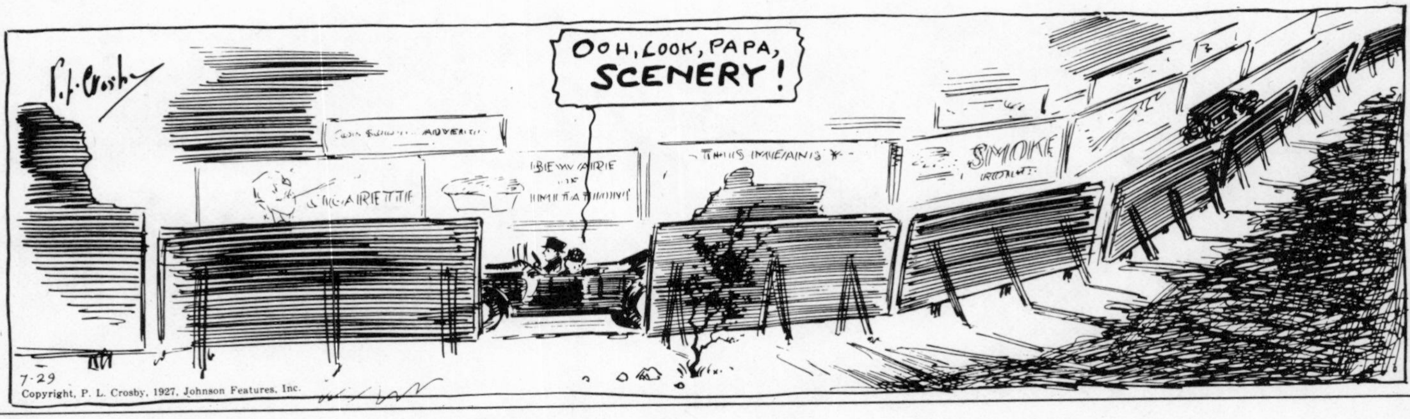
P. L. Crosby
OOH, LOOK, PAPA, SCENERY!
SMOKE
7-29
Copyright, P. L. Crosby, 1927, Johnson Features, Inc.

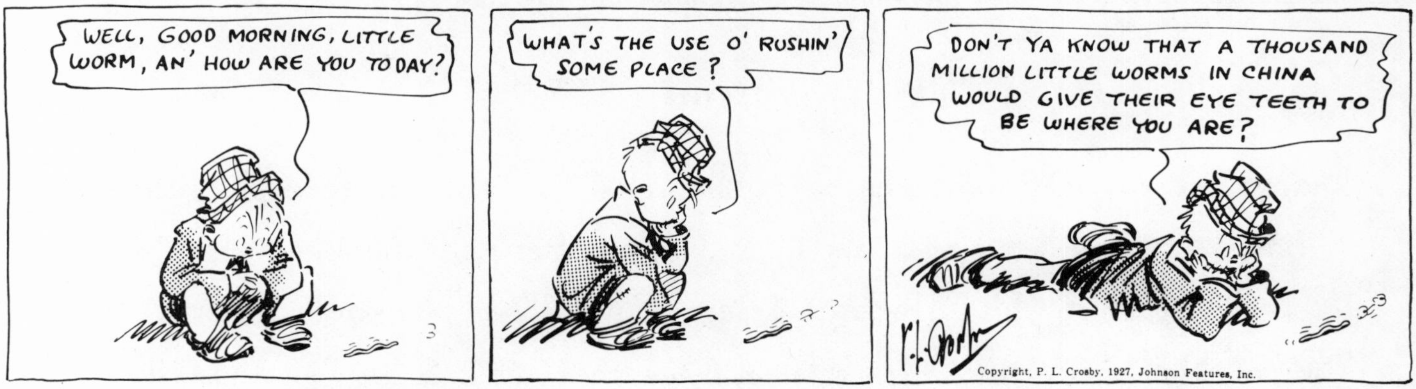
WELL, GOOD MORNING, LITTLE WORM, AN' HOW ARE YOU TODAY?
WHAT'S THE USE O' RUSHIN' SOME PLACE?
DON'T YA KNOW THAT A THOUSAND MILLION LITTLE WORMS IN CHINA WOULD GIVE THEIR EYE TEETH TO BE WHERE YOU ARE?
Copyright, P. L. Crosby, 1927, Johnson Features, Inc.

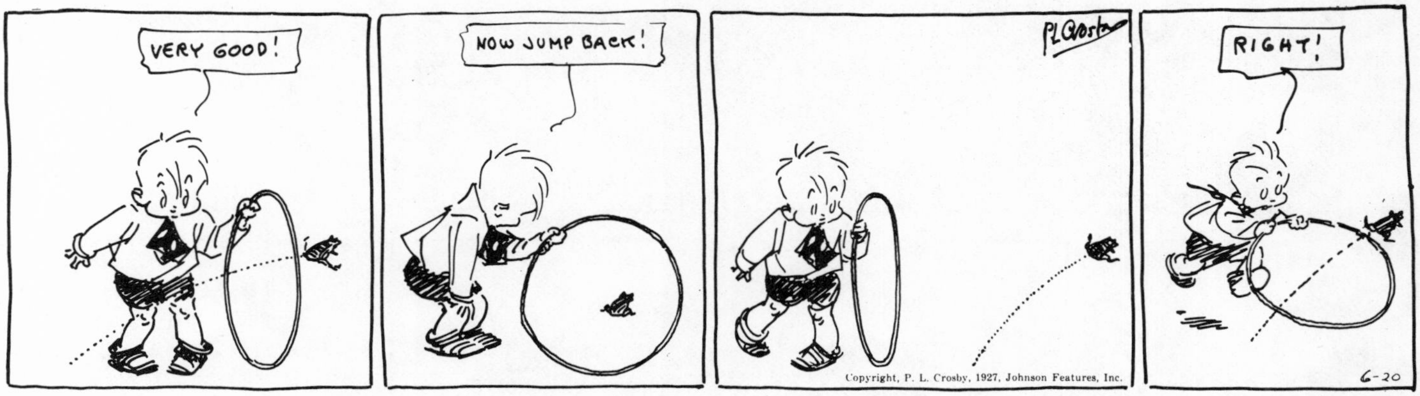
VERY GOOD!
NOW JUMP BACK!
RIGHT!
Copyright, P. L. Crosby, 1927, Johnson Features, Inc.
6-20

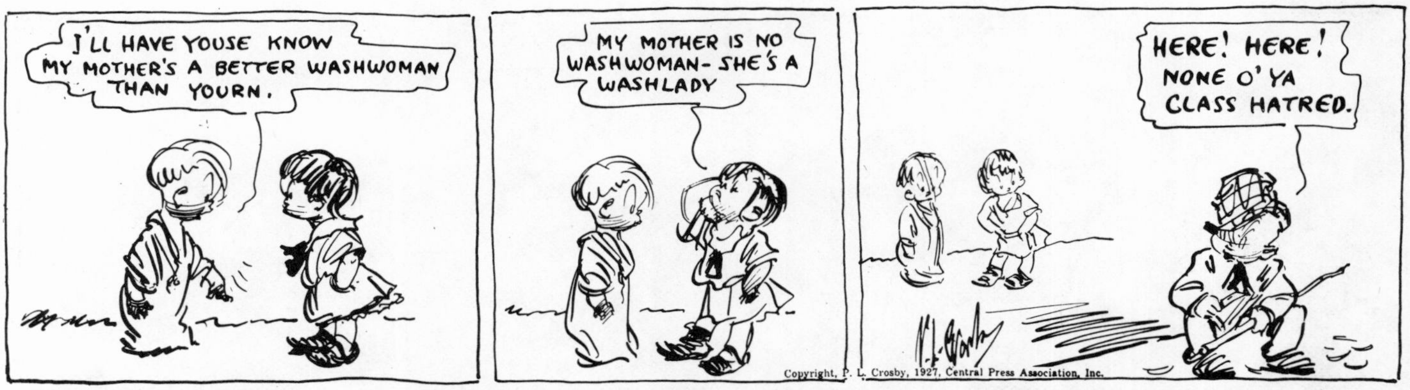
I'LL HAVE YOUSE KNOW MY MOTHER'S A BETTER WASHWOMAN THAN YOURN.
MY MOTHER IS NO WASHWOMAN- SHE'S A WASHLADY
HERE! HERE! NONE O' YA CLASS HATRED.
Copyright, P. L. Crosby, 1927, Central Press Association, Inc.

Skippy Themes

Sports

Although Crosby loved sports, he was not himself a natural athlete (except for the early boxing prowess he claimed, and his known riding and shooting skills). Still, he never outgrew his early hero worship of sports champions or his passion for sports. Crosby's insecurity as an athlete is reflected in Skippy's enthusiastic ineptitude. Like his creator, Skippy often pronounced his failures as victories.

C'MON, SECOND, LET'S HAVE IT!
5-30

OH, NO WONDER! I GOT SOMEBODY ELSE'S SKATES.
Copyright, P. L. Crosby, 1927, Central Press Association, Inc.

ARE YA HOIT?
NO-WHY?
S'LONG, FELLERS, I GOTTA BE GOIN'
JUST AS I THOUGHT— I AM HURT.
Copyright, 1928, Percy L. Crosby, Central Press Assn., Inc.

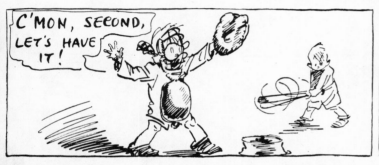

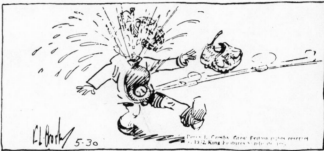

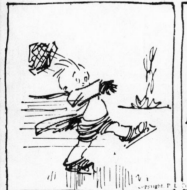

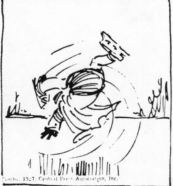

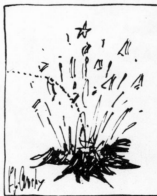

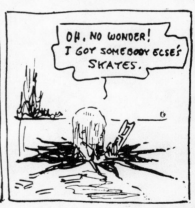

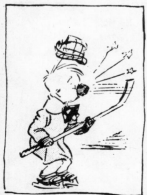

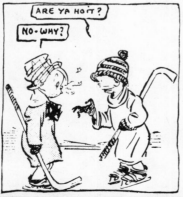

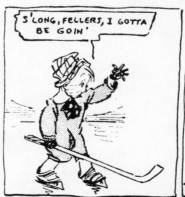

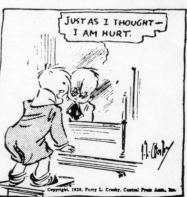

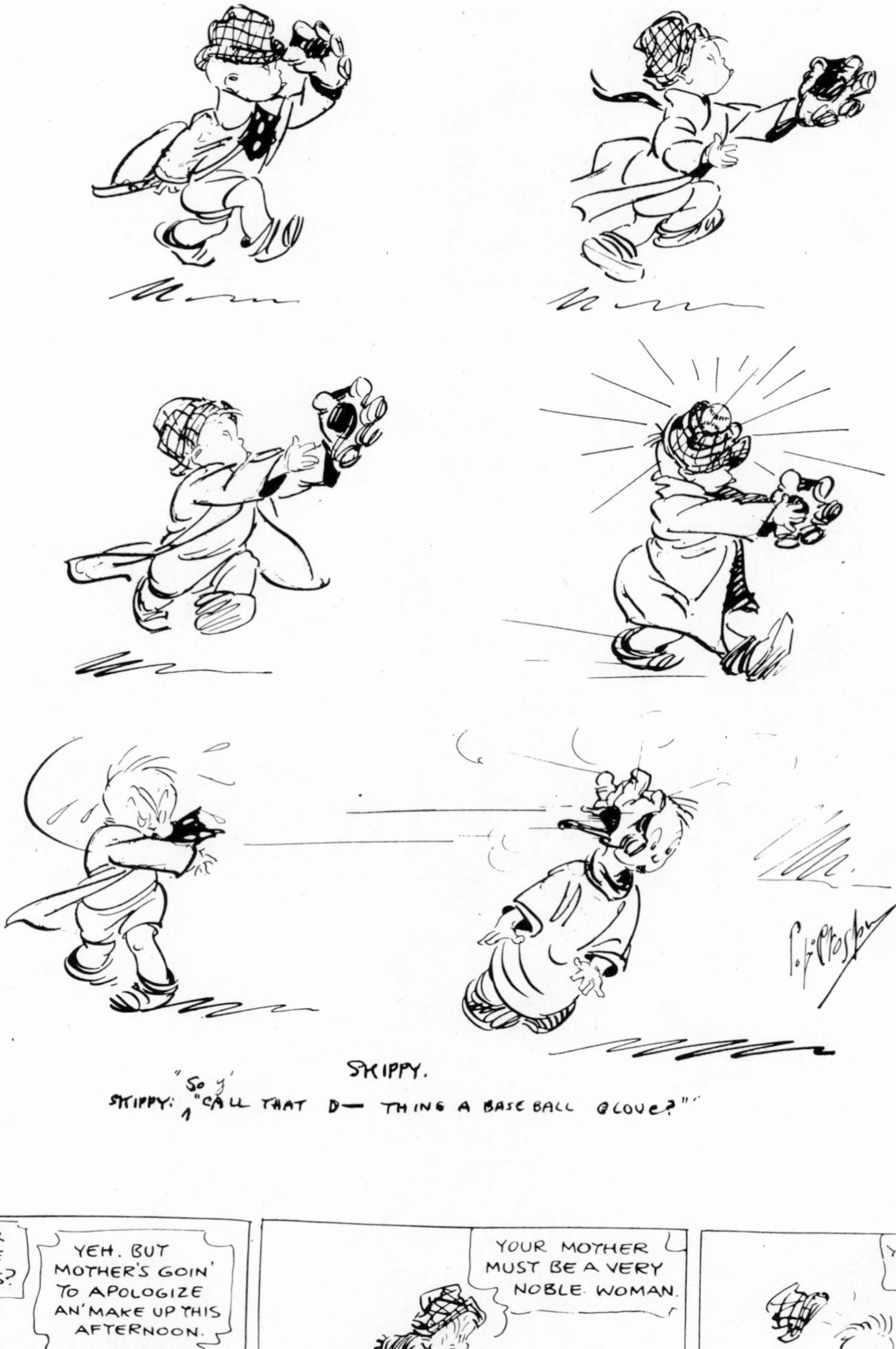

SKIPPY.

SKIPPY: "So y' CALL THAT D— THING A BASE BALL GLOVE?"

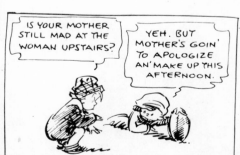

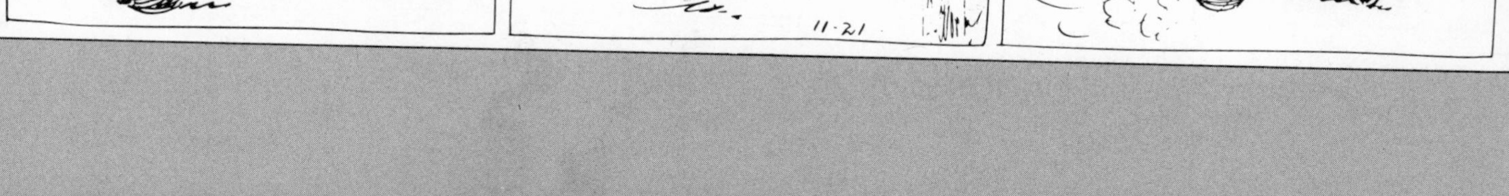
IS YOUR MOTHER STILL MAD AT THE WOMAN UPSTAIRS?
YEH. BUT MOTHER'S GOIN' TO APOLOGIZE AN' MAKE UP THIS AFTERNOON.
YOUR MOTHER MUST BE A VERY NOBLE WOMAN.
YOU'RE RIGHT, SHE IS! AN' BESIDES, WE'RE GETTIN' LOW ON SUGAR.
11-21

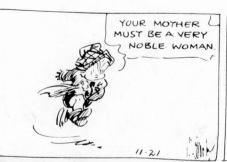

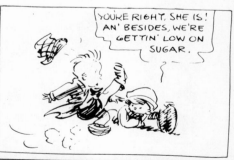

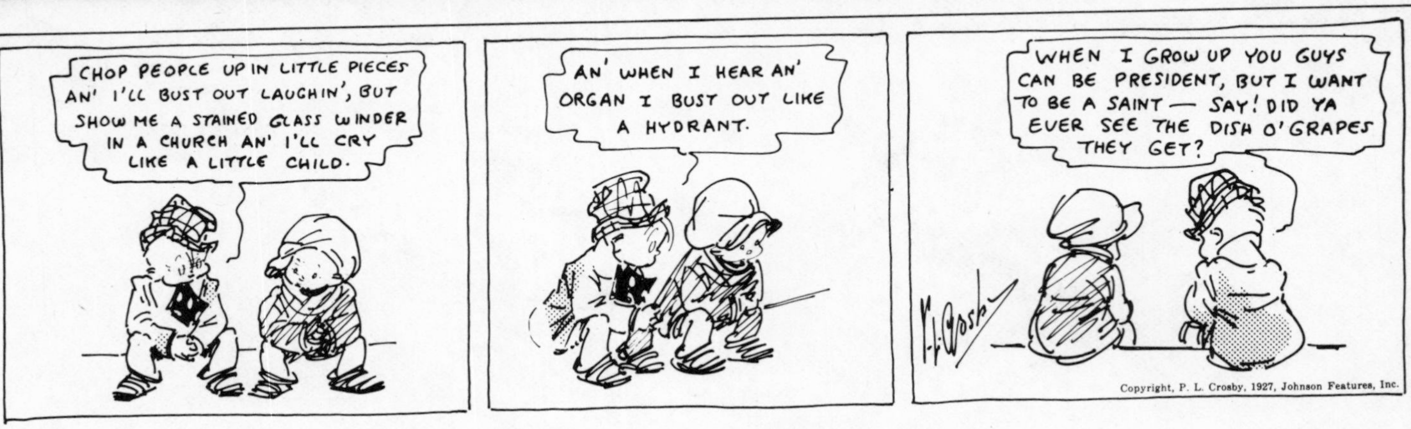
CHOP PEOPLE UP IN LITTLE PIECES AN' I'LL BUST OUT LAUGHIN', BUT SHOW ME A STAINED GLASS WINDER IN A CHURCH AN' I'LL CRY LIKE A LITTLE CHILD.
AN' WHEN I HEAR AN' ORGAN I BUST OUT LIKE A HYDRANT.
WHEN I GROW UP YOU GUYS CAN BE PRESIDENT, BUT I WANT TO BE A SAINT — SAY! DID YA EVER SEE THE DISH O' GRAPES THEY GET?
Copyright, P. L. Crosby, 1927, Johnson Features, Inc.

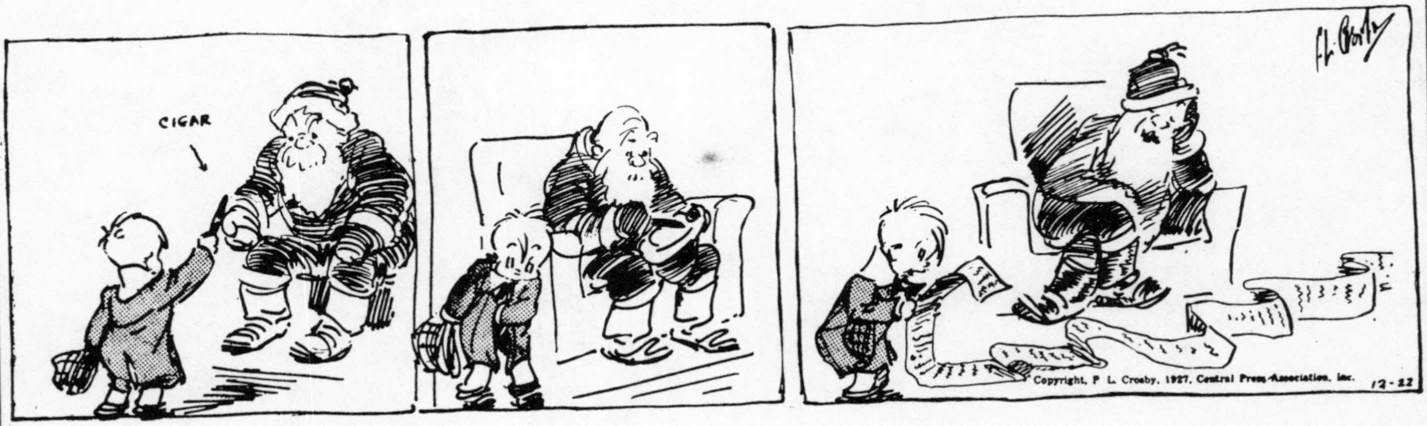
CIGAR
Copyright, P L Crosby, 1927, Central Press Association, Inc.
12-22

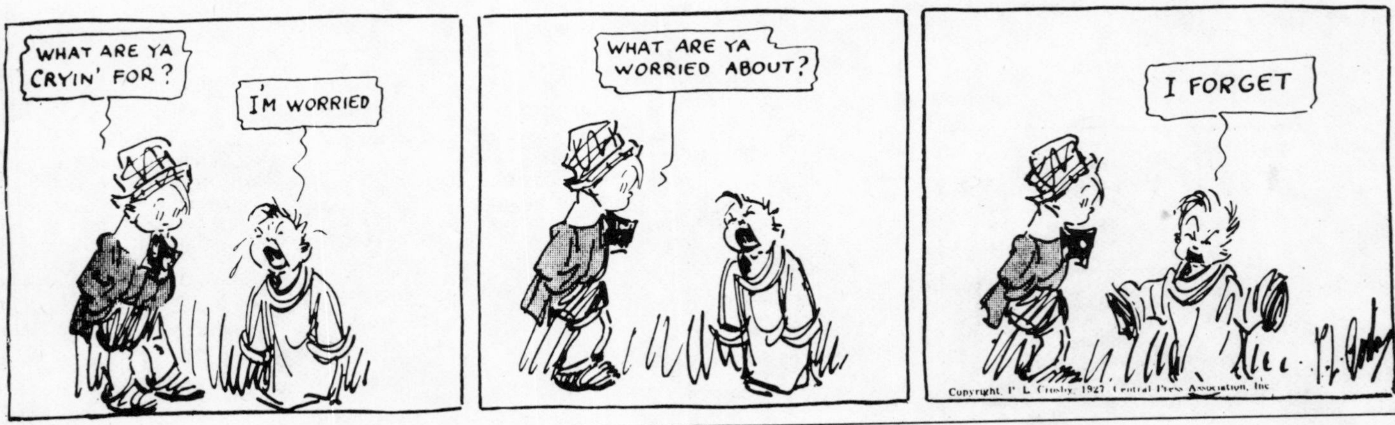
WHAT ARE YA CRYIN' FOR?
I'M WORRIED
WHAT ARE YA WORRIED ABOUT?
I FORGET
Copyright, P. L. Crosby, 1927, Central Press Association, Inc

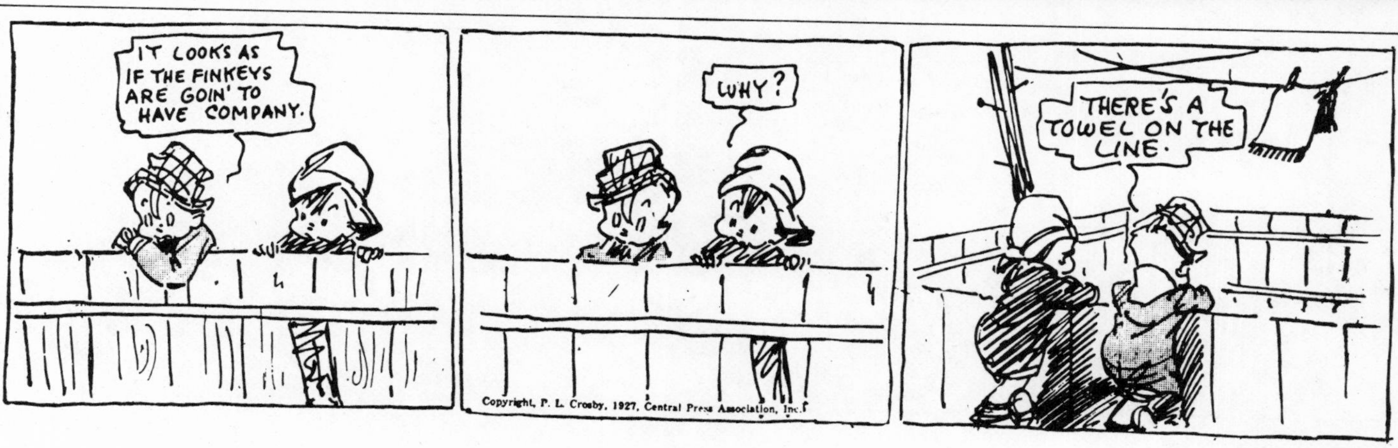
IT LOOKS AS IF THE FINKEYS ARE GOIN' TO HAVE COMPANY.
WHY?
Copyright, P. L. Crosby, 1927, Central Press Association, Inc.
THERE'S A TOWEL ON THE LINE.

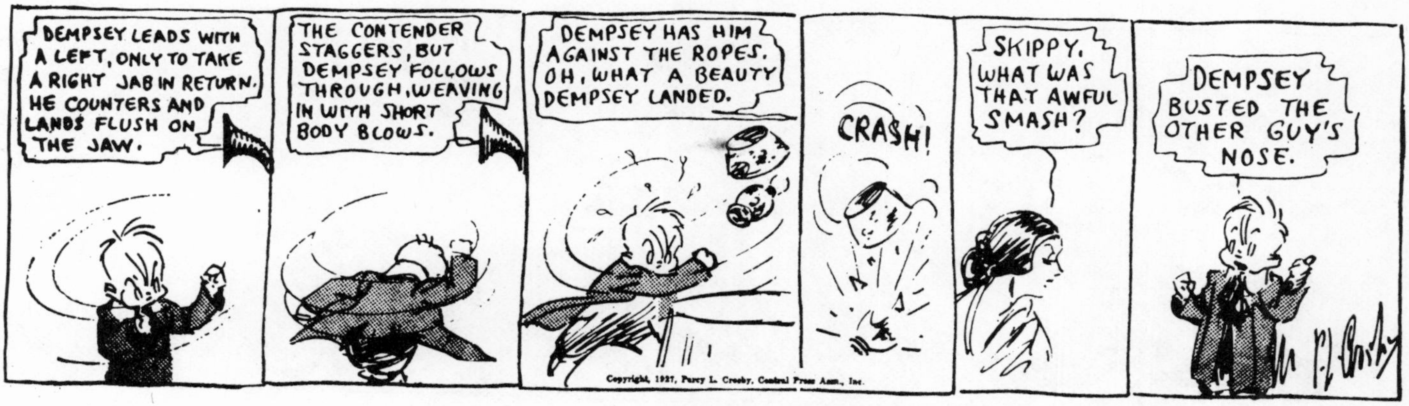
DEMPSEY LEADS WITH A LEFT, ONLY TO TAKE A RIGHT JAB IN RETURN. HE COUNTERS AND LANDS FLUSH ON THE JAW.
THE CONTENDER STAGGERS, BUT DEMPSEY FOLLOWS THROUGH, WEAVING IN WITH SHORT BODY BLOWS.
DEMPSEY HAS HIM AGAINST THE ROPES. OH, WHAT A BEAUTY DEMPSEY LANDED.
Copyright, 1927, Percy L. Crosby, Central Press Assn., Inc.
CRASH!
SKIPPY, WHAT WAS THAT AWFUL SMASH?
DEMPSEY BUSTED THE OTHER GUY'S NOSE.

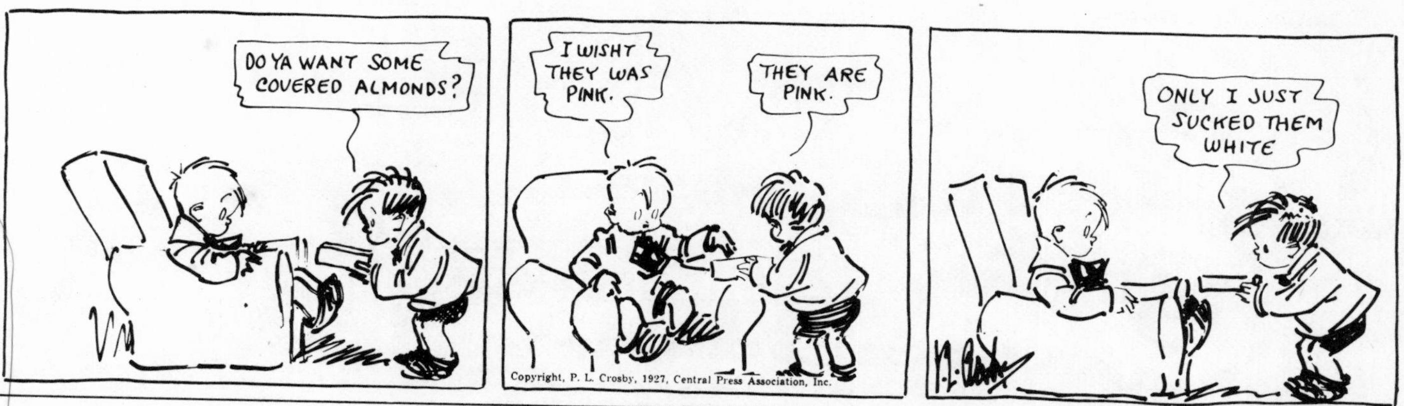
DO YA WANT SOME COVERED ALMONDS?
I WISHT THEY WAS PINK.
THEY ARE PINK.
Copyright, P. L. Crosby, 1927, Central Press Association, Inc.
ONLY I JUST SUCKED THEM WHITE

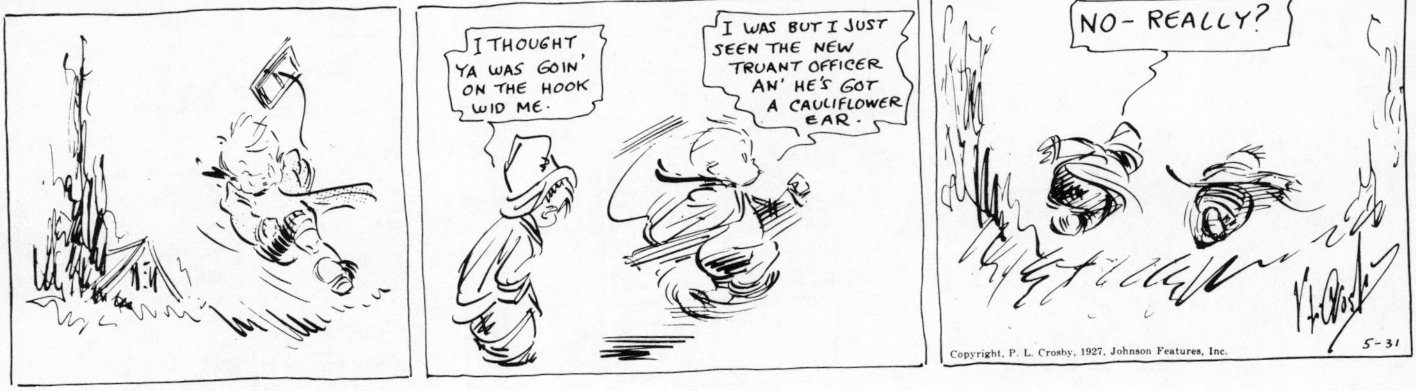
I THOUGHT YA WAS GOIN' ON THE HOOK WID ME.
I WAS BUT I JUST SEEN THE NEW TRUANT OFFICER AN' HE'S GOT A CAULIFLOWER EAR.
NO-REALLY?
Copyright, P. L. Crosby, 1927, Johnson Features, Inc.
5-31

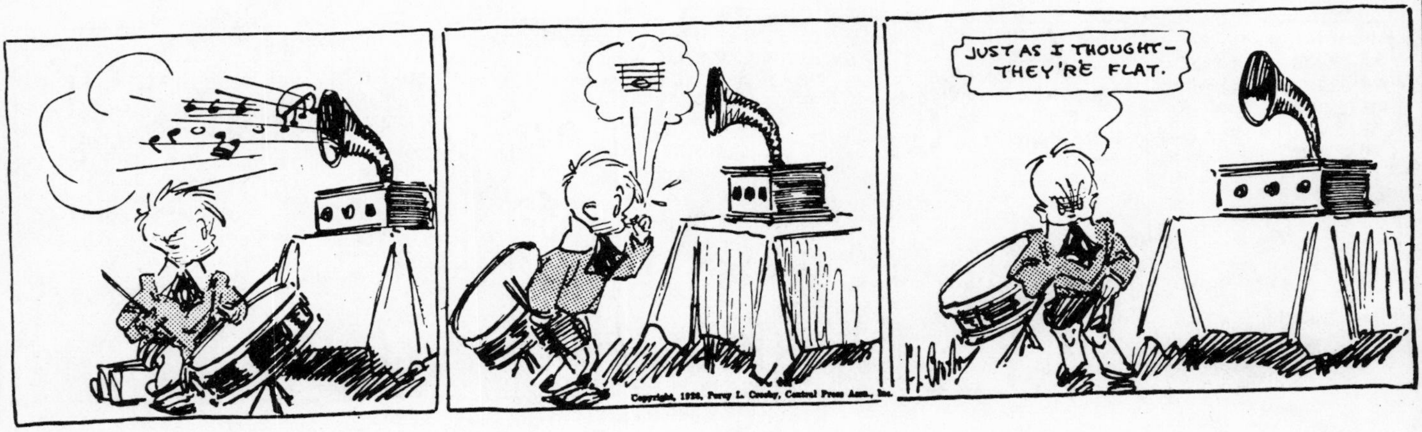
JUST AS I THOUGHT- THEY'RE FLAT.
Copyright, 1928, Percy L. Crosby, Central Press Assn., Inc.

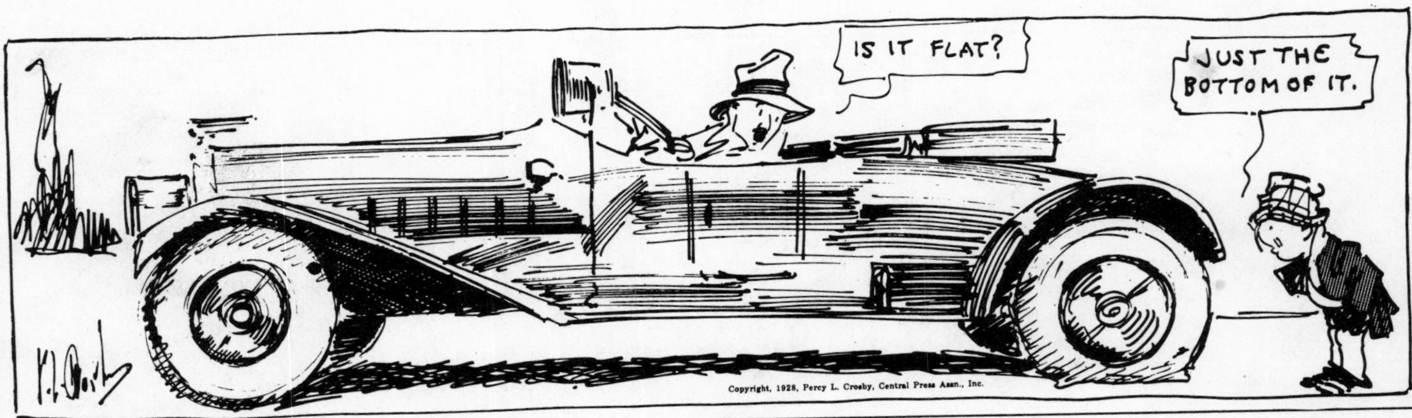
IS IT FLAT?
JUST THE BOTTOM OF IT.
Copyright, 1928, Percy L. Crosby, Central Press Assn., Inc.

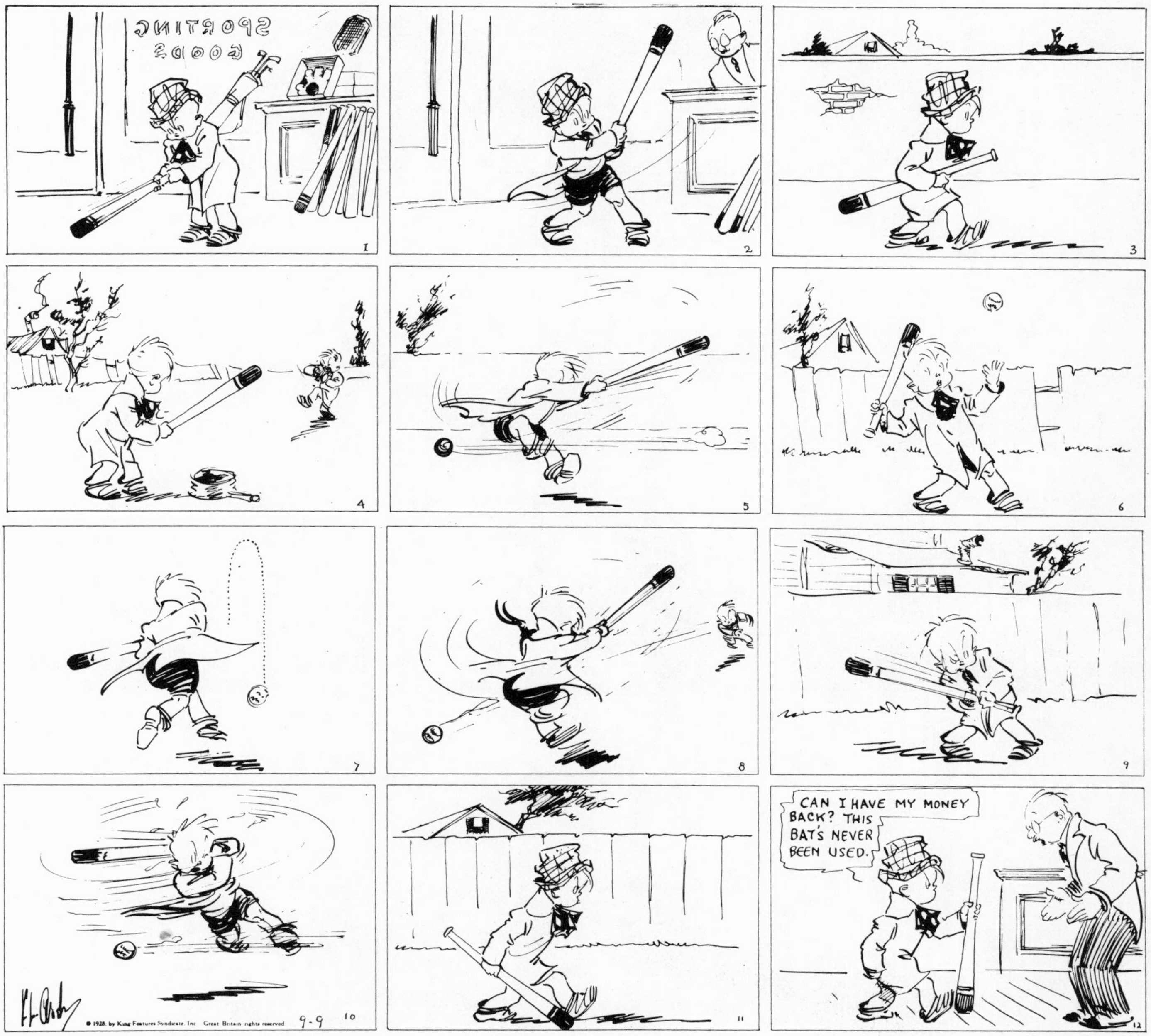
SPORTING GOODS
CAN I HAVE MY MONEY BACK? THIS BAT'S NEVER BEEN USED.
© 1928, by King Features Syndicate, Inc. Great Britain rights reserved
9-9

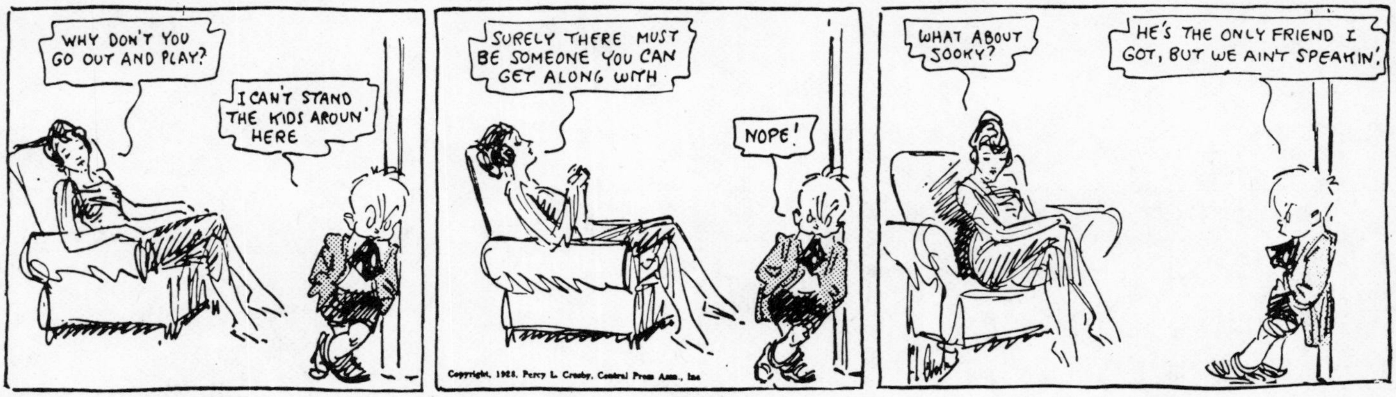
WHY DON'T YOU GO OUT AND PLAY?
I CAN'T STAND THE KIDS AROUN' HERE
SURELY THERE MUST BE SOMEONE YOU CAN GET ALONG WITH
NOPE!
WHAT ABOUT SOOKY?
HE'S THE ONLY FRIEND I GOT, BUT WE AIN'T SPEAKIN'.
Copyright, 1928, Percy L. Crosby, Central Press Assn., Inc

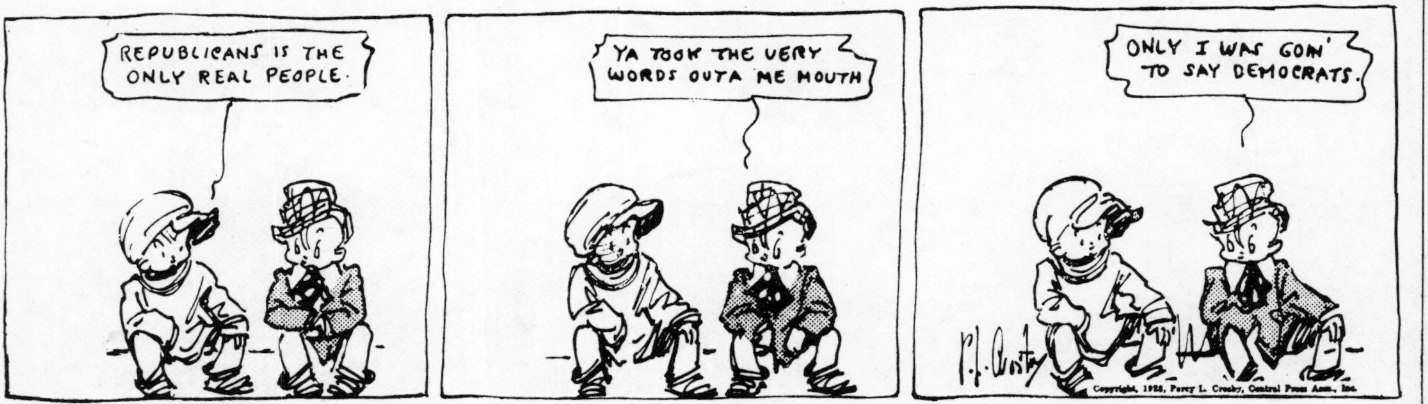
REPUBLICANS IS THE ONLY REAL PEOPLE.
YA TOOK THE VERY WORDS OUTA ME MOUTH
ONLY I WAS GOIN' TO SAY DEMOCRATS.
Copyright, 1928, Percy L. Crosby, Central Press Assn., Inc.

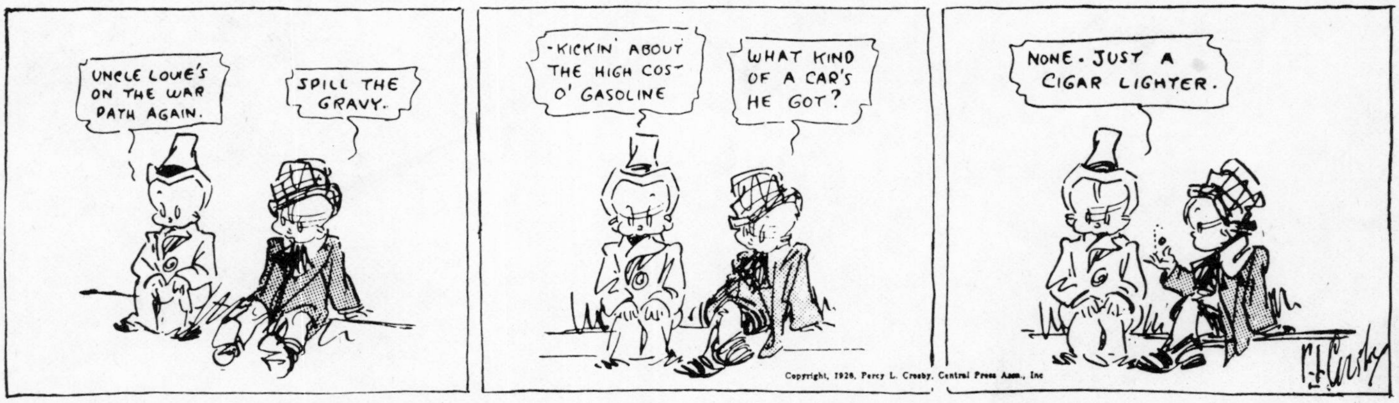
UNCLE LOUIE'S ON THE WAR PATH AGAIN.
SPILL THE GRAVY.
-KICKIN' ABOUT THE HIGH COS- O' GASOLINE
WHAT KIND OF A CAR'S HE GOT?
NONE. JUST A CIGAR LIGHTER.
Copyright, 1928, Percy L. Crosby, Central Press Assn., Inc

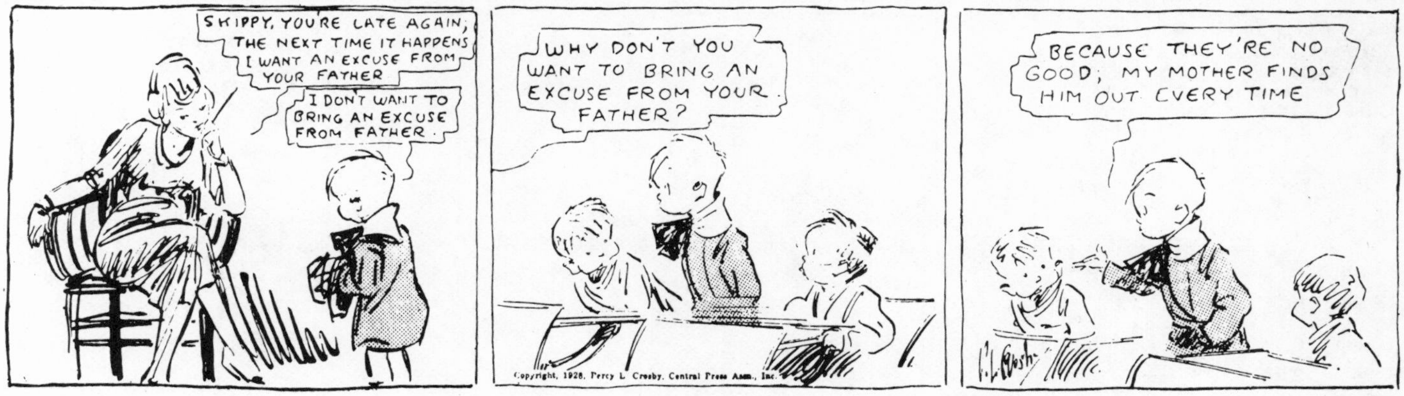
SKIPPY, YOU'RE LATE AGAIN; THE NEXT TIME IT HAPPENS I WANT AN EXCUSE FROM YOUR FATHER
I DON'T WANT TO BRING AN EXCUSE FROM FATHER.
WHY DON'T YOU WANT TO BRING AN EXCUSE FROM YOUR FATHER?
BECAUSE THEY'RE NO GOOD; MY MOTHER FINDS HIM OUT EVERY TIME
Copyright, 1928, Percy L. Crosby, Central Press Assn., Inc.

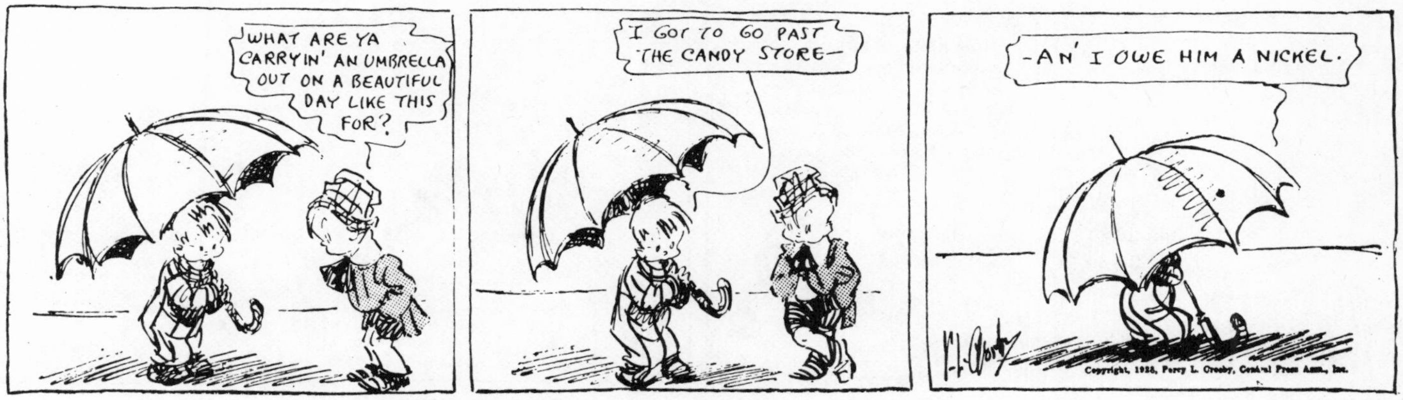
WHAT ARE YA CARRYIN' AN UMBRELLA OUT ON A BEAUTIFUL DAY LIKE THIS FOR?
I GOT TO GO PAST THE CANDY STORE—
-AN' I OWE HIM A NICKEL.
Copyright, 1928, Percy L. Crosby, Central Press Assn., Inc.

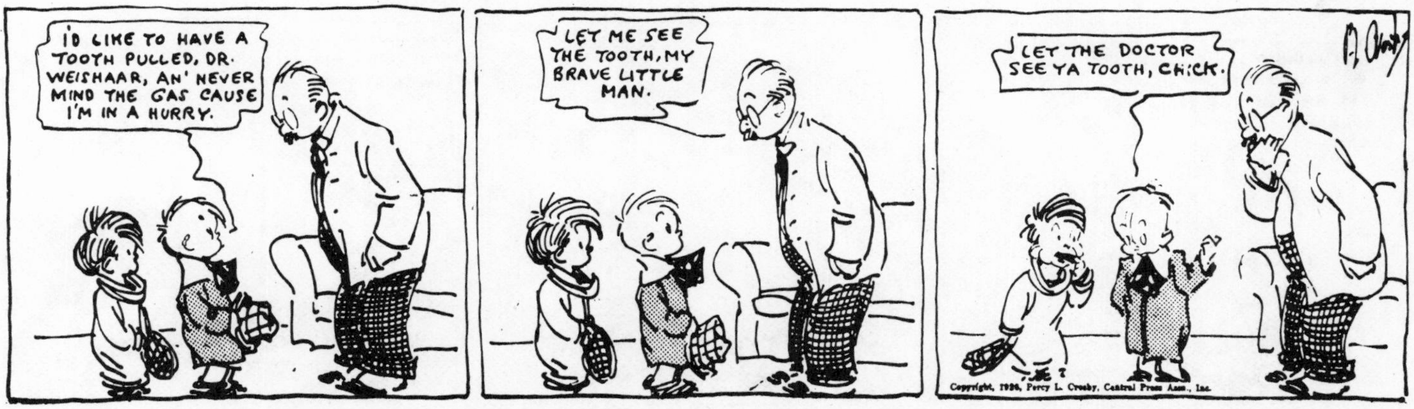
I'D LIKE TO HAVE A TOOTH PULLED, DR. WEISHAAR, AN' NEVER MIND THE GAS CAUSE I'M IN A HURRY.
LET ME SEE THE TOOTH, MY BRAVE LITTLE MAN.
LET THE DOCTOR SEE YA TOOTH, CHICK.
Copyright, 1928, Percy L. Crosby, Central Press Assn., Inc.

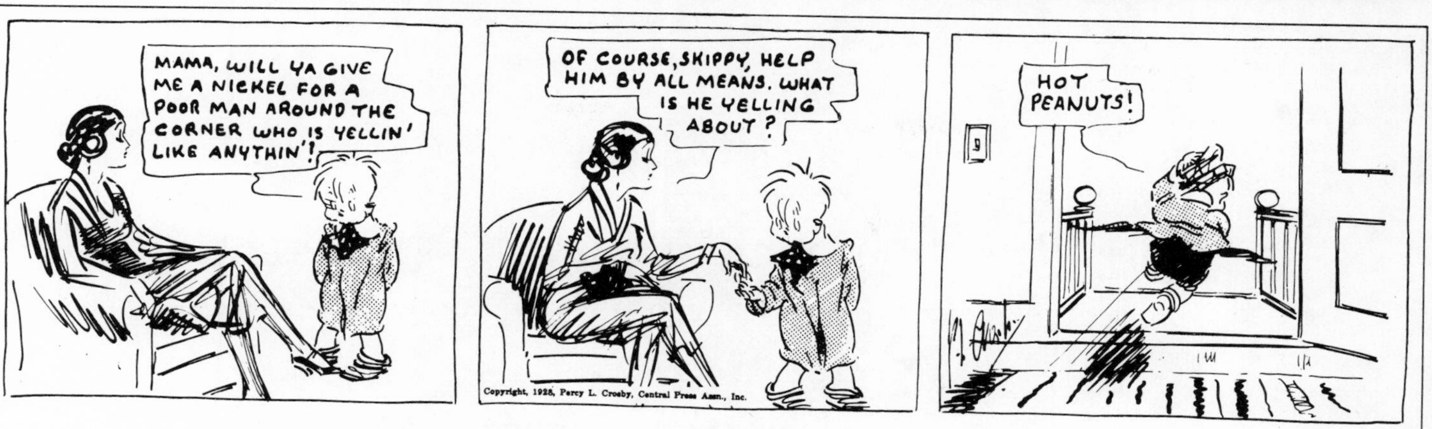
MAMA, WILL YA GIVE ME A NICKEL FOR A POOR MAN AROUND THE CORNER WHO IS YELLIN' LIKE ANYTHIN'!
OF COURSE, SKIPPY, HELP HIM BY ALL MEANS. WHAT IS HE YELLING ABOUT?
Copyright, 1928, Percy L. Crosby, Central Press Assn., Inc.
HOT PEANUTS!

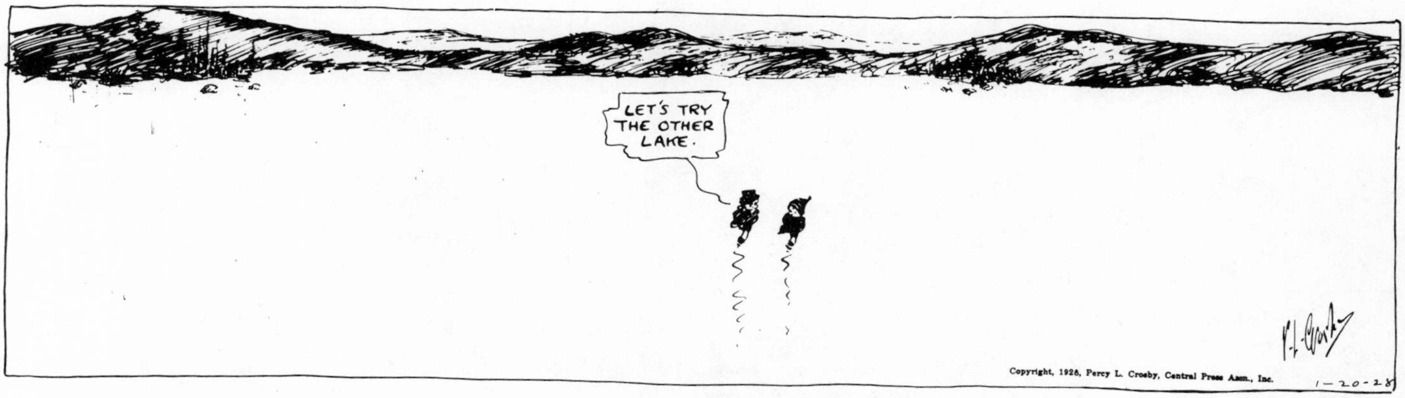
LET'S TRY THE OTHER LAKE.
Copyright, 1928, Percy L. Crosby, Central Press Assn., Inc.
1-20-28

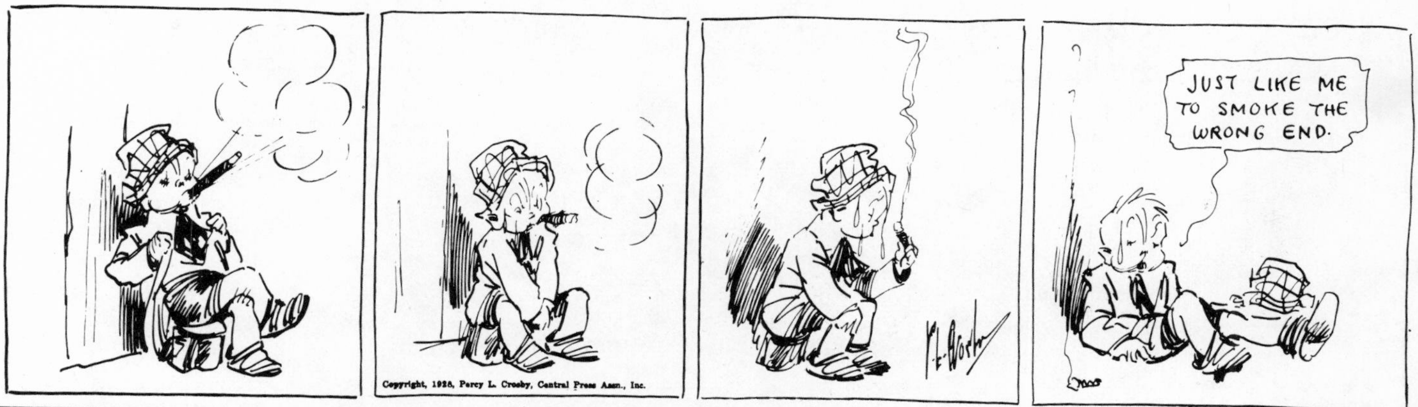
Copyright, 1928, Percy L. Crosby, Central Press Assn., Inc.
JUST LIKE ME TO SMOKE THE WRONG END.

Skippy Themes

Butch O'Leary

Skippy's *bête noire* was a neighborhood tough, Butch O'Leary. A single glare from Butch was enough to evaporate Skippy's normal bravado.

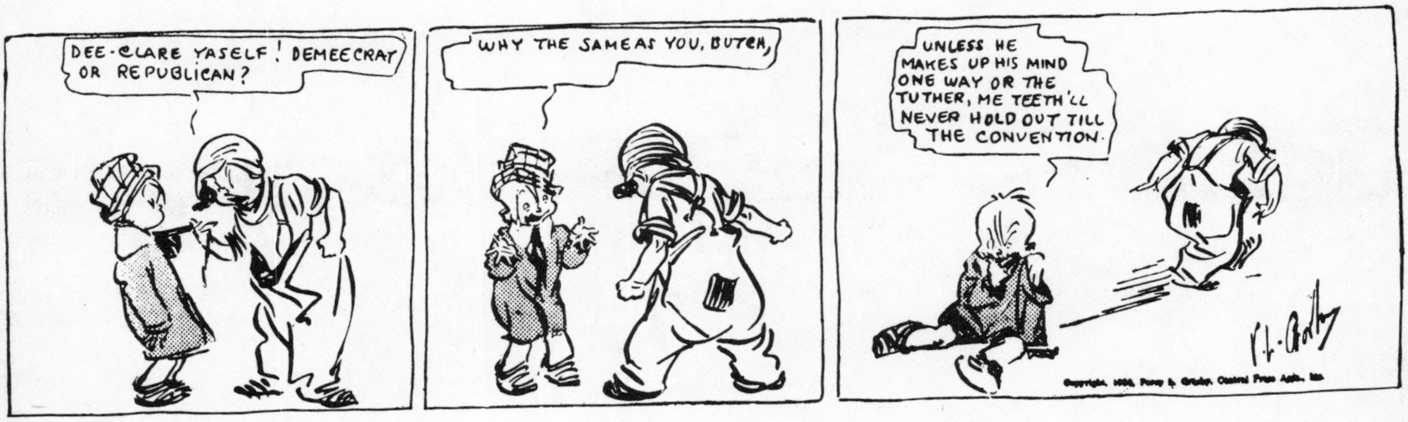
DEE-CLARE YASELF! DEMEECRAT OR REPUBLICAN?
WHY THE SAMEAS YOU, BUTCH,
UNLESS HE MAKES UP HIS MIND ONE WAY OR THE TUTHER, ME TEETH'LL NEVER HOLD OUT TILL THE CONVENTION.

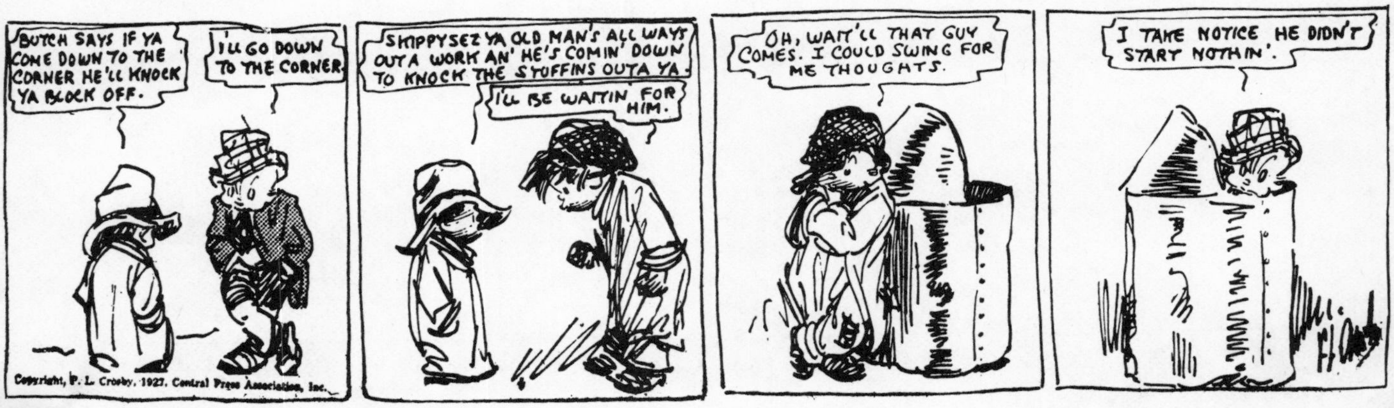
BUTCH SAYS IF YA COME DOWN TO THE CORNER HE'LL KNOCK YA BLOCK OFF.
I'LL GO DOWN TO THE CORNER.
SKIPPY SEZ YA OLD MAN'S ALL WAYS OUTA WORK AN' HE'S COMIN' DOWN TO KNOCK THE STUFFINS OUTA YA.
I'LL BE WAITIN' FOR HIM.
OH, WAIT'LL THAT GUY COMES. I COULD SWING FOR ME THOUGHTS.
I TAKE NOTICE HE DIDN'T START NOTHIN'.
Copyright, P. L. Crosby, 1927, Central Press Association, Inc.

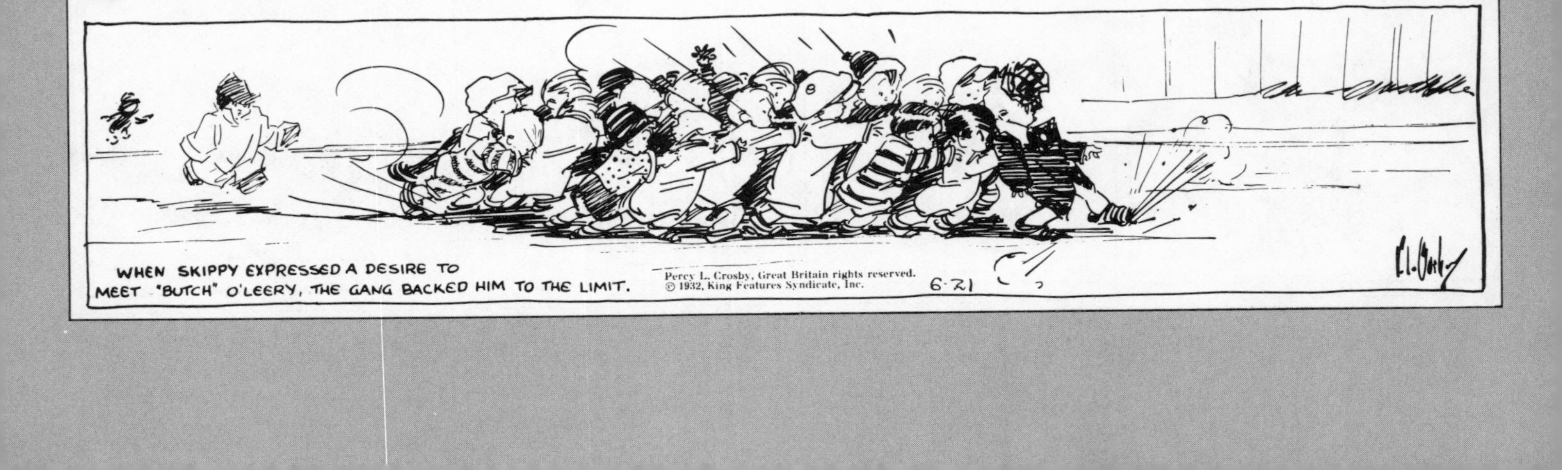
WHEN SKIPPY EXPRESSED A DESIRE TO MEET "BUTCH" O'LEERY, THE GANG BACKED HIM TO THE LIMIT.
Percy L. Crosby, Great Britain rights reserved.
© 1932, King Features Syndicate, Inc.
6-21

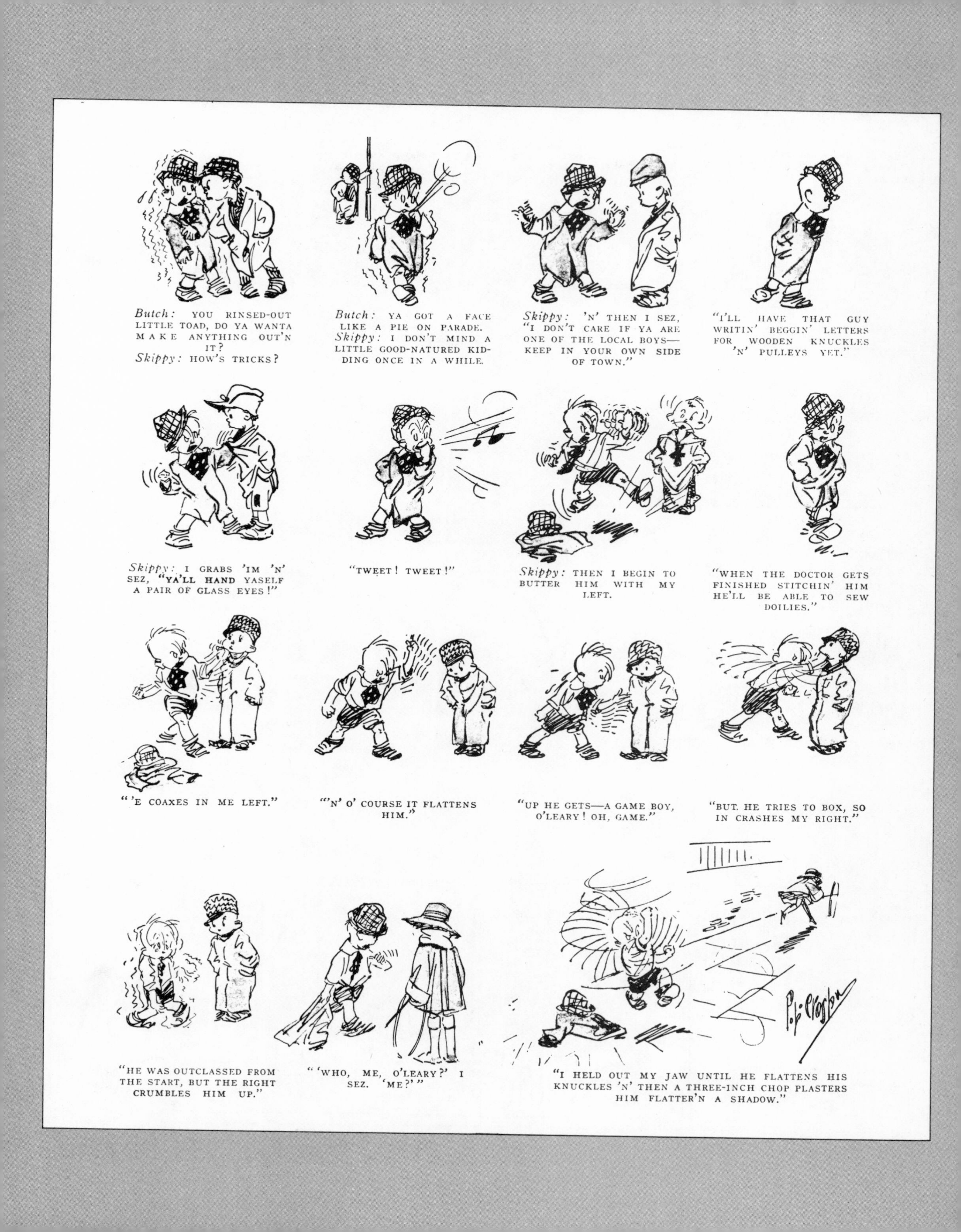
Butch: YOU RINSED-OUT LITTLE TOAD, DO YA WANTA MAKE ANYTHING OUT'N IT?
Skippy: HOW'S TRICKS?
Butch: YA GOT A FACE LIKE A PIE ON PARADE.
Skippy: I DON'T MIND A LITTLE GOOD-NATURED KIDDING ONCE IN A WHILE.
Skippy: 'N' THEN I SEZ, "I DON'T CARE IF YA ARE ONE OF THE LOCAL BOYS—KEEP IN YOUR OWN SIDE OF TOWN."
"I'LL HAVE THAT GUY WRITIN' BEGGIN' LETTERS FOR WOODEN KNUCKLES 'N' PULLEYS YET."
Skippy: I GRABS 'IM 'N' SEZ, "**YA'LL HAND** YASELF A PAIR OF GLASS EYES!"
"TWEET! TWEET!"
Skippy: THEN I BEGIN TO BUTTER HIM WITH MY LEFT.
"WHEN THE DOCTOR GETS FINISHED STITCHIN' HIM HE'LL BE ABLE TO SEW DOILIES."
"'E COAXES IN ME LEFT."
"'N' O' COURSE IT FLATTENS HIM."
"UP HE GETS—A GAME BOY, O'LEARY! OH, GAME."
"BUT. HE TRIES TO BOX, SO IN CRASHES MY RIGHT."
"HE WAS OUTCLASSED FROM THE START, BUT THE RIGHT CRUMBLES HIM UP."
"'WHO, ME, O'LEARY?' I SEZ. 'ME?'"
"I HELD OUT MY JAW UNTIL HE FLATTENS HIS KNUCKLES 'N' THEN A THREE-INCH CHOP PLASTERS HIM FLATTER'N A SHADOW."

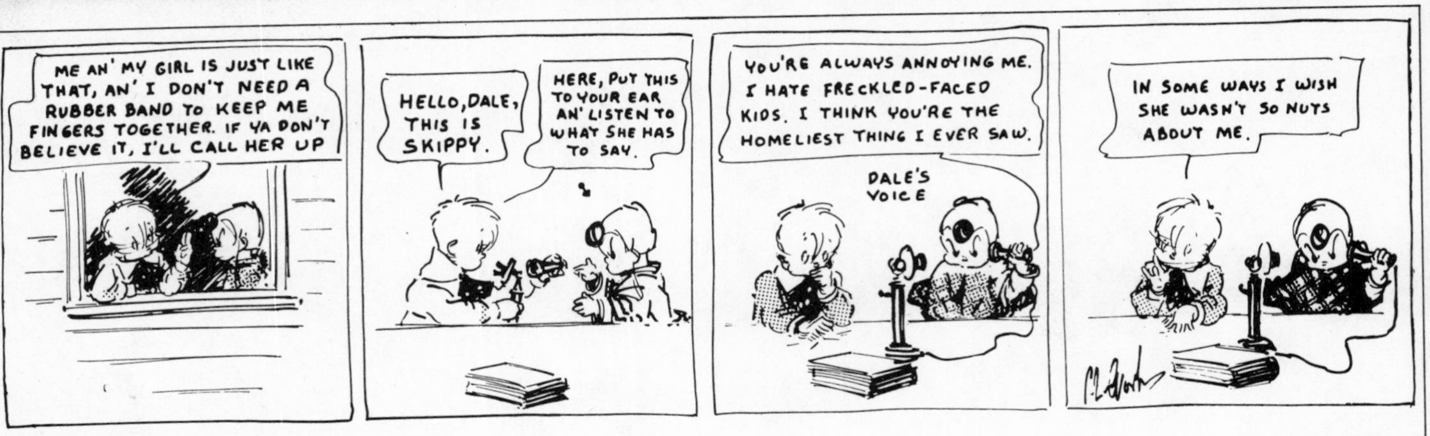
ME AN' MY GIRL IS JUST LIKE THAT, AN' I DON'T NEED A RUBBER BAND TO KEEP ME FINGERS TOGETHER. IF YA DON'T BELIEVE IT, I'LL CALL HER UP
HELLO, DALE, THIS IS SKIPPY.
HERE, PUT THIS TO YOUR EAR AN' LISTEN TO WHAT SHE HAS TO SAY.
YOU'RE ALWAYS ANNOYING ME. I HATE FRECKLED-FACED KIDS. I THINK YOU'RE THE HOMELIEST THING I EVER SAW.
DALE'S VOICE
IN SOME WAYS I WISH SHE WASN'T SO NUTS ABOUT ME.

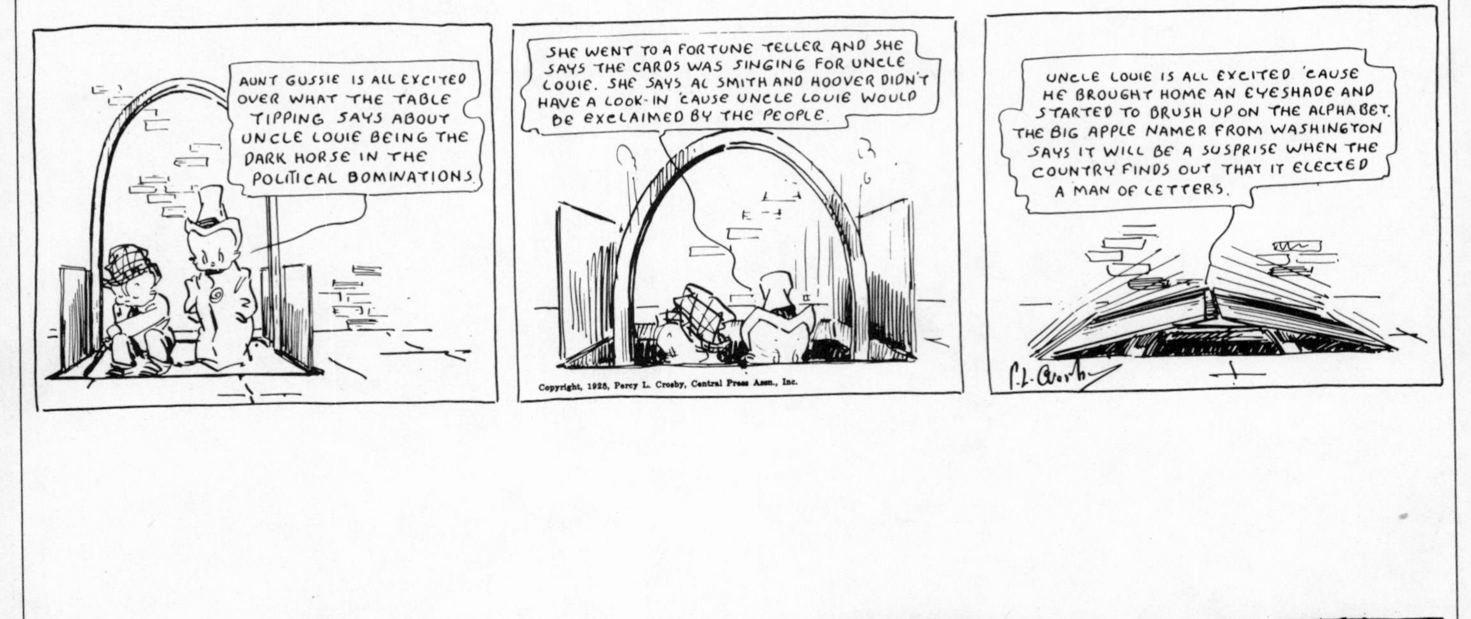
AUNT GUSSIE IS ALL EXCITED OVER WHAT THE TABLE TIPPING SAYS ABOUT UNCLE LOUIE BEING THE DARK HORSE IN THE POLITICAL BOMINATIONS.
SHE WENT TO A FORTUNE TELLER AND SHE SAYS THE CARDS WAS SINGING FOR UNCLE LOUIE. SHE SAYS AL SMITH AND HOOVER DIDN'T HAVE A LOOK-IN 'CAUSE UNCLE LOUIE WOULD BE EXCLAIMED BY THE PEOPLE.
Copyright, 1928, Percy L. Crosby, Central Press Assn., Inc.
UNCLE LOUIE IS ALL EXCITED 'CAUSE HE BROUGHT HOME AN EYESHADE AND STARTED TO BRUSH UP ON THE ALPHABET. THE BIG APPLE NAMER FROM WASHINGTON SAYS IT WILL BE A SUSPRISE WHEN THE COUNTRY FINDS OUT THAT IT ELECTED A MAN OF LETTERS.

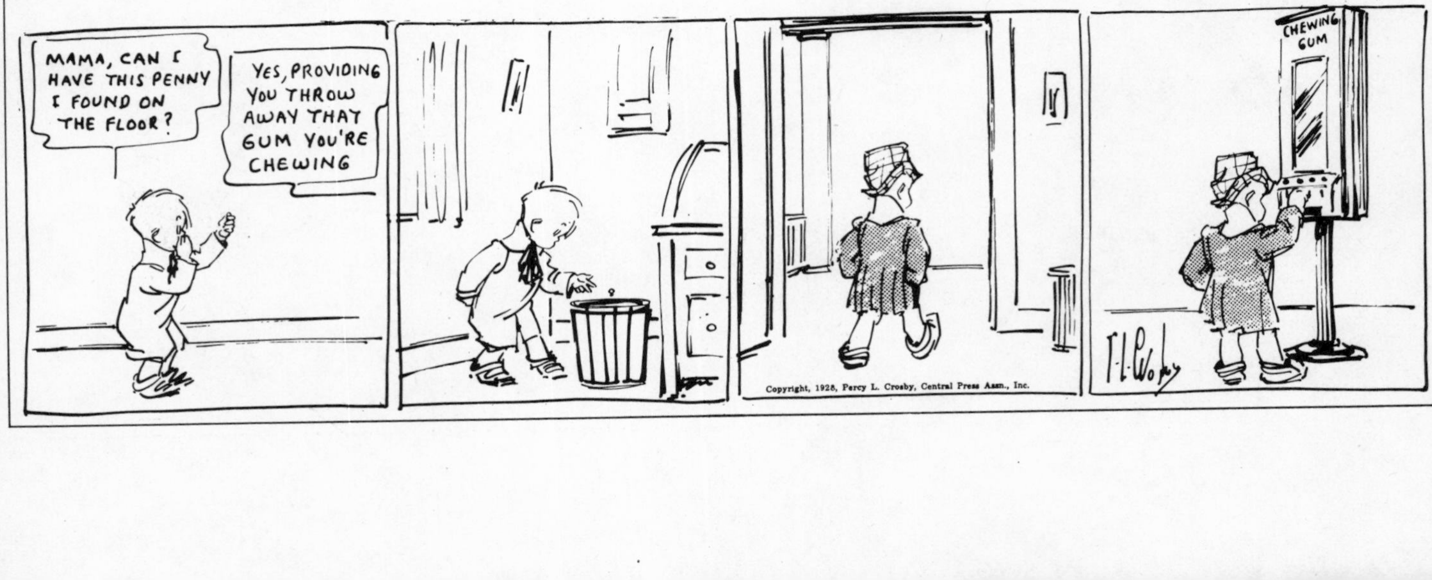
MAMA, CAN I HAVE THIS PENNY I FOUND ON THE FLOOR?
YES, PROVIDING YOU THROW AWAY THAT GUM YOU'RE CHEWING
Copyright, 1928, Percy L. Crosby, Central Press Assn., Inc.
CHEWING GUM

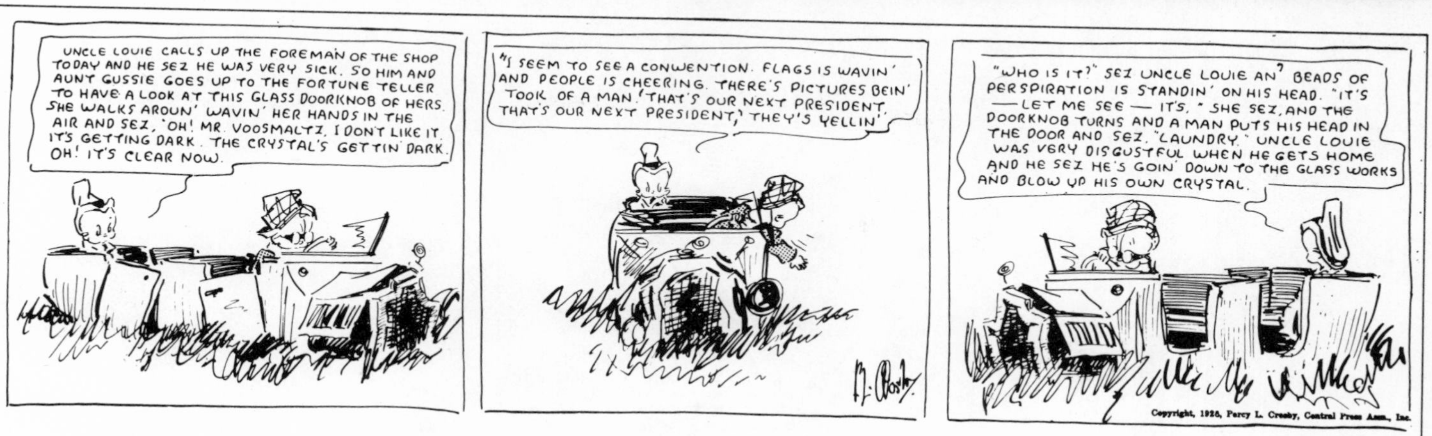
UNCLE LOUIE CALLS UP THE FOREMAN OF THE SHOP TODAY AND HE SEZ HE WAS VERY SICK. SO HIM AND AUNT GUSSIE GOES UP TO THE FORTUNE TELLER TO HAVE A LOOK AT THIS GLASS DOORKNOB OF HERS. SHE WALKS AROUN' WAVIN' HER HANDS IN THE AIR AND SEZ, "OH! MR. VOOSMALTZ, I DON'T LIKE IT. IT'S GETTING DARK. THE CRYSTAL'S GETTIN' DARK. OH! IT'S CLEAR NOW.
"I SEEM TO SEE A CONWENTION. FLAGS IS WAVIN' AND PEOPLE IS CHEERING. THERE'S PICTURES BEIN' TOOK OF A MAN. 'THAT'S OUR NEXT PRESIDENT. THAT'S OUR NEXT PRESIDENT,' THEY'S YELLIN'.
"WHO IS IT?" SEZ UNCLE LOUIE AN' BEADS OF PERSPIRATION IS STANDIN' ON HIS HEAD. "IT'S — LET ME SEE — IT'S," SHE SEZ, AND THE DOORKNOB TURNS AND A MAN PUTS HIS HEAD IN THE DOOR AND SEZ, "LAUNDRY." UNCLE LOUIE WAS VERY DISGUSTFUL WHEN HE GETS HOME AND HE SEZ HE'S GOIN' DOWN TO THE GLASS WORKS AND BLOW UP HIS OWN CRYSTAL.
Copyright, 1928, Percy L. Crosby, Central Press Assn., Inc.

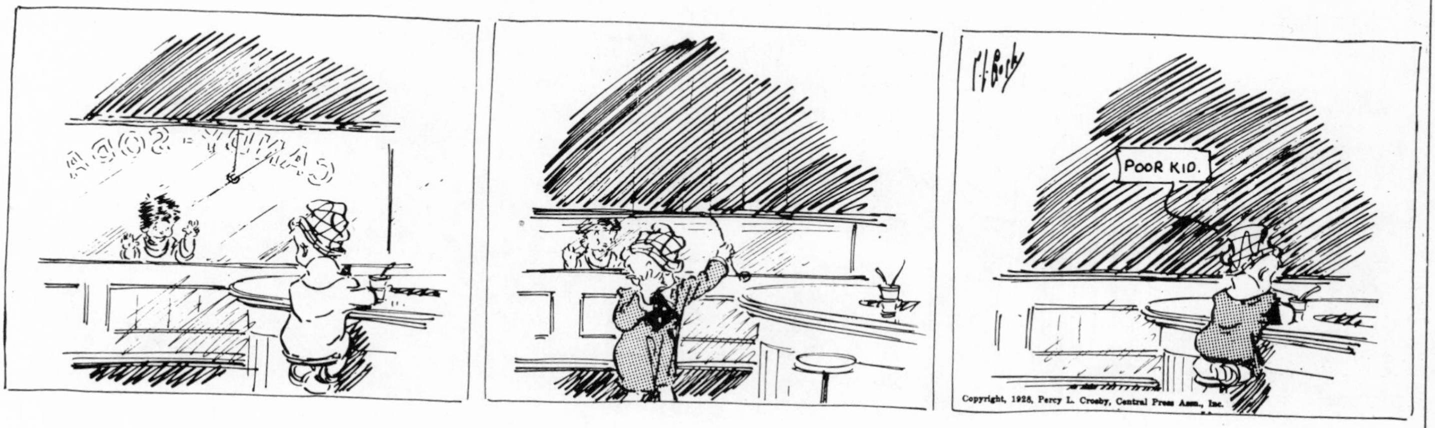
POOR KID.
Copyright, 1928, Percy L. Crosby, Central Press Assn., Inc.

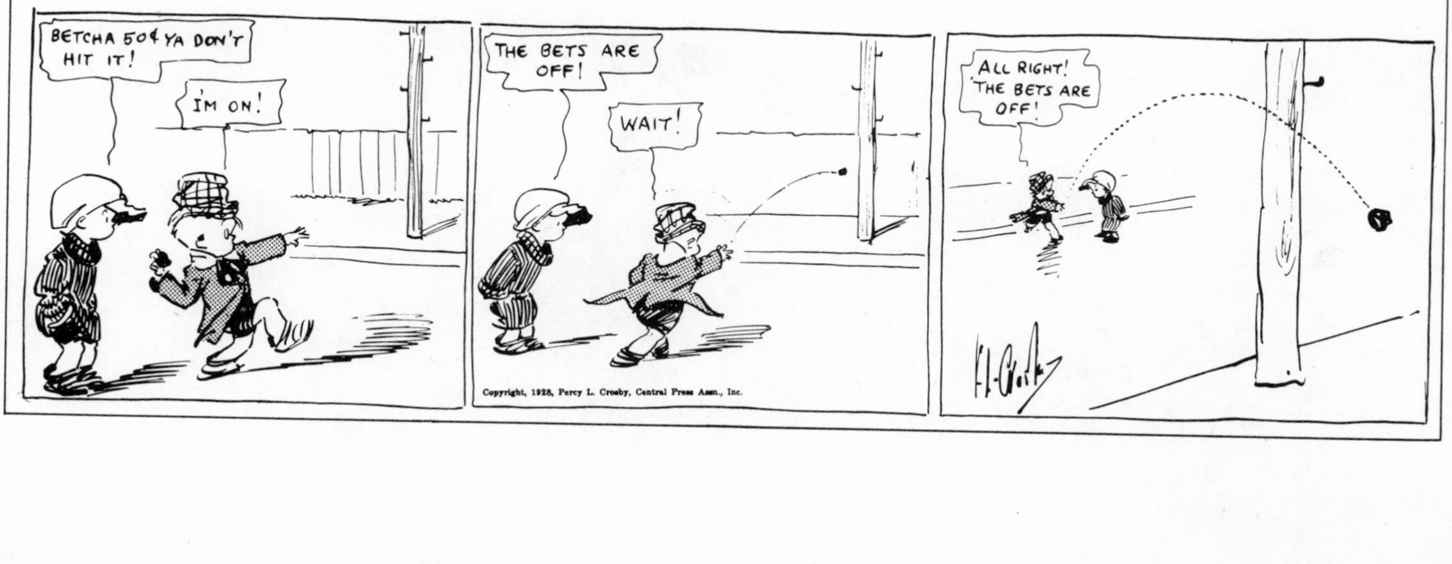
BETCHA 50¢ YA DON'T HIT IT!
I'M ON!
THE BETS ARE OFF!
WAIT!
ALL RIGHT! THE BETS ARE OFF!
Copyright, 1928, Percy L. Crosby, Central Press Assn., Inc.

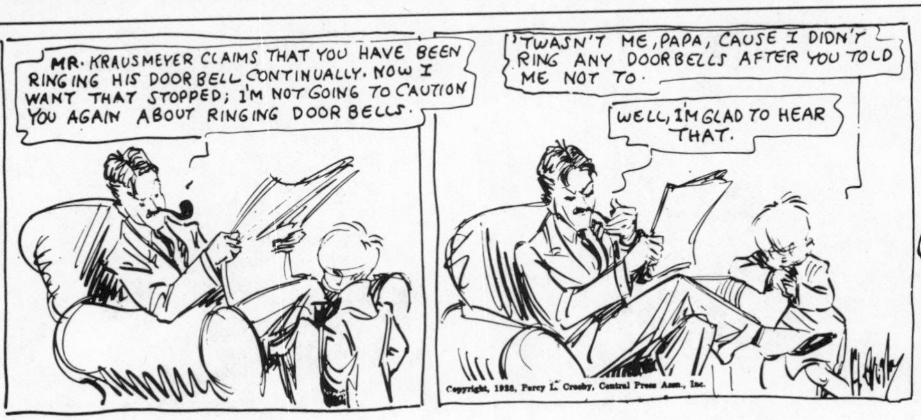
MR. KRAUSMEYER CLAIMS THAT YOU HAVE BEEN RINGING HIS DOORBELL CONTINUALLY. NOW I WANT THAT STOPPED; I'M NOT GOING TO CAUTION YOU AGAIN ABOUT RINGING DOOR BELLS.
'TWASN'T ME, PAPA, CAUSE I DIDN'T RING ANY DOORBELLS AFTER YOU TOLD ME NOT TO.
WELL, I'M GLAD TO HEAR THAT.
Copyright, 1928, Percy L. Crosby, Central Press Assn., Inc.
I MIGHT O' ROLLED A COUPLE O' COBBLE STONES IN THE HALL WAY, BUT DOORBELLS — NEVER!
1-25

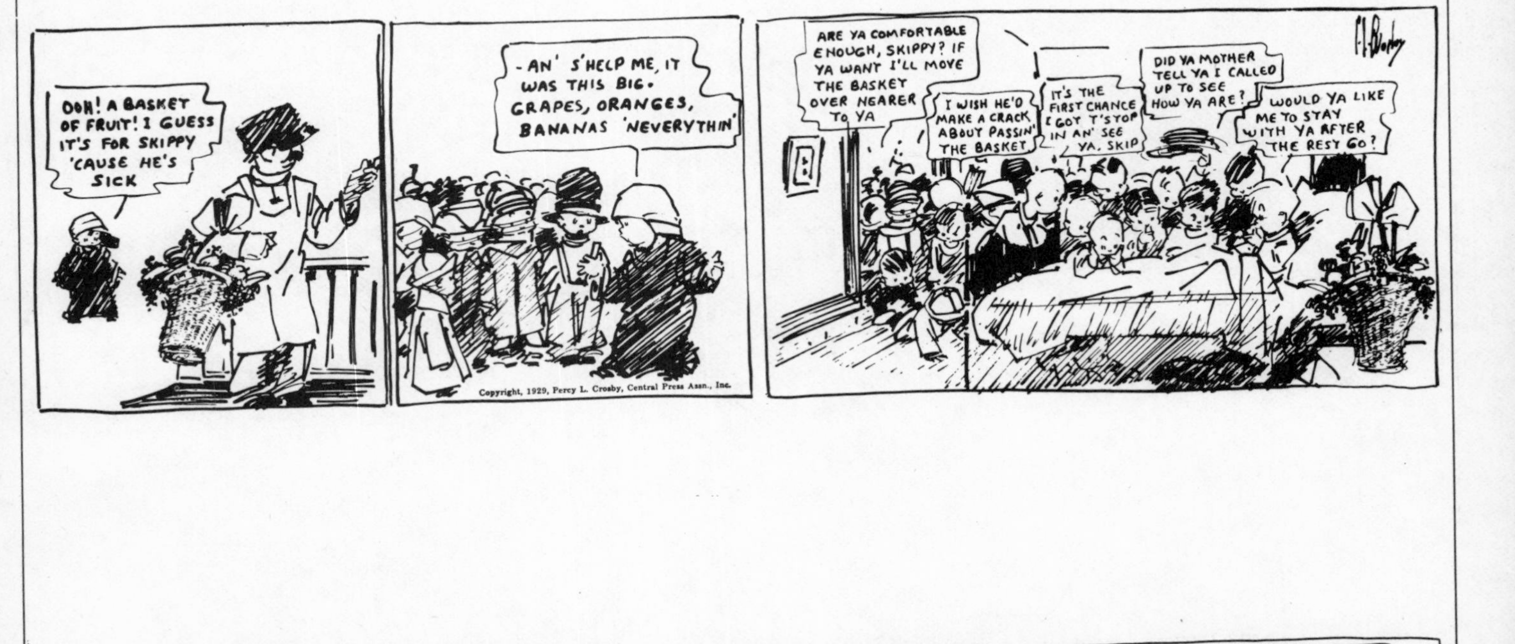
OOH! A BASKET OF FRUIT! I GUESS IT'S FOR SKIPPY 'CAUSE HE'S SICK
- AN' S'HELP ME, IT WAS THIS BIG. GRAPES, ORANGES, BANANAS 'NEVERYTHIN'
Copyright, 1929, Percy L. Crosby, Central Press Assn., Inc.
ARE YA COMFORTABLE ENOUGH, SKIPPY? IF YA WANT I'LL MOVE THE BASKET OVER NEARER TO YA
I WISH HE'D MAKE A CRACK ABOUT PASSIN' THE BASKET.
IT'S THE FIRST CHANCE I GOT T'STOP IN AN' SEE YA, SKIP
DID YA MOTHER TELL YA I CALLED UP TO SEE HOW YA ARE?
WOULD YA LIKE ME TO STAY WITH YA AFTER THE REST GO?

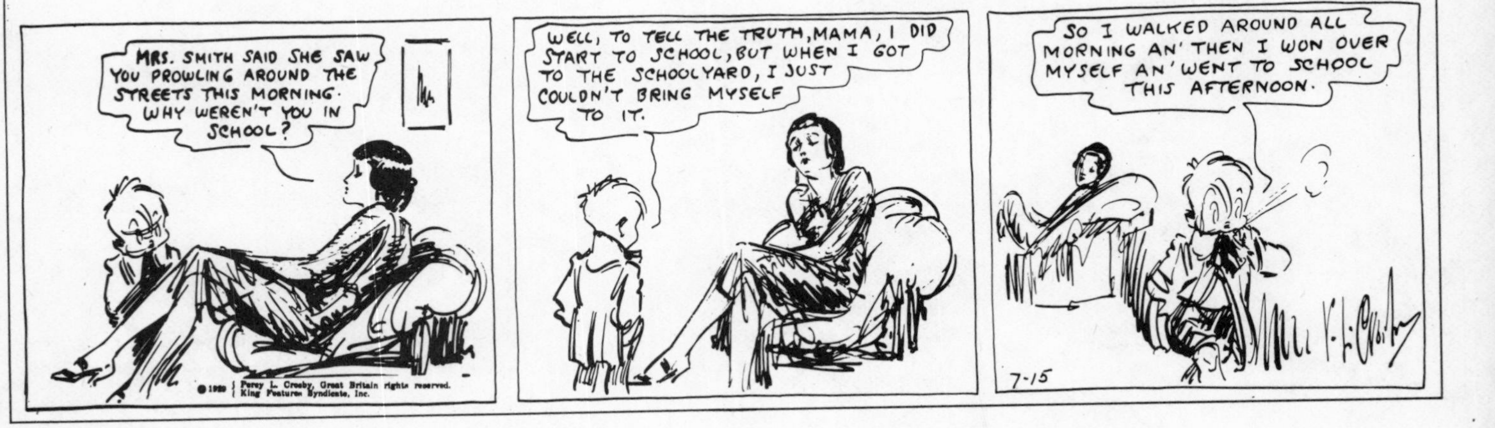
MRS. SMITH SAID SHE SAW YOU PROWLING AROUND THE STREETS THIS MORNING. WHY WEREN'T YOU IN SCHOOL?
© 1929 Percy L. Crosby, Great Britain rights reserved. King Features Syndicate, Inc.
WELL, TO TELL THE TRUTH, MAMA, I DID START TO SCHOOL, BUT WHEN I GOT TO THE SCHOOLYARD, I JUST COULDN'T BRING MYSELF TO IT.
SO I WALKED AROUND ALL MORNING AN' THEN I WON OVER MYSELF AN' WENT TO SCHOOL THIS AFTERNOON.
7-15

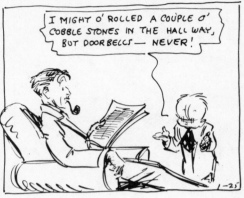

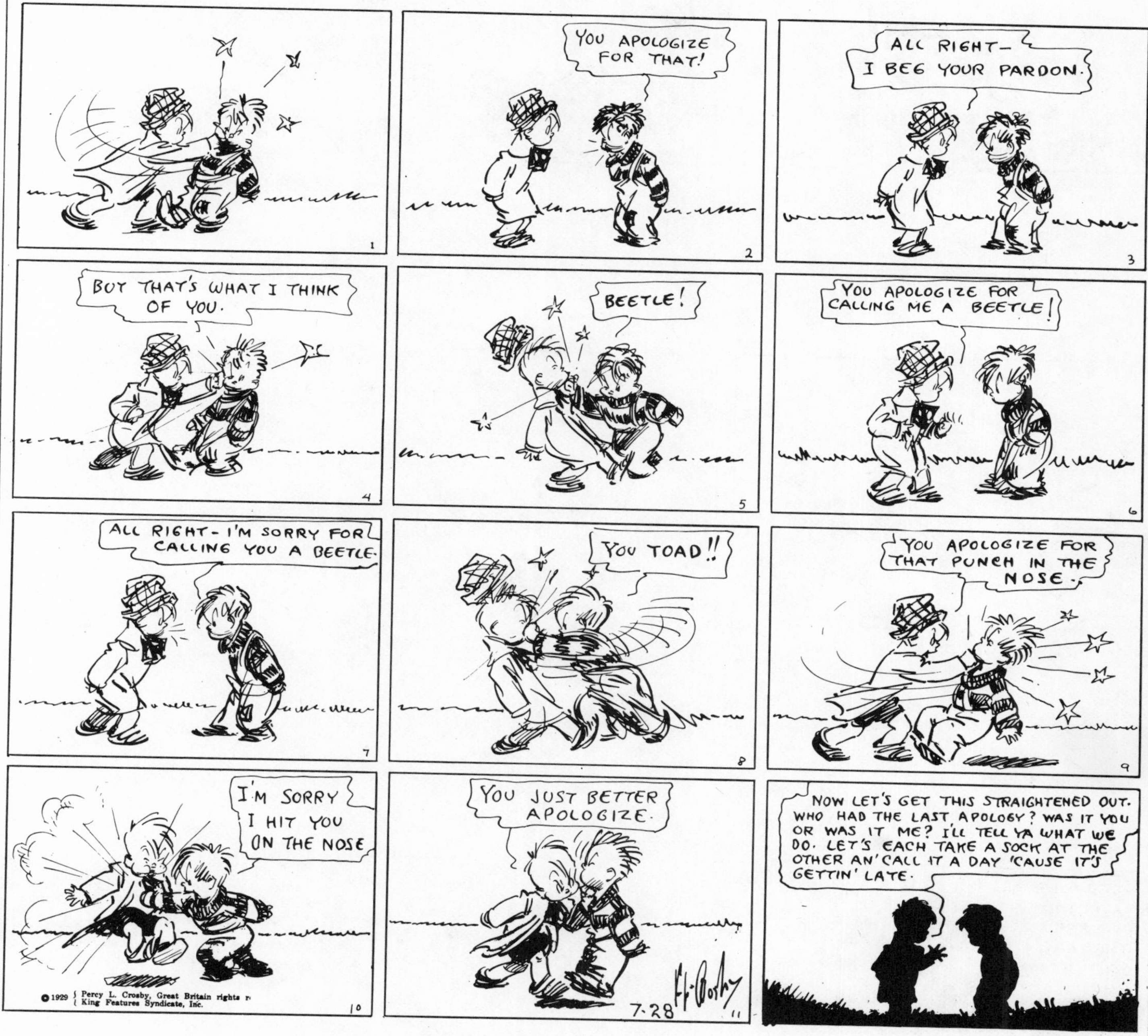
YOU APOLOGIZE FOR THAT!
ALL RIGHT— I BEG YOUR PARDON.
BUT THAT'S WHAT I THINK OF YOU.
BEETLE!
YOU APOLOGIZE FOR CALLING ME A BEETLE!
ALL RIGHT - I'M SORRY FOR CALLING YOU A BEETLE.
YOU TOAD!!
YOU APOLOGIZE FOR THAT PUNCH IN THE NOSE.
I'M SORRY I HIT YOU ON THE NOSE
© 1929 Percy L. Crosby, Great Britain rights r King Features Syndicate, Inc.
YOU JUST BETTER APOLOGIZE.
7-28
NOW LET'S GET THIS STRAIGHTENED OUT. WHO HAD THE LAST APOLOGY? WAS IT YOU OR WAS IT ME? I'LL TELL YA WHAT WE DO. LET'S EACH TAKE A SOCK AT THE OTHER AN' CALL IT A DAY 'CAUSE IT'S GETTIN' LATE.

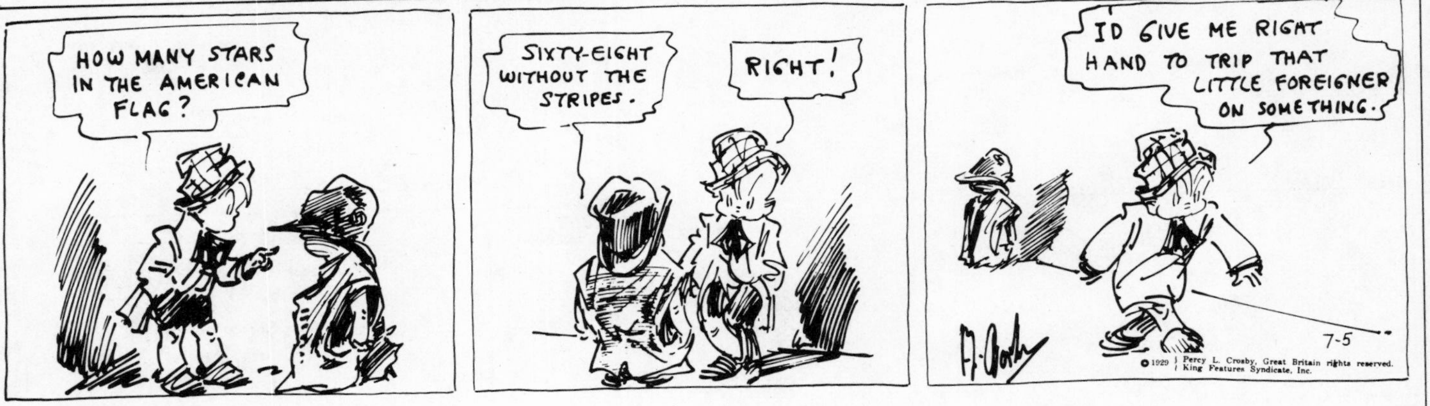
HOW MANY STARS IN THE AMERICAN FLAG?
SIXTY-EIGHT WITHOUT THE STRIPES.
RIGHT!
ID GIVE ME RIGHT HAND TO TRIP THAT LITTLE FOREIGNER ON SOMETHING.
7-5
© 1929 Percy L. Crosby, Great Britain rights reserved. King Features Syndicate, Inc.

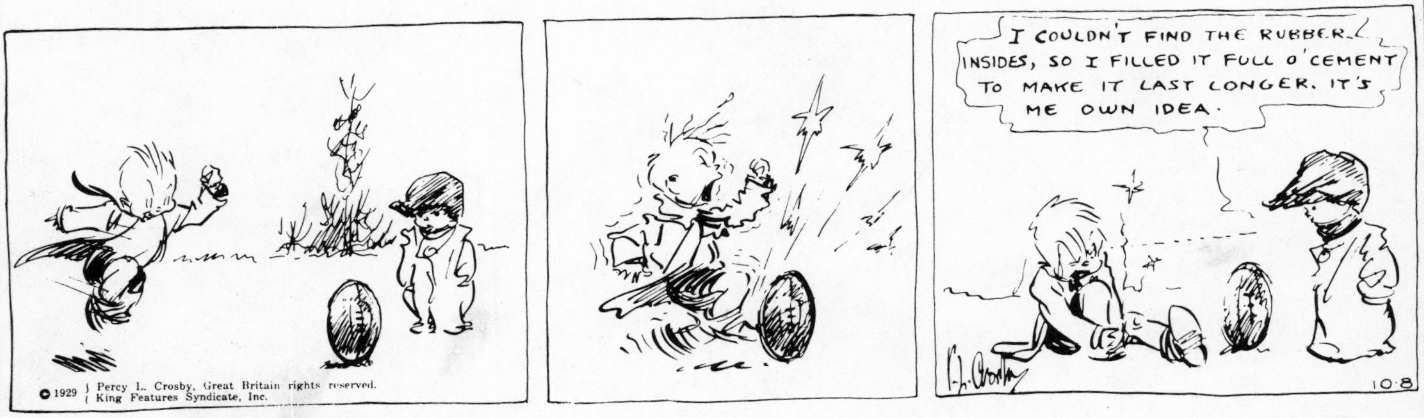
© 1929 Percy L. Crosby, Great Britain rights reserved. King Features Syndicate, Inc.
I COULDN'T FIND THE RUBBER INSIDES, SO I FILLED IT FULL O'CEMENT TO MAKE IT LAST LONGER. IT'S ME OWN IDEA.
10-8

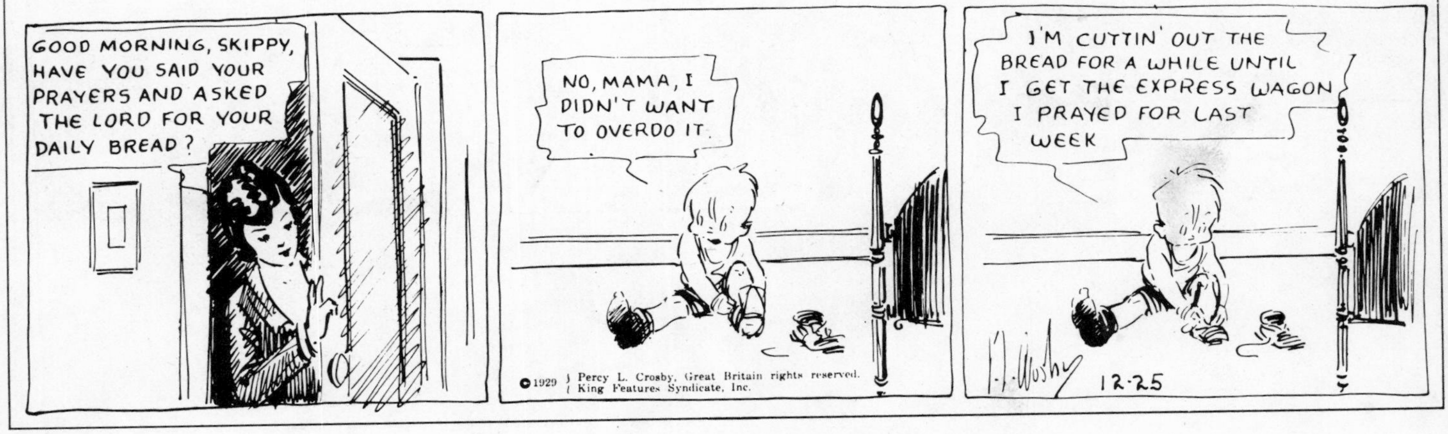
GOOD MORNING, SKIPPY, HAVE YOU SAID YOUR PRAYERS AND ASKED THE LORD FOR YOUR DAILY BREAD?
NO, MAMA, I DIDN'T WANT TO OVERDO IT.
© 1929 Percy L. Crosby, Great Britain rights reserved. King Features Syndicate, Inc.
I'M CUTTIN' OUT THE BREAD FOR A WHILE UNTIL I GET THE EXPRESS WAGON I PRAYED FOR LAST WEEK
12-25

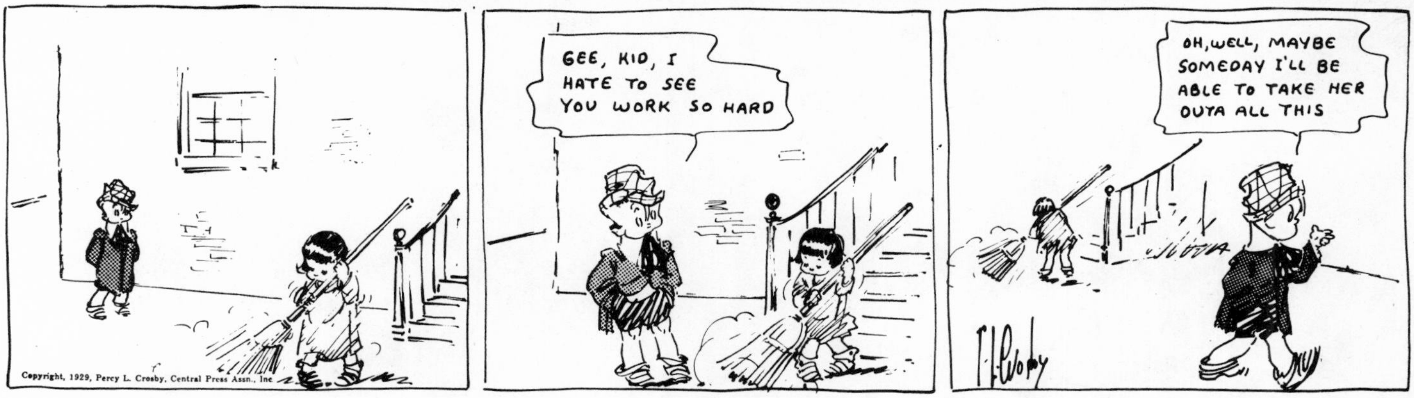
GEE, KID, I HATE TO SEE YOU WORK SO HARD
OH, WELL, MAYBE SOMEDAY I'LL BE ABLE TO TAKE HER OUTA ALL THIS
Copyright, 1929, Percy L. Crosby, Central Press Assn., Inc

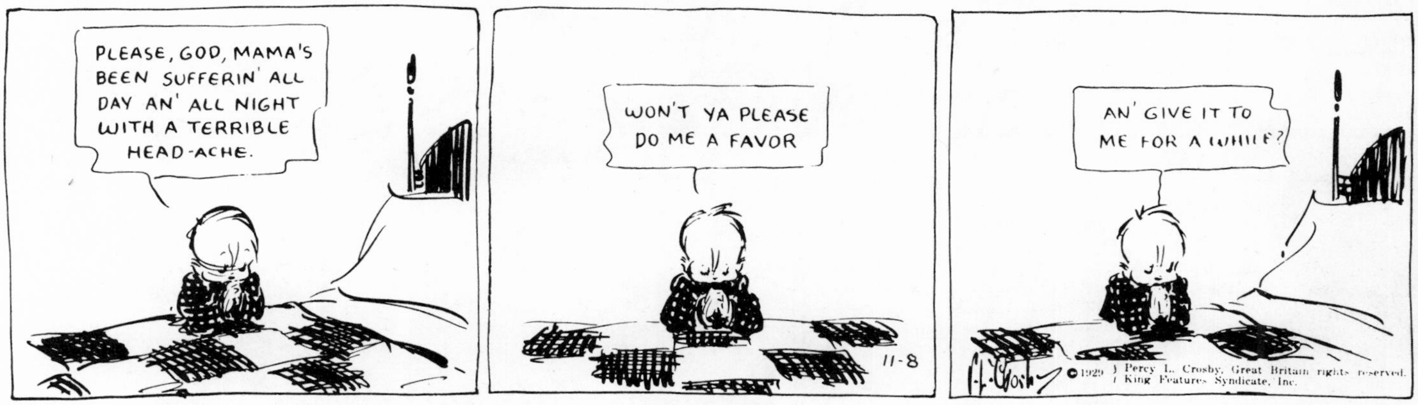
PLEASE, GOD, MAMA'S BEEN SUFFERIN' ALL DAY AN' ALL NIGHT WITH A TERRIBLE HEAD-ACHE.
WON'T YA PLEASE DO ME A FAVOR
AN' GIVE IT TO ME FOR A WHILE?
11-8
© 1929, Percy L. Crosby, Great Britain rights reserved. King Features Syndicate, Inc.

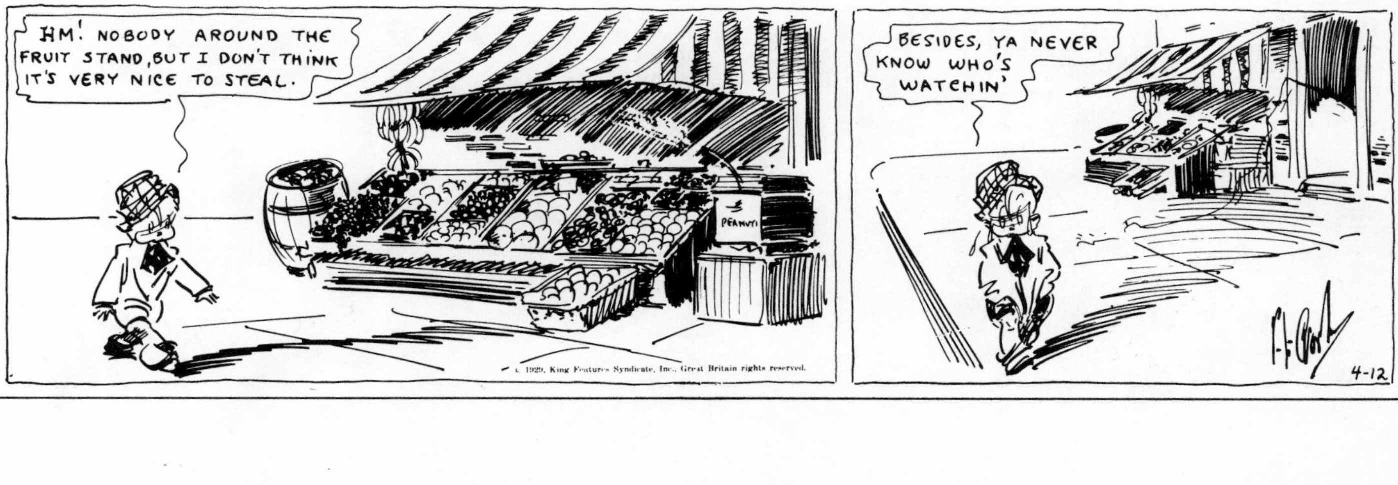
HM! NOBODY AROUND THE FRUIT STAND, BUT I DON'T THINK IT'S VERY NICE TO STEAL.
PEANUTS
© 1929, King Features Syndicate, Inc., Great Britain rights reserved.
BESIDES, YA NEVER KNOW WHO'S WATCHIN'
4-12

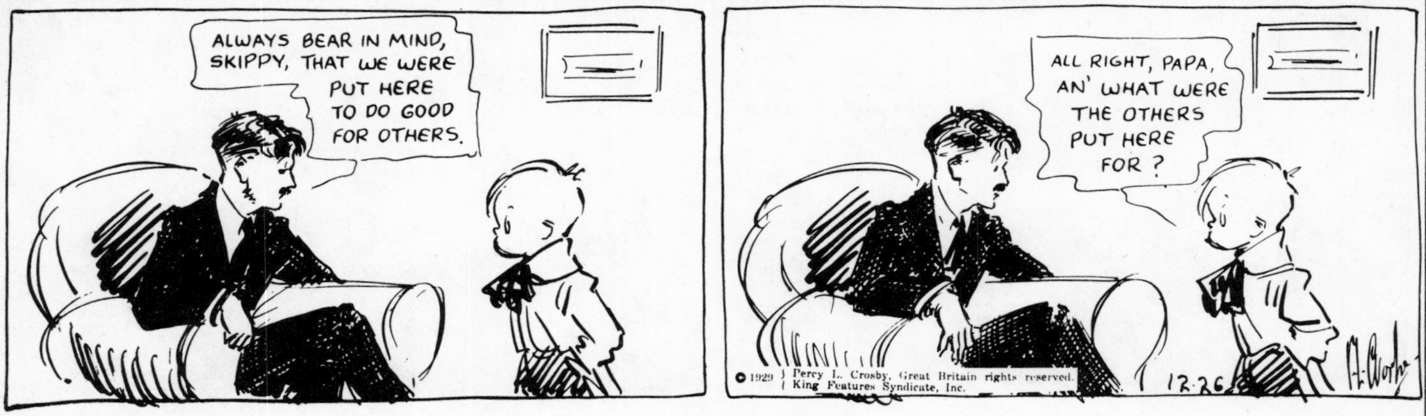
ALWAYS BEAR IN MIND, SKIPPY, THAT WE WERE PUT HERE TO DO GOOD FOR OTHERS.
ALL RIGHT, PAPA, AN' WHAT WERE THE OTHERS PUT HERE FOR ?
© 1929 Percy L. Crosby, Great Britain rights reserved. King Features Syndicate, Inc.
12-26

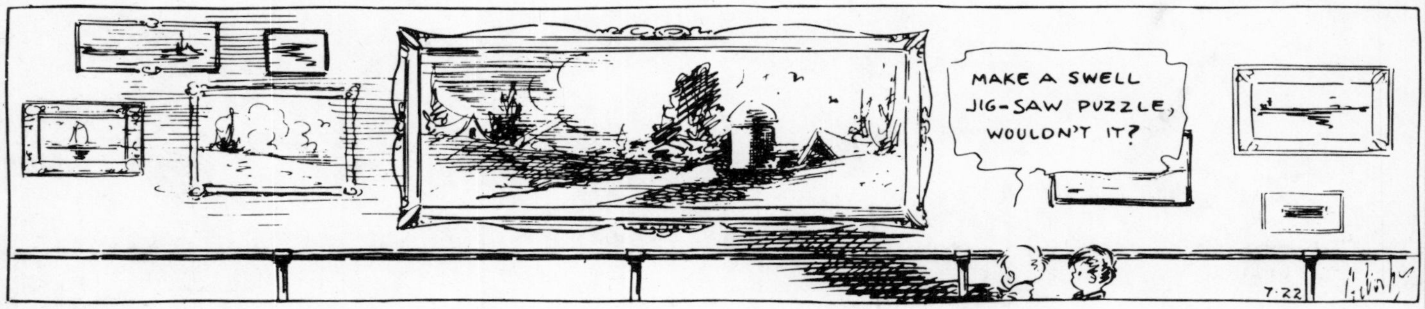
MAKE A SWELL JIG-SAW PUZZLE, WOULDN'T IT?
7-22

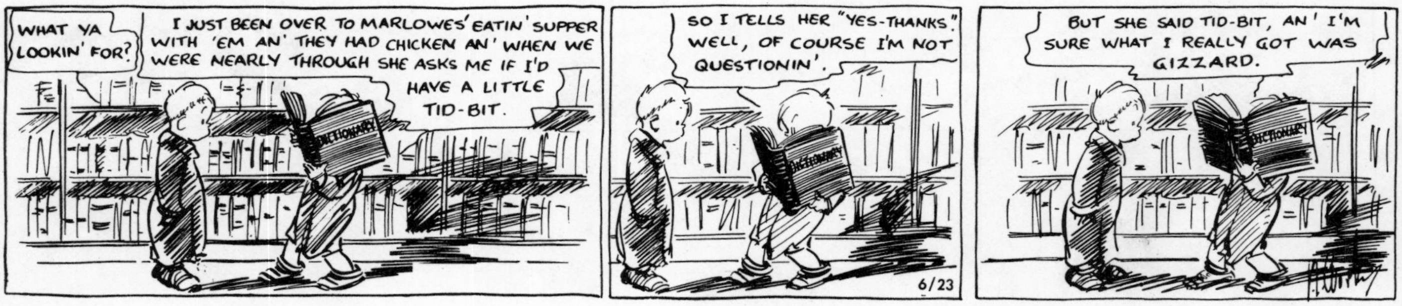
WHAT YA LOOKIN' FOR?
I JUST BEEN OVER TO MARLOWES' EATIN' SUPPER WITH 'EM AN' THEY HAD CHICKEN AN' WHEN WE WERE NEARLY THROUGH SHE ASKS ME IF I'D HAVE A LITTLE TID-BIT.
DICTIONARY
SO I TELLS HER "YES-THANKS." WELL, OF COURSE I'M NOT QUESTIONIN'.
6/23
BUT SHE SAID TID-BIT, AN' I'M SURE WHAT I REALLY GOT WAS GIZZARD.

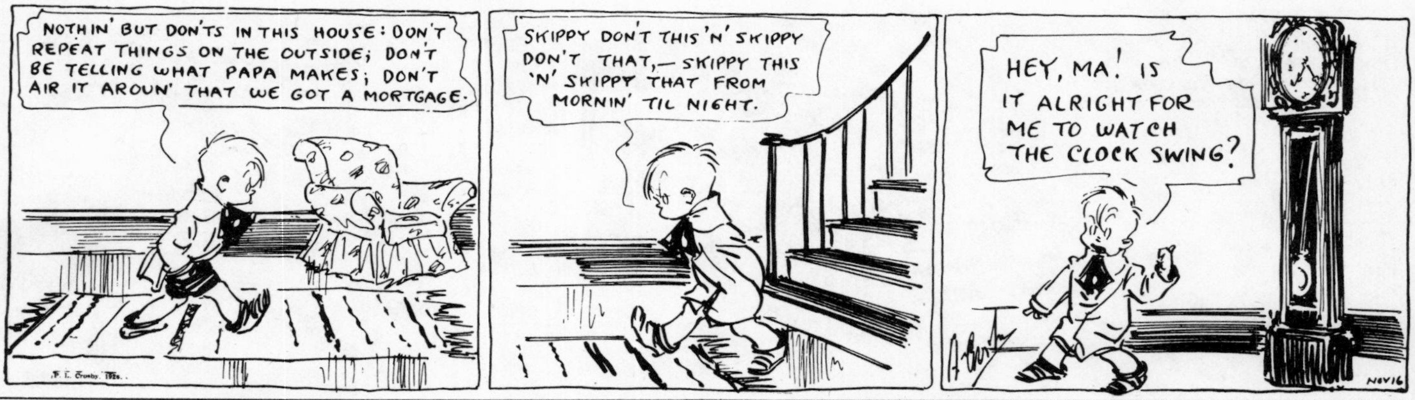
NOTHIN' BUT DON'TS IN THIS HOUSE: DON'T REPEAT THINGS ON THE OUTSIDE; DON'T BE TELLING WHAT PAPA MAKES; DON'T AIR IT AROUN' THAT WE GOT A MORTGAGE.
SKIPPY DON'T THIS 'N' SKIPPY DON'T THAT,— SKIPPY THIS 'N' SKIPPY THAT FROM MORNIN' TIL NIGHT.
HEY, MA! IS IT ALRIGHT FOR ME TO WATCH THE CLOCK SWING?
NOV 16

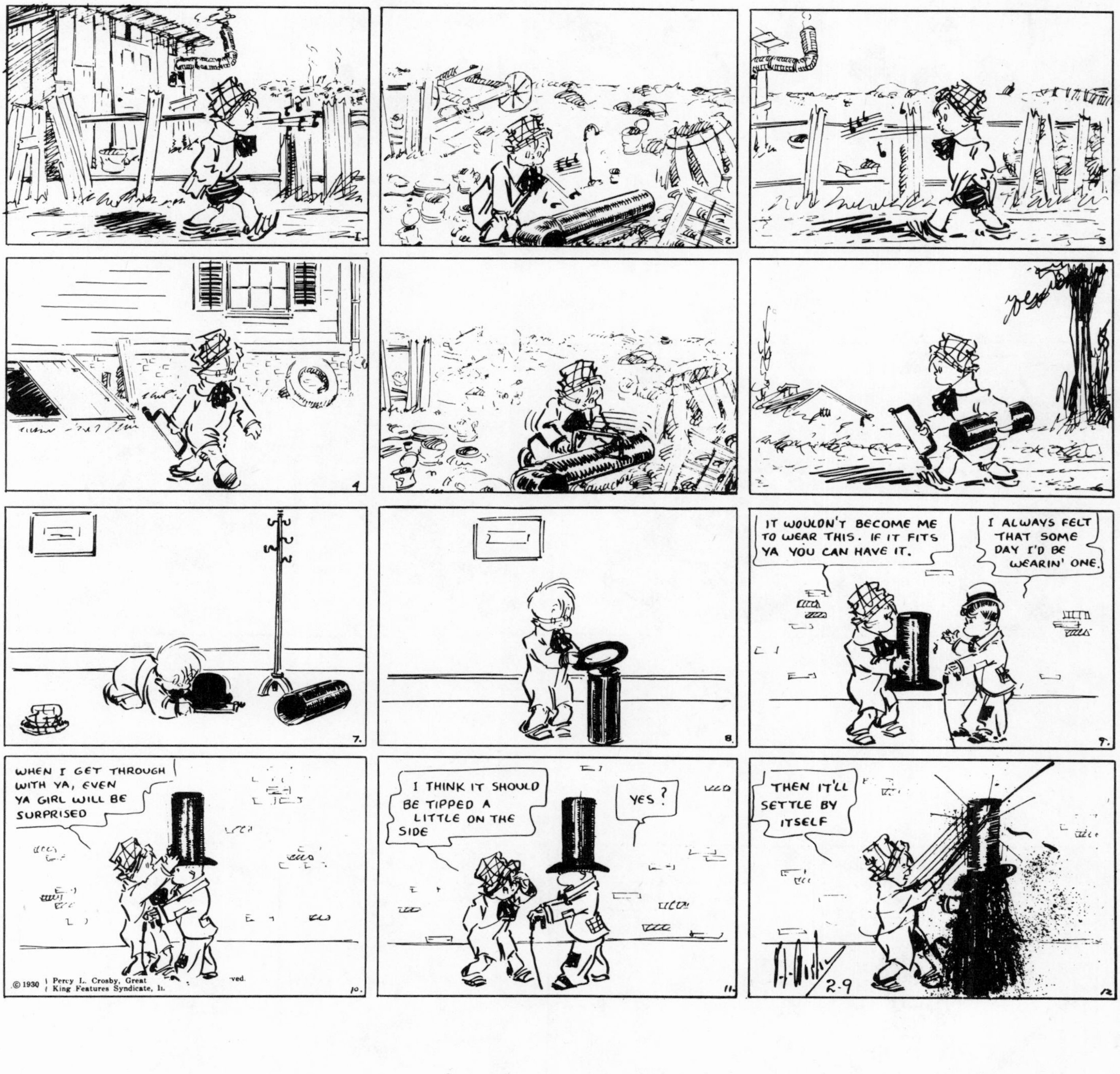
IT WOULDN'T BECOME ME TO WEAR THIS. IF IT FITS YA YOU CAN HAVE IT.
I ALWAYS FELT THAT SOME DAY I'D BE WEARIN' ONE.
WHEN I GET THROUGH WITH YA, EVEN YA GIRL WILL BE SURPRISED
I THINK IT SHOULD BE TIPPED A LITTLE ON THE SIDE
YES ?
THEN IT'LL SETTLE BY ITSELF
© 1930 Percy L. Crosby, Great
King Features Syndicate, In.
ved.
2-9

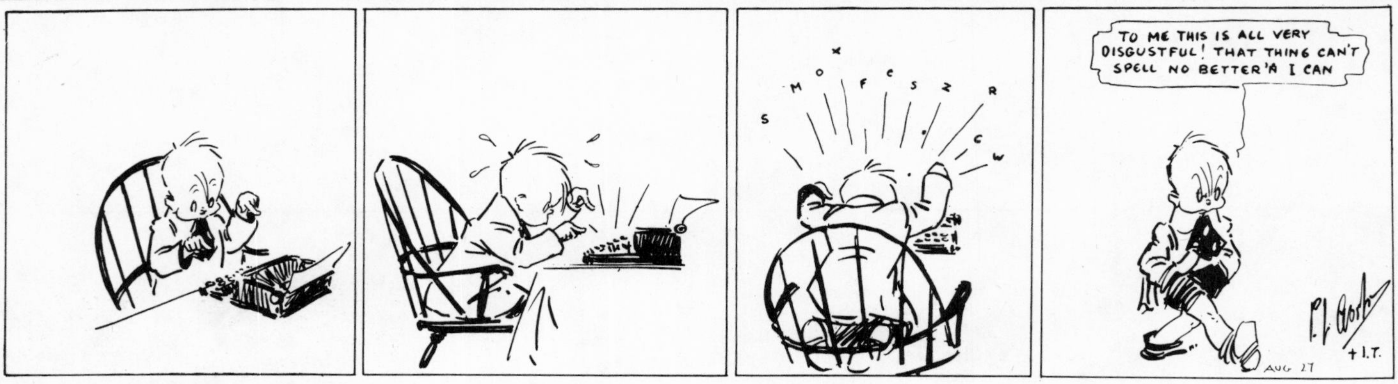
S M O X F C S Z R C W
TO ME THIS IS ALL VERY DISGUSTFUL! THAT THING CAN'T SPELL NO BETTER'A I CAN
AUG 27

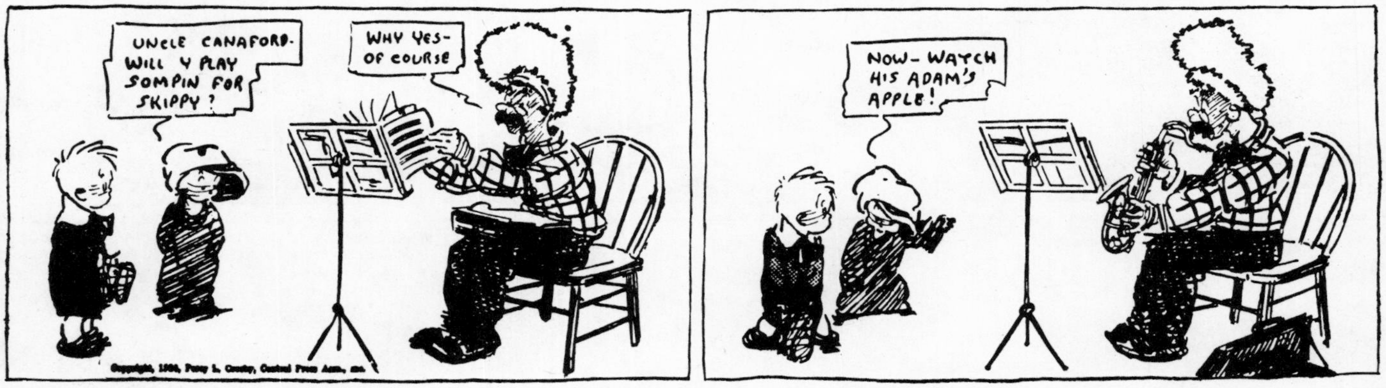
UNCLE CANAFORD. WILL Y PLAY SOMPIN FOR SKIPPY?
WHY YES- OF COURSE
NOW- WATCH HIS ADAM'S APPLE!

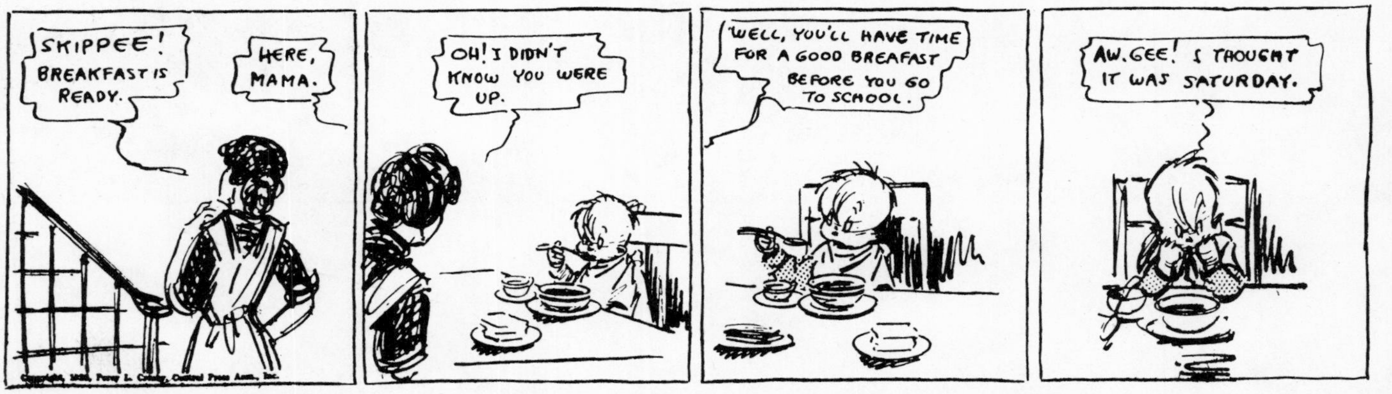
SKIPPEE! BREAKFAST IS READY.
HERE, MAMA.
OH! I DIDN'T KNOW YOU WERE UP.
WELL, YOU'LL HAVE TIME FOR A GOOD BREAFAST BEFORE YOU GO TO SCHOOL.
AW, GEE! I THOUGHT IT WAS SATURDAY.

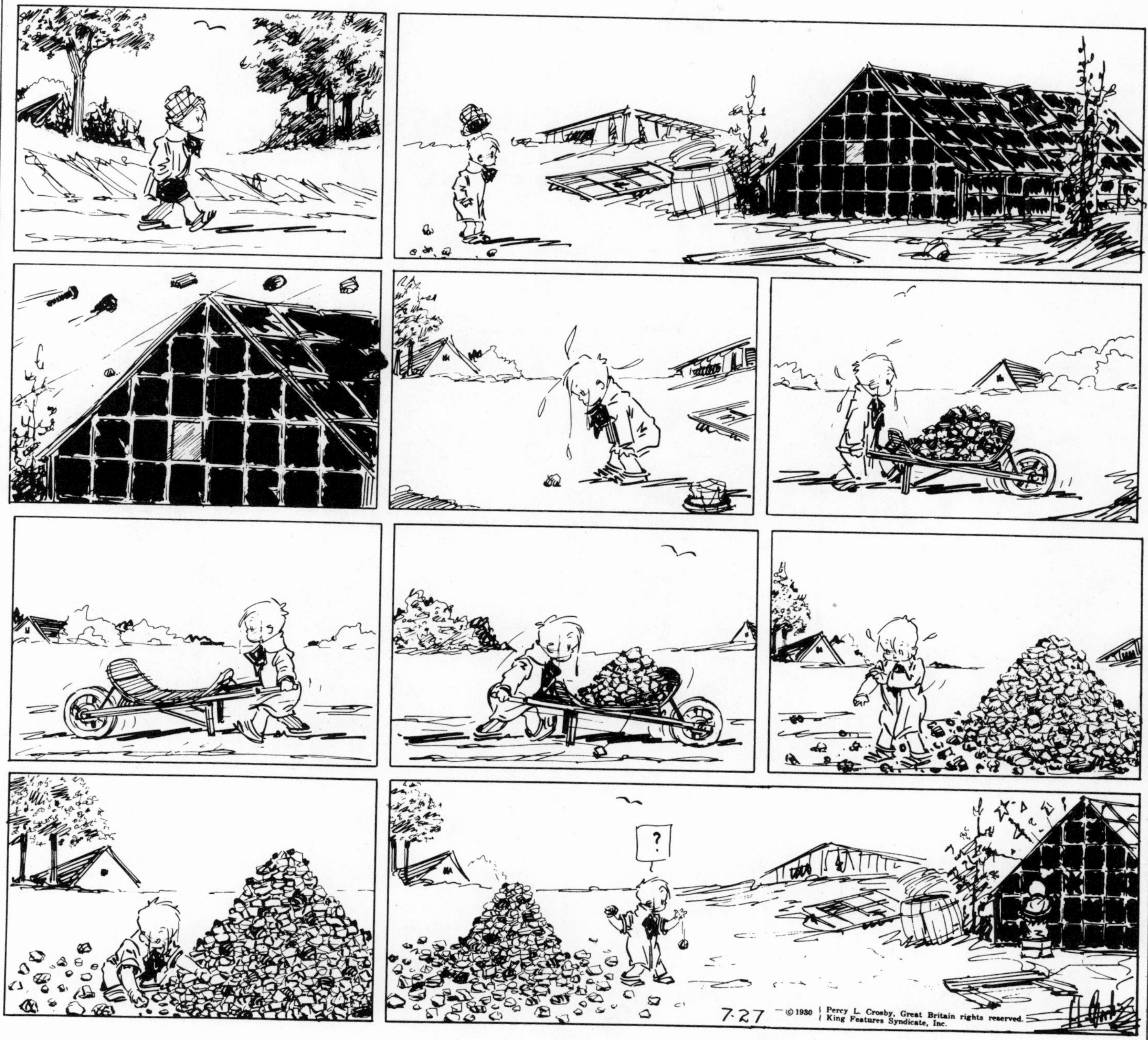
?
7-27
© 1930 Percy L. Crosby, Great Britain rights reserved.
King Features Syndicate, Inc.

Skippy Themes

Animals

Crosby's favorite animal was the horse, but there were many others he drew into *Skippy* episodes. He loved animals, knew that they hold a great fascination for the young, and perceived their possibilities for good visual humor. A marvelous anatomist and draftsman, most likely he also included them just for the sheer joy of drawing them.

Copyright, P. L. Crosby, 1927, Johnson Features, Inc

THEY MAKE BILLIARD BALLS OUT O' THEM HORNS.
© 1931 Percy L. Crosby, Great Britain rights reserved. King Features Syndicate, Inc.
BUT NOT UNTIL HE'S THROUGH WITH THEM.
8-8

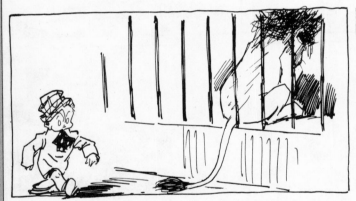

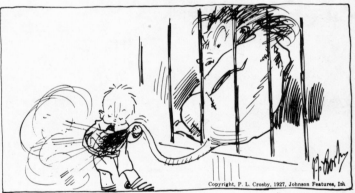

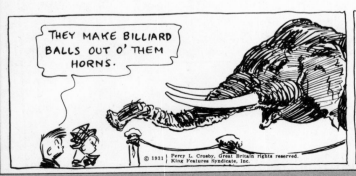

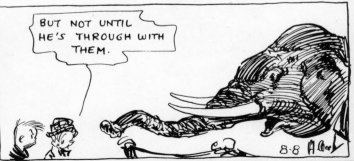

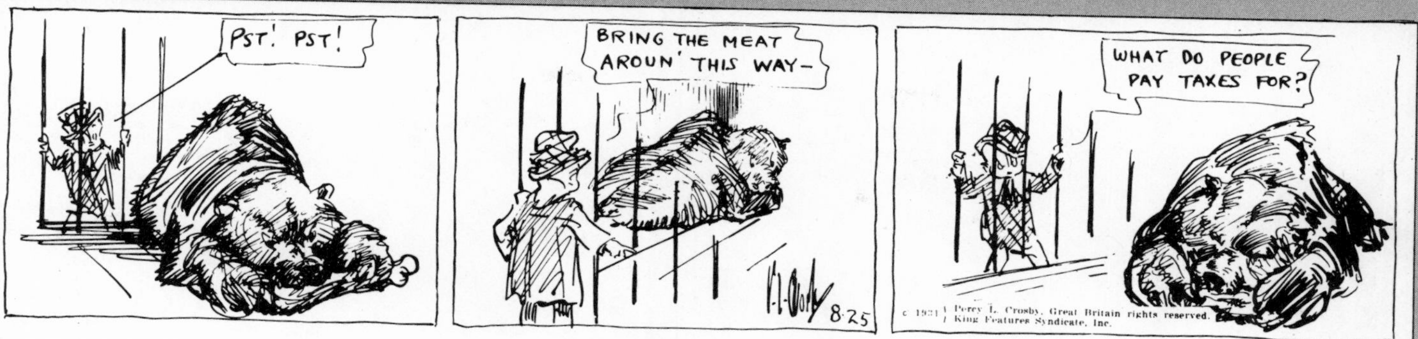
PST! PST!
BRING THE MEAT AROUN' THIS WAY-
8·25
WHAT DO PEOPLE PAY TAXES FOR?
c 1931 Percy L. Crosby, Great Britain rights reserved. King Features Syndicate, Inc.

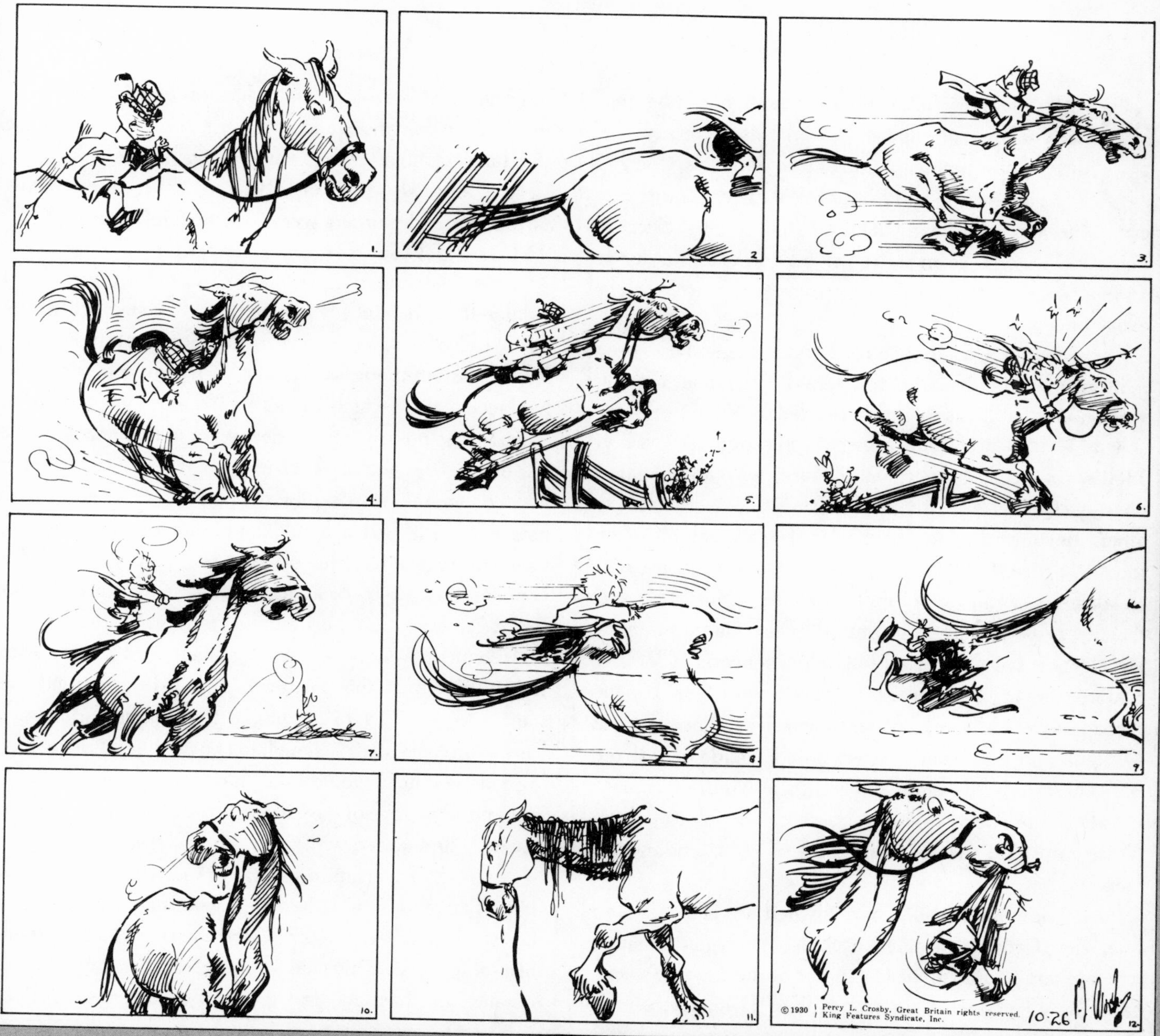
1.
2
3.
4.
5.
6.
7.
8.
9.
10.
11.
© 1930 Percy L. Crosby, Great Britain rights reserved. King Features Syndicate, Inc.
10·26
12.

5 / THE CREATIVE YEARS

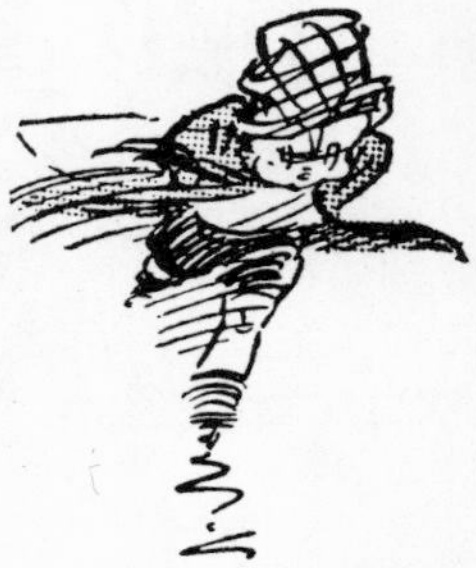

Crosby's career following the creation of *Skippy* became one of almost bewildering diversity: he thrived as a painter, as an author of novels, poetry, and philosophy, and as a political propagandist and critic. He was at the height of his creative powers. Success in one area would seem to trigger a burst of creativity in another—as if there were a compulsion to prove himself in everything.

"America was going on the greatest, gaudiest spree in history," wrote F. Scott Fitzgerald of the time. Crosby was on a spree all his own. He reveled in New York life. It was as if he were still a boy standing goggle-eyed in Holt's, the neighborhood candy store, with an unlimited charge account. Crosby flitted from one world to the other, devouring them all like favorite chocolates—the theater, opera, ballet, art galleries, museums, music halls, speakeasies, and nightclubs. Passionate about music and theater, he could be as enraptured by Toscanini conducting La Scala at Carnegie Hall or the concerts of Walter Damrosch (an admirer of Crosby's work) as by the Broadway of Alfred Lunt and Lynn Fontanne, Eugene O'Neill, and Al Jolson. He was an aficionado of both the ballet at the Metropolitan and boxing at Madison Square Garden. He spent so many hours at the Metropolitan Museum of Art that he knew most of the attendants by name.

By now internationally renowned as cartoonist and humorist, Crosby attracted a circle of talented friends, among them Marc Connelly, author of the classic American play *The Green Pastures*; Robert Benchley, author and humorist; Harold Ross, editor of *The New Yorker*; and Robert E. Sherwood, then editor of *Life* magazine and later Pulitzer Prize–winning playwright of *Idiot's Delight* and *Abe Lincoln in Illinois*. His closest fellow cartoonists and painters were George McManus, H. T. Webster, and Guy Hoff.

For the first time in his life, Crosby was able to indulge his penchant for fine clothes. His suits were now Brooks Brothers, he designed a Japanese-style monogram for his custom-made shirts, and in addition to his usual Malacca cane (which he had affected since his early twenties) he now sported a derby hat and spats. Despite all the newly acquired veneer, however, Crosby remained, in the words of Connelly, "fundamentally an innocent." He had a childlike, boyish quality, and, as Connelly recalled, "He could be so young—I loved his youngness." Crosby could also be cocky, even arrogant at times, but this, too, was fundamentally a naïveté. Crosby and Connelly were once traveling together on a train, with Percy staring at the passing countryside apparently in some reverie. "I'd like to have three million dollars," Percy suddenly said, "enough to live on the rest of my life. You know what I would do, Marc—go to the Far East, and find some sage of the Orient. . . ." Then he turned to Connelly and added with great relish, "*And trip him up!*"

Crosby's wartime marriage to Gertrude crumbled in the early twenties, and after a few years of legal separation they were divorced in 1927. Gertrude received custody of their only child, Patricia. Throughout his life, when a romance or marriage faded Crosby was disconsolate.

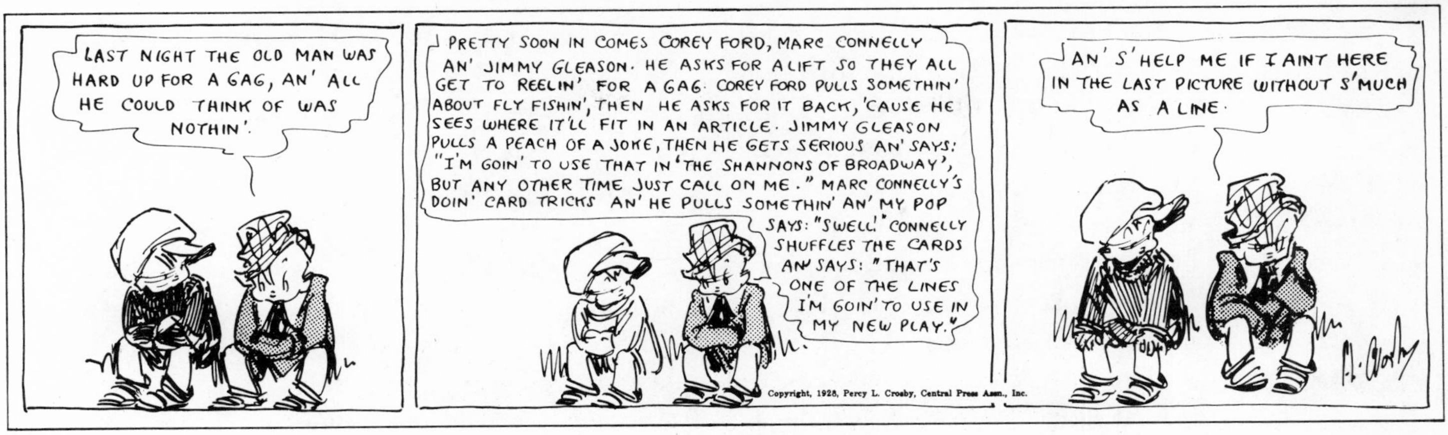
LAST NIGHT THE OLD MAN WAS HARD UP FOR A GAG, AN' ALL HE COULD THINK OF WAS NOTHIN'.
PRETTY SOON IN COMES COREY FORD, MARC CONNELLY AN' JIMMY GLEASON. HE ASKS FOR A LIFT SO THEY ALL GET TO REELIN' FOR A GAG. COREY FORD PULLS SOMETHIN' ABOUT FLY FISHIN', THEN HE ASKS FOR IT BACK, 'CAUSE HE SEES WHERE IT'LL FIT IN AN ARTICLE. JIMMY GLEASON PULLS A PEACH OF A JOKE, THEN HE GETS SERIOUS AN' SAYS: "I'M GOIN' TO USE THAT IN 'THE SHANNONS OF BROADWAY', BUT ANY OTHER TIME JUST CALL ON ME." MARC CONNELLY'S DOIN' CARD TRICKS AN' HE PULLS SOMETHIN' AN' MY POP SAYS: "SWELL!" CONNELLY SHUFFLES THE CARDS AN' SAYS: "THAT'S ONE OF THE LINES I'M GOIN' TO USE IN MY NEW PLAY."
Copyright, 1928, Percy L. Crosby, Central Press Assn., Inc.
AN' S'HELP ME IF I AINT HERE IN THE LAST PICTURE WITHOUT S'MUCH AS A LINE.

And it was at those vulnerable times that he seemed to hold a particular fascination for women—perhaps a challenge for them as well. It was part of Crosby's boyish charm, and he knew it. "Never feel sorry for yourself unless you can get a woman thinking the same way." He was especially attracted to the glamour and vitality of women of the theater. One such romantic interest was Libby Holman, the noted torch singer and star of the *Garrick Gaities*. They often made the rounds of the nightclubs—to Harlem to see the revue at Connie's Inn with Louis Armstrong and his Orchestra, or to the Cotton Club where Duke Ellington, Ethel Waters, or Bill "Bojangles" Robinson might be performing. When he saw Ina Claire in *The Gold Diggers*, he was "carried into the realms of ecstasy," not knowing at the time she was an avid *Skippy* fan. She later became his close friend, as did such other actresses as Colleen Moore, Elsie Janis, and Marilyn Miller. Percy could be charming, witty, and attentive, and the creator of *Skippy* was probably as glamorous to those women as they were to him. Even so, Crosby was always shy with beautiful women. He once confessed, "I was one who adored women—really taken off my feet when I beheld a beautiful face and a gorgeous figure of a woman, but sometimes, in fact all times, my knees buckled and my tongue froze to the roof of my mouth if such a one approached me. The virile part of me alone wanted to plunge forward, at any cost, to grasp the desired one, but my holier self held me in check like a charioteer who tightens the reins to keep speeding horses from galloping into the grandstands. If I hadn't been cursed with this other self, it would have been far different for me. Who shoved this sanctimonious self into my passionate being?"

About this time, Crosby had to contend with another paradox in his makeup. Journalists and cartoonists of the period were notoriously hard drinkers, and it wasn't long before Crosby, up to then a teetotaler, began to drink. The man who had so often written passionately about the evils of alcohol gradually became addicted himself, and by the end of the twenties it was a serious problem. Not only did he frequent the speakeasies, Crosby also drank heavily at his clubs. A thriving institution of the time, New York clubs attracted many of the leading figures from the art, theater, sports, and business worlds. Oliver Herford, the satirist for *Vanity Fair*, proposed Crosby's membership to the noted theatrical club the Players. Crosby was also a member of the Salmagundi Club on lower Fifth Avenue, a venerable institution whose members comprised a who's who of the arts, and for a time he maintained an apartment in the Hotel Seymour, which housed the Coffee House Club, another favorite. There, as well as at the weekly luncheons at the Dutch Treat Club, Crosby would dine with such luminaries as George Abbott, Jerome Kern, Ring Lardner, John Barrymore, Rube Goldberg, Heywood Broun, and Frank Crowninshield, editor of *Vanity Fair*.

As with so many other heavy drinkers, the chemistry of alcohol would temporarily alter Crosby's personality. Like the classic drunk in Charlie Chaplin's *City Lights*, he would awake the morning after with little or no recollection of what had transpired. The first escapades were minor, and had minor, although embarrassing, repercussions, such as being asked to resign from the Players Club. But, as time went on, these antics were to have more serious effects on his personal relations with friends, business associates, and family. *Newsweek* reported what must have been an epic binge. At the end of a tour of New York speakeasies, Crosby woke up to find himself in a Cleveland railway yard. After taxiing to yet another all-night watering hole, Crosby was somehow knocked out during a raid by federal agents, and he awoke in a Cleveland jail. The escapade had a typical Crosby ending. The jailkeeper was charmed by Percy, who in turn called the prison the nicest place he had ever seen. He remained there several days, drawing *Skippy* pictures for the jailer's son.

A colleague and favorite drinking companion was C. D. Russell, creator of *Pete, the Tramp*. On one occasion both men were well into a night of serious drinking when Percy suddenly realized he needed a set of *Skippy* dailies for the following day. C. D. was too drunk to assist, but Percy got out the paper and pen and, without penciling, inked in six dailies, complete with dialogue, in an hour and a half—then passed out. However true or apocryphal, such Crosby stories grew, undoubtedly embellished in their retelling. They often involved drinking bouts, but other seemingly bizarre incidents added to the Crosby legend as well. Herblock (Herbert Block), the noted political cartoonist and an admirer of Crosby's work, recounts one story as an example of Crosby's flamboyant style. An insurance salesman came to Crosby's studio one day unannounced and launched into a sales pitch. Crosby, in the middle of inking a page, never said a word, but slowly washed his brush out in a goldfish bowl that sat on his taboret. He opened a drawer, picked up a pistol, took careful aim, and shot the fish and the bowl into smithereens. Then he calmly replaced the gun and resumed inking. The astonished salesman stuffed his papers into his case and made a shaky departure. Herblock admired the Crosby method of getting rid of salesmen—but thought it hard on goldfish.

Crosby's frenetic life hardly disguised his growing isolation and loneliness. One time he threw an elegant dinner party at his house in Douglaston, Long Island, which degenerated, as usual, into an all-night bacchanal. Jack Shuttleworth, a friend, awoke early in the morning to find Percy alone on the lawn, still in white tie and tails, a melancholy figure quietly painting a watercolor of the sunrise.

By 1929, Crosby found himself weary of Broadway glitter and unsatisfied with bachelor life. He yearned for a devoted wife and family and a home in the country. When in a euphoric mood, Crosby could think of himself as a genius and believe that all geniuses were monogamous by nature. He idealized the memory of his parents' marriage and wanted to duplicate it. Pure, everlasting love was part of the knighthood legends, and in this, too, Crosby's life was an extended acting-out of the dreams of his boyhood.

About 1927, Crosby began to write prose vignettes of Skippy for *Life*, usually to run along with the Skippy cartoons. Their success led Crosby to undertake a Skippy novel. To finish the final draft, he went off on a writing vacation with his good friend, Corey Ford, a popular humorist and one of the original contributors to *The New Yorker* magazine. Ford and Crosby both loved the outdoors and would often flee the pressures of New York for their favorite retreat, a farmhouse near Freedom, New Hampshire. Crosby was not without humor about his bucolic sojourns in the Granite State: "In New Hampshire, the slogan is: 'Be Free or Die.' What's the sense of being free in New Hampshire?"

Crosby returned to New York with the complete manuscript. His publisher, George Putnam of G. P. Putnam's Sons, assigned him his own secretary. Crosby was impressed with more than her secretarial ability. As he later described their meeting: "A cursory glance revealed that she was rather tall and had the finest figure I ever saw. . . . I could hardly take my eyes from her. . . . She had great poise and moved with graceful rhythm. . . . I wondered with all her poise and dignity and haughty manner, could she be like Zola's Nana?" When she finished typing the entire novel, Crosby invited her to celebrate with a night on the town. It was a memorable evening in the grand Crosby manner, starting with a ride around Central Park in a horse-drawn Victoria, a dinner

Dale and Percy just after their marriage in New York

at the Biltmore, the theater (the original production of *Show Boat* starring Paul Robeson and Helen Morgan), and ending with a drive to her Westchester home in a chauffeured limousine. Crosby was in love again. The Lone Knight had found his princess. She was Agnes Dale Locke, a graduate of Vassar, who had joined the Putnam firm just a year before. They were married on April 4, 1929.

The Crosbys sailed for Europe for their honeymoon on the *Ile de France* and took a villa perched on a Normandy cliff overlooking the English Channel near Dieppe. It was a romantic idyll: concerts and the ballet; the roulette tables at the casino; prowling the countryside; trips to the Château d'Arques and Rouen through fields of wheat and poppies; sketching and painting excursions; and exploring the chalk cliffs along the beach (where Crosby one day sketched the picture *Rat Hunter*, of a French waif, later bought by the British Museum). Percy

had an almost mystical revelation one day on his way to Dieppe, a moment that profoundly affected his life. "Never had I experienced the loneliness that I felt. . . . I walked as one who belonged to Purgatory—the astral plane; walked as one utterly lost and out of harmony with the world. I was going mad, I thought, everything had changed . . . I was suffocating from within. Some philosopher once said that nature abhors a vacuum; my sensation was, if such a thing is conceivable, that a vacuum had been chased by the entire world and had at last found refuge in me." He reached Dieppe through a downpour of rain, and finally, seated at a café, drenched to the skin, he ordered a glass of wine. As the wine passed his lips, he suddenly knew what this thing was and what he had to do. He vowed never to touch a drop of liquor again. The vow was to last seven years.

Several weeks after the Crosbys returned from Europe, the stock market crashed. Crosby lost little—much of his money was by now invested in Virginia real estate. The couple moved to McLean, Virginia, near Washington, D.C., where Percy bought a fine old home, "The Beeches." After a few years, the Crosbys transferred to an even more elaborate estate of two hundred acres, described as one of the showplaces of northern

Rat Hunter

Rat Hunter, a wash drawing done on the Normandy coast during the honeymoon trip, recounted in Crosby's book, *A Cartoonist's Philosophy*. Original in the collection of the British Museum.

Virginia. It was Percy's Shangri-La. He built an iron fence with two imposing stone pillars at the entrance gate with a plaque inscribed RIDGELAWN. He installed a tennis court. The stable housed four riding horses—his favorites were named Skippy, Sooky, and Eagle. The eighteen-room colonial stone mansion was situated on a hill commanding an extensive view across the upper Potomac to Washington. Reached by a long, tree-lined drive, the house itself was screened by ancient white oaks. A studio was connected to the main building by an arched breezeway. Crosby did all the interior decorating himself—Flemish tapestries, oriental rugs, and antiques—and installed great stone fireplaces. To one side of the center hall was his favorite room—a library of over seven thousand carefully selected books. The staff at Ridgelawn consisted of a registered nurse for the children—his son, Skippy, and three daughters, Barbara, Joan, and Carol—a secretary, two maids, a cook, a chauffeur for the yellow Packard 8, a foreman, and several handymen to care for the grounds. Percy would often take one of his favorite stallions through the woodlands of his estate, and periodically he would visit the 1,500-acre farm he had acquired nearby. The press reported that Crosby reveled in his new role of "country squire." That was not quite accurate. It was actually, again, a realization of his boyhood fantasy—the Lone Knight on a white charger, sallying forth from his castle to protect his deeded lands.

Life at Ridgelawn seems in retrospect almost too perfect, as if it had been taking place on a Hollywood set. Enthusiastic about tennis, Crosby took private lessons with a pro (to his dismay, his wife Dale continued to beat him). An expert shot, he enjoyed target practice (Crosby even designed and patented an invention for firearms, an ingenious device that incorporated a pistol in the stock of a rifle) and was also adept at throwing the long knife. He romped with the children on the lawn, indulged them with expensive toys such as an elaborate fire engine and an expensive reproduction of his Packard, and told them stories (often episodes of *Skippy*) under a huge oak, their favorite play area. Holidays were always special occasions, carefully stage-managed by Crosby for the children. The eggs for the Easter hunt were painted with *Skippy* characters, the elaborate Fourth of July fireworks

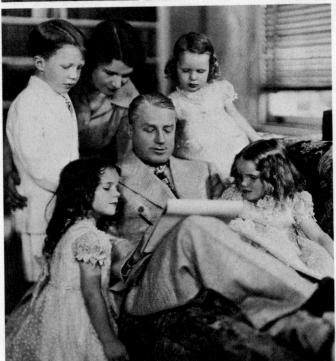

The Squire of Ridgelawn. Bottom photo *(clockwise around Crosby from upper left)*: Skippy, Dale, Carol, Joan, Barbara.

were augmented by a fleet from the local fire department, and Christmas usually included a visit from Santa, a role played by the handyman but directed by Crosby. Percy was proud of his beautiful family—his wife and children were all uncommonly attractive—but while his georgic life fulfilled his familial desires, it was only a backdrop for an ever expanding professional life.

Dale now took charge of his business affairs, finances, and correspondence. He acquired an agent to handle the growing Skippy empire—contracts for the Skippy novels and a radio show, and others such as with Standard Oil (for which he agreed to do thirty-four posters at a thousand dollars each).

Hollywood too was quick to see the potential of Skippy. After protracted negotiations, Paramount bought the film rights for $25,000, a considerable sum in Depression times, and signed some of its leading talent to the picture, including veteran director Norman Taurog, Joseph L. Mankiewicz, noted film scenarist, and Don Marquis, author of *Archie and Mehitabel*. Skippy was played by Jackie Cooper, and Robert Coogan, the five-year-old brother of Jackie Coogan, co-star of Charlie Chaplin's *The Kid*, made his film debut in the role of Sooky. Many of the scenes were filmed on location at an actual shantytown near San Bernardino, California.

In April, 1931, Skippy opened simultaneously at the New York and Brooklyn Paramount theaters, and 260,000 New Yorkers saw the picture the first week. The reviews were unanimous raves and the film was an immediate box-office hit. When time came for the Academy Awards, Taurog won Best Director. Jackie Cooper had been nominated for Best Actor, and, although Lionel Barrymore won the award, the role of Skippy established Cooper as a child star.

The movie was a success in the eyes of everyone except Percy Crosby. "Paramount mangled my novel," he would write over and over again. In truth, the film bore little resemblance to Crosby's novel. The pathos of Sooky's death, for example, was replaced by the plight of a stray mongrel dog. Crosby never forgave Hollywood or anyone connected with the film, although he sent Cooper a gold watch inscribed "in appreciation of your perfect portrayal of Skippy." For a time, Cooper was so identified with the role that he was billed as "Skippy" in personal appearances throughout the country. Infuriated, Crosby instituted a suit to prevent such use of the name. Later that year, he had to endure a second, previously contracted film, *Sooky*, with Cooper and Coogan in the same roles. Despite an offer from MGM of $50,000 for a third film, Crosby was so embittered that he never allowed another Skippy movie to be made.

The constant pressure of deadlines on the *Skippy* newspaper strip forced Percy to turn for assistance to an old friend, Richard Reddy. When the nineteen-year-old Crosby won first prize in the Edison contest, twenty-one-year-old Reddy won the second and third prizes, and they had celebrated their good fortune together. Both had attended the Art Students League and had worked together on the *Globe* and the *Herald*. Reddy, an artist of exceptional talent, remained as assistant on *Skippy* to the end of Crosby's career.

In the ten years from 1928 to 1937, Crosby turned out 3,650 episodes of *Skippy*; ten books of fiction, philosophy, politics, drawings, and cartoons; numerous pamphlets and essays; and held a dozen exhibitions of his oils, watercolors, lithography, drypoint, and drawings in New York, Washington, Paris, London, and Rome. All this frenetic activity and accomplishment was made possible, in part, by one special ability—his incredible speed.

(text continues on page 84)

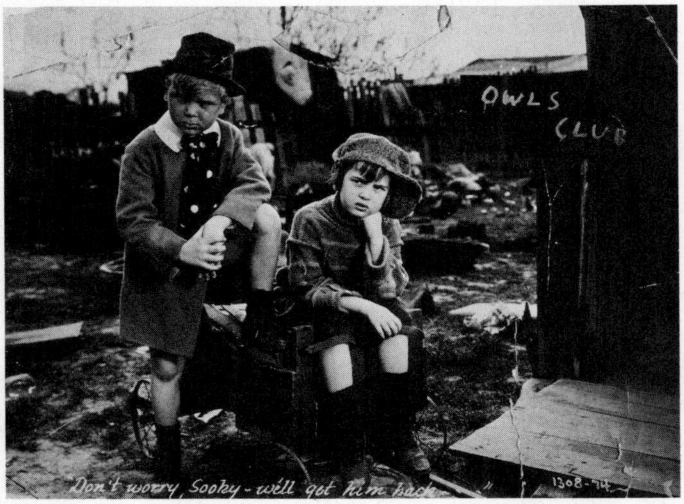
OWLS
CLUB
Don't worry, Sooky - we'll get him back
1308-74

A publicity still from the movie *Skippy*: Jackie Cooper as Skippy, and Robert Coogan as Sooky

Encores

Crosby was never reluctant to repeat an idea in his cartoons. Often he adapted drawings first done for *Life* magazine to the *Skippy* newspaper strip, refining and improving upon the originals, and occasionally he would meet the never-ending deadline pressure of the strip with the very same drawings (though not without several years having intervened). At least he never resorted to the device of some cartoonists who, behind in their schedules, had been known to insert a notice that a particular cartoon was "reprinted by popular demand." Apparently he was confident that the repetitions would either not be noticed or be accepted simply as an encore worth seeing again.

Copyright, P. L. Crosby, 1927, Central Press Association, Inc.
DID YOU KILL THE TURKEY FOR TOMORROW?
NO, MA, I WENT OUT THERE, BUT I THOUGHT IT WOULD BE BETTER IF HE GOT A GOOD NIGHT'S REST FIRST 'CAUSE HE'S GOT SUCH A HARD DAY BEFORE HIM TOMORROW.

Percy Crosby

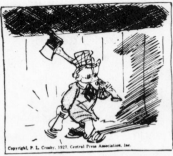

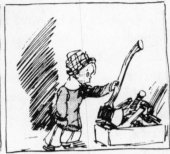

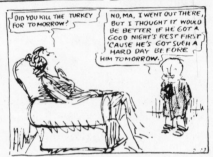

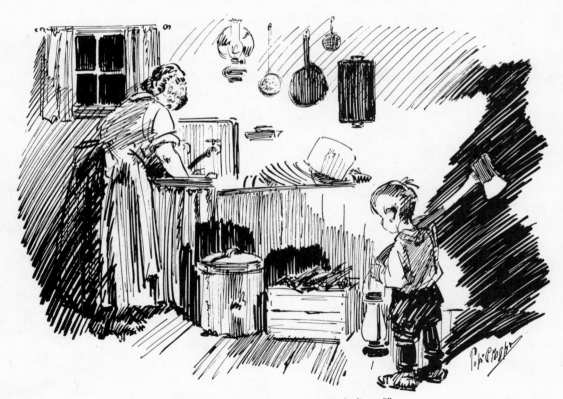

"Did you kill the rooster for to-morrow's dinner?"
"No, Ma, I went out there, but I thought it would be better if the poor fellow got a good night's rest first 'cause he's got such a hard day before him to-morrow."

BUTCH SAYS IF YA COME DOWN TO THE CORNER HE'LL KNOCK YA BLOCK OFF.
I'LL GO DOWN TO THE CORNER.
Copyright, P. L. Crosby. 1927. Central Press Association, Inc.
SKIPPY SEZ YA OLD MAN'S ALL WAYS OUTA WORK AN' HE'S COMIN' DOWN TO KNOCK THE STUFFINS OUTA YA.
I'LL BE WAITIN FOR HIM.
OH, WAIT'LL THAT GUY COMES. I COULD SWING FOR ME THOUGHTS.
I TAKE NOTICE HE DIDN'T START NOTHIN'.

BUTCH SEZ IF YA COME DOWN ON THE CORNER HE'LL KNOCK THE STUFFIN' OUT OF YA.
TELL HIM I'LL GO DOWN THERE ALL I WANT TO.
HE KNOCK THE STUFFIN' OUTA ME — I LOVE THAT.
SKIPPY SEZ YOUR A BIG STIFF AN' YOUR OLD MAN'S ALWAYS OUTA WOIK AN' HE'S COMIN' DOWN AN' KNOCK YA FROM UNDER YOUR HAT!
OH! IF I COULD GET ME HANDS ON THAT SKIPPY! I CAN EVEN SWING FOR ME THOUGHTS.
RUSH
—AN' THEN ANUDDER LEFT, AN' A RIGHT AN' THEN, OH! AN' THEN ME AWFUL UPPERCUT!
RUSH
STILL I GOTTA PULL ME UPPERCUT IF I WANT TO SAVE MESELF THE EXPENSE OF A HOISE.
GIVE ME A STAND-UP, HUH! JUST FOR THAT I WON'T PULL ME UPPERCUT!
Percy L. Crosby, Great Britain rights reserved © 1936, King Features Syndicate, Inc.
I NOTICE HE DIDN'T START NOTHIN'!

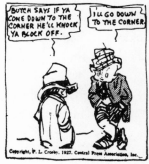

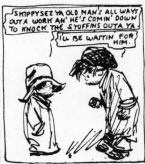

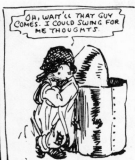

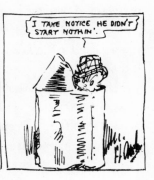

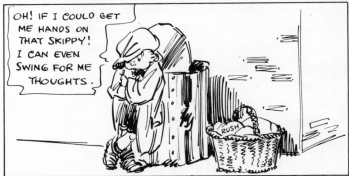

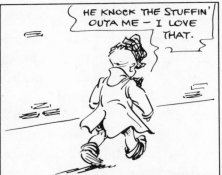

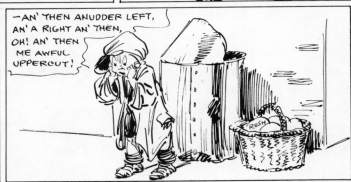

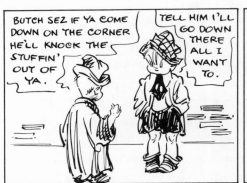

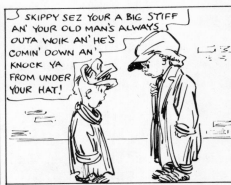

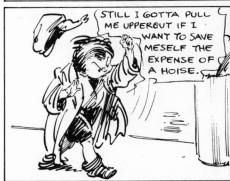

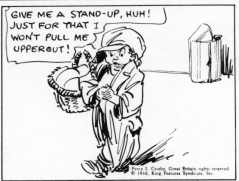

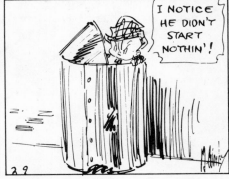

Crosby was able, when pressed, to turn out a year's work on the *Skippy* strip (with Reddy's help) in several months, freeing his energies and time for his myriad other pursuits.

Crosby's reputation as an author was growing. His novel *Skippy*, serialized in the *Ladies' Home Journal*, was a financial and critical success. (The publisher, George P. Putnam, and his wife, the noted aviatrix Amelia Earhart, were Crosby's friends. Putnam gave him a most favorable contract—fifteen-percent royalty, instead of the usual ten. Rights were also sold to Grosset and Dunlap for another edition which eventually sold fifty thousand copies.) Perhaps Crosby's most engaging literary quality was his ability to re-create the mind, mood, and idiom of children with deceptive simplicity. As William Rose Benét observed in the *Saturday Review of Literature*, "The artlessness of *Skippy* is the most difficult art, brought off with a casualness that amazes. An enduring contribution to the art of this period as well as to the literature."

In his next book, *Dear Sooky*, composed of diarylike letters from Skippy to his pal in Heaven, Crosby delved further into Skippy's persona. Perhaps the highest praise accorded *Dear Sooky* came from Robert Sherwood in *Scribner's Magazine*: "To say that Skippy is human is to underestimate him. He is both superhuman and supernatural. . . . It is all very well to say that no small boy could write in that apostrophic style, but Peter Pan accomplished a feat successfully, and what goes for Peter Pan goes double for Skippy."

There was a subtle change in Crosby's next, and last, Skippy book, *Skippy Rambles*. It consisted of twenty-six short essays, each a dialogue between Skippy and one of his pals—Yappy, Somerset, Sniffles, Yacob, and others. The humor was more heavily laden with philosophical and political comment and covered such subjects as the soul, cosmology, war, art, the church, economy, and advertising. Crosby's writing was becoming more and more a vehicle for his personal beliefs—political, social, and religious. It had crossed the line from entertainment to polemic, and the charm, humor, and essential naïveté of Skippy were being lost in the process. This dichotomy became more apparent in *A Cartoonist's Philosophy*, published in 1931. The first half is a charming account of Crosby's honeymoon trip to Europe—humorous, at times moving, with vivid characterizations of people he met. The second half, however, beginning with his return to New York and his disillusionment with what he saw as the city's hypocrisy and greed, swiftly develops into a political and religious tract. It made the book unacceptable for commercial publishers, and their rejection of it became the subject of the book's foreword when Crosby published it privately: "This book has been published by the author for the reason that eight prominent publishing houses saw no commercial possibilities in such a volume. Moreover, it was intimated that should the author embark upon so foolish a venture as to publish it as it now stands, his supposed public would turn against him. If one must eventually decide between the freedom of thought and gold, the author prefers the formlessness that accepts no mold save that ordained by the Creator." From then on, all his books carried the imprint "Percy Crosby, Publisher" or "Freedom Press," which Crosby established in 1936. *The New York Times* found "many a nugget of sound philosophy scattered through *A Cartoonist's Philosophy*," and wondered whether eight publishers might not have made a mistake. Financially, they had not. Crosby lost a huge sum on the venture, as well as on the subsequent works he published.

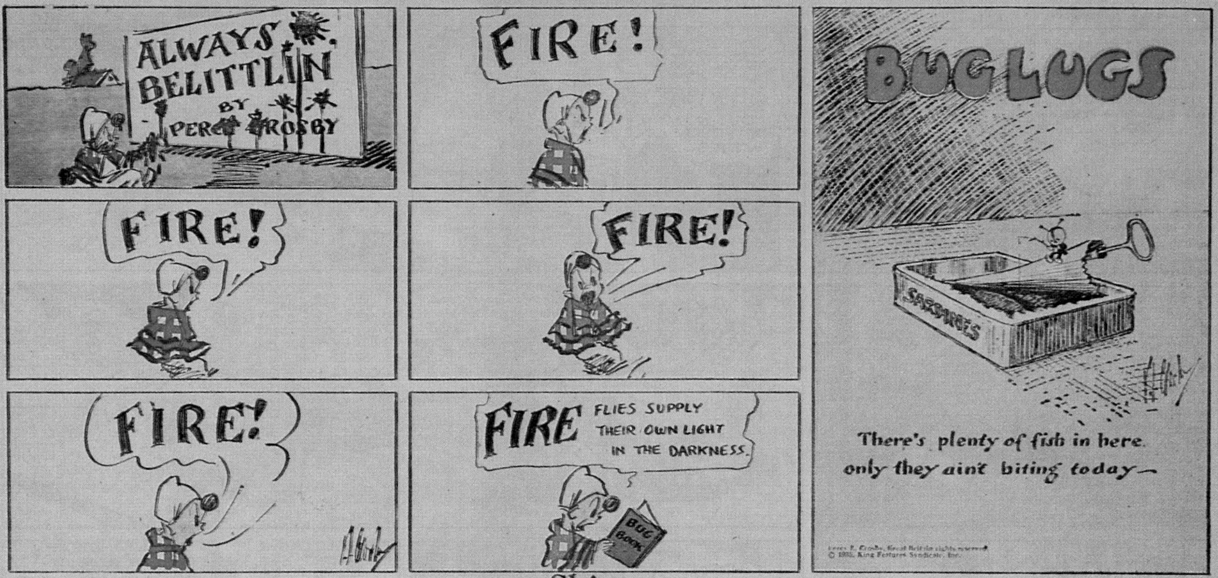
ALWAYS BELITTLIN
BY
PERCY CROSBY
FIRE!
FIRE!
FIRE!
FIRE!
FIRE
FLIES SUPPLY THEIR OWN LIGHT IN THE DARKNESS.
BUG BOOK
BUGLUGS
SARDINES
There's plenty of fish in here only they ain't biting today—

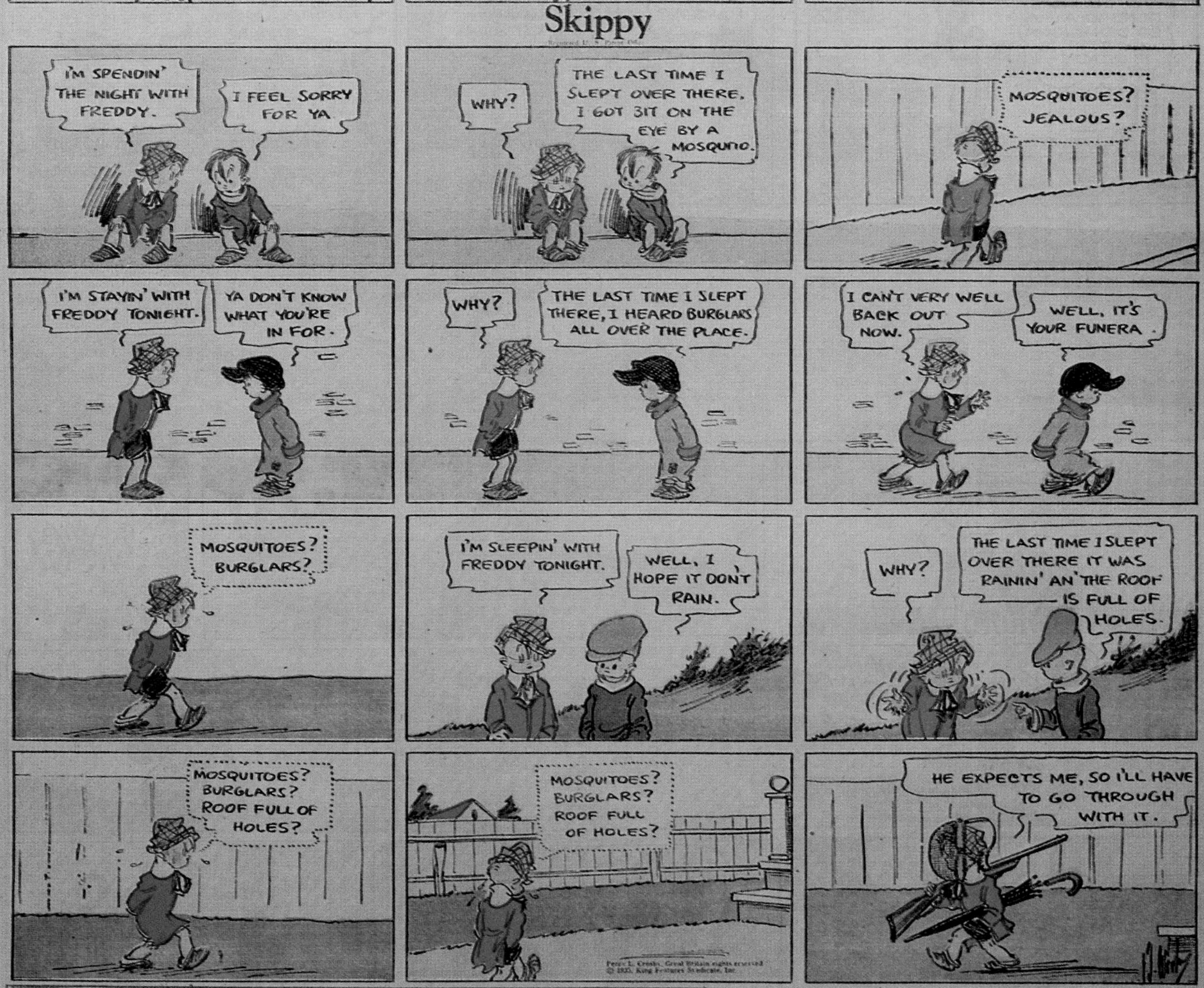
Skippy
I'M SPENDIN' THE NIGHT WITH FREDDY.
I FEEL SORRY FOR YA
WHY?
THE LAST TIME I SLEPT OVER THERE, I GOT BIT ON THE EYE BY A MOSQUITO.
MOSQUITOES? JEALOUS?
I'M STAYIN' WITH FREDDY TONIGHT.
YA DON'T KNOW WHAT YOU'RE IN FOR.
WHY?
THE LAST TIME I SLEPT THERE, I HEARD BURGLARS ALL OVER THE PLACE.
I CAN'T VERY WELL BACK OUT NOW.
WELL, IT'S YOUR FUNERA
MOSQUITOES? BURGLARS?
I'M SLEEPIN' WITH FREDDY TONIGHT.
WELL, I HOPE IT DON'T RAIN.
WHY?
THE LAST TIME I SLEPT OVER THERE IT WAS RAININ' AN' THE ROOF IS FULL OF HOLES.
MOSQUITOES? BURGLARS? ROOF FULL OF HOLES?
MOSQUITOES? BURGLARS? ROOF FULL OF HOLES?
HE EXPECTS ME, SO I'LL HAVE TO GO THROUGH WITH IT.

Skippy's Quaint Sayings Are Also in the Daily Inquirer

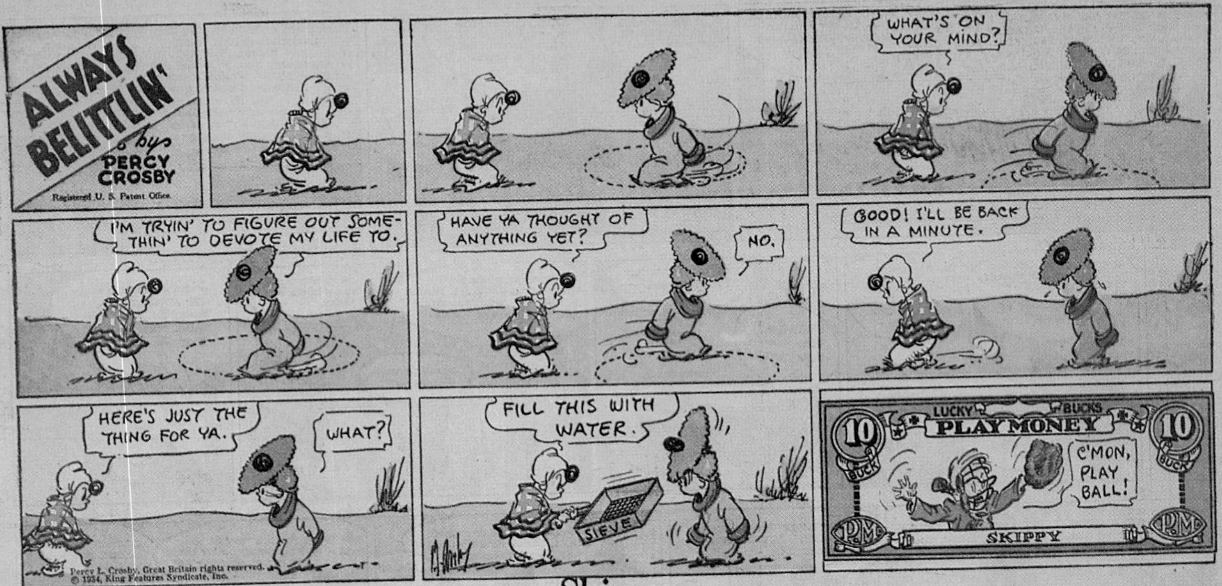
ALWAYS BELITTLIN'
by PERCY CROSBY
Registered U. S. Patent Office.
WHAT'S ON YOUR MIND?
I'M TRYIN' TO FIGURE OUT SOMETHIN' TO DEVOTE MY LIFE TO.
HAVE YA THOUGHT OF ANYTHING YET?
NO.
GOOD! I'LL BE BACK IN A MINUTE.
HERE'S JUST THE THING FOR YA.
WHAT?
FILL THIS WITH WATER.
SIEVE
Percy L. Crosby, Great Britain rights reserved.
© 1934, King Features Syndicate, Inc.
LUCKY BUCKS
PLAY MONEY
10
BUCK
C'MON, PLAY BALL!
SKIPPY

Skippy

Registered U. S. Patent Office

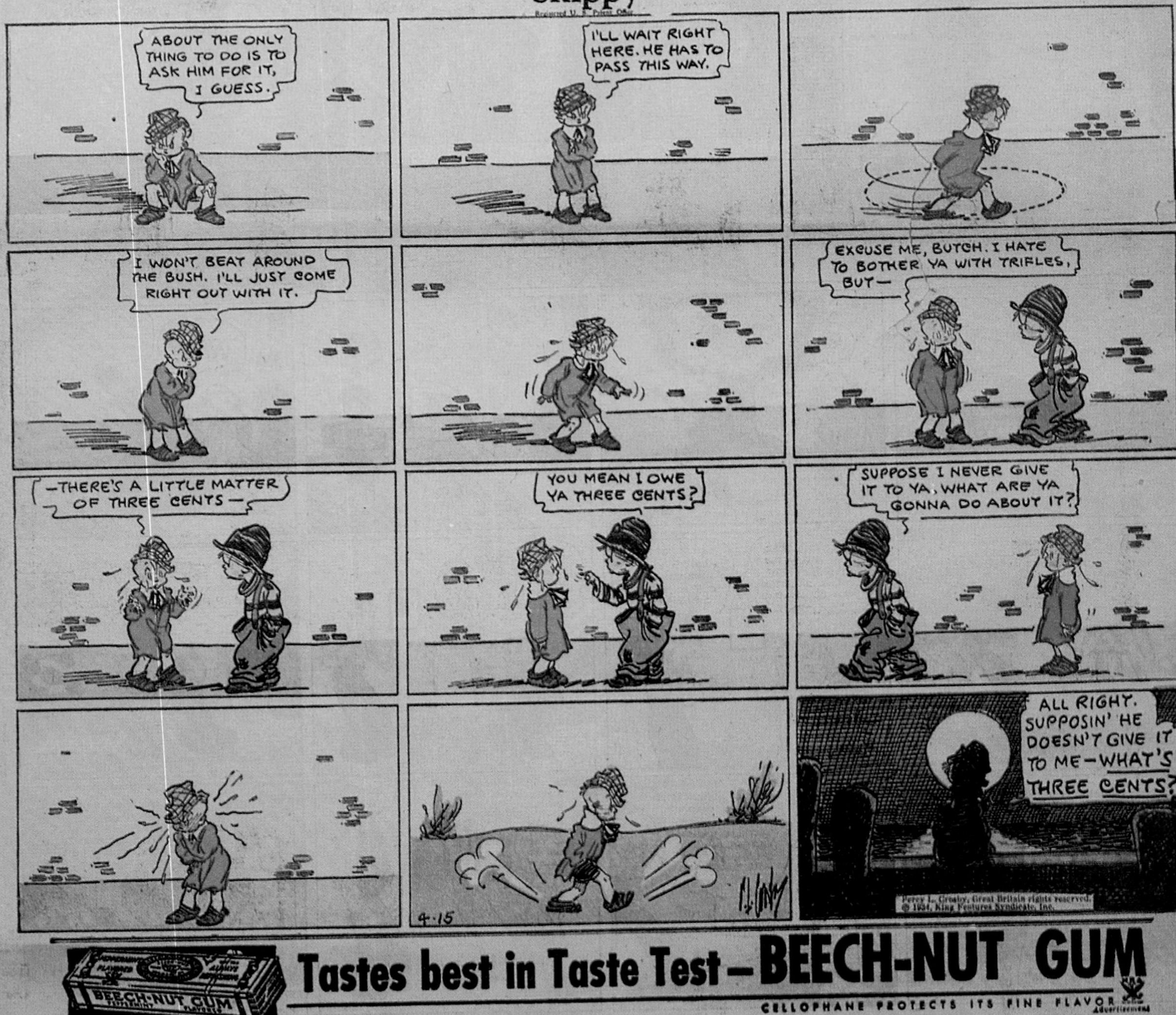
ABOUT THE ONLY THING TO DO IS TO ASK HIM FOR IT, I GUESS.
I'LL WAIT RIGHT HERE. HE HAS TO PASS THIS WAY.
I WON'T BEAT AROUND THE BUSH. I'LL JUST COME RIGHT OUT WITH IT.
EXCUSE ME, BUTCH. I HATE TO BOTHER YA WITH TRIFLES, BUT—
—THERE'S A LITTLE MATTER OF THREE CENTS—
YOU MEAN I OWE YA THREE CENTS?
SUPPOSE I NEVER GIVE IT TO YA, WHAT ARE YA GONNA DO ABOUT IT?
ALL RIGHT. SUPPOSIN' HE DOESN'T GIVE IT TO ME—WHAT'S THREE CENTS?
4-15
Percy L. Crosby, Great Britain rights reserved.
© 1934, King Features Syndicate, Inc.

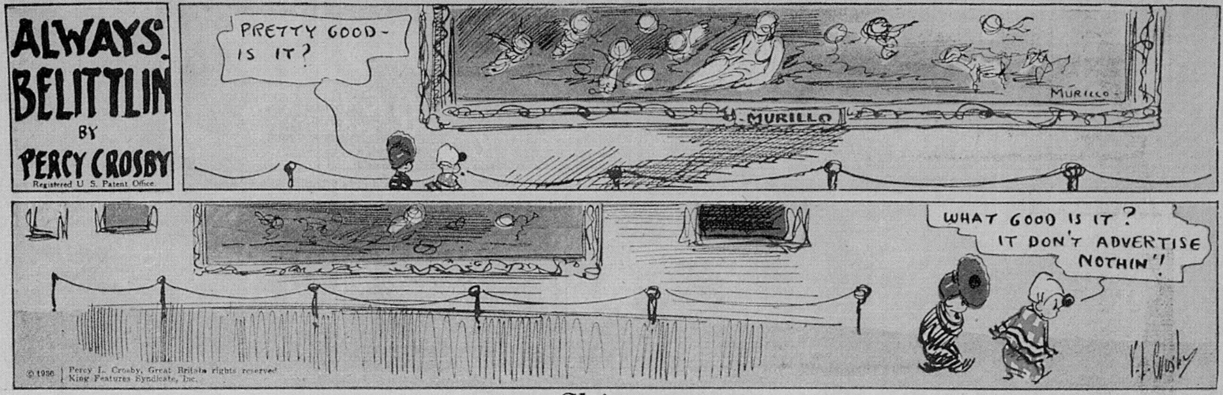
ALWAYS BELITTLIN
BY
PERCY CROSBY
Registered U. S. Patent Office
PRETTY GOOD - IS IT?
MURILLO
WHAT GOOD IS IT? IT DON'T ADVERTISE NOTHIN'!
© 1930 Percy L. Crosby, Great Britain rights reserved
King Features Syndicate, Inc.

Skippy

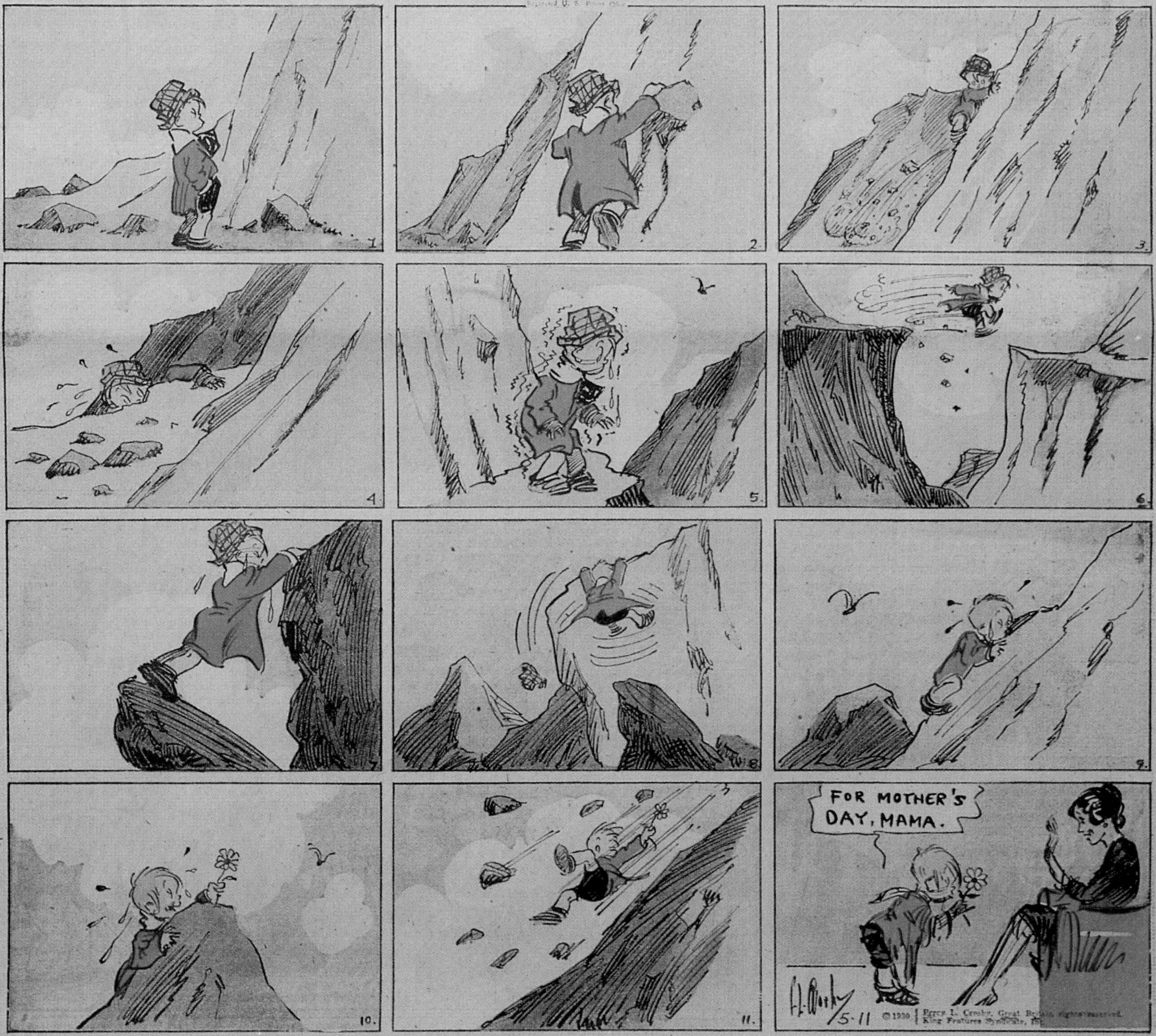
FOR MOTHER'S DAY, MAMA.
5-11

Watch for Skippy Every Morning in the Public Ledger

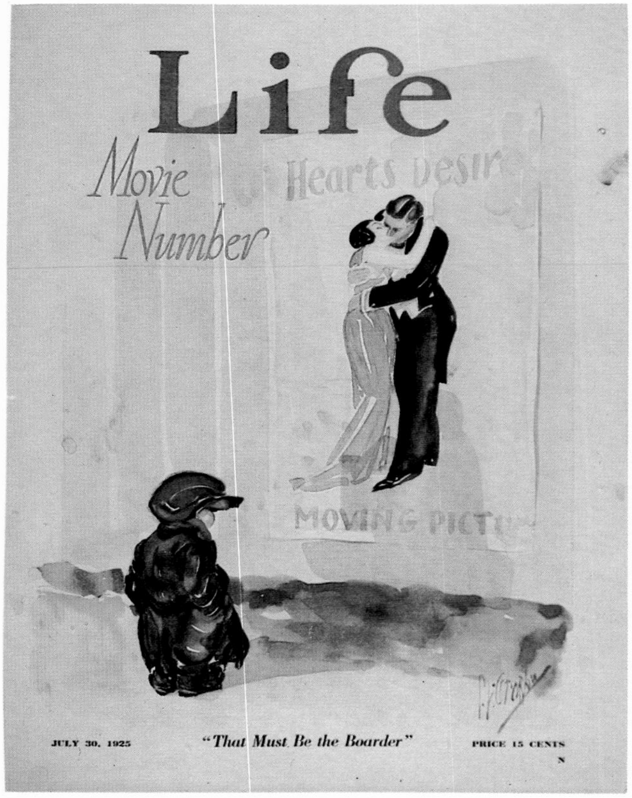
Life
Movie Number
Hearts Desir
MOVING PICTU
JULY 30, 1925
"That Must Be the Boarder"
PRICE 15 CENTS

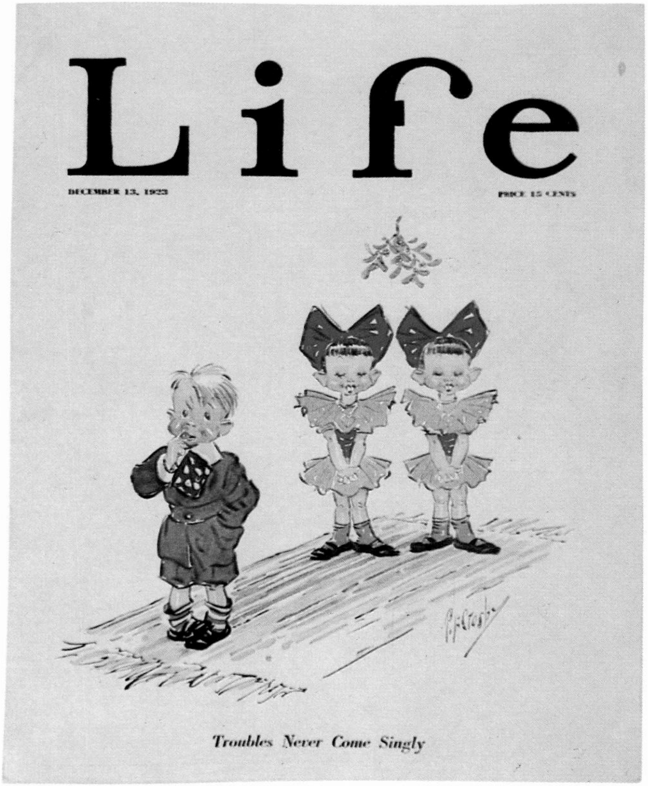
Life
DECEMBER 13, 1923
PRICE 15 CENTS
Troubles Never Come Singly

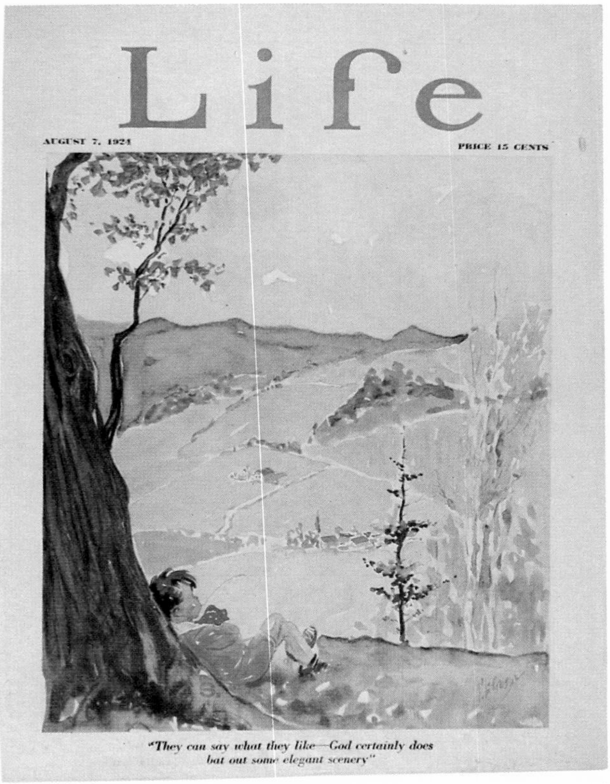
Life
AUGUST 7, 1924
PRICE 15 CENTS
"They can say what they like—God certainly does bat out some elegant scenery"

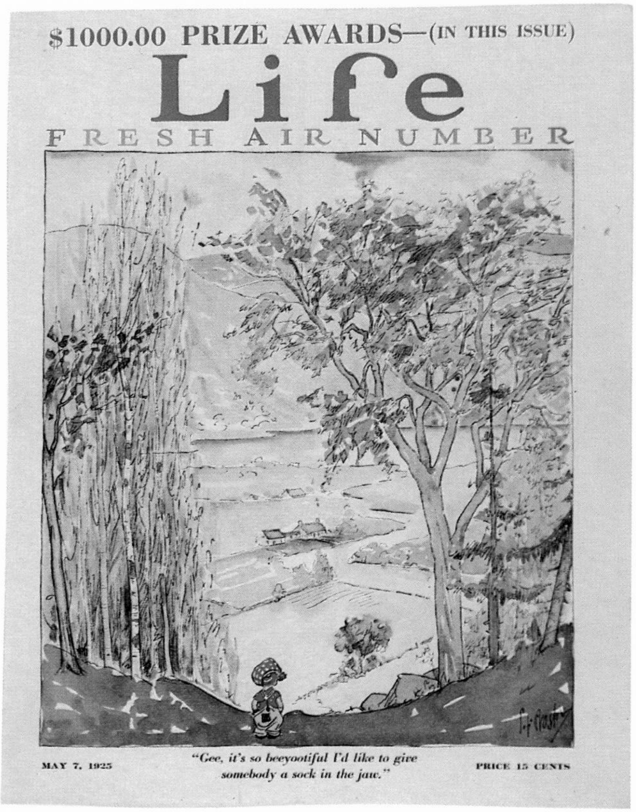
$1000.00 PRIZE AWARDS—(IN THIS ISSUE)
Life
FRESH AIR NUMBER
MAY 7, 1925
"Gee, it's so beeyootiful I'd like to give somebody a sock in the jaw."
PRICE 15 CENTS

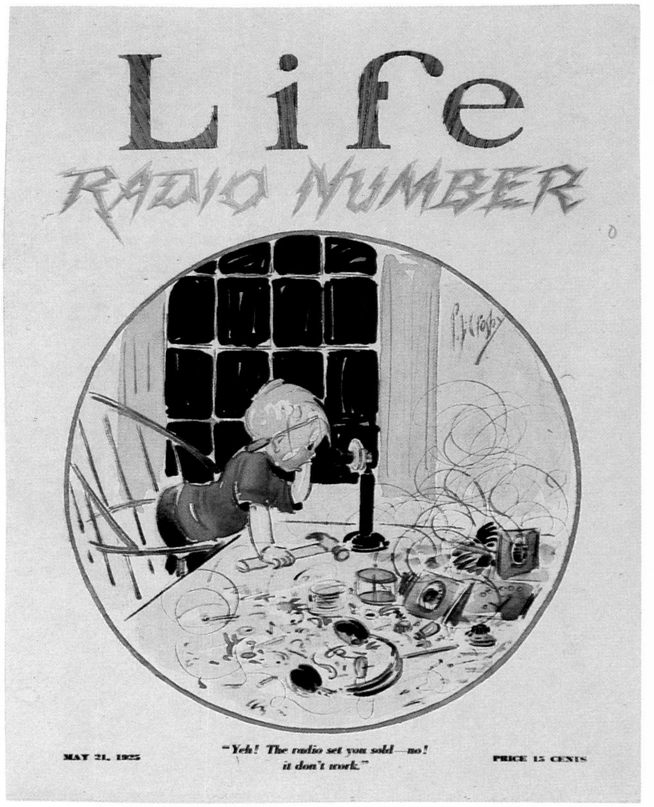
Life
RADIO NUMBER
MAY 21, 1925
"Yeh! The radio set you sold—no! it don't work."
PRICE 15 CENTS

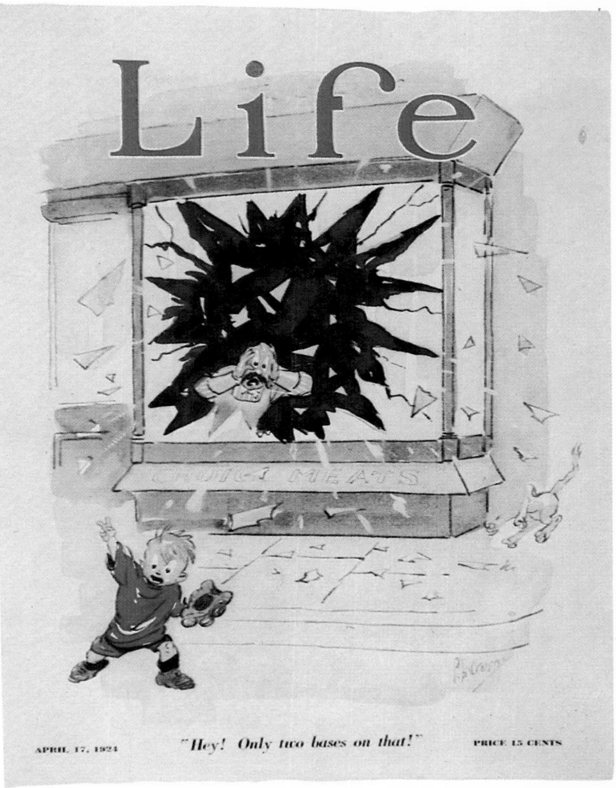
Life
APRIL 17, 1924
"Hey! Only two bases on that!"
PRICE 15 CENTS

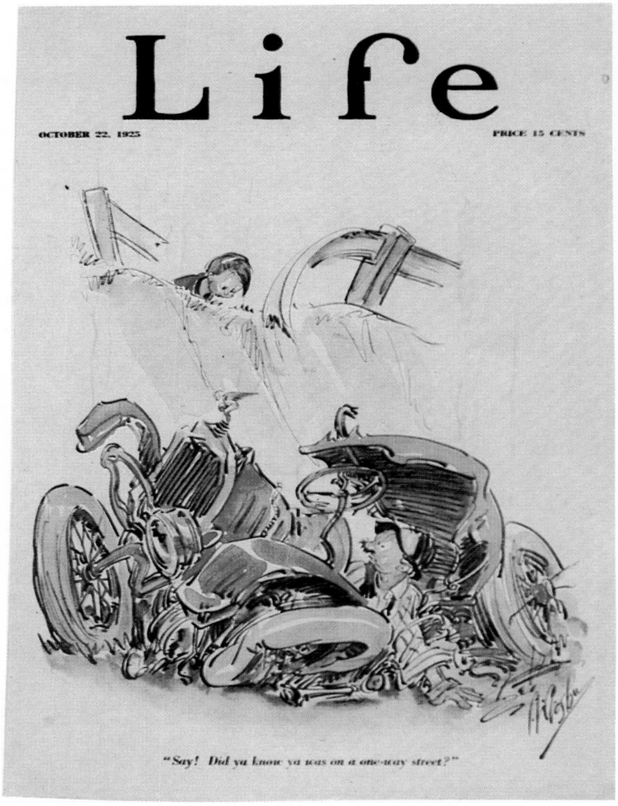
Life
OCTOBER 22, 1925
PRICE 15 CENTS
"Say! Did ya know ya was on a one-way street?"

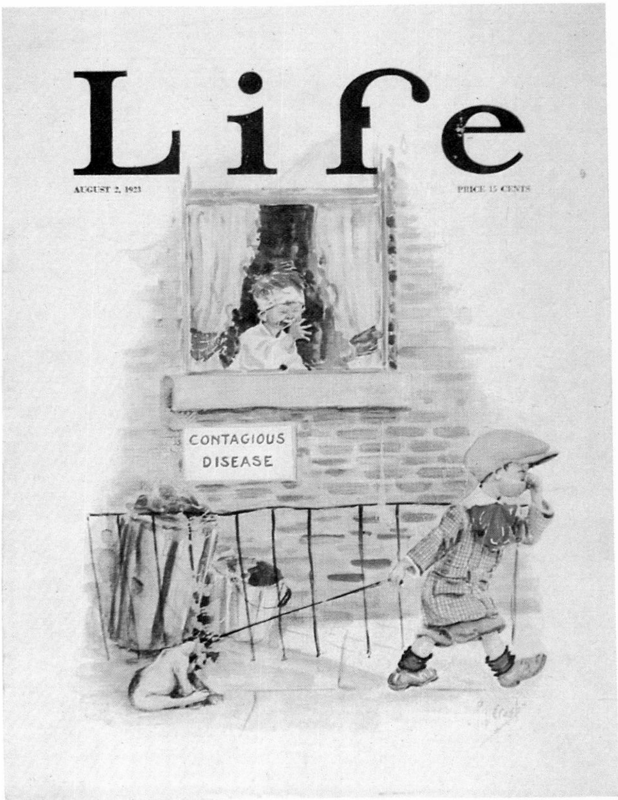
Life
AUGUST 2, 1923
PRICE 15 CENTS
CONTAGIOUS DISEASE

The Home Stretch (watercolor)

"A Curious Sort of Lightning"

As a young man, Percy Crosby sat in the fourth row of the orchestra at the Metropolitan Opera House intent on the dancing feet of Anna Pavlova. Crosby loved ballet. When only sixteen, he had first seen Pavlova perform with Nijinsky and was enthralled. This time, however, something strange happened. He seemed to see Pavlova's feet in slow motion. "I was startled. Nothing like that ever happened before," Crosby remembered. "Then my vision changed, and rapid motion resumed. If there was any time my sense of motion was awakened and transferred to the drawing, it was that night. From that time on, I began to make drawings of the dance. Even so, never did I go out for motion in art—that is, deliberately. The drawings just came."

Deliberate or not, motion became the hallmark of Crosby's work. The portrayal of one intense moment of supreme physical effort (be it with dancer, boxer, diver, or racehorse) had a purity and an elemental joy that seemed to satisfy the soul of Percy Crosby. It was the simple truth that he sought, one that

he could control, one that the world couldn't complicate, muddy, or destroy. When he sought it in life—in a woman, in politics, or even in his cartoons (subject to the pressures of editors and syndicates)—he was continually disappointed. It was the clean, swift, simply conceived drawings that sustained him. Seemingly without effort, Crosby gave that quality of life in line that all artists hope to attain. Edward Alden Jewell, art critic of *The New York Times*, called Crosby "the greatest apostle of motion in the field of art" and described his drawings: "Man or animal in violent action are as quick as a streak of lightning, a curious sort of lightning, that despite speed, always has time to be specifically formed. . . . These divers and dancers and speed-maddened horses represent more than just feats of surface virtuosity. . . . Ceasing, in large measure, to be strictly individual shapes, they become symbols of an idea. We see them as, in the truer sense of the word, abstractions."

The futurists, who held their first exhibition in Paris, might have influenced Crosby, for the concept of motion was part of

New York (lithograph)

Just Before the Bell (oil)

the futurist manifesto. They scorned the monotony of the nude; their gods were motion and speed, with which they hoped to transform and revolutionize art. Crosby, however, did not resort to the simultaneity of futurism. His figures, etched in a few eloquent lines, seemed to suggest the preceding motion as well as the action about to occur. He was a master of summing up the action of successive movements in one penetrating image, an image without that arbitrary fidelity to one specific action that often results in a frozen or mechanical portrayal.

Since the birth of the comic strip in 1895, there has been a continuous interplay with the fine arts. Crosby continued the American tradition started by the pioneer cartoonist-painters, George Luks (*The Yellow Kid*) and Lionel Feininger (*The Kin-Der-Kids* and *Wee Willie Winkie's World*). Among the noted painters and illustrators who found the comic strip a unique form of artistic expression were James Montgomery Flagg (*Nervy Nat*), John Held, Jr. (*Margy*), Russell Patterson (*Mamie*), and John Sloan. None, however, worked so

successfully in both disciplines—the comic strip and the fine arts—as did Percy Crosby.

In 1928, the Anderson Gallery in New York held Crosby's first exhibition, an ambitious show of oil paintings, watercolors, lithography, drypoint drawings, and cartoons. Included was a lithograph of Pavlova, of which one reviewer noted: "Enthusiasts of the dance would study the few swift lines that were the essence of the dancer, and talked of Pavlova as if she were there before them."

Crosby viewed sports as serious dramatic art, and they became one of his principal subjects: horse racing, polo, boxing, ice skating, football, diving, and others. He saw them as primal symbols of motion. In his series of sports lithographs, Crosby seemed to abandon the hint of bitterness and tragedy in his cartoons, and to celebrate the wholesome rite of physical strength and beauty. He freed himself in these drawings from the world of corruptible things for a purity of ideals. The honor which Crosby cherished above all others was the Silver Medal

Lone Cowboy (watercolor)

for his lithograph of a diver, *Jackknife*, awarded at the International Art Exhibition celebrating the 1932 Olympic games in Los Angeles.

In 1933, Crosby's work was exhibited at the Corcoran Gallery of Art in Washington, D.C., the Richmond Academy of Art in Richmond, Virginia, and the Macbeth Gallery in New York (the latter exhibition limited to sports subjects, to Crosby's regret). One reviewer observed: "Sketches seemingly reeled off in seconds are the result of arduous experimentation. Intense practice by the trial and error method produced figures of amazing activity." Actually, few of Crosby's subjects were drawn from life. More usually they were done entirely from memory. Many critics, noting the unique pulsating, rhythmic movement in Crosby's painting and drawing, wondered how much music had to do with his art. Certainly it was one of his lifelong passions. He would almost always work to the accompaniment of a symphony or an opera.

A major exhibition of Crosby's art—138 oils, watercolors, drawings, and prints—opened at the Jacques Seligmann & Fils Galleries on the Rue de la Paix in Paris in 1934. It formed the first one-man show by an American artist that this conservative French gallery had ever hung. When informed by his agent that it was then common for artists to pay critics to review their shows for the Paris press, Crosby was indignant. He wrote René Seligmann, director of the New York branch of the gallery: "If I had billions of dollars at my disposal, I would never pay a critic for any words of praise. . . . Critics have the right to say anything they want in regard to my work, whether it be praise or censure. . . . I stand on my own feet at all times and am not afraid of severe criticism and am not unduly moved by praise. I say this because I am absolutely aware of the quality of my work. I hope you will not deem me unduly confident, but at the same time, if the artist did not possess this quality and believe in his own work, he would not be able to produce works of art." Crosby's confidence proved justified. The French critics were unanimous in their praise. They saw

Dancers (drypoint)

his work in the context of European graphic traditions of Grosz and Toulouse-Lautrec. (*Art Digest* reported, "France is thrilled by the creator of *Skippy*.")

Equally successful shows followed in Rome and London. The National Gallery of Modern Art in Rome acquired the lithograph *At the Garden*, as well as two sepia studies. The British Museum acquired three pictures: *The Rat Hunter of Dieppe*, a character study in sepia ink wash of a ragged urchin, one of the cliffdwellers who inhabited the French coast; and two lithographs, *The Cabby*, a humorous but faithful portrait of a New York hansom cab driver in Central Park, and *Cross Shot*, a polo scene at Meadowbrook, Long Island. The English critics affirmed that Crosby had, indeed, made the transition. "Crosby is not only a comic strip artist, and in the extensive range of his almost whirlwind art, shows a somewhat bewildering versatility. . . .

"We find that this American is not only a mirth-maker, but a brilliant draftsman, delighting in conveying with a shorthand technique wonderful effects of speed, force, and spirit."

The Crosby show, returning from Europe in 1936, opened at the Jacques Seligmann Gallery in New York and later that year at the Robert C. Vose Gallery in Boston. It now included a series of watercolors and lithographs, *Impressions of the West*, completed during a recent trip to California. *Art Digest* praised the new work: "In the character drawings and sports subjects, there is a great deal of gusto and that peculiar, indefinable Crosby touch, but his landscapes reveal him as a nature lover, deeply meditative before a far range of mountains or a great expanse of blue sea."

At times, however, Crosby seemed not quite ready to accept his transition from cartoonist to serious artist. He experienced moods of despair and self-doubt, nurtured by such critiques as that in *Art News*: "He leaves the humble routine of cartooning for a number of pictorial flights more ambitious than successful. Possessed of an exuberant talent and elastic fancy, Mr. Crosby has sketched and drawn and painted a vast series of incidents

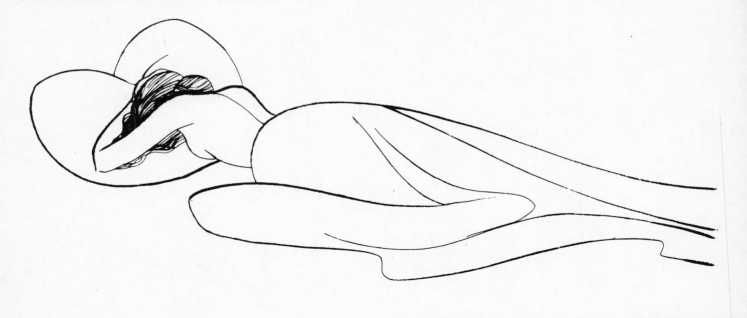

Reclining figure (drypoint)

that have to do with sports and rhythmic dancing and the
thousand and one activities that would engage the roving eye of
an illustrator bent on extending his borders. But it is only too
true that it is his 'Skippy' self that in the end wins the day."

But when the Louvre acquired several works from the
Seligmann exhibition, Crosby felt he had won his battle for
acceptance as a fine artist. One of the acquisitions was a
watercolor study in purple, rose, and green of a cowboy riding
a pony across a Western plain, the horse and rider silhouetted
against the sunset sky. Titled *Lone Cowboy*, it was appropriately symbolic of Percy Crosby, the Lone Knight. This time,
victorious.

Gull (lithograph)

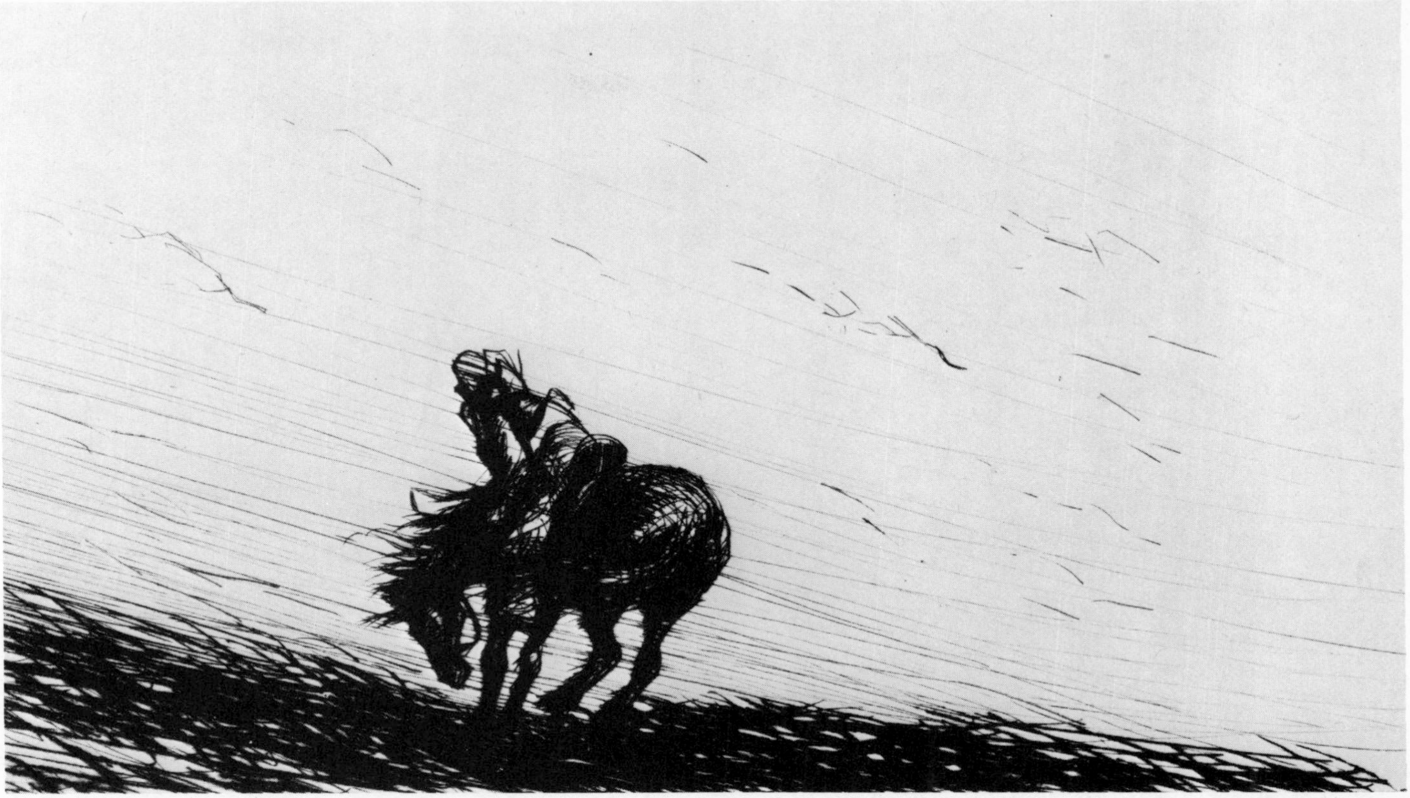

Cowboy leaning into wind (ink drawing)

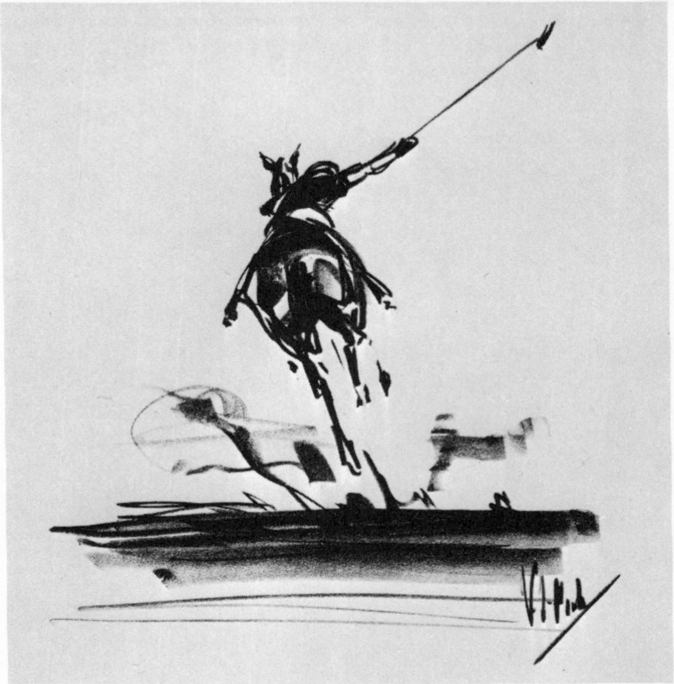

Clear Field Ahead (lithograph)

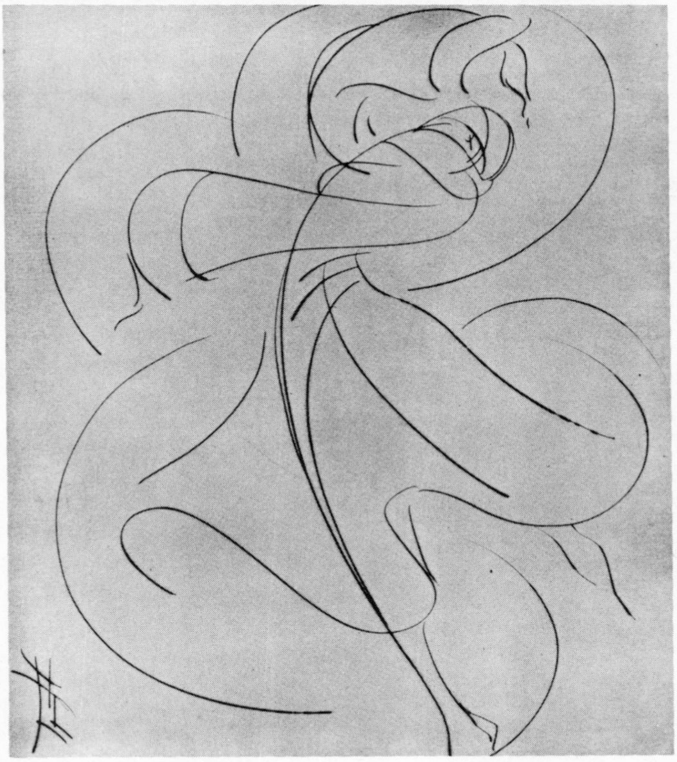

Figure Skater (drypoint)

Oui Madame (wash)

Standing figure (drypoint)

Jackknife (ink drawing)

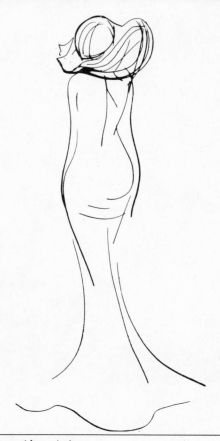

Flamenco dancer (lithograph)

6 / THE MAD PATRIOT

It is hard to determine exactly where Crosby's implacable opposition to communism began, but, even after it became the essential focus of his politics and he had been generally accepted as a right-winger, his viewpoint remained undoctrinaire. Today he might be regarded as a strict libertarian. His passionate concerns were for freedom of the press and the rights of the individual, against censorship of any kind and tyranny whether from the Right or the Left. As vigorous in his opposition to Naziism and its virulent anti-Semitism as he was to communism, Crosby saw bigotry in any guise as "the cancer of the soul."

Crosby's first political cartoons since his days on the *Call* appeared in the *Brooklyn Eagle* and in *Life* magazine in the early 1920s. One, drawn for the *Eagle*, was an attack upon the Ku Klux Klan and was met with opposition from local Klan sympathizers. Characteristically, this only succeeded in stirring Crosby to combat. Considering the KKK "the most glaring example of mob brutality and sadism, screening itself behind the safe portals of religion," he sketched another cartoon titled "Like the Moth, It Works in the Dark"; it showed a beady-eyed moth with a glaring white body, labeled KKK, steadily working its destructive way across the American flag. The editor of *Life* insisted that it be offered to Gibson to do the finished drawing. Crosby was reluctant, but it would have been ungracious not to defer to his mentor, Gibson. The cartoon appeared in a double-page spread (but unsigned by Gibson) and was widely praised as one of the most powerful cartoon attacks on the Klan. Crosby felt "like a mother who had renounced all rights to her child." By then he was completely politicized, and it wasn't long before he refused to do any humorous cartoons for *Life* unless they also printed his political articles and cartoons. *Life*, now under new management, refused. Jack Shuttleworth, art editor of the rival *Judge*, seized the opportunity and purchased fifty of Crosby's cartoons for his magazine. And, as part of the deal, he agreed to publish a two-column article by Crosby each week, subject to editing only for libel.

On the nine books and pamphlets Crosby was to publish from 1932, only two—*Sports Drawings* (1933), a handsome collection of his watercolors, lithographs, and drypoints, and *Rays* (1937), a small book of poetry—were not concerned with politics and philosophy. When *Life* magazine refused to publish an anti-Prohibition article, Crosby felt compelled to resort to a new tactic to get his ideas to the public. He ran the complete article as a paid advertisement at regular page rates in the *Washington Herald*. Then Columbia Broadcasting System canceled a scheduled radio speech, also on Prohibition, as being too controversial. When they tried to persuade Crosby to discuss Skippy's philosophy instead, he refused and published his entire planned speech in the *New York Sun* at a cost of $3,200. Again and again, Crosby's articles and cartoons would appear as paid ads, often double spreads, in the *Washington Herald*, the *Washington Post*, *The New York Times*, and the *New York Sun*. In addition to Prohibition and the Anti-Saloon League, the subjects that engaged his crusading opposition were pacifism, the chairman of the Armed Forces Appropriations Committee, gangsterism, naval disarmament, atheism, bootleggers, and communists. In one two-year period alone, Crosby spent over thirty thousand dollars for such editorials. The *New Republic* called him "The Mad Patriot."

Although Crosby initially supported Franklin D. Roosevelt during his first campaign in 1932, the President soon became the object of some of Crosby's most bitter attacks, mainly on the issue of Prohibition. His hatred of Roosevelt grew out of fear that FDR was usurping undue power, and he expressed it in the most vitriolic language. He characterized the President as "crazed by power" and claimed the original mold for the New Deal was made in Moscow. FDR's fireside chats were described as "talking from the Moscow Room of the Spite House." A Crosby-paid editorial in the *New York Sun*, "Machine Gunning for Peace," amazed even some of Roosevelt's severest critics. As Drew Pearson and Robert S. Allen reported in their column, "The Washington Merry-Go-Round": "Full of the most scathing indictments, the advertisement was written and paid for by Percy Crosby, author of the comic strip *Skippy*. Twice Crosby urged his readers: 'Never wound a snake, but kill it.' Although the Secret Service has investigated him, there's not much it can do about indirect threats of this kind." A careful reading of the article shows that Crosby was referring to a potential aggressor as the snake to be killed, but, as the article was a general attack on Roosevelt's leadership, it was interpreted as a threat to the President. (Ironically, an editorial in the communist *Daily Worker* attacked the "Crosby Manifesto" as "an incitement to the assassination

"A Man Who Gets Mad"

From the time of his first newspaper job on the *New York Call* as an editorial cartoonist, Crosby was obsessed with politics. He drew political cartoons throughout his career—for various newspapers and books, for *Life* magazine, and even, in his last years, while confined in the mental ward of Kings Park Veterans' Hospital. Whenever he felt passionately about an issue, which was often, he drew a slashing cartoon and, if rejected, published it at his own expense. Beginning as early as 1928, he couldn't resist occasionally injecting his political views into *Skippy*—often to the detriment of the strip.

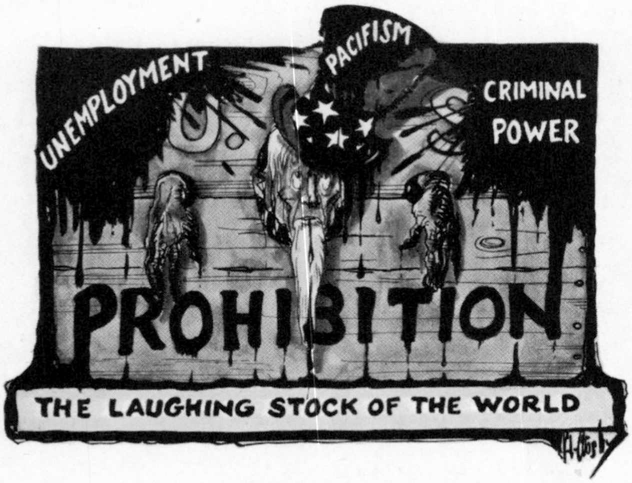
UNEMPLOYMENT
PACIFISM
CRIMINAL POWER
PROHIBITION
THE LAUGHING STOCK OF THE WORLD

IT LIVES BY WHAT THE *SUCKERS* BRING IN.

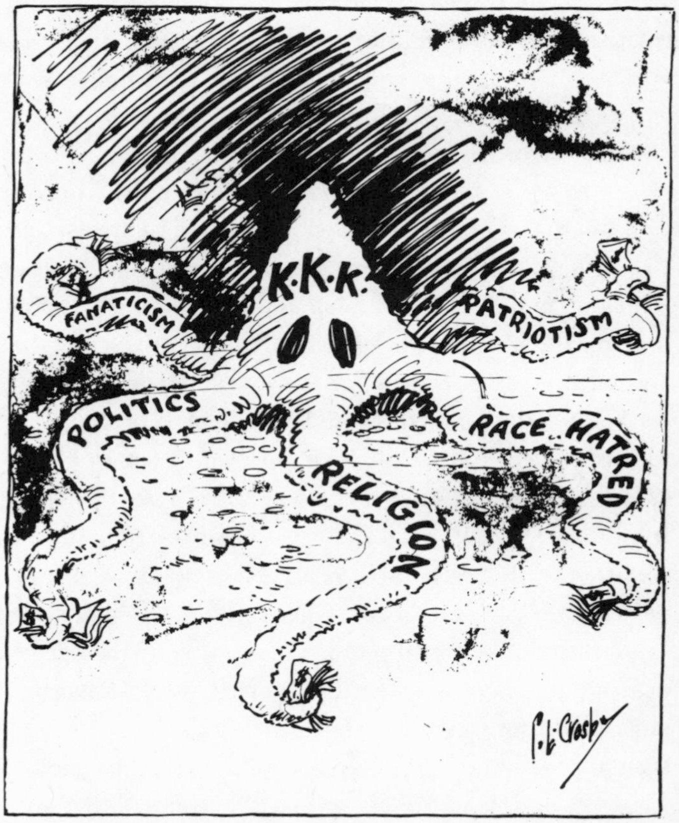
K.K.K.
FANATICISM
PATRIOTISM
POLITICS
RACE HATRED
RELIGION

of the President of the United States. It is a call to terrorism and murder. It is an approval for treason and civil war. . . . This is *Skippy* with a swastika.")

If FDR was Crosby's target at the top of American society, his target at the bottom was Al Capone. In an ad published simultaneously in the *New York World* and the *Washington Times*, Crosby attacked the Chicago racketeer: "You cannot salute your flag with a clear conscience until Al Capone is knocked off the throne erected by the Anti-Saloon League. I . . . refuse to pay homage to this Chicago monarch. He has neither enough money nor enough lead to make me change my mind. By this plurality of one vote, I make myself the leader opposing the existing gunman autocracy in the United States." *Time* magazine reported on the ad in an article, "Crosby Versus Capone," quoting Crosby as saying that if invited he would go to Chicago to meet Al Capone in his own territory, without gun permit or bodyguard. The crusading cartoonist was soon invited to give his views at a banquet of the Universal Fellowship Foundation in Chicago. Crosby explained in his speech that he was merely carrying on the campaign he had waged in his strip for three months. In the *Skippy* sequence, a flashily dressed gangster called Spumone headed a gang known as the "Jacketeers." The *Chicago Post* ran a story on Crosby's appearance under the headline "Lone Crusader for Dry Reform Visits Chicago, Wars on Gangs." (Again, Crosby was cast in the role of the Knight.) What particularly irritated Crosby was the fact that Capone had once compared himself to the barons of the Middle Ages who demanded payment for protecting the goods and lives of their vassals. The temerity of the gangster to invoke *his*

ARMY AND NAVY ECONOMY CUT

WHAT'S ALL THIS PAN AMERICAN STUFF I SEE IN THE PAPERS?
THE PAN AMERICA STUFF STARTED OFF'N VESEY STREET, BY YOUR BELITTLIN', AN NOW IT'S TAKIN' AVIATORS AN' WARSHIPS TO PRESS OUT THE WRINKLES.
CONGRESS CAN'T BLUFF ME.
THE MAP O' THE UNITED STATES IS LIKE AN OPEN HAND, READY TO SHAKE WITH SOUTH AMERICA; BUT IT'S GUYS JUST LIKE YOU THAT'S TRYIN' TO MAKE A FIST OUT OF IT.
Copyright, 1928, Percy L. Crosby, Central Press Assn., Inc.

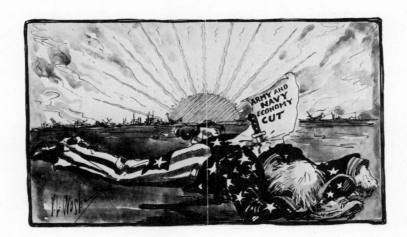

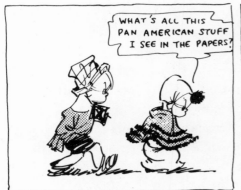

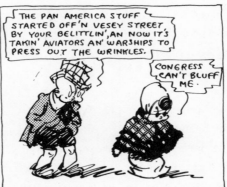

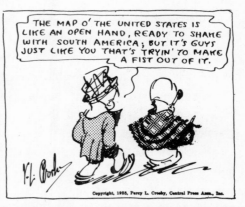

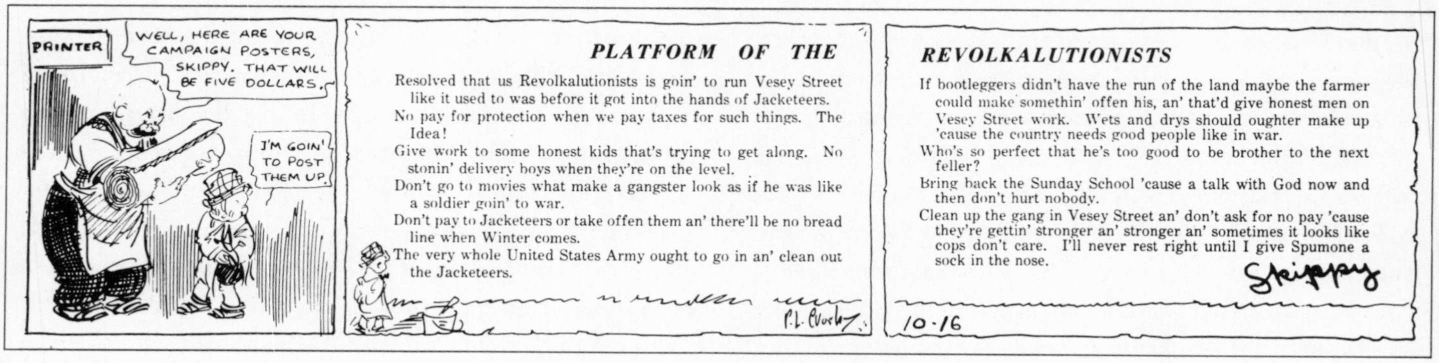

Comic panel text:

PRINTER

WELL, HERE ARE YOUR CAMPAIGN POSTERS, SKIPPY. THAT WILL BE FIVE DOLLARS.

I'M GOIN' TO POST THEM UP.

PLATFORM OF THE

Resolved that us Revolkalutionists is goin' to run Vesey Street like it used to was before it got into the hands of Jacketeers.

No pay for protection when we pay taxes for such things. The Idea!

Give work to some honest kids that's trying to get along. No stonin' delivery boys when they're on the level.

Don't go to movies what make a gangster look as if he was like a soldier goin' to war.

Don't pay to Jacketeers or take offen them an' there'll be no bread line when Winter comes.

The very whole United States Army ought to go in an' clean out the Jacketeers.

P.L. Crosby

REVOLKALUTIONISTS

If bootleggers didn't have the run of the land maybe the farmer could make somethin' offen his, an' that'd give honest men on Vesey Street work. Wets and drys should oughter make up 'cause the country needs good people like in war.

Who's so perfect that he's too good to be brother to the next feller?

Bring back the Sunday School 'cause a talk with God now and then don't hurt nobody.

Clean up the gang in Vesey Street an' don't ask for no pay 'cause they're gettin' stronger an' stronger an' sometimes it looks like cops don't care. I'll never rest right until I give Spumone a sock in the nose.

Skippy

10-16

---

era! "When Capone refers to the Middles Ages, he perhaps forgets that in those days, there were Knights who rode alone, and under the shield of 'Honor and Truth,' opposed to barbaric customs and needless bloodshed. Their code was Chivalry, which was born of decency. When Capone says, 'Like them, I sell protection, security, and peace,' he has one man right here in Chicago to whom he *cannot* sell protection nor security, at any price."

In time Crosby was to express the fear that Capone was after him and might kidnap his children. The specter may have been prompted by the hysteria sweeping the country in the wake of the Lindbergh kidnapping, but whatever its basis it was interpreted then and in Crosby's later years as sheer paranoia, as were other claims of persecution. Most of these involved the federal government. From 1932 on, Crosby maintained that he was followed on trips to and from Washington, that his phones were being tapped and his mail intercepted. The Pearson-Allen column is one of the few actual corroborations of such hounding, though in 1933 the Internal Revenue Service did bring a deficiency claim against Crosby and his corporation, Skippy, Inc., for over forty-three thousand dollars. Crosby concluded that the action was related to his political views, and he even had the temerity to publicly question Roosevelt's own taxes and challenge the President to make them public. Then, in 1937, the IRS included Crosby in a list of "tax dodgers" and claimed he owed a sum in excess of sixty thousand dollars. Crosby was quoted in *Newsweek*; "I believe I made myself very clear on the issue. . . . I am a citizen who is willing to pay any amount of taxes under the Constitutional form of government, and that willingly, but it is from a citizen who shall never pay toll to a one-man government at any price." Crosby's battle with the IRS continued for years and, like many other of his quixotic struggles, was doomed to failure.

Although *Skippy* was syndicated by Hearst's King Features Syndicate, Crosby owned the copyright and never considered himself a syndicate employee. His position certainly didn't deter him from attacking William Randolph Hearst or his chief editorial writer, Arthur Brisbane, both of whom he accused of being communist dupes because of their favorable editorials and articles on the USSR and their early support of Roosevelt. Hearst, one of the pioneer developers of the comic strip, greatly admired Crosby's talent as a cartoonist and, despite the continued attacks, was not about to sever their relationship—and lose Crosby to a rival syndicate.

Crosby's political polemics were receiving national attention on radio and in the press. General Douglas MacArthur, then Army Chief of Staff, wrote thanking Crosby for a series of cartoons which he called one of the most important single factors in the fight against proposed cuts in army appropriations. While time has proved many of Crosby's positions wrong, it has also shown some to be prophetic. In *Patriotism*, written ten years before Pearl Harbor, Crosby wrote: "Japan will suddenly discover that she had no war with China, and realizing the opportunity of a lifetime, will make a swift call on America. . . . The next war will give America no time for preparation. It may be over before America ever gets started, due to her state of obvious unpreparedness."

One Memorial Day, *Skippy* attempted to awaken the patriotism of the nation with a four-hundred-word monologue on disarmament and pacifism. Crosby remarked with some understatement that he detected a slight restlessness on the part of the syndicate in regard to the cartoon's propriety. (Hearst, however, attached his seal of approval in a telegram to Crosby: "PLEASE THANK SKIPPY FOR HIS GRAND PRAYER, THERE ARE STILL A LOT OF GOOD AMERICANS WHO ARE PRAYING WITH HIM.") The editor of the *Des Moines Register and Tribune* registered a vigorous protest to the syndicate, stating in part: "My understanding is that we pay for a *Skippy* strip and that Percy Crosby is to entertain our readers with what he puts into that strip. . . . We shall be grateful if you will persuade Mr. Crosby . . . that we want comic strips that amuse, that do not preach." Crosby's reply was typical: "One wonders if the readers of the *Des Moines Register* are allowed to stay up after 9 o'clock. The author has always found that the American people are perfectly capable of accepting or rejecting an idea without having any editorial assistance, and takes this opportunity to inform him that Percy Crosby takes orders from no editor as to what he shall or shall not write or draw." Crosby then proceeded to have the paper crossed off the list of *Skippy* subscribers.

Until that time, the introduction of politics had been taboo in newspaper comic strips. While there was a detectable coloration in *Little Orphan Annie* reflecting the ultraconservative philosophy of its creator, Harold Gray, Crosby was the first to break the unwritten law against injecting specific political issues into a strip. He began an evolution that flowered in the political and social allegories of Al Capp's *Li'l Abner* and Walt Kelly's *Pogo* and was completed only recently when Garry Trudeau's comic strip, *Doonesbury*, was awarded the Pulitzer Prize for editorial cartoons. In *Skippy*'s time, however, Crosby's use of politics was generally cited as further evidence of his eccentricity.

"Percy Crosby, brilliant and subtle, is a man who gets mad. Not angry, mad. At fakery and fraud—and gangdom and prohibition," wrote one critic. Gradually, however, Crosby seemed to be at war with himself as much as with those he attacked. In 1936, Crosby deliberately broke the vow of abstinence he had made on his honeymoon seven years before. "How could I attack fear and proclaim freedom for humanity if my gesture of abstinence from alcohol imprisoned my soul?" he rationalized. From then on, his drinking undoubtedly contributed to episodes of bizarre behavior, hardly as amusing as his earlier peccadilloes. Visitors reported Crosby and his foreman shooting at "intruders" on the estate in the middle of the night. On another occasion, a guest at Ridgelawn reported that Crosby had installed a machine gun at the top of the staircase, threatening to give any intruder "a bellyful of lead." (Dale denies the incident and recalls no such weapon ever in the house. But, even if apocryphal, the story became part of the Crosby legend.)

Dale recalls that living with Percy at the time was "like driving on top of a volcano—you never knew when it would erupt. He was about ten men rolled into one—each a different personality." The marriage was disintegrating. After one particularly violent scene in February 1939, Percy drove off to Florida. He returned two weeks later full of remorse and contrition, bearing gifts for Dale and the children, but his family was not there to receive them. Dale had left home a short time before and filed suit for divorce. The press reported that the decree charged "acts of cruelty, including an alleged assault that sent Mrs. Crosby to the hospital with a broken nose. . . . A temporary injunction restrained the cartoonist from assaulting or injuring his wife and from interfering or communicating with his wife or children." He never again saw Dale or his children: Skippy, then nine, Barbara Dale, seven, Joan Carolyn, six, and Carol, five.

The divorce was devastating to Crosby. "The philosopher searches for the secret of existence and loses his own in the search," Crosby wrote. He began a painful search for a new existence. He moved back to Manhattan and soon went on a spending spree, which he could ill afford. In a further attempt to raise his spirits, he took a trip to Hawaii, but becoming more and more depressed he abruptly returned to New York. He entered Presbyterian Hospital to be treated for exhaustion and a troubling infection on his arm. With deadlines again closing in, he was forced to set up a studio in the hospital room. As Crosby recalled: "I still had to turn out a Sunday page as well as six *Skippy* strips. . . . How could I ever make the public laugh when my heart was breaking?"

Just one thing could shake Crosby from his depression—romance. One day, Carolyn Soper, the chief dietitian, entered his hospital room. Crosby later recorded the dialogue: "'The nurses told me you are famous, Mr. Crosby, and I laughed.' 'You laughed? Why?' 'My mother loves *Skippy* so much in the *Boston Herald* that she named our dog Skippy.'" Carolyn and Percy never forgot their first date at the New York World's Fair after Percy's recovery. They dined at the Hungarian Restaurant. It was a romantic evening, violinists hovered over them; they were in love and soon had lost all track of time. The fair closed for the night and the gates had to be opened for them to leave. Crosby, forty-eight, married Miss Soper, thirty-three, of Littleton, New Hampshire, in May 1940, and they honeymooned in Venice, Florida.*

*Crosby had obtained his own divorce from Dale in Florida, claiming mental cruelty and desertion. However, as the Virginia divorce was not final, he was guilty of bigamy in that state.

It was a brief happy interlude. Crosby's financial condition was now critical. To satisfy his tax claims, the divorce settlement, legal fees, and alimony, he was forced to sell his beloved estate, Ridgelawn, for a fraction of its value. The 1,500-acre farm and other Virginia properties were awarded to Dale. Even the equity in most of his insurance policies was assigned to the government. To make matters worse, his income from *Skippy* had been dropping steadily. The stress and tension brought on cycles of severe illness. Friends and associates found him increasingly difficult, and King Features Syndicate had to send emissaries to discuss his barrage of complaints, mostly about what he claimed was dismal reproduction of the strip.

The occasional diatribes in the *Skippy* strip became more frequent, more surreal. Some days were almost solid dialogue. In the past, Crosby had been able to move from one discipline to another—painting, writing, cartooning, and politics. Now, under extreme mental stress, the

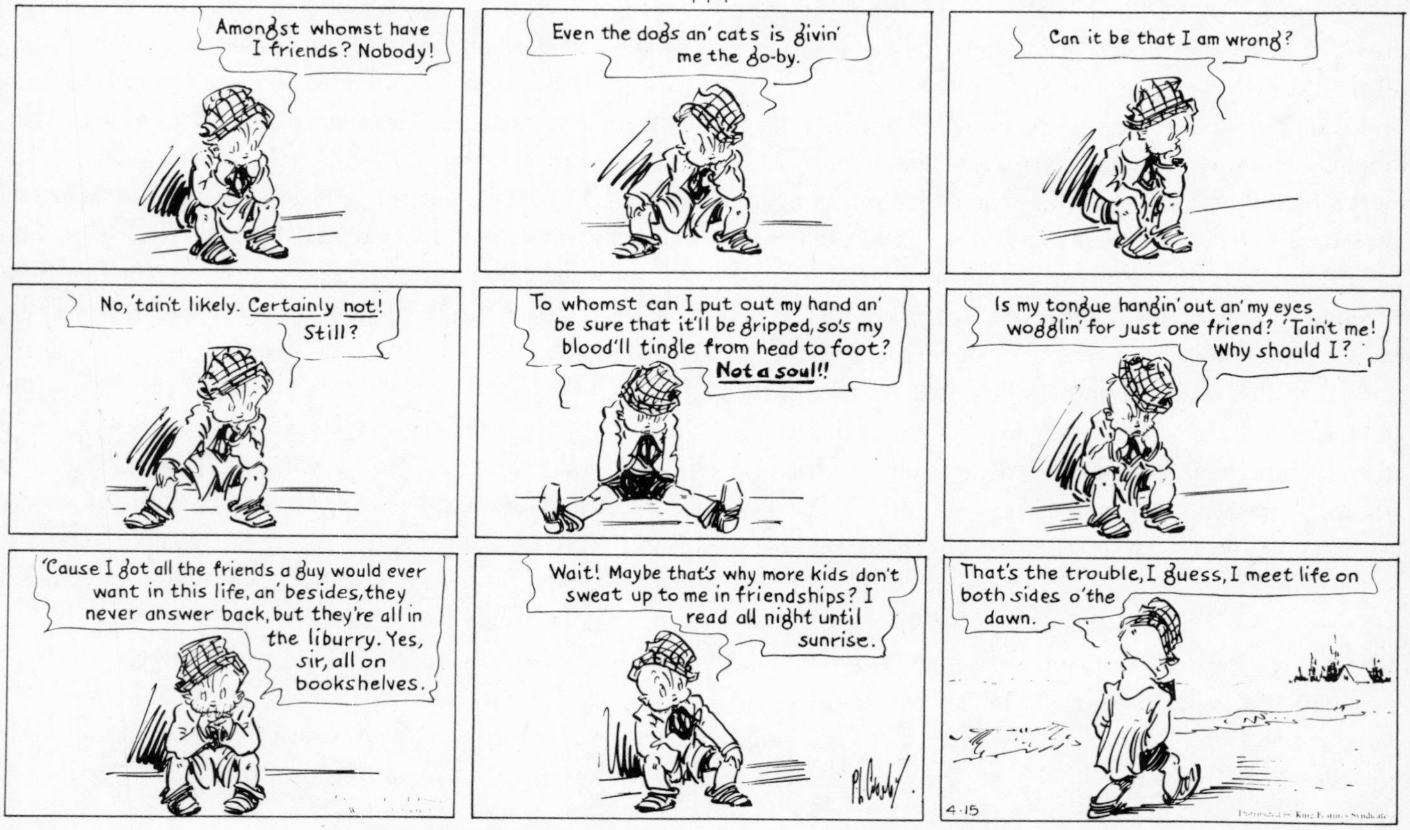
Amongst whomst have I friends? Nobody!
Even the dogs an' cats is givin' me the go-by.
Can it be that I am wrong?
No, 'tain't likely. Certainly not!
Still?
To whomst can I put out my hand an' be sure that it'll be gripped, so's my blood'll tingle from head to foot?
Not a soul!!
Is my tongue hangin' out an' my eyes wogglin' for just one friend? 'Tain't me! Why should I?
'Cause I got all the friends a guy would ever want in this life, an' besides, they never answer back, but they're all in the liburry. Yes, sir, all on bookshelves.
Wait! Maybe that's why more kids don't sweat up to me in friendships? I read all night until sunrise.
That's the trouble, I guess, I meet life on both sides o' the dawn.
4-15

A Sunday *Skippy* cartoon (down to one-third of a page) from the strip's last year

boundaries became blurred, and one intruded into the other to the detriment of all. Irked by the fact that *Skippy* had been "mutilated" on Sunday to a third of a page (because of the newsprint shortage), Crosby sent a 337-word night letter to the editor of every paper on the *Skippy* list, serving notice that unless King Features met his terms for a return to the half page *Skippy* would play hookey from their pages. Crosby soon withdrew the threat, explaining that he might have been overemphatic because the crisis came while he was studying military history and was right in the middle of the battle of Waterloo. Crosby's reading of Waterloo proved appropriate. Less than six months later, after long negotiations, Crosby and King Features were unable to agree on a new contract. On December 8, 1945, Crosby's fifty-fourth birthday, *Skippy*, age twenty, died.

The next years were desperate ones for Crosby. His resources were dwindling and nothing was coming in. He tried to get work everywhere. Carolyn was forced to resume work as a nurse. Then Crosby's mother suddenly died. To contain his grief, he plunged into painting oils and watercolors, sometimes for weeks on end. Other times, he would write furiously on politics, or dash off outlines of future novels. He was like a bloodied, besieged knight, flailing out in all directions. His desperate efforts to preserve his dignity are reminiscent of a character he observed at the gambling casino in Dieppe and described in *A Cartoonist's Philosophy*: "He was approaching the casino and the sunlight shot through a curved crack in the rim of his derby, leaving a streak of light in the shadow of his forehead. It was the cruelest gash of sunlight I had ever seen, for it appeared to be laughing at the man being slowly crushed under respectability's last stand."

Efforts to revive *Skippy* failed. The accumulation of emotional and financial catastrophes led to even heavier drinking. It was a pernicious cycle that produced waves of shame and guilt, and a loss of self-respect leading to ever deeper depression. His creativity deteriorated along with his self-image. He couldn't cope with the mounting despair. His sister Gladys was listening to the radio when she first heard the news. Millions of others read the Associated Press wire story: PERCY CROSBY IN HOSPITAL WITH SLASHED WRISTS—New York, December 18—Percy L. Crosby, 57, Creator of the comic strip, *Skippy*, has been admitted to Bellevue Hospital's Psychiatric Ward, authorities there said today. Mr. Crosby, who began his career as author of World War I battle cartoons . . . was admitted yesterday the hospital said . . . with lacerations of both wrists and chest injuries." A short time later, over the Christmas holiday, always Crosby's most vulnerable time of depression and melancholia, he was transferred to the mental ward of Kings Park Veterans' Hospital on Long Island. The self-destructive demons that had been pursuing Crosby for so long finally struck him down. At Kings Park, Crosby began the strangest and, in many ways, the most creative years of his career—a psychic odyssey from which he never returned.

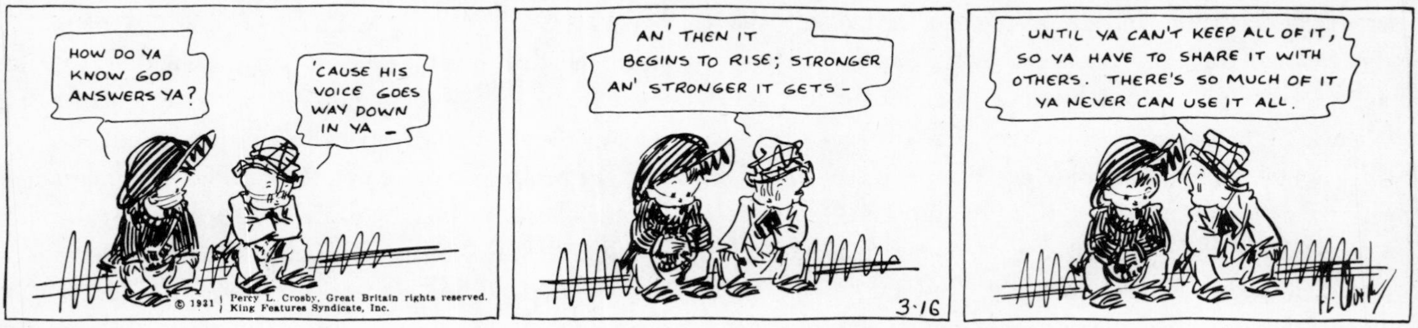
HOW DO YA KNOW GOD ANSWERS YA?
'CAUSE HIS VOICE GOES WAY DOWN IN YA –
© 1931 | Percy L. Crosby, Great Britain rights reserved. | King Features Syndicate, Inc.
AN' THEN IT BEGINS TO RISE; STRONGER AN' STRONGER IT GETS –
3-16
UNTIL YA CAN'T KEEP ALL OF IT, SO YA HAVE TO SHARE IT WITH OTHERS. THERE'S SO MUCH OF IT YA NEVER CAN USE IT ALL.

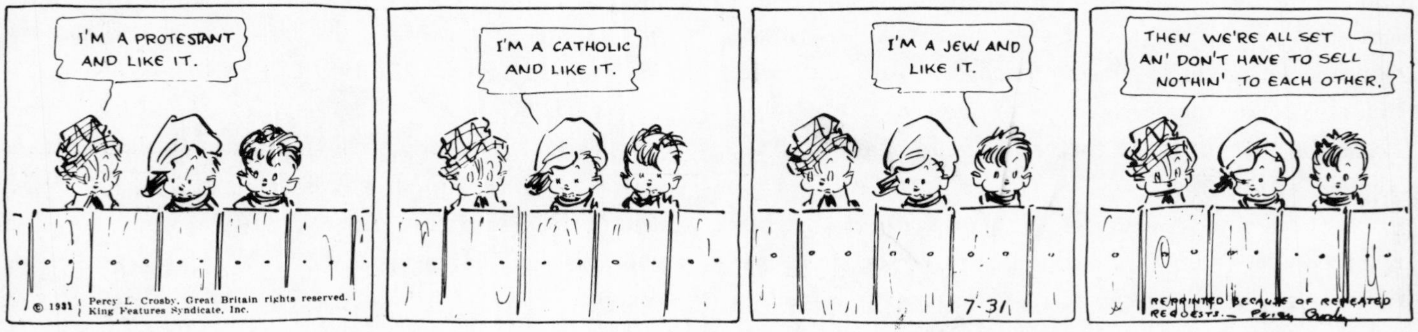
I'M A PROTESTANT AND LIKE IT.
© 1931 | Percy L. Crosby, Great Britain rights reserved. | King Features Syndicate, Inc.
I'M A CATHOLIC AND LIKE IT.
I'M A JEW AND LIKE IT.
7-31
THEN WE'RE ALL SET AN' DON'T HAVE TO SELL NOTHIN' TO EACH OTHER.
REPRINTED BECAUSE OF REPEATED REQUESTS. – Percy Crosby

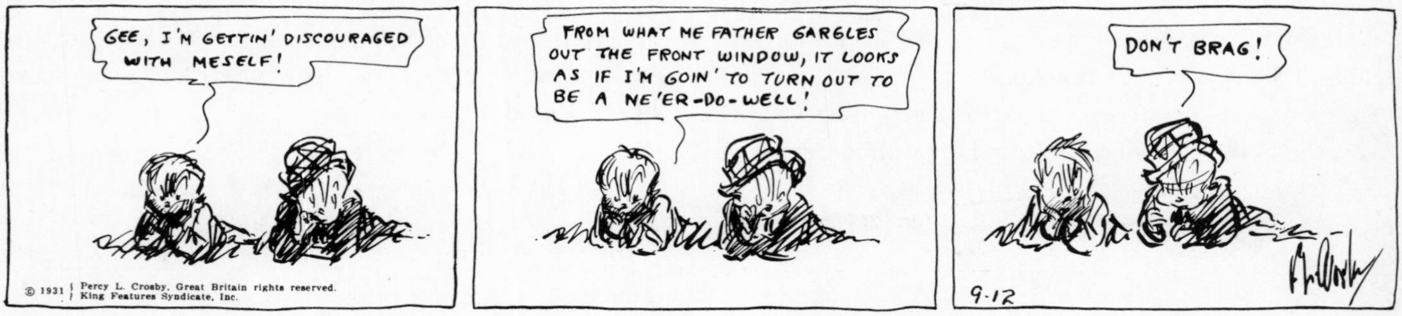
GEE, I'M GETTIN' DISCOURAGED WITH MESELF!
© 1931 | Percy L. Crosby, Great Britain rights reserved. | King Features Syndicate, Inc.
FROM WHAT ME FATHER GARGLES OUT THE FRONT WINDOW, IT LOOKS AS IF I'M GOIN' TO TURN OUT TO BE A NE'ER-DO-WELL!
DON'T BRAG!
9-12

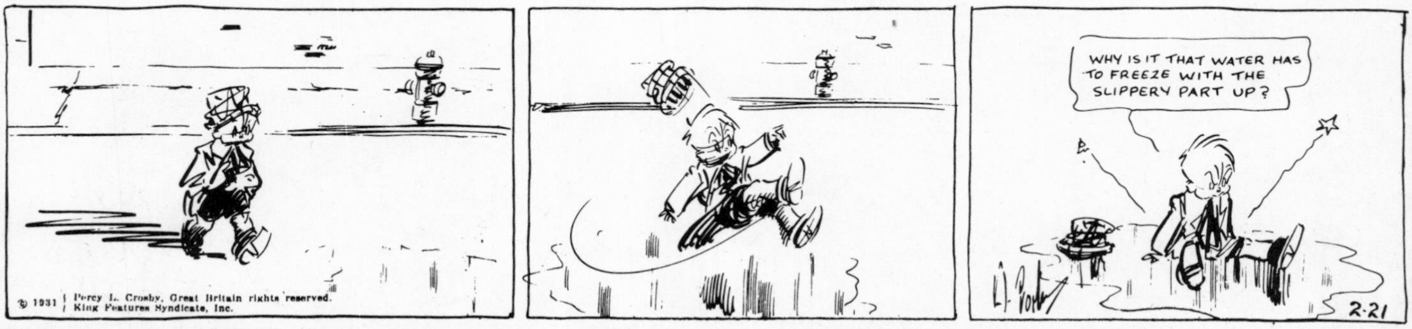
© 1931 | Percy L. Crosby, Great Britain rights reserved. | King Features Syndicate, Inc.
WHY IS IT THAT WATER HAS TO FREEZE WITH THE SLIPPERY PART UP?
2-21

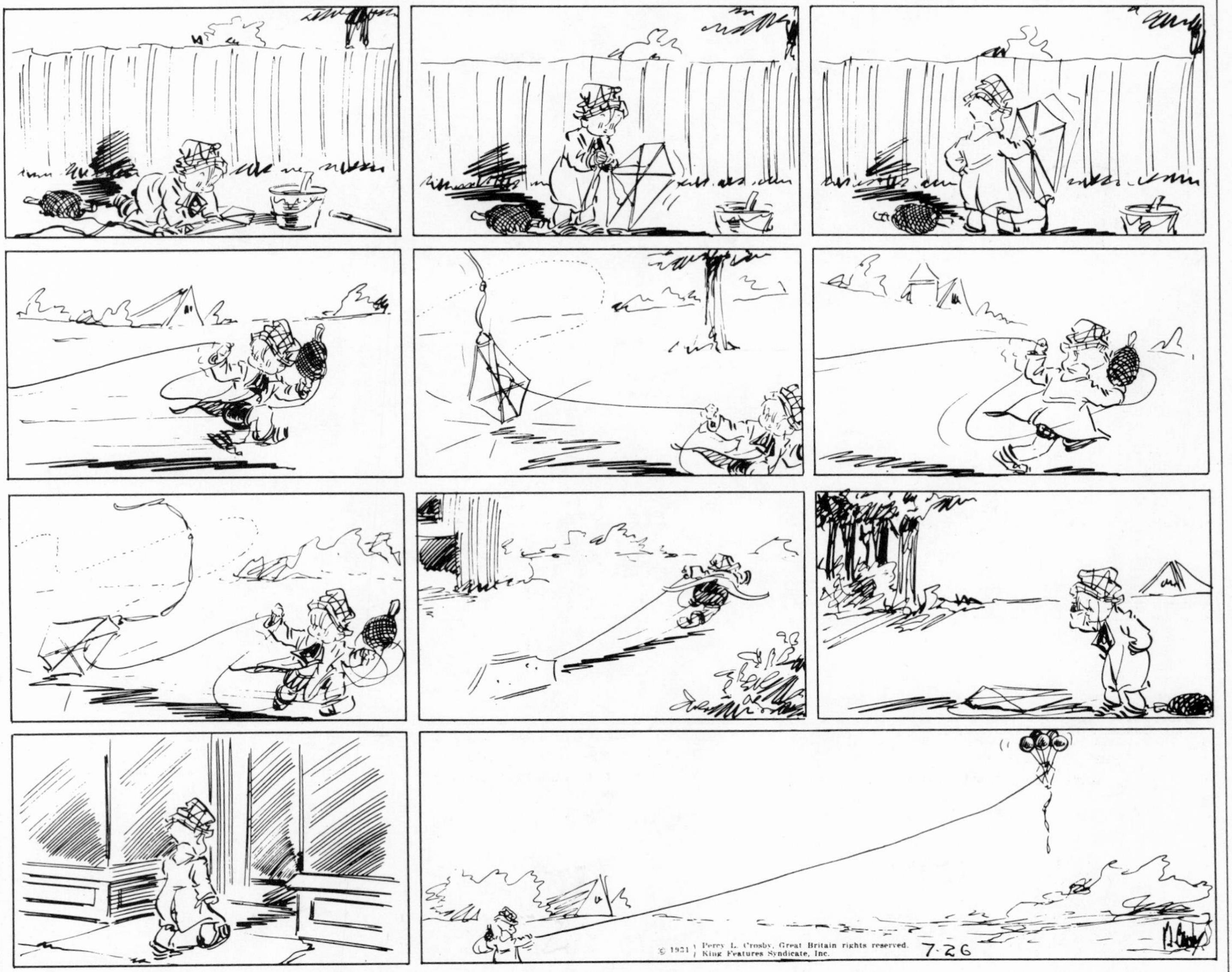
© 1931 Percy L. Crosby, Great Britain rights reserved.
King Features Syndicate, Inc.
7-26

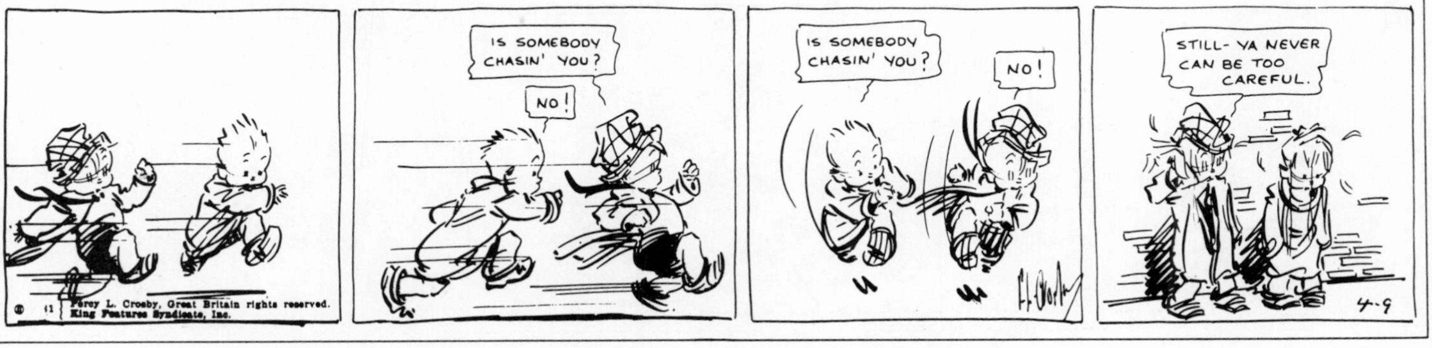
© 41 Percy L. Crosby, Great Britain rights reserved.
King Features Syndicate, Inc.
IS SOMEBODY CHASIN' YOU?
NO!
IS SOMEBODY CHASIN' YOU?
NO!
STILL- YA NEVER CAN BE TOO CAREFUL.
4-9

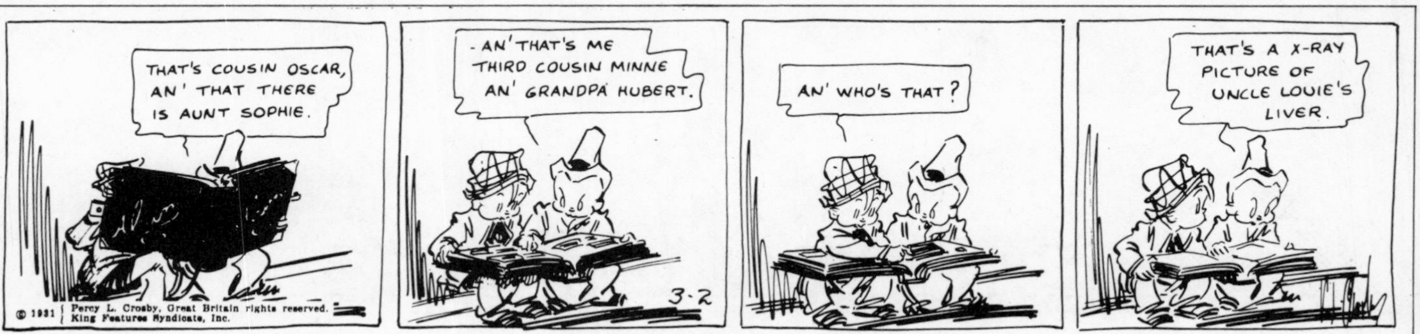
THAT'S COUSIN OSCAR, AN' THAT THERE IS AUNT SOPHIE.
- AN' THAT'S ME THIRD COUSIN MINNE AN' GRANDPA HUBERT.
AN' WHO'S THAT?
THAT'S A X-RAY PICTURE OF UNCLE LOUIE'S LIVER.
© 1931 Percy L. Crosby, Great Britain rights reserved. King Features Syndicate, Inc.
3-2

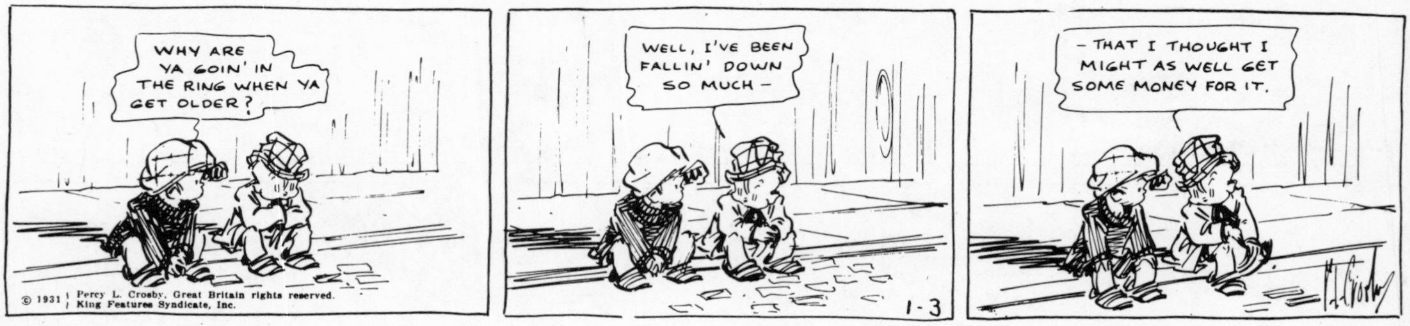
WHY ARE YA GOIN' IN THE RING WHEN YA GET OLDER?
WELL, I'VE BEEN FALLIN' DOWN SO MUCH -
- THAT I THOUGHT I MIGHT AS WELL GET SOME MONEY FOR IT.
© 1931 Percy L. Crosby, Great Britain rights reserved. King Features Syndicate, Inc.
1-3

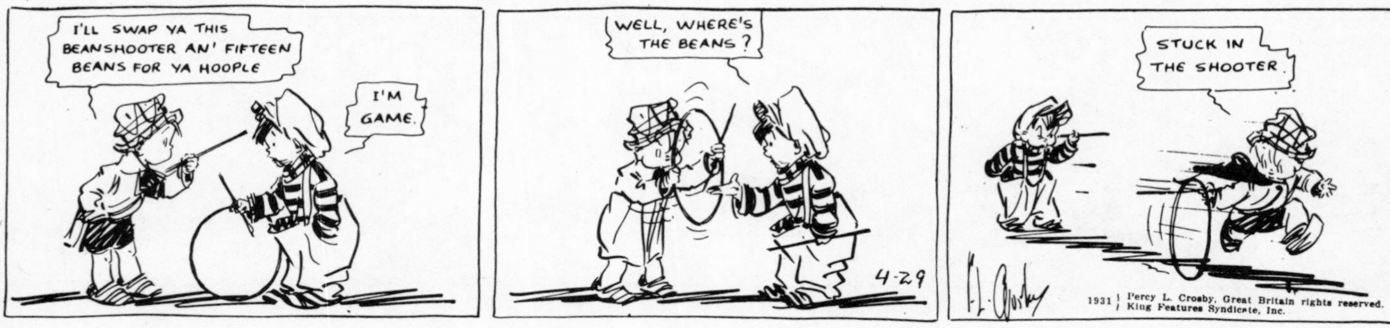
I'LL SWAP YA THIS BEANSHOOTER AN' FIFTEEN BEANS FOR YA HOOPLE
I'M GAME.
WELL, WHERE'S THE BEANS?
STUCK IN THE SHOOTER.
4-29
1931 Percy L. Crosby, Great Britain rights reserved. King Features Syndicate, Inc.

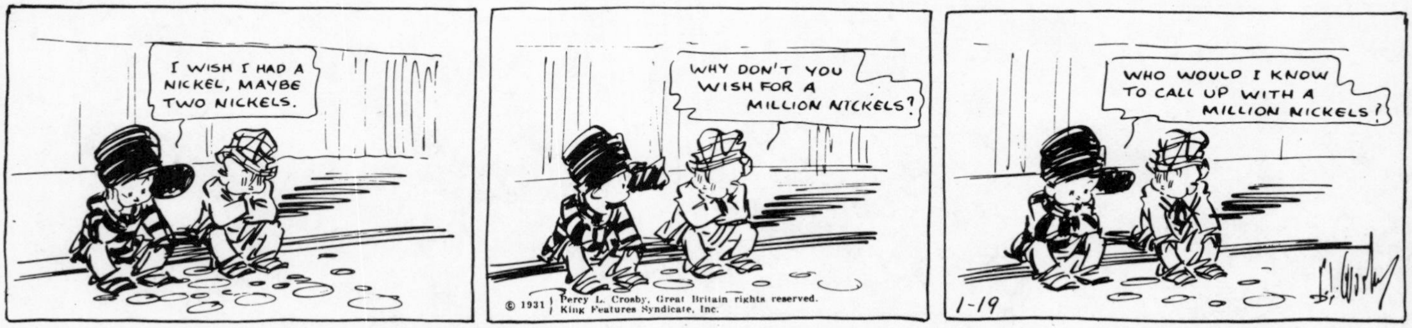
I WISH I HAD A NICKEL, MAYBE TWO NICKELS.
WHY DON'T YOU WISH FOR A MILLION NICKELS?
WHO WOULD I KNOW TO CALL UP WITH A MILLION NICKELS?
© 1931 Percy L. Crosby, Great Britain rights reserved. King Features Syndicate, Inc.
1-19

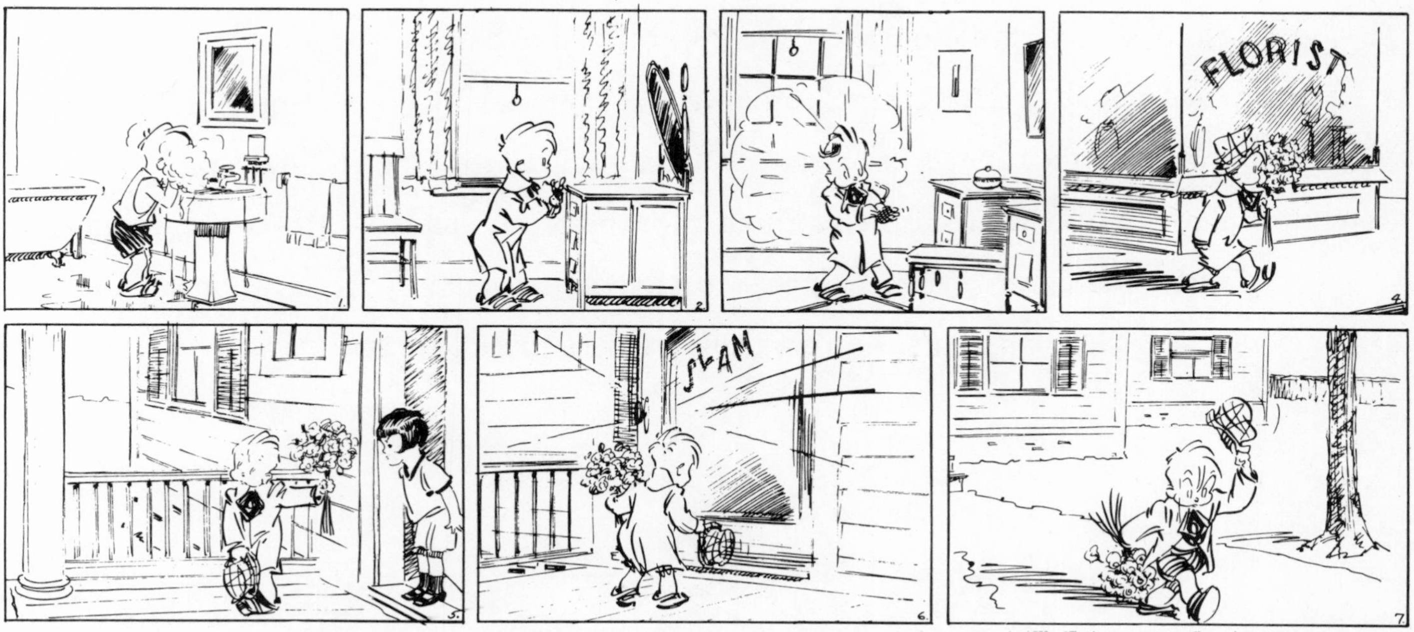
FLORIST
SLAM
SKIPPY LOVES MARY
© 1931 Percy L. Crosby, Great Britain rights reserved. King Features Syndicate, Inc.
1-25

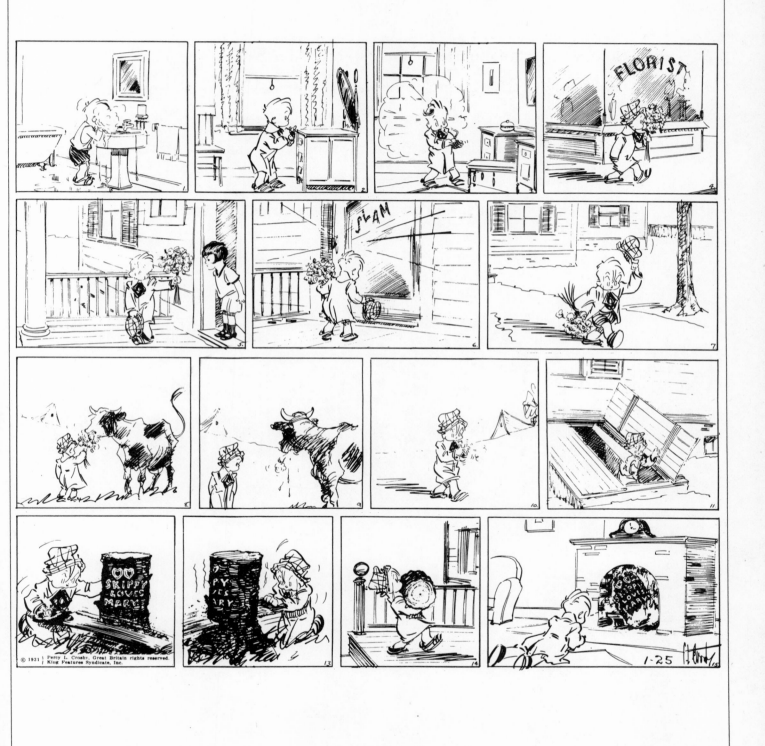

Romance

Crosby's boyhood infatuations were the inspiration for Skippy's romantic interludes. Skippy, like Crosby, is the eternal romantic, forever seeking his perfect love. One of Skippy's first episodes concerns his disappointing search for "the girl in the pink dress" (remindful today of Charlie Brown's longing for the pretty but never-to-be approached "little red-haired girl"). Skippy's romances were as full of frustrations, disappointments, and disasters as were those of his creator.

GOD BLESS PAPA AN' MAMA.
AN' GRANDMA AN' GRANDPA AN' CANST NOT THOU MAKE THE GIRL IN THE PINK RED DRESS GIVE ME A TUMBLE?
BUT IF THOU CANST NOT AN' SHE'S EVER SICK, TELL THE ANGELS I GOT SIXTY SEVEN CENTS UNDER THE CORNER CARPET AN' IT'S ALL FOR HER.
Copyright, P. L. Crosby, 1927, Johnson Features, Inc.
6-29

OH! ARE THOSE FLOWERS FOR ME?
YES, IF YA KEEP STEADY COMPANY WITH ME
OH! I CAN'T DO THAT!
8-26
TAKE ONE!
© 1931 | Percy L. Crosby, Great Britain rights reserv | King Features Syndicate, Inc.

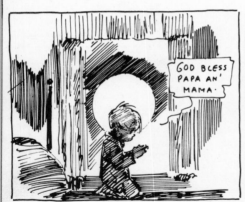

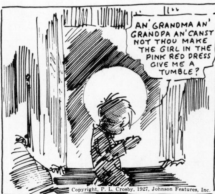

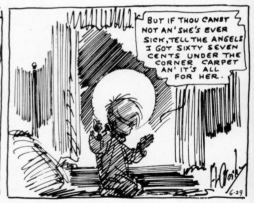

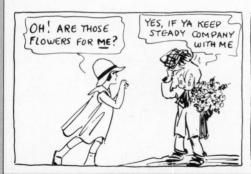

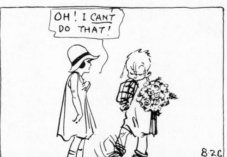

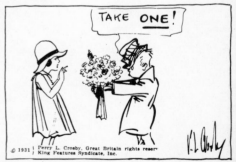

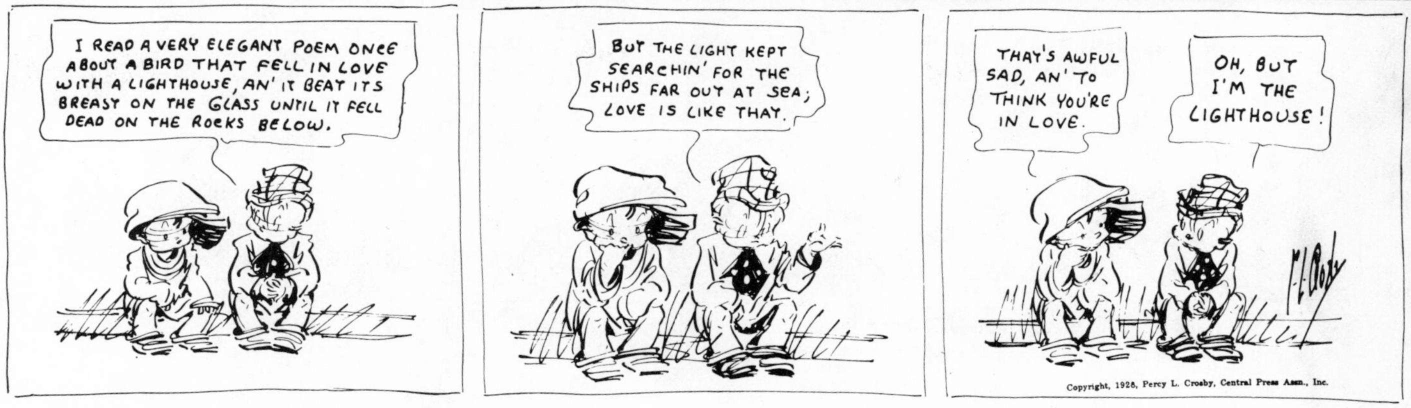
I READ A VERY ELEGANT POEM ONCE ABOUT A BIRD THAT FELL IN LOVE WITH A LIGHTHOUSE, AN' IT BEAT ITS BREAST ON THE GLASS UNTIL IT FELL DEAD ON THE ROCKS BELOW.
BUT THE LIGHT KEPT SEARCHIN' FOR THE SHIPS FAR OUT AT SEA; LOVE IS LIKE THAT.
THAT'S AWFUL SAD, AN' TO THINK YOU'RE IN LOVE.
OH, BUT I'M THE LIGHTHOUSE!
P. L. Crosby
Copyright, 1928, Percy L. Crosby, Central Press Assn., Inc.

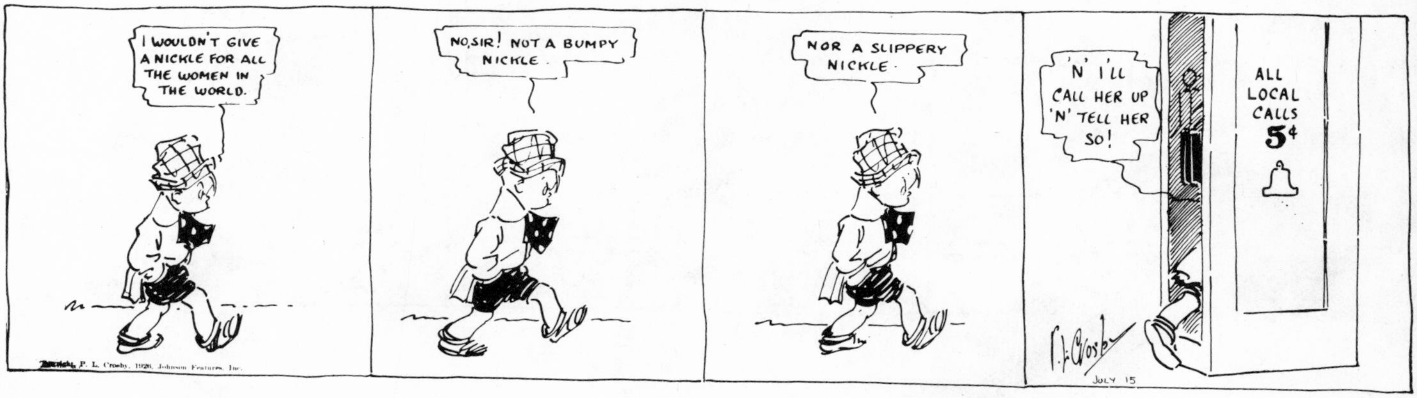
I WOULDN'T GIVE A NICKLE FOR ALL THE WOMEN IN THE WORLD.
NO, SIR! NOT A BUMPY NICKLE.
NOR A SLIPPERY NICKLE.
'N' I'LL CALL HER UP 'N' TELL HER SO!
ALL LOCAL CALLS 5¢
P. L. Crosby
JULY 15
P. L. Crosby, 1926, Johnson Features, Inc.

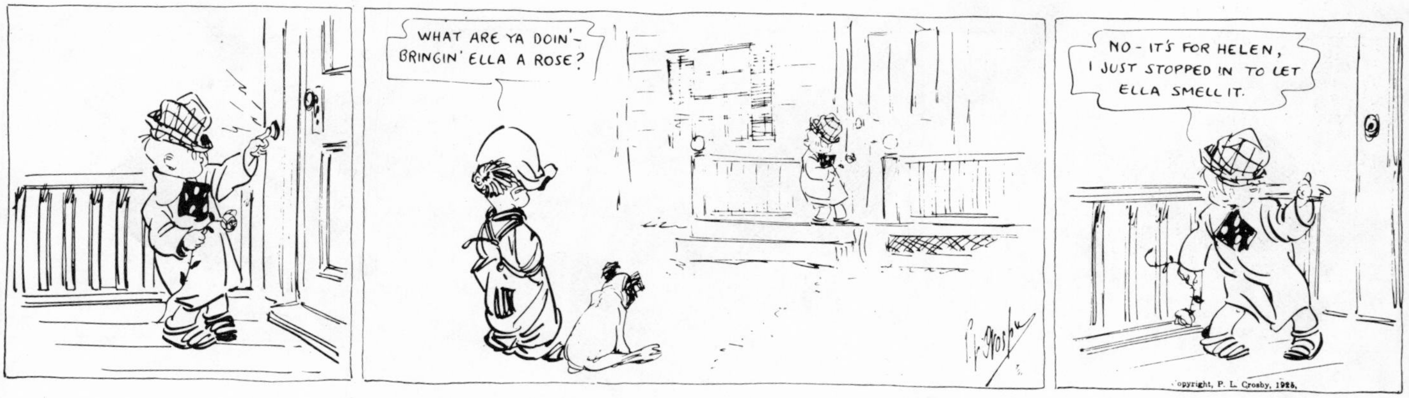
WHAT ARE YA DOIN'- BRINGIN' ELLA A ROSE?
P. L. Crosby
NO - IT'S FOR HELEN, I JUST STOPPED IN TO LET ELLA SMELL IT.
Copyright, P. L. Crosby, 1926.

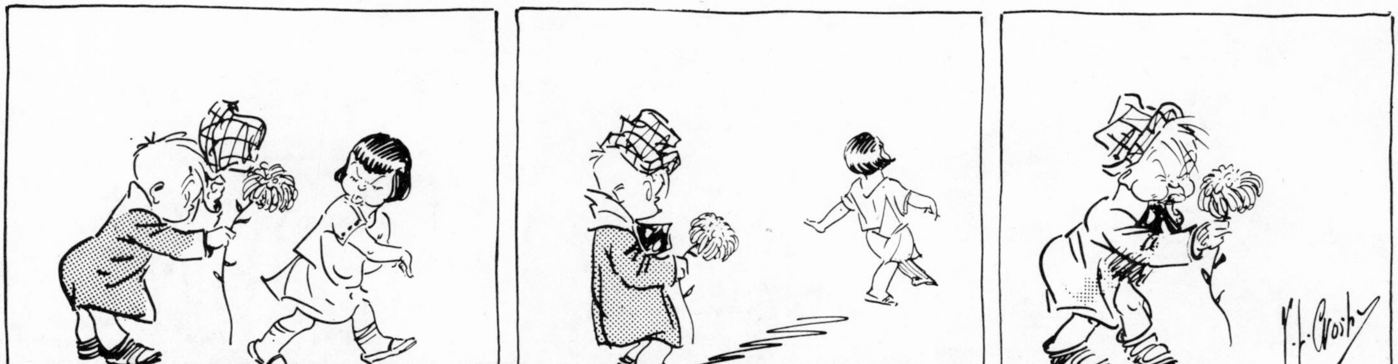
Copyright, P. L. Crosby, 1927, Johnson Features, Inc.
P. L. Crosby

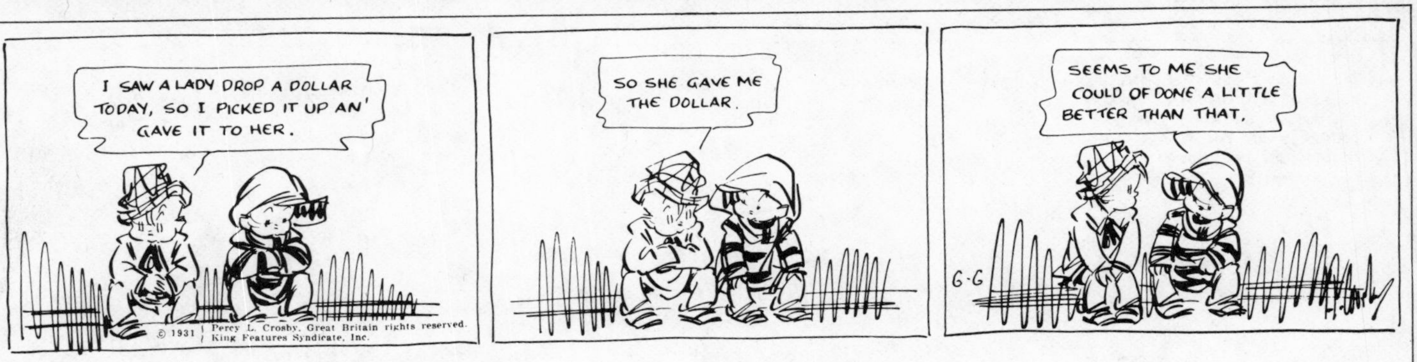
I SAW A LADY DROP A DOLLAR TODAY, SO I PICKED IT UP AN' GAVE IT TO HER.
© 1931 Percy L. Crosby, Great Britain rights reserved. King Features Syndicate, Inc.
SO SHE GAVE ME THE DOLLAR.
SEEMS TO ME SHE COULD OF DONE A LITTLE BETTER THAN THAT.
6.6

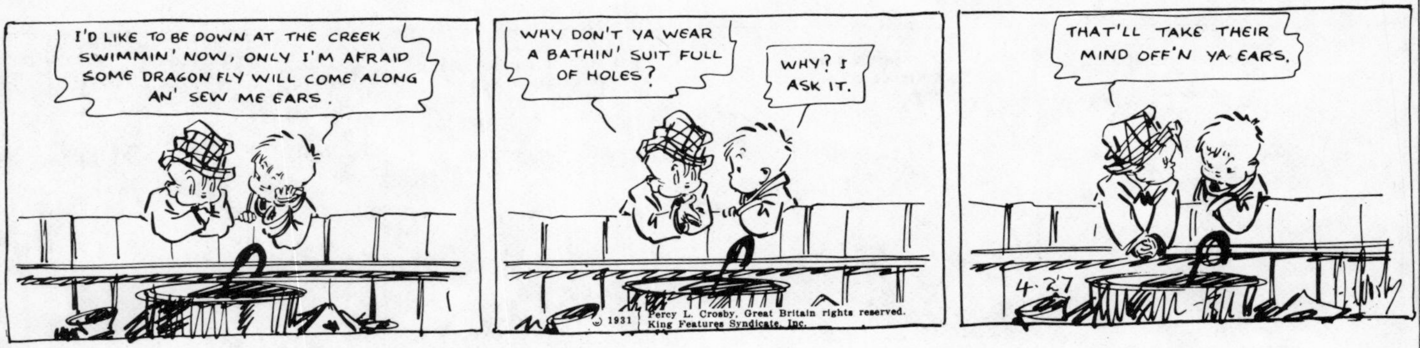
I'D LIKE TO BE DOWN AT THE CREEK SWIMMIN' NOW, ONLY I'M AFRAID SOME DRAGON FLY WILL COME ALONG AN' SEW ME EARS.
WHY DON'T YA WEAR A BATHIN' SUIT FULL OF HOLES?
WHY? I ASK IT.
© 1931 Percy L. Crosby, Great Britain rights reserved. King Features Syndicate, Inc.
THAT'LL TAKE THEIR MIND OFF'N YA EARS.
4.27

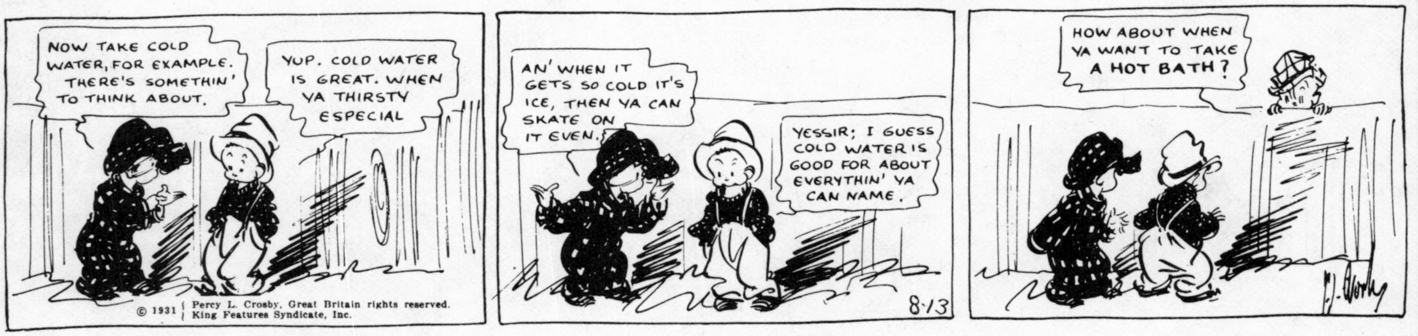
NOW TAKE COLD WATER, FOR EXAMPLE. THERE'S SOMETHIN' TO THINK ABOUT.
YUP. COLD WATER IS GREAT. WHEN YA THIRSTY ESPECIAL
© 1931 Percy L. Crosby, Great Britain rights reserved. King Features Syndicate, Inc.
AN' WHEN IT GETS SO COLD IT'S ICE, THEN YA CAN SKATE ON IT EVEN.
YESSIR; I GUESS COLD WATER IS GOOD FOR ABOUT EVERYTHIN' YA CAN NAME.
8.13
HOW ABOUT WHEN YA WANT TO TAKE A HOT BATH?

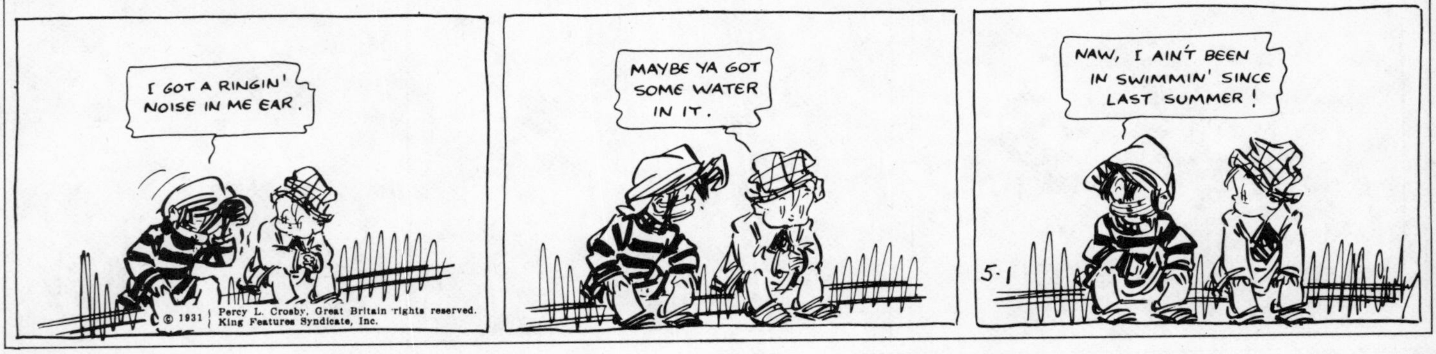
I GOT A RINGIN' NOISE IN ME EAR.
© 1931 Percy L. Crosby, Great Britain rights reserved. King Features Syndicate, Inc.
MAYBE YA GOT SOME WATER IN IT.
NAW, I AIN'T BEEN IN SWIMMIN' SINCE LAST SUMMER!
5.1

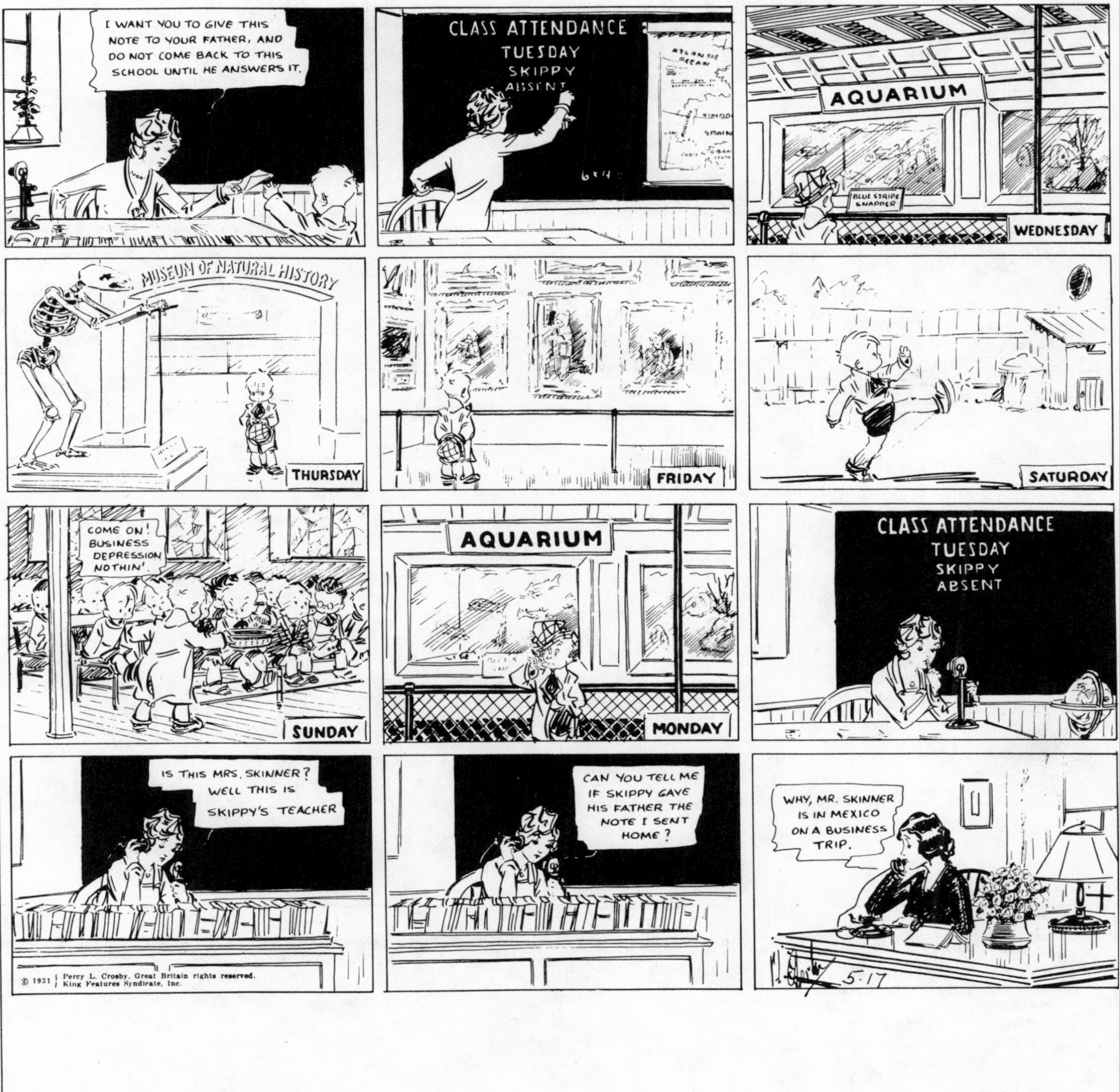
I WANT YOU TO GIVE THIS NOTE TO YOUR FATHER, AND DO NOT COME BACK TO THIS SCHOOL UNTIL HE ANSWERS IT.
CLASS ATTENDANCE
TUESDAY
SKIPPY
ABSENT
AQUARIUM
BLUE STRIPE SNAPPER
WEDNESDAY
MUSEUM OF NATURAL HISTORY
THURSDAY
FRIDAY
SATURDAY
COME ON! BUSINESS DEPRESSION NOTHIN'.
SUNDAY
AQUARIUM
MONDAY
CLASS ATTENDANCE
TUESDAY
SKIPPY
ABSENT
IS THIS MRS. SKINNER? WELL THIS IS SKIPPY'S TEACHER
CAN YOU TELL ME IF SKIPPY GAVE HIS FATHER THE NOTE I SENT HOME?
WHY, MR. SKINNER IS IN MEXICO ON A BUSINESS TRIP.
© 1931 Percy L. Crosby, Great Britain rights reserved. King Features Syndicate, Inc.
5-17

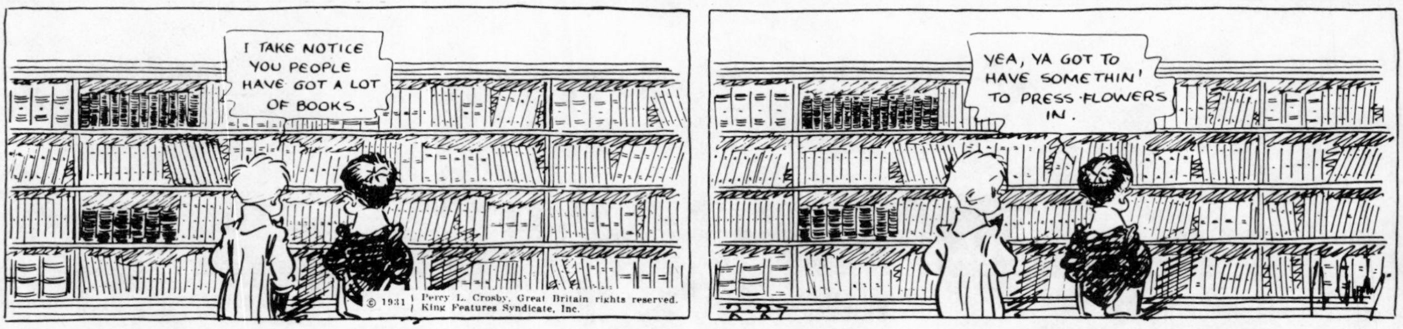
I TAKE NOTICE YOU PEOPLE HAVE GOT A LOT OF BOOKS.
© 1931 Percy L. Crosby, Great Britain rights reserved. King Features Syndicate, Inc.
YEA, YA GOT TO HAVE SOMETHIN' TO PRESS FLOWERS IN.

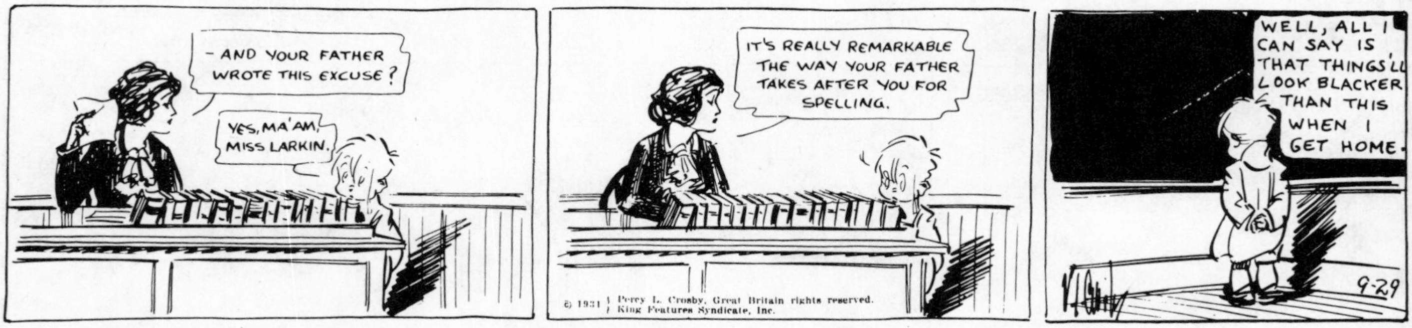
—AND YOUR FATHER WROTE THIS EXCUSE?
YES, MA'AM, MISS LARKIN.
IT'S REALLY REMARKABLE THE WAY YOUR FATHER TAKES AFTER YOU FOR SPELLING.
© 1931 Percy L. Crosby, Great Britain rights reserved. King Features Syndicate, Inc.
WELL, ALL I CAN SAY IS THAT THINGS'LL LOOK BLACKER THAN THIS WHEN I GET HOME.
9-29

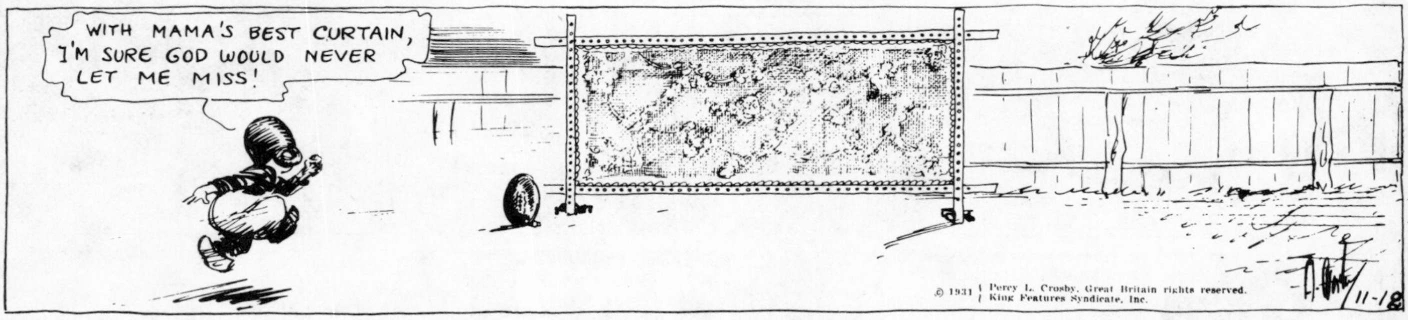
WITH MAMA'S BEST CURTAIN, I'M SURE GOD WOULD NEVER LET ME MISS!
© 1931 Percy L. Crosby, Great Britain rights reserved. King Features Syndicate, Inc.
11-18

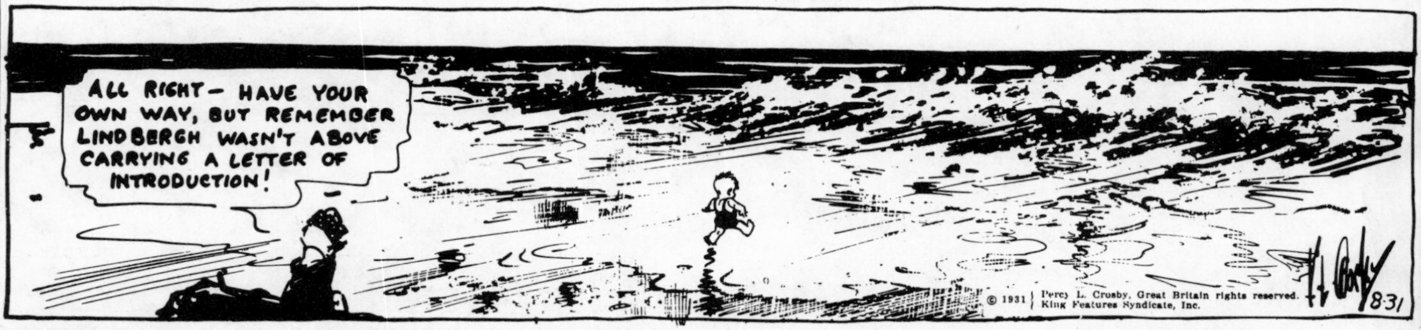
ALL RIGHT— HAVE YOUR OWN WAY, BUT REMEMBER LINDBERGH WASN'T ABOVE CARRYING A LETTER OF INTRODUCTION!
© 1931 Percy L. Crosby, Great Britain rights reserved. King Features Syndicate, Inc.
8-31

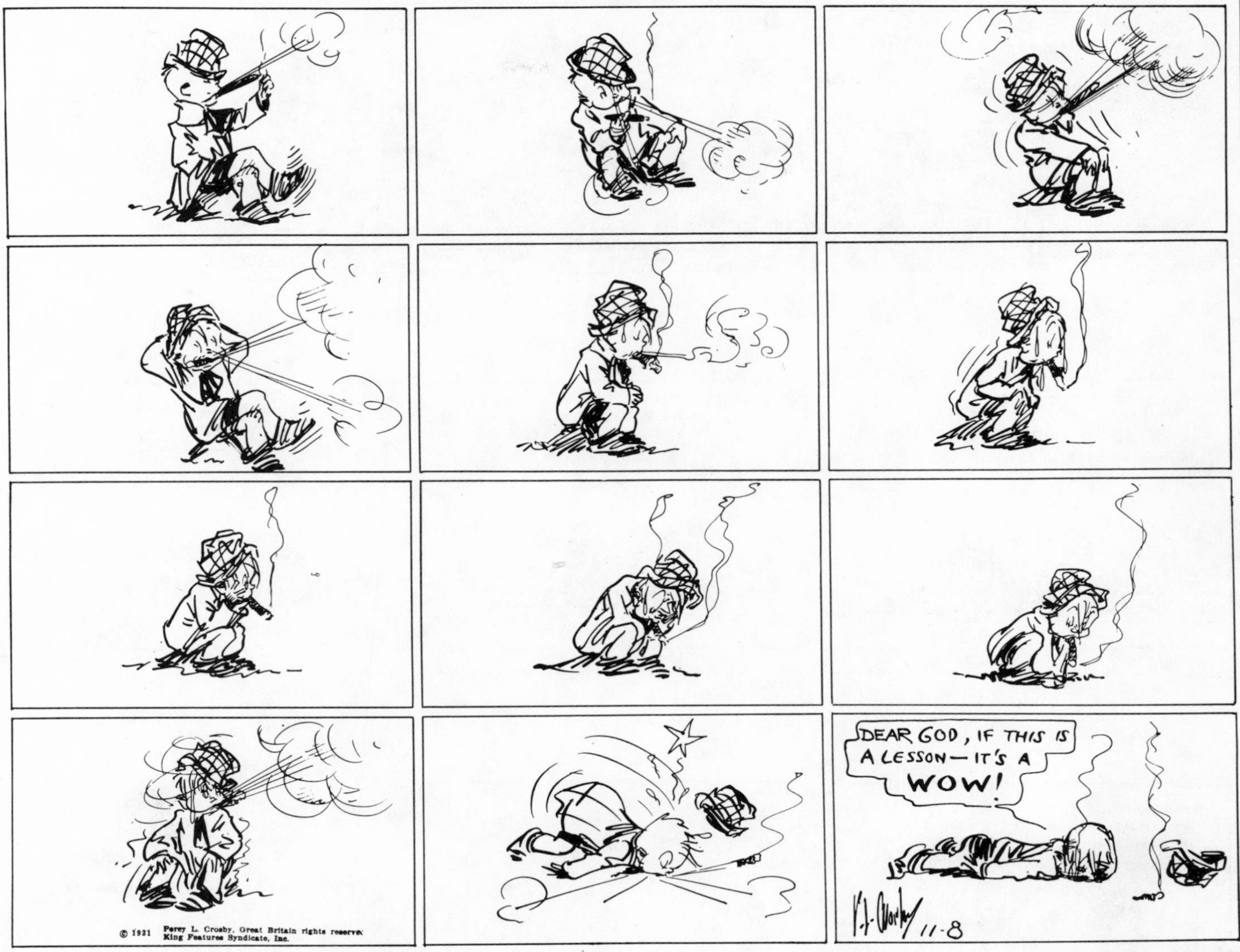
DEAR GOD, IF THIS IS A LESSON—IT'S A WOW!
© 1931 Percy L. Crosby, Great Britain rights reserved. King Features Syndicate, Inc.
11-8

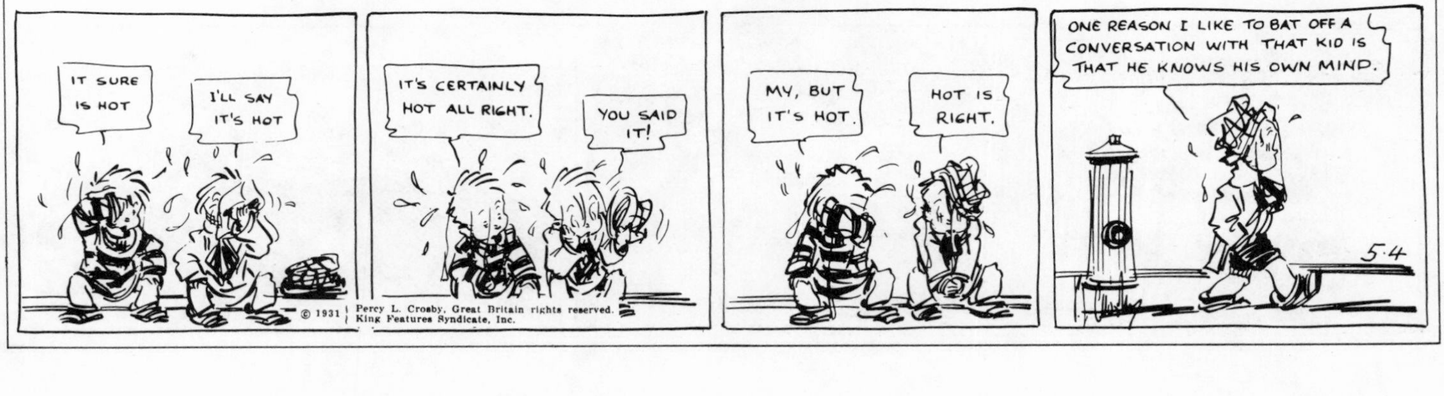
IT SURE IS HOT
I'LL SAY IT'S HOT
IT'S CERTAINLY HOT ALL RIGHT.
YOU SAID IT!
MY, BUT IT'S HOT.
HOT IS RIGHT.
ONE REASON I LIKE TO BAT OFF A CONVERSATION WITH THAT KID IS THAT HE KNOWS HIS OWN MIND.
© 1931 Percy L. Crosby, Great Britain rights reserved. King Features Syndicate, Inc.
5-4

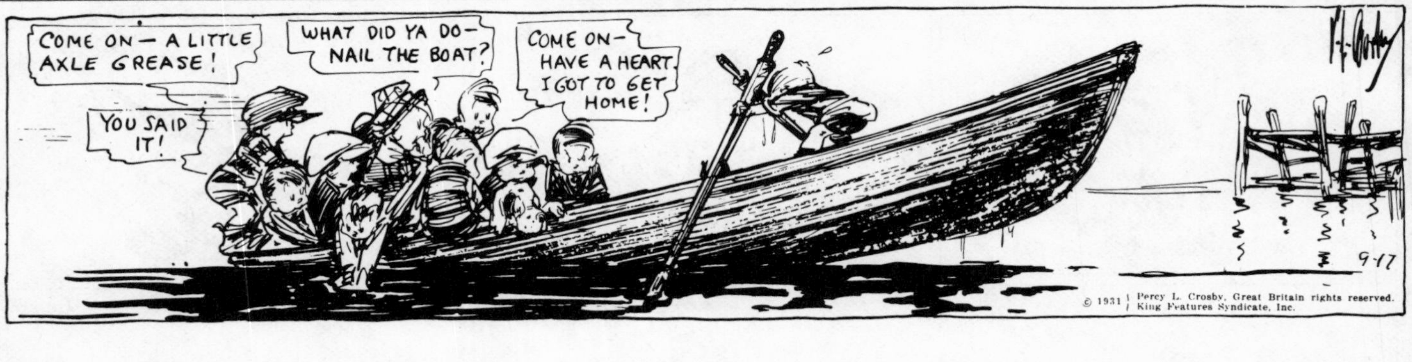
COME ON — A LITTLE AXLE GREASE!
YOU SAID IT!
WHAT DID YA DO — NAIL THE BOAT?
COME ON — HAVE A HEART. I GOT TO GET HOME!
9-17
© 1931 Percy L. Crosby, Great Britain rights reserved. King Features Syndicate, Inc.

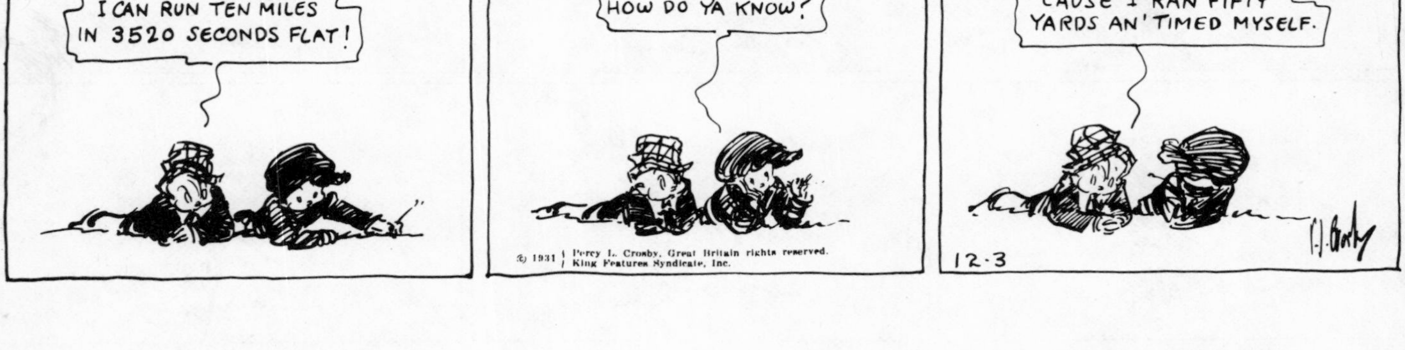
I CAN RUN TEN MILES IN 3520 SECONDS FLAT!
HOW DO YA KNOW?
© 1931 Percy L. Crosby, Great Britain rights reserved. King Features Syndicate, Inc.
'CAUSE I RAN FIFTY YARDS AN' TIMED MYSELF.
12-3

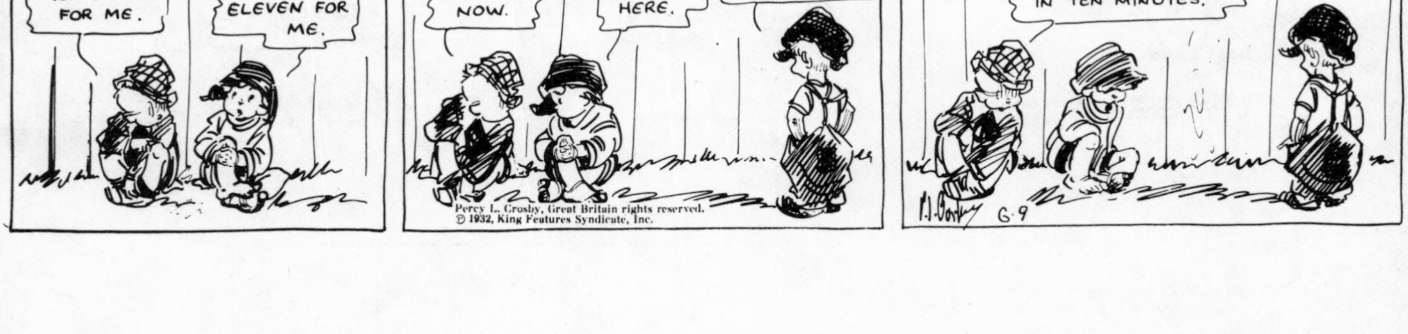
THAT MAKES TEN THINGS FOR ME.
NOW IT'S ELEVEN FOR ME.
FIFTEEN WITH ME NOW.
FOURTEEN HERE.
WHATEVER ARE YA DOIN'?
Percy L. Crosby, Great Britain rights reserved. © 1932, King Features Syndicate, Inc.
JUST SEEIN' HOW MANY THINGS WE CAN FORGET IN TEN MINUTES.
6-9

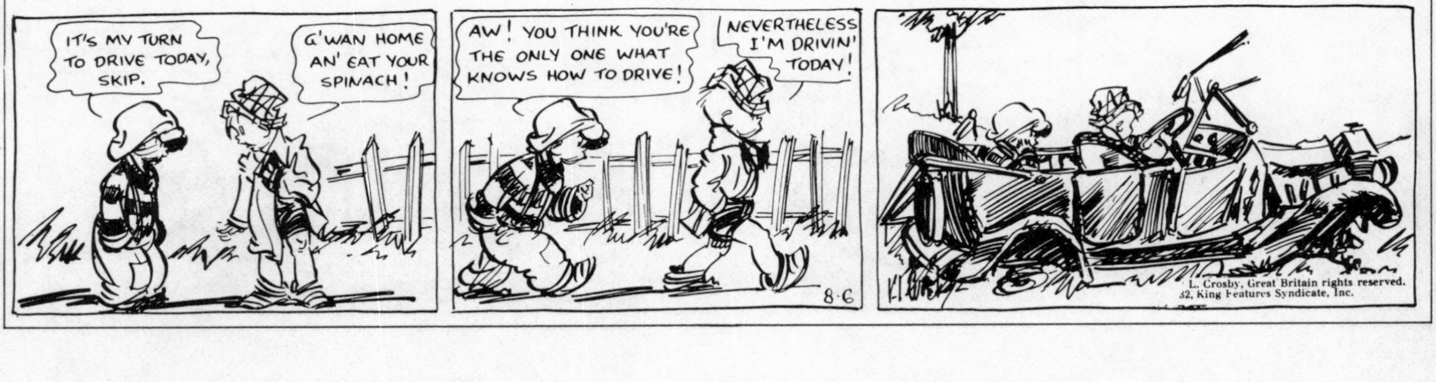
IT'S MY TURN TO DRIVE TODAY, SKIP.
G'WAN HOME AN' EAT YOUR SPINACH!
AW! YOU THINK YOU'RE THE ONLY ONE WHAT KNOWS HOW TO DRIVE!
NEVERTHELESS I'M DRIVIN' TODAY!
8-6
L. Crosby, Great Britain rights reserved.
32, King Features Syndicate, Inc.

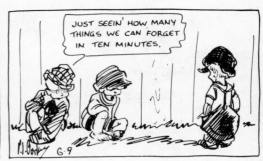

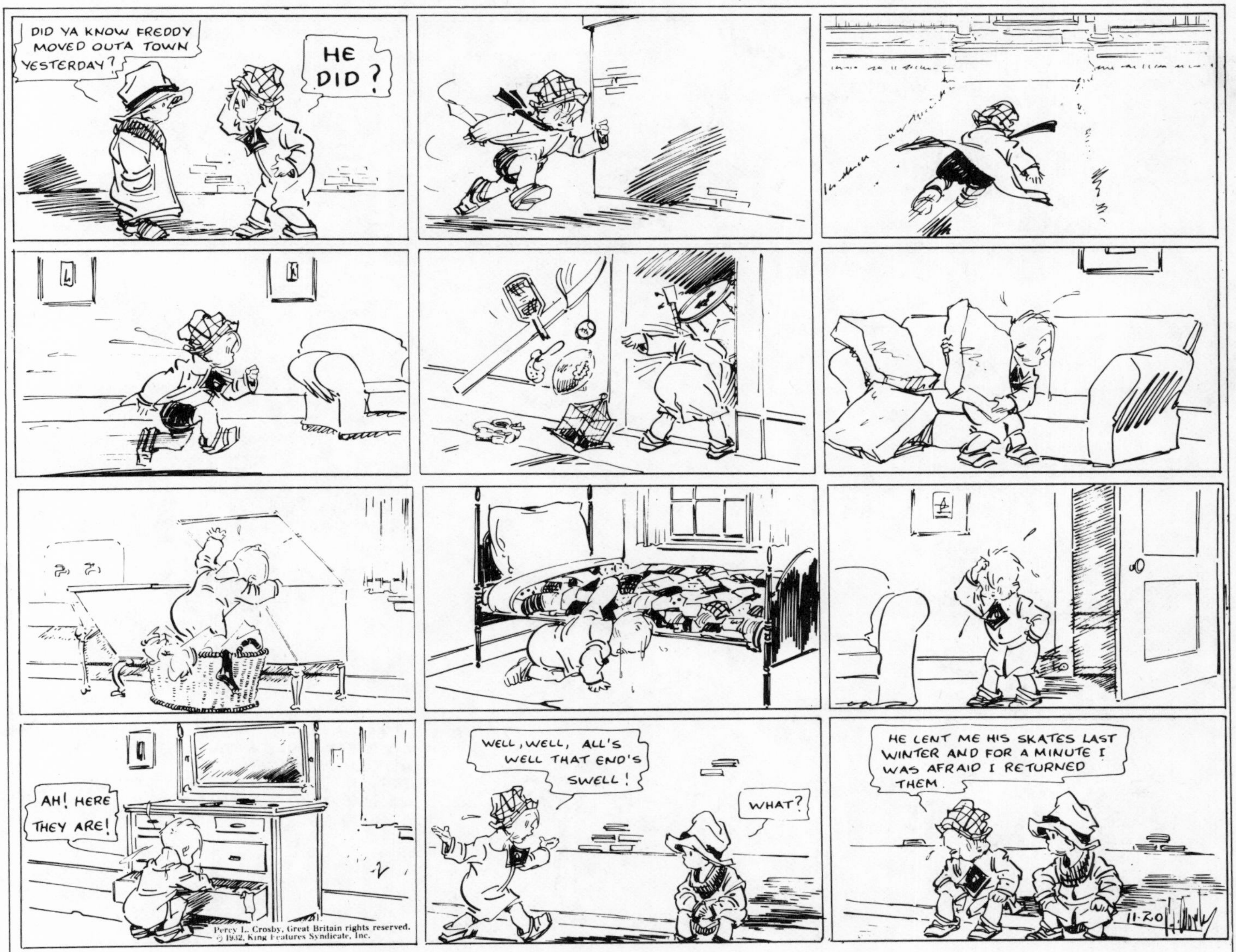
DID YA KNOW FREDDY MOVED OUTA TOWN YESTERDAY?
HE DID?
AH! HERE THEY ARE!
Percy L. Crosby, Great Britain rights reserved.
© 1932, King Features Syndicate, Inc.
WELL, WELL, ALL'S WELL THAT END'S SWELL!
WHAT?
HE LENT ME HIS SKATES LAST WINTER AND FOR A MINUTE I WAS AFRAID I RETURNED THEM.
11-20

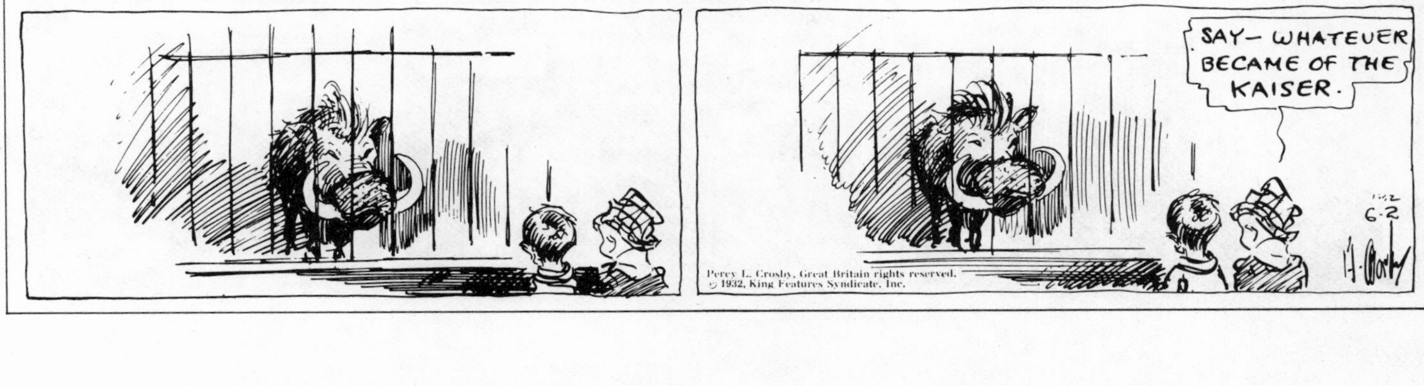
SAY— WHATEVER BECAME OF THE KAISER.
6-2
Percy L. Crosby, Great Britain rights reserved.
© 1932, King Features Syndicate, Inc.

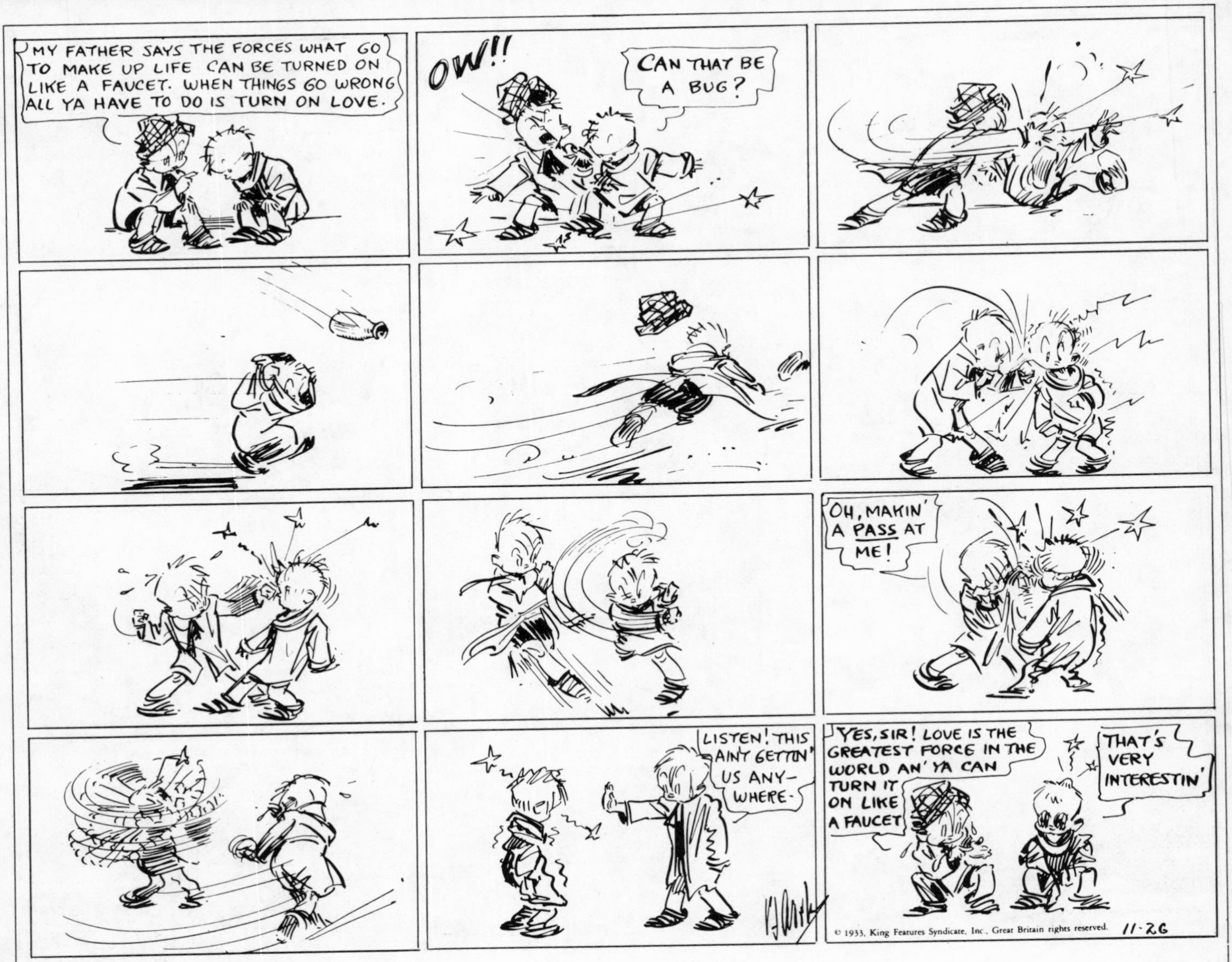
MY FATHER SAYS THE FORCES WHAT GO TO MAKE UP LIFE CAN BE TURNED ON LIKE A FAUCET. WHEN THINGS GO WRONG ALL YA HAVE TO DO IS TURN ON LOVE.
OW!!
CAN THAT BE A BUG?
OH, MAKIN' A PASS AT ME!
LISTEN! THIS AIN'T GETTIN' US ANY-WHERE.
YES, SIR! LOVE IS THE GREATEST FORCE IN THE WORLD AN' YA CAN TURN IT ON LIKE A FAUCET
THAT'S VERY INTERESTIN'
© 1933, King Features Syndicate, Inc., Great Britain rights reserved.
11-26

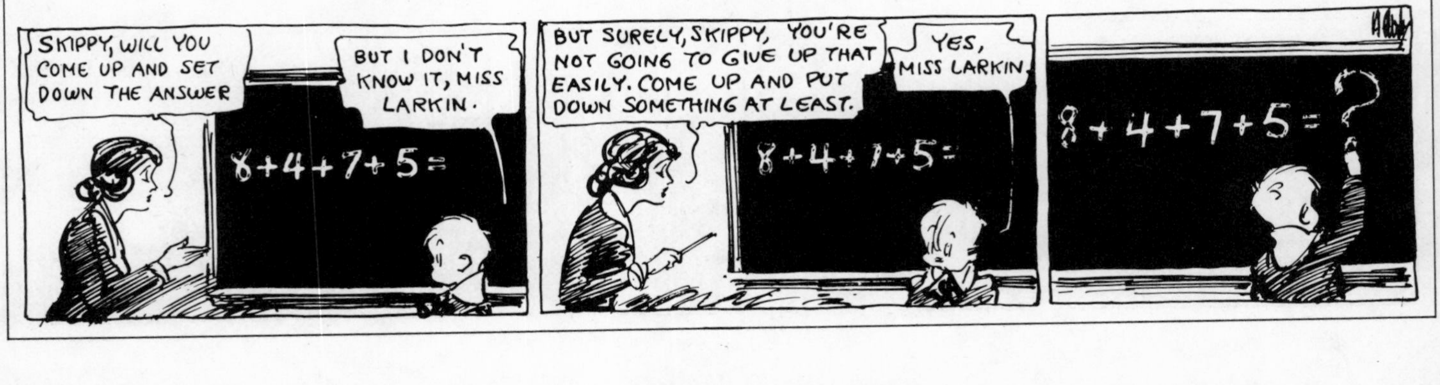
SKIPPY, WILL YOU COME UP AND SET DOWN THE ANSWER
BUT I DON'T KNOW IT, MISS LARKIN.
8+4+7+5=
BUT SURELY, SKIPPY, YOU'RE NOT GOING TO GIVE UP THAT EASILY. COME UP AND PUT DOWN SOMETHING AT LEAST.
YES, MISS LARKIN.
8+4+7+5=
8+4+7+5=?

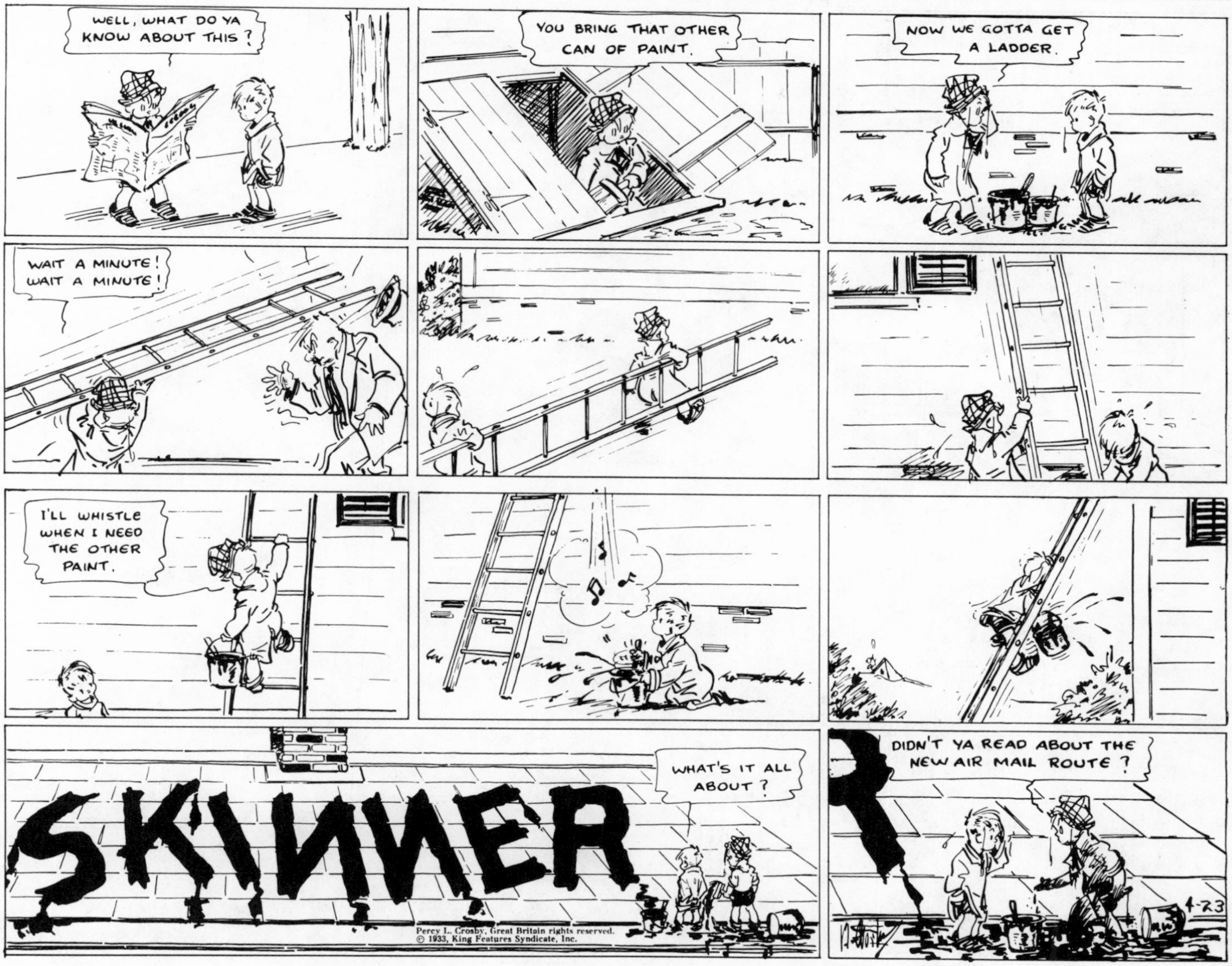
WELL, WHAT DO YA KNOW ABOUT THIS?
YOU BRING THAT OTHER CAN OF PAINT.
NOW WE GOTTA GET A LADDER.
WAIT A MINUTE! WAIT A MINUTE!
I'LL WHISTLE WHEN I NEED THE OTHER PAINT.
SKINNER
WHAT'S IT ALL ABOUT?
DIDN'T YA READ ABOUT THE NEW AIR MAIL ROUTE?
4-23
Percy L. Crosby, Great Britain rights reserved.
© 1933, King Features Syndicate, Inc.

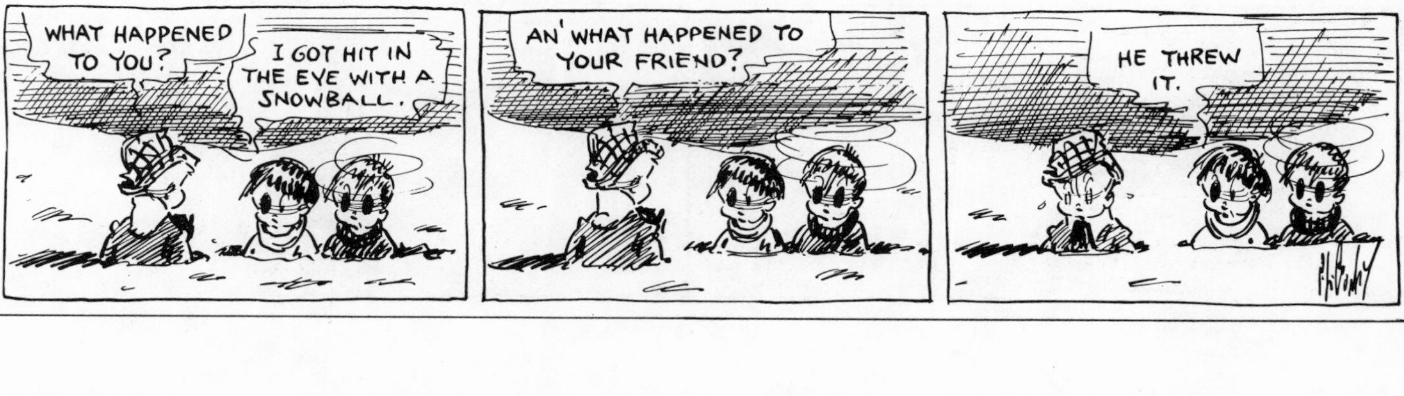
WHAT HAPPENED TO YOU?
I GOT HIT IN THE EYE WITH A SNOWBALL.
AN' WHAT HAPPENED TO YOUR FRIEND?
HE THREW IT.

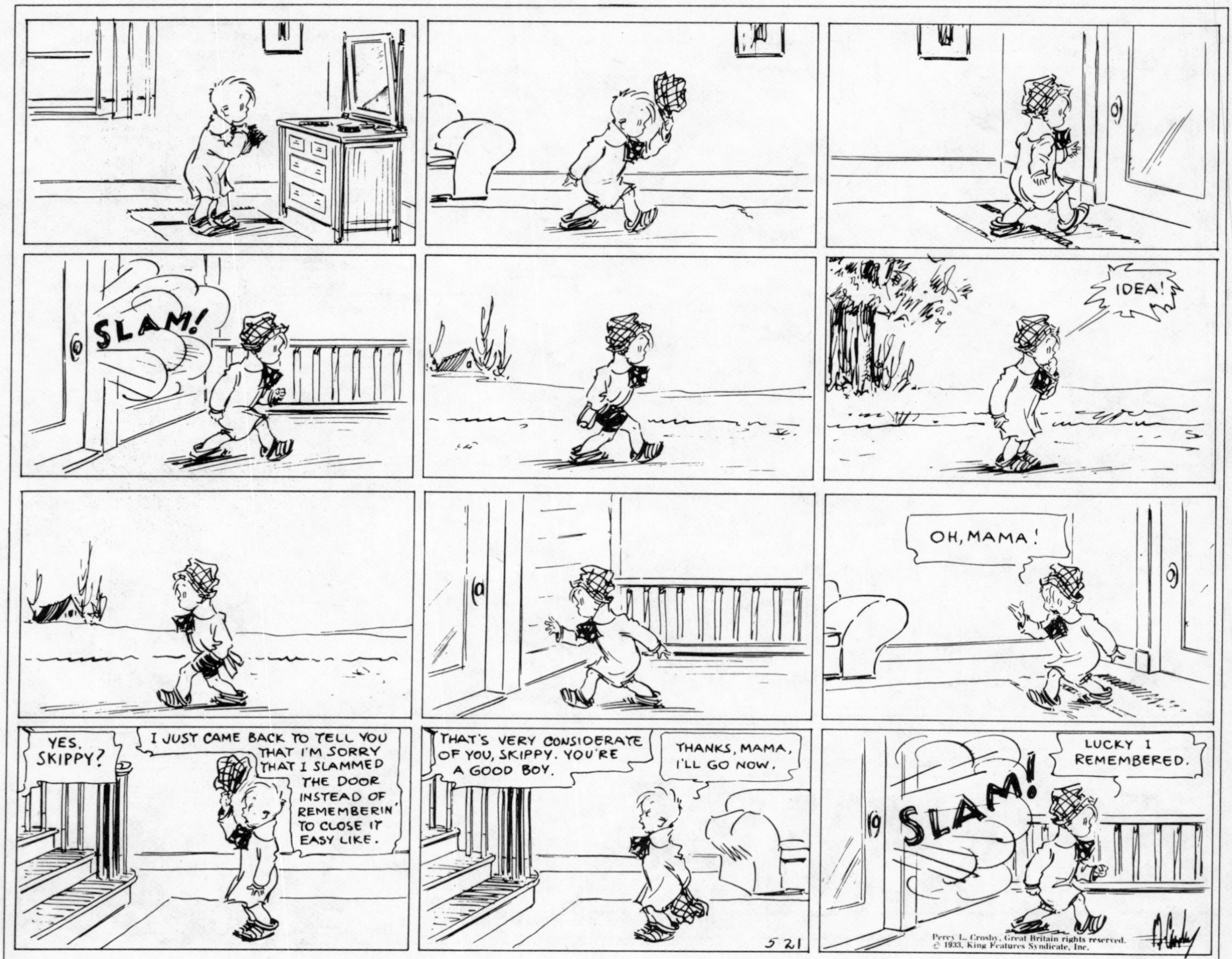
SLAM!
IDEA!
OH, MAMA!
YES, SKIPPY?
I JUST CAME BACK TO TELL YOU THAT I'M SORRY THAT I SLAMMED THE DOOR INSTEAD OF REMEMBERIN' TO CLOSE IT EASY LIKE.
THAT'S VERY CONSIDERATE OF YOU, SKIPPY. YOU'RE A GOOD BOY.
THANKS, MAMA, I'LL GO NOW.
5 21
SLAM!
LUCKY I REMEMBERED.
Percy L. Crosby, Great Britain rights reserved.
© 1933, King Features Syndicate, Inc.

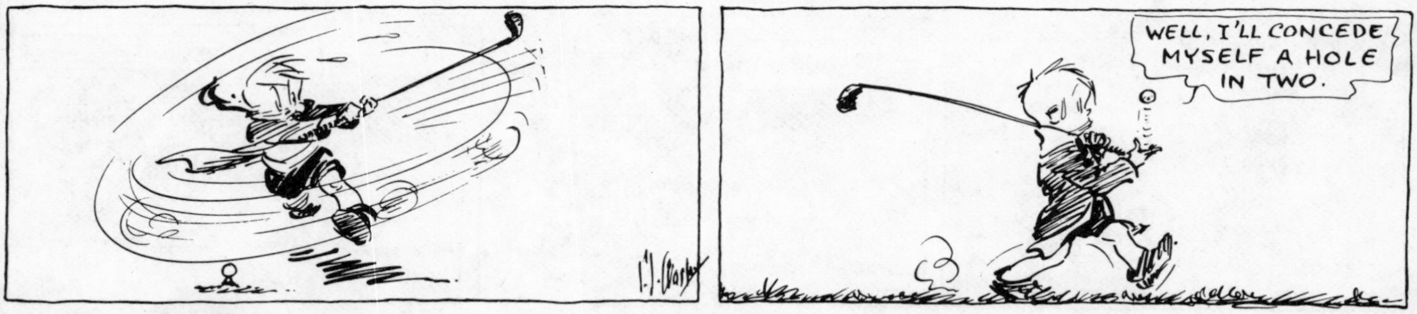
WELL, I'LL CONCEDE MYSELF A HOLE IN TWO.

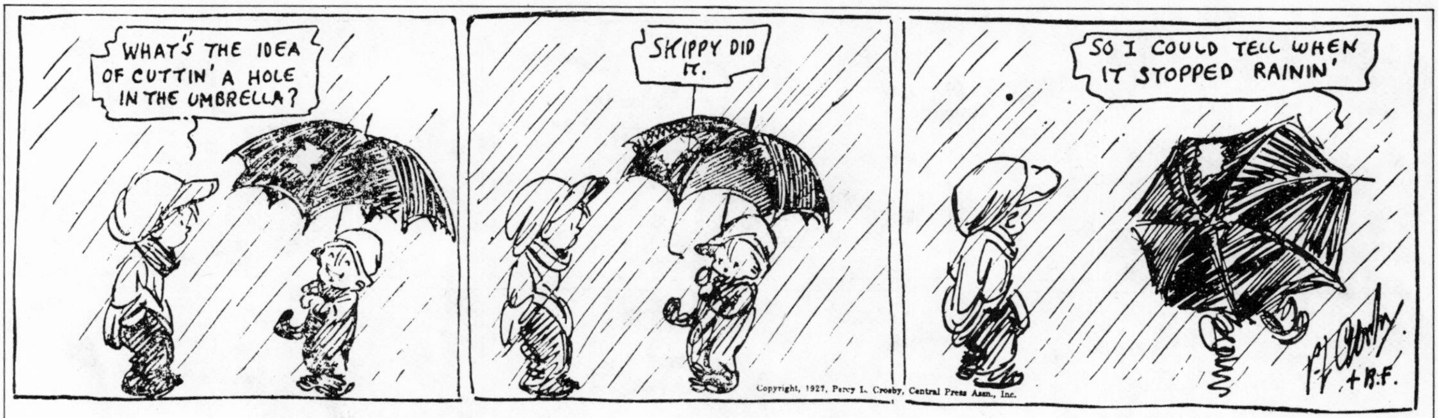
WHAT'S THE IDEA OF CUTTIN' A HOLE IN THE UMBRELLA?
SKIPPY DID IT.
SO I COULD TELL WHEN IT STOPPED RAININ'
Copyright, 1927, Percy L. Crosby, Central Press Assn., Inc.

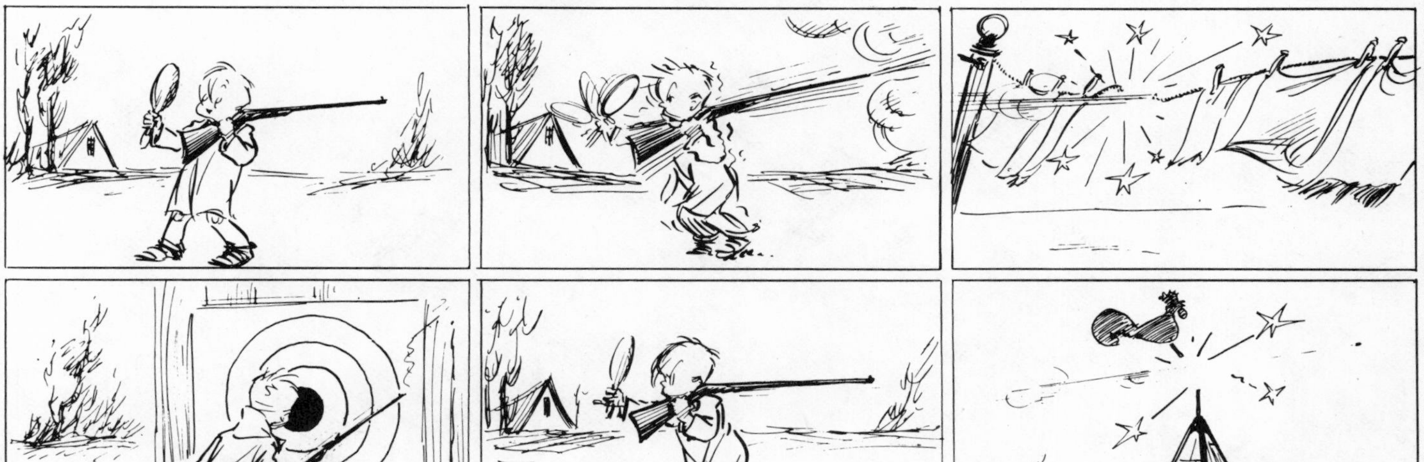
SAY! YA KNOW THOSE BULLETS YA SENT ME? WELL, THEY'RE ALL BLANKS!
rcy L. Crosby, Great Britain rights reserved.
© 1933, King Features Syndicate, Inc.
11-19

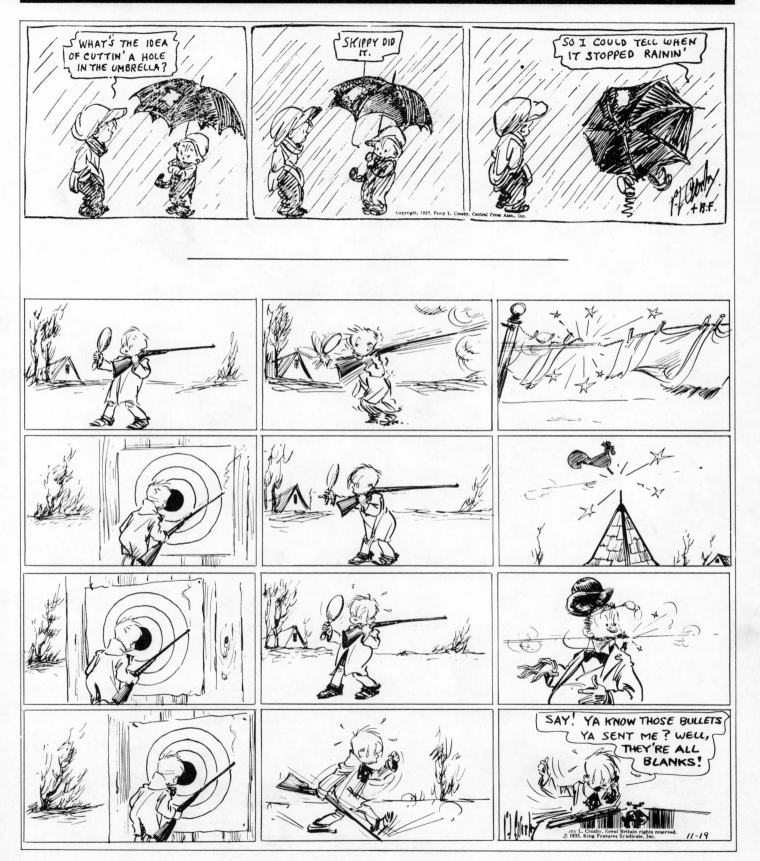

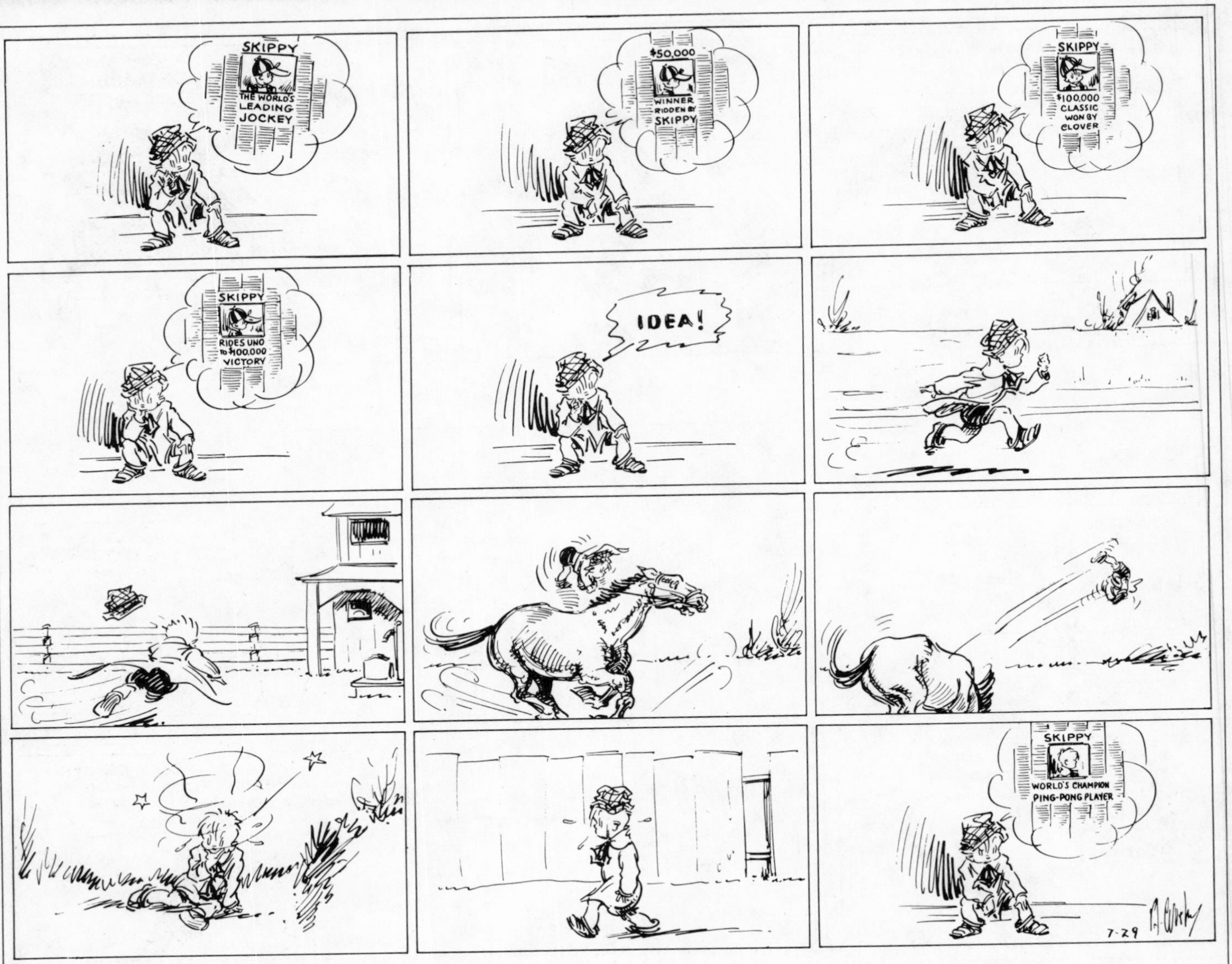
SKIPPY
THE WORLD'S LEADING JOCKEY
$50,000
WINNER RIDDEN BY SKIPPY
SKIPPY
$100,000 CLASSIC WON BY CLOVER
SKIPPY
RIDES UNO TO $100,000 VICTORY
IDEA!
SKIPPY
WORLD'S CHAMPION PING-PONG PLAYER
7-29

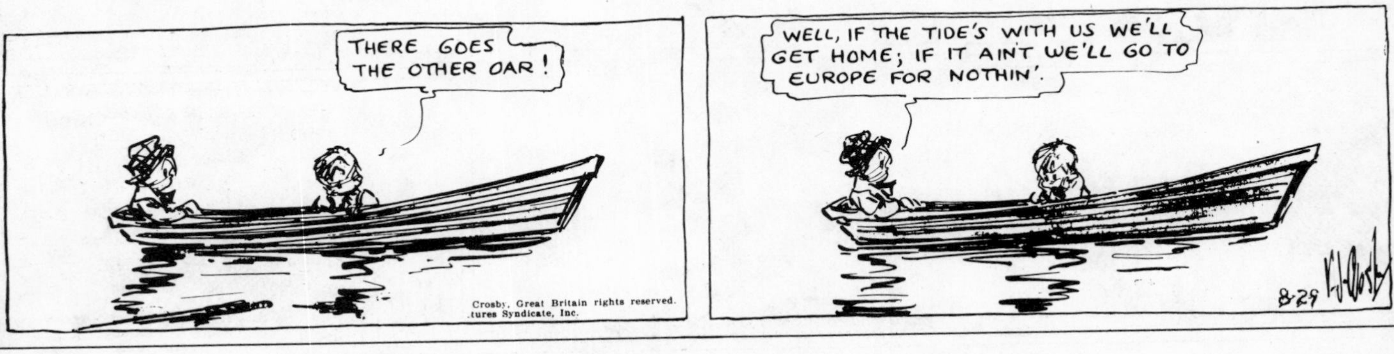
THERE GOES THE OTHER OAR!
Crosby, Great Britain rights reserved.
.tures Syndicate, Inc.
WELL, IF THE TIDE'S WITH US WE'LL GET HOME; IF IT AIN'T WE'LL GO TO EUROPE FOR NOTHIN'.
8-29

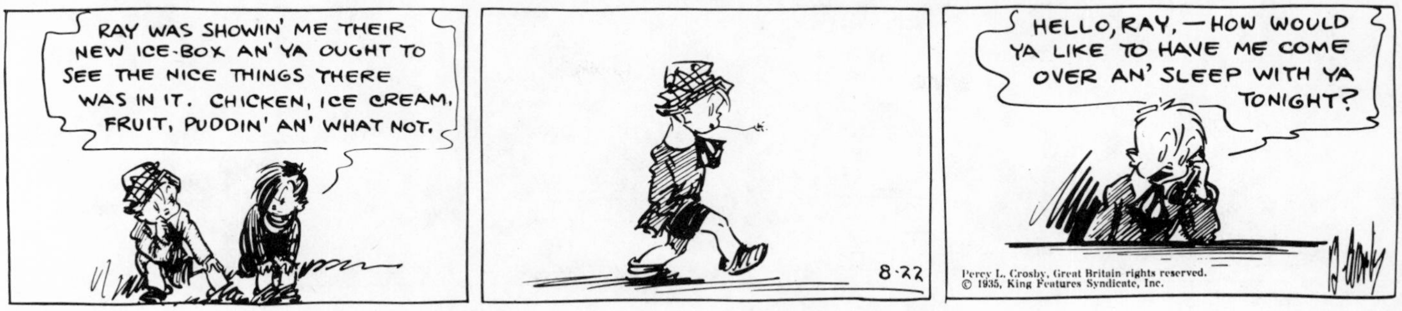
RAY WAS SHOWIN' ME THEIR NEW ICE-BOX AN' YA OUGHT TO SEE THE NICE THINGS THERE WAS IN IT. CHICKEN, ICE CREAM, FRUIT, PUDDIN' AN' WHAT NOT.
8-22
HELLO, RAY, —HOW WOULD YA LIKE TO HAVE ME COME OVER AN' SLEEP WITH YA TONIGHT?
Percy L. Crosby, Great Britain rights reserved.
© 1935, King Features Syndicate, Inc.

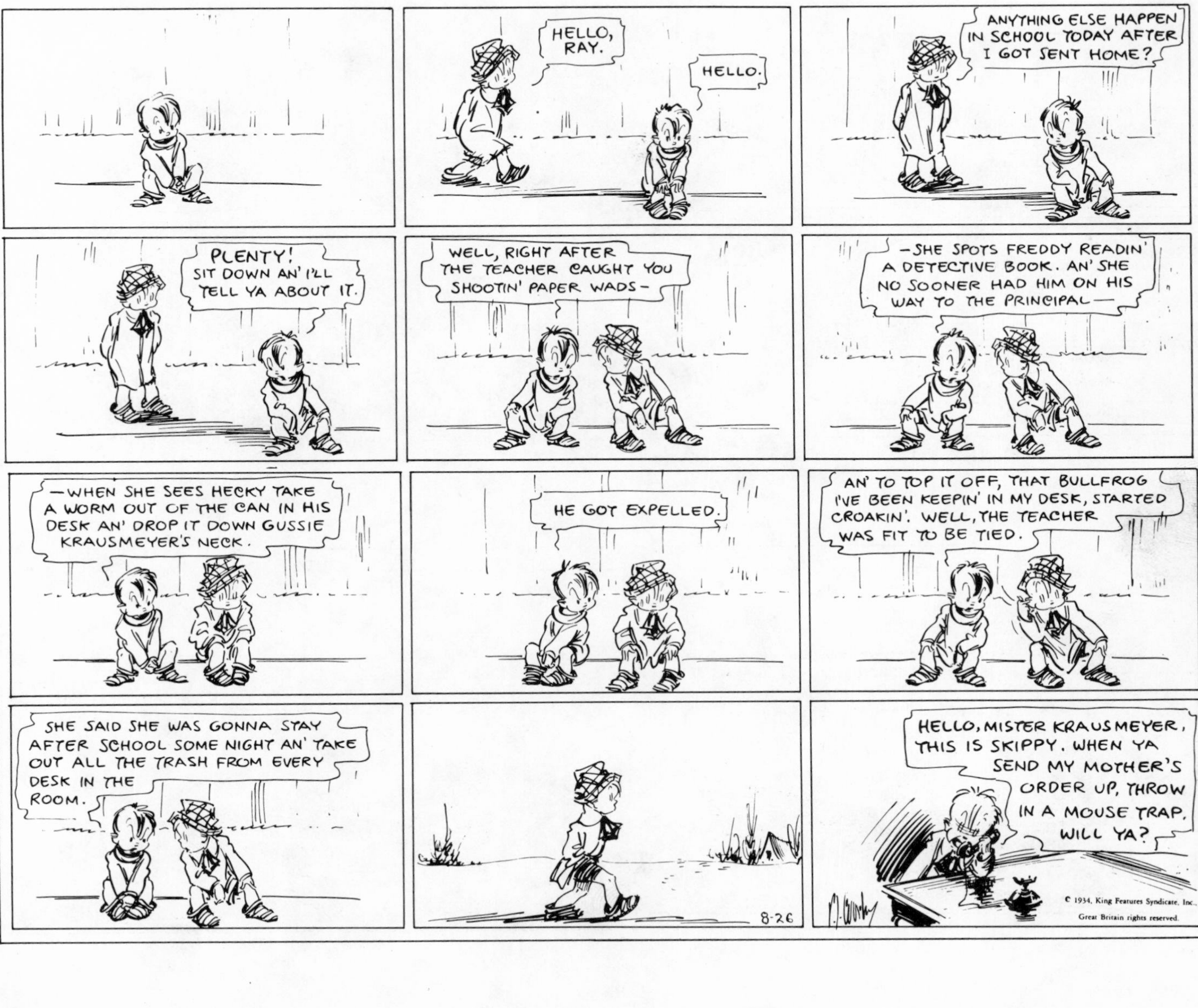
HELLO, RAY.
HELLO.
ANYTHING ELSE HAPPEN IN SCHOOL TODAY AFTER I GOT SENT HOME?
PLENTY! SIT DOWN AN' I'LL TELL YA ABOUT IT.
WELL, RIGHT AFTER THE TEACHER CAUGHT YOU SHOOTIN' PAPER WADS—
—SHE SPOTS FREDDY READIN' A DETECTIVE BOOK. AN' SHE NO SOONER HAD HIM ON HIS WAY TO THE PRINCIPAL—
—WHEN SHE SEES HECKY TAKE A WORM OUT OF THE CAN IN HIS DESK AN' DROP IT DOWN GUSSIE KRAUSMEYER'S NECK.
HE GOT EXPELLED.
AN' TO TOP IT OFF, THAT BULLFROG I'VE BEEN KEEPIN' IN MY DESK, STARTED CROAKIN'. WELL, THE TEACHER WAS FIT TO BE TIED.
SHE SAID SHE WAS GONNA STAY AFTER SCHOOL SOME NIGHT AN' TAKE OUT ALL THE TRASH FROM EVERY DESK IN THE ROOM.
8-26
HELLO, MISTER KRAUSMEYER, THIS IS SKIPPY. WHEN YA SEND MY MOTHER'S ORDER UP, THROW IN A MOUSE TRAP, WILL YA?
© 1934, King Features Syndicate, Inc.
Great Britain rights reserved.

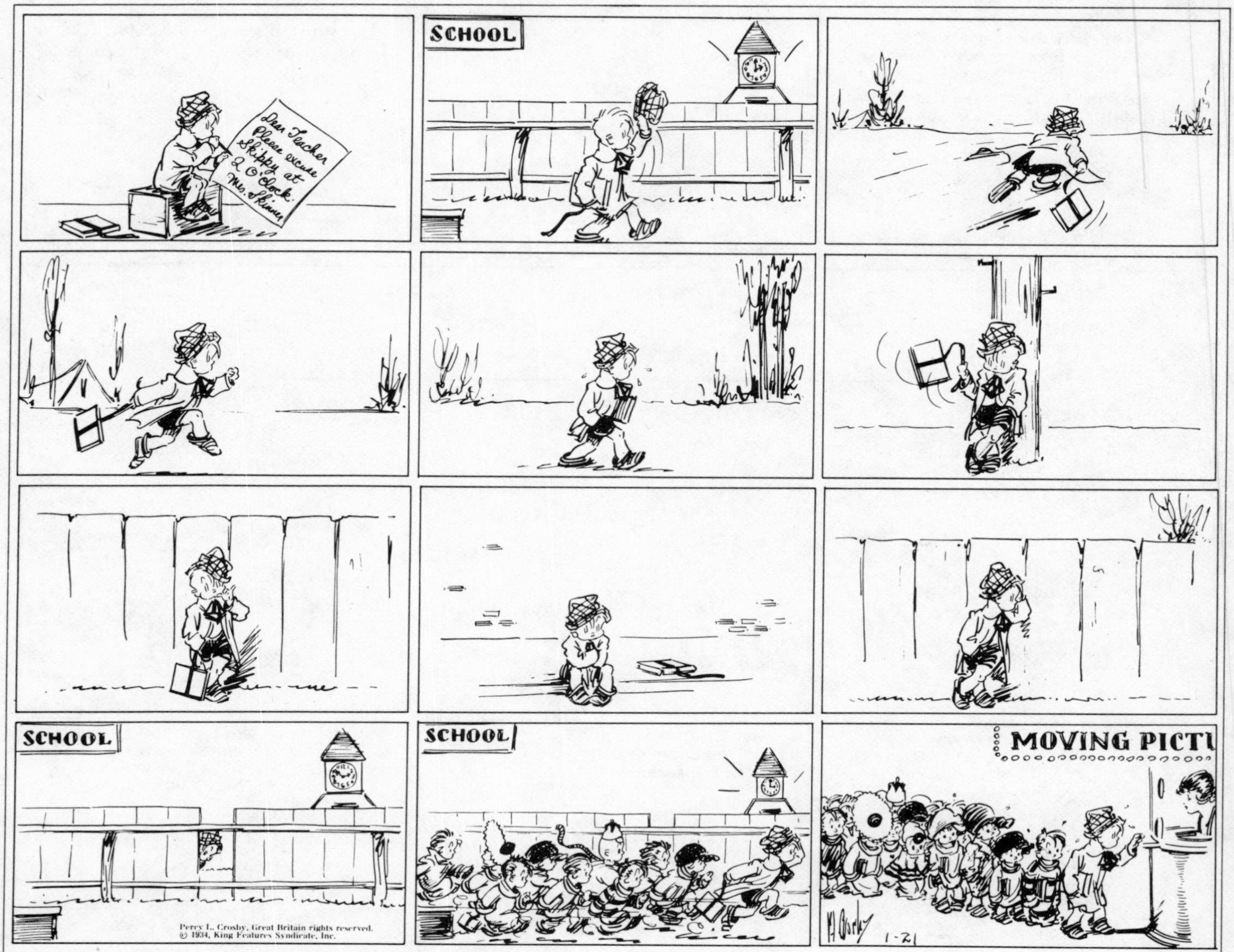
Dear Teacher
Please excuse
Skippy at
2 O'clock.
Mr. Skinner
SCHOOL
SCHOOL
SCHOOL
MOVING PICTU
Percy L. Crosby, Great Britain rights reserved.
© 1934, King Features Syndicate, Inc.
1-21

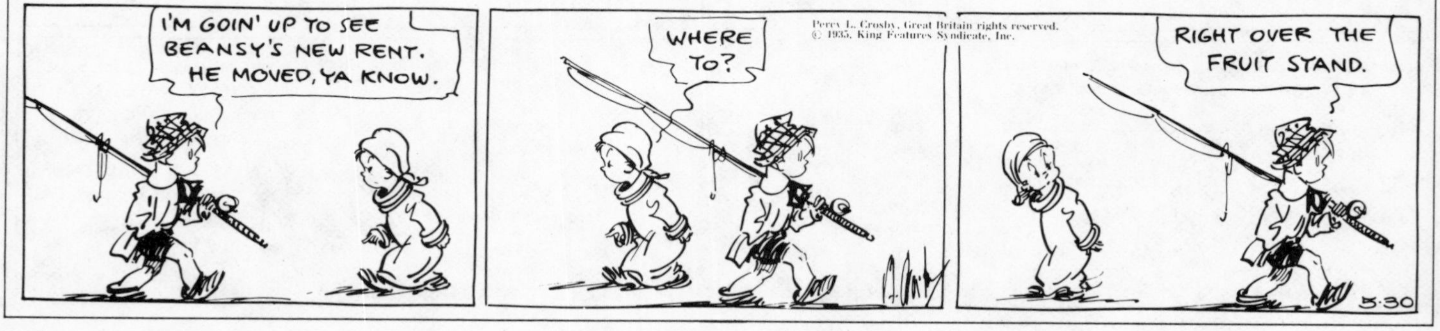
I'M GOIN' UP TO SEE BEANSY'S NEW RENT. HE MOVED, YA KNOW.
WHERE TO?
Percy L. Crosby, Great Britain rights reserved.
© 1935, King Features Syndicate, Inc.
RIGHT OVER THE FRUIT STAND.
5-30

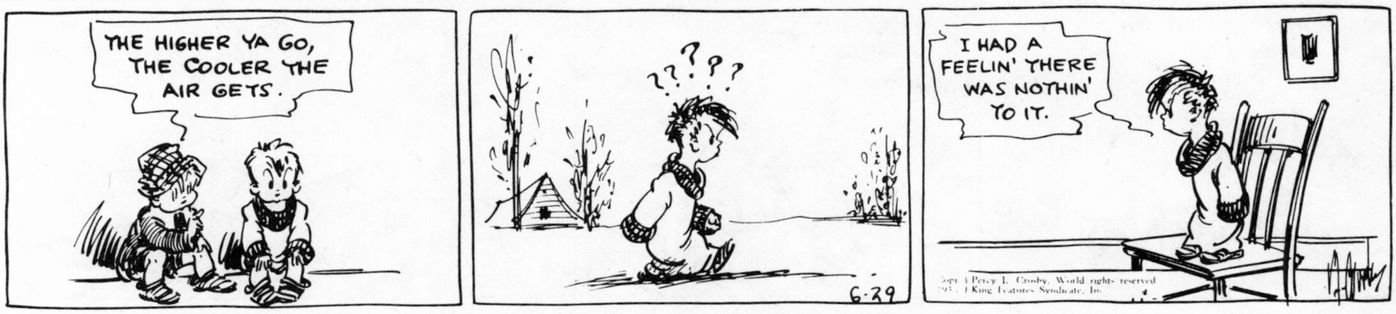
THE HIGHER YA GO, THE COOLER THE AIR GETS.
???
I HAD A FEELIN' THERE WAS NOTHIN' TO IT.
Percy L. Crosby, World rights reserved
King Features Syndicate, Inc
6-29

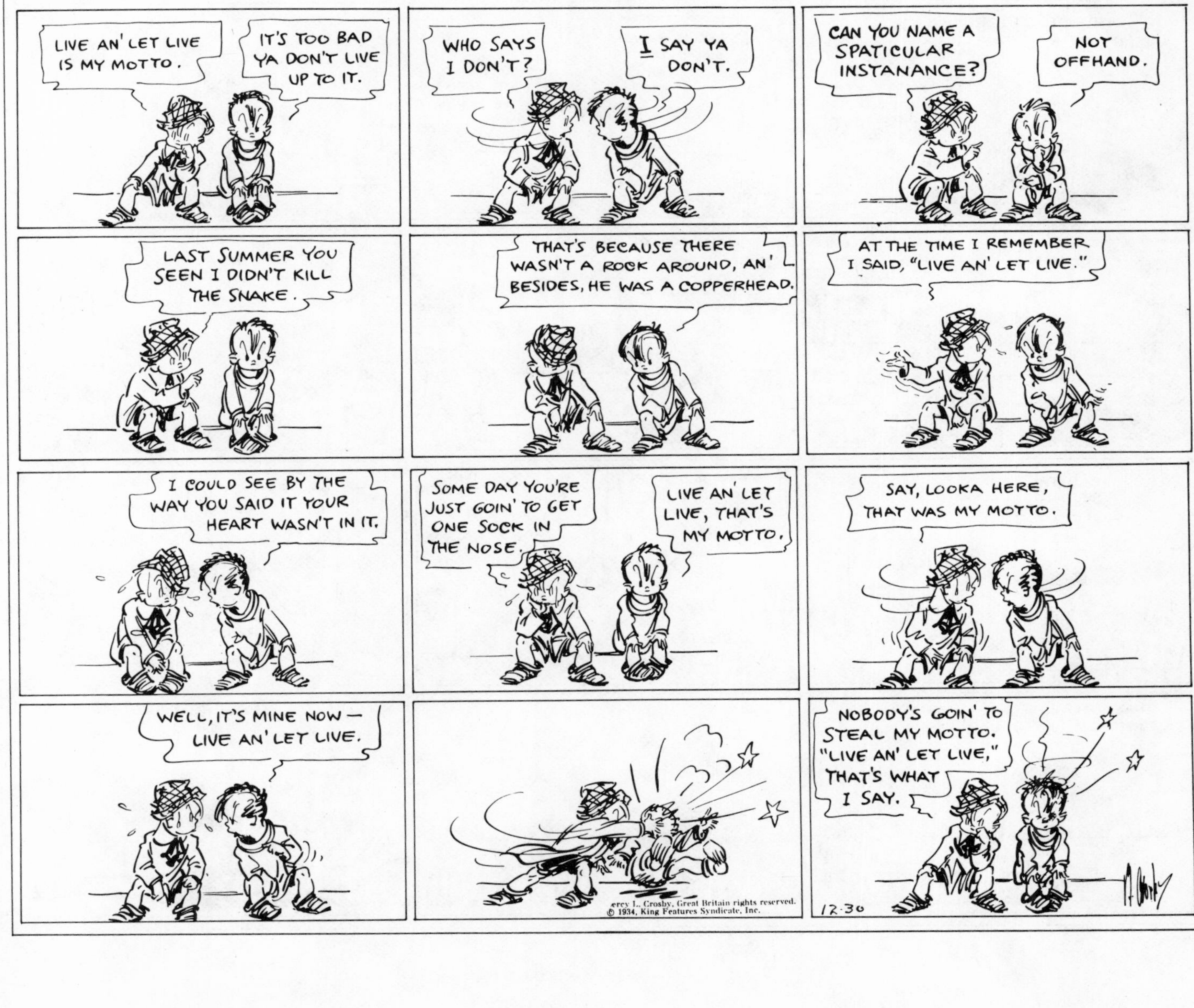
LIVE AN' LET LIVE IS MY MOTTO.
IT'S TOO BAD YA DON'T LIVE UP TO IT.
WHO SAYS I DON'T?
I SAY YA DON'T.
CAN YOU NAME A SPATICULAR INSTANANCE?
NOT OFFHAND.
LAST SUMMER YOU SEEN I DIDN'T KILL THE SNAKE.
THAT'S BECAUSE THERE WASN'T A ROCK AROUND, AN' BESIDES, HE WAS A COPPERHEAD.
AT THE TIME I REMEMBER I SAID, "LIVE AN' LET LIVE."
I COULD SEE BY THE WAY YOU SAID IT YOUR HEART WASN'T IN IT.
SOME DAY YOU'RE JUST GOIN' TO GET ONE SOCK IN THE NOSE.
LIVE AN' LET LIVE, THAT'S MY MOTTO.
SAY, LOOKA HERE, THAT WAS MY MOTTO.
WELL, IT'S MINE NOW — LIVE AN' LET LIVE.
ercy L. Crosby, Great Britain rights reserved.
© 1934, King Features Syndicate, Inc.
NOBODY'S GOIN' TO STEAL MY MOTTO. "LIVE AN' LET LIVE," THAT'S WHAT I SAY.
12-30

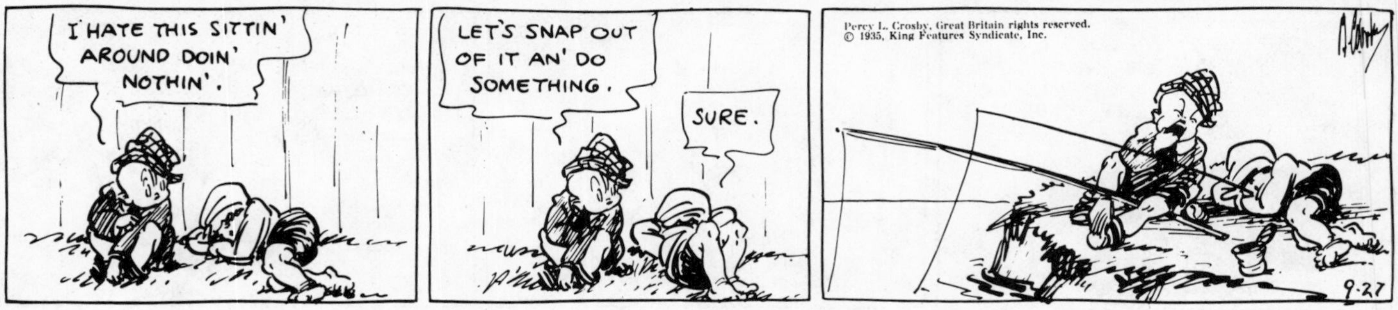
I HATE THIS SITTIN' AROUND DOIN' NOTHIN'.
LET'S SNAP OUT OF IT AN' DO SOMETHING.
SURE.
Percy L. Crosby, Great Britain rights reserved.
© 1935, King Features Syndicate, Inc.
9-27

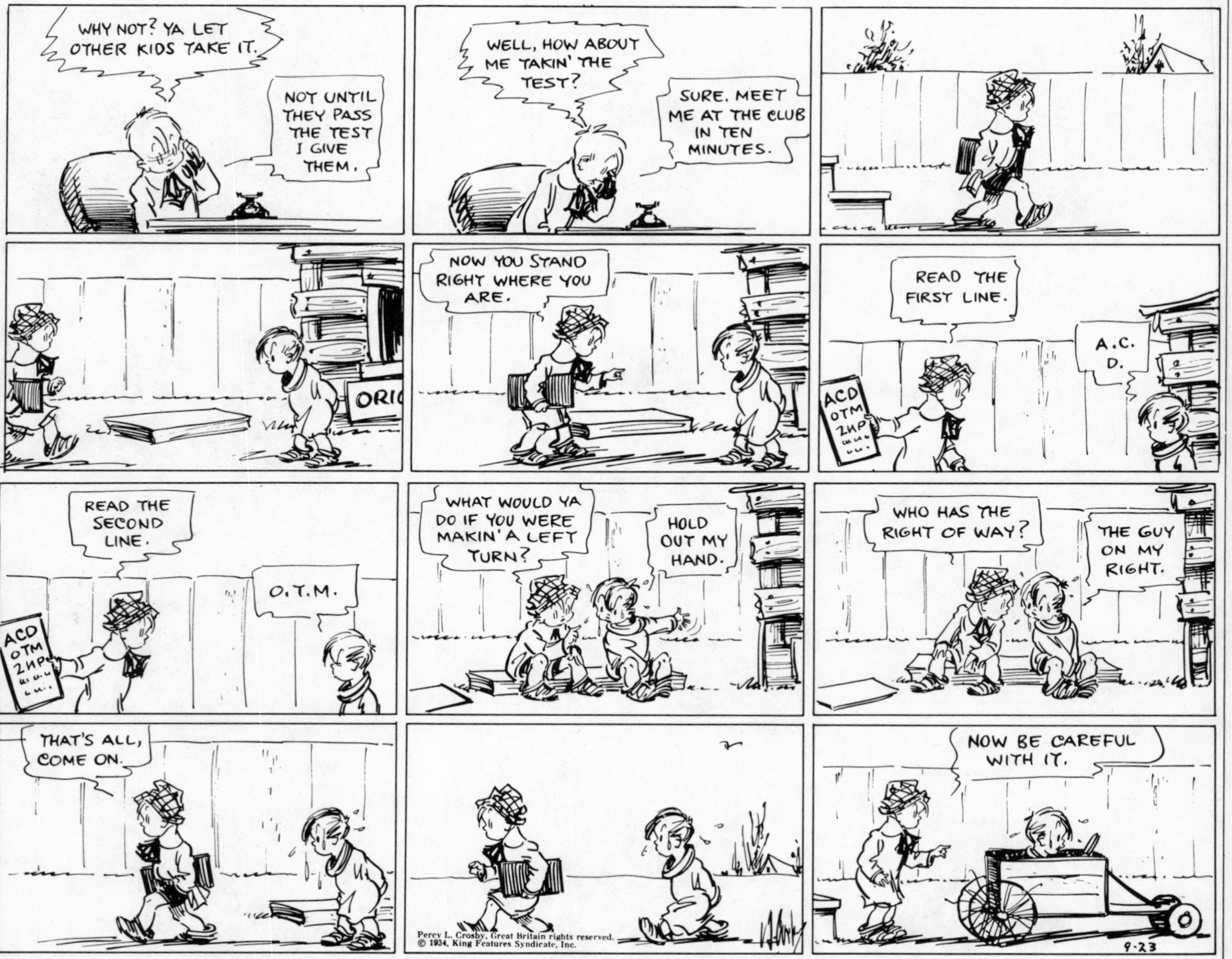
WHY NOT? YA LET OTHER KIDS TAKE IT.
NOT UNTIL THEY PASS THE TEST I GIVE THEM.
WELL, HOW ABOUT ME TAKIN' THE TEST?
SURE. MEET ME AT THE CLUB IN TEN MINUTES.
ORI
NOW YOU STAND RIGHT WHERE YOU ARE.
READ THE FIRST LINE.
A. C. D.
ACD OTM 2HP
READ THE SECOND LINE.
O. T. M.
WHAT WOULD YA DO IF YOU WERE MAKIN' A LEFT TURN?
HOLD OUT MY HAND.
WHO HAS THE RIGHT OF WAY?
THE GUY ON MY RIGHT.
THAT'S ALL, COME ON.
Percy L. Crosby, Great Britain rights reserved.
© 1934, King Features Syndicate, Inc.
NOW BE CAREFUL WITH IT.
9-23

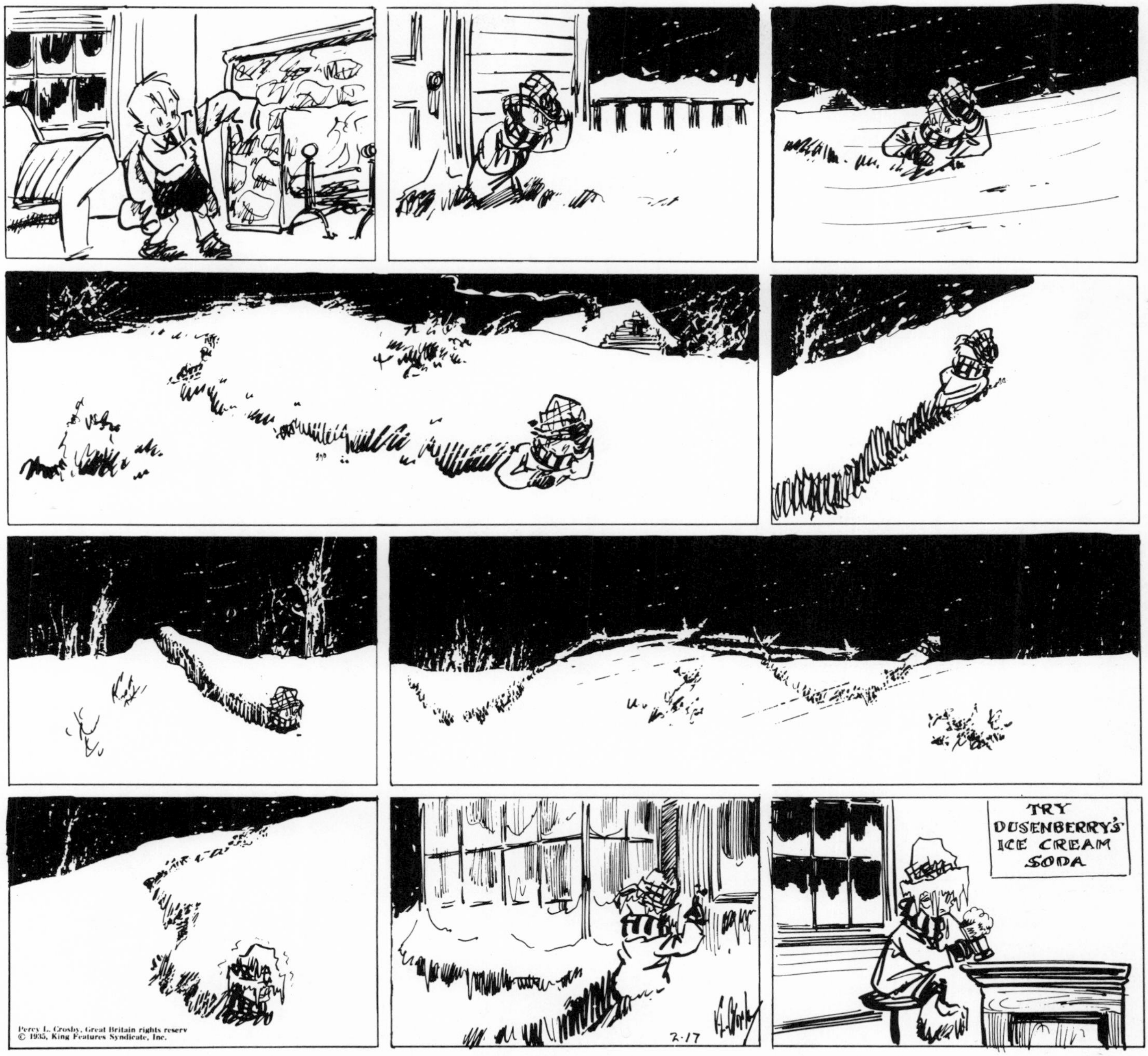
TRY DUSENBERRY'S ICE CREAM SODA
Percy L. Crosby, Great Britain rights reserv
© 1935, King Features Syndicate, Inc.
2·17

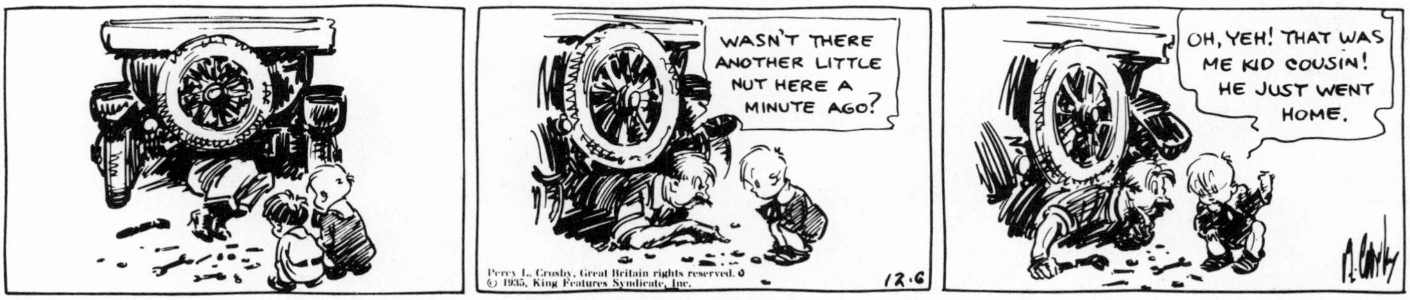
WASN'T THERE ANOTHER LITTLE NUT HERE A MINUTE AGO?
OH, YEH! THAT WAS ME KID COUSIN! HE JUST WENT HOME.
Percy L. Crosby, Great Britain rights reserved.
© 1935, King Features Syndicate, Inc.
12·6

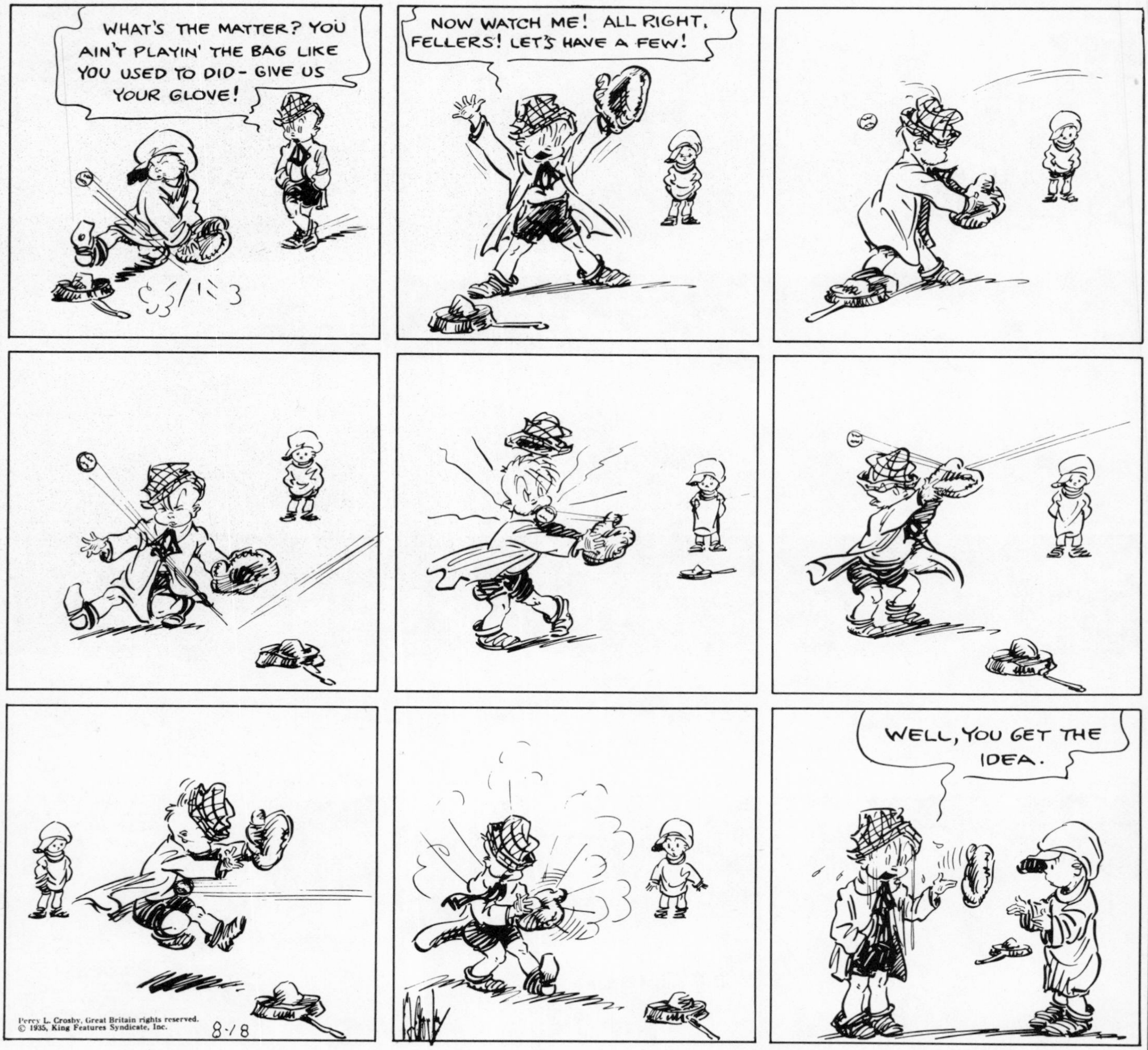
WHAT'S THE MATTER? YOU AIN'T PLAYIN' THE BAG LIKE YOU USED TO DID - GIVE US YOUR GLOVE!
NOW WATCH ME! ALL RIGHT, FELLERS! LET'S HAVE A FEW!
WELL, YOU GET THE IDEA.
Percy L. Crosby, Great Britain rights reserved.
© 1935, King Features Syndicate, Inc.
8-18

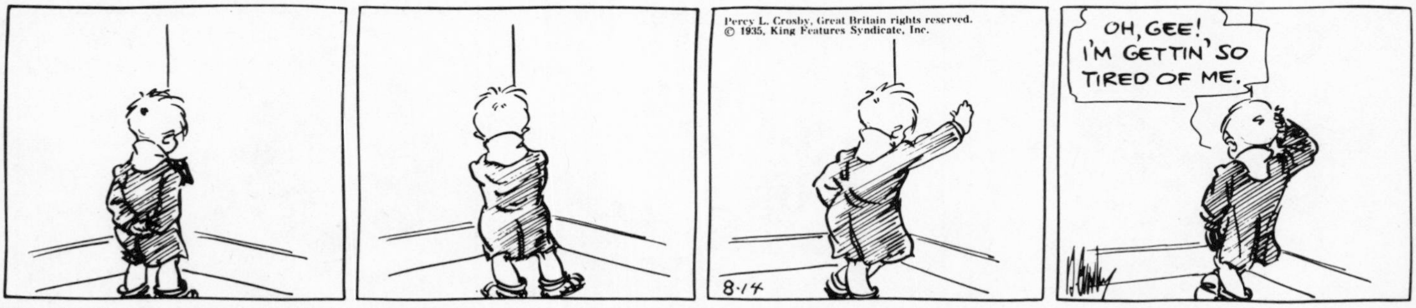
Percy L. Crosby, Great Britain rights reserved.
© 1935, King Features Syndicate, Inc.
8-14
OH, GEE! I'M GETTIN' SO TIRED OF ME.

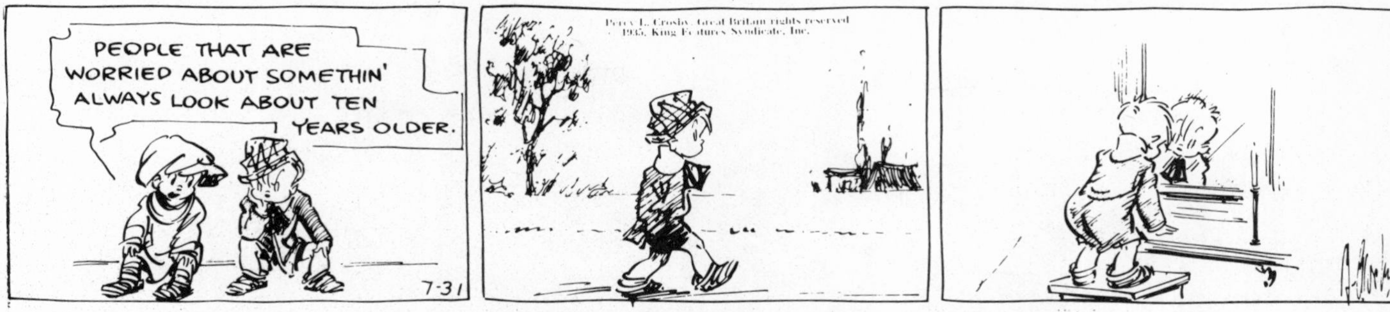
PEOPLE THAT ARE WORRIED ABOUT SOMETHIN' ALWAYS LOOK ABOUT TEN YEARS OLDER.
7-31
Percy L. Crosby, Great Britain rights reserved © 1935, King Features Syndicate, Inc.

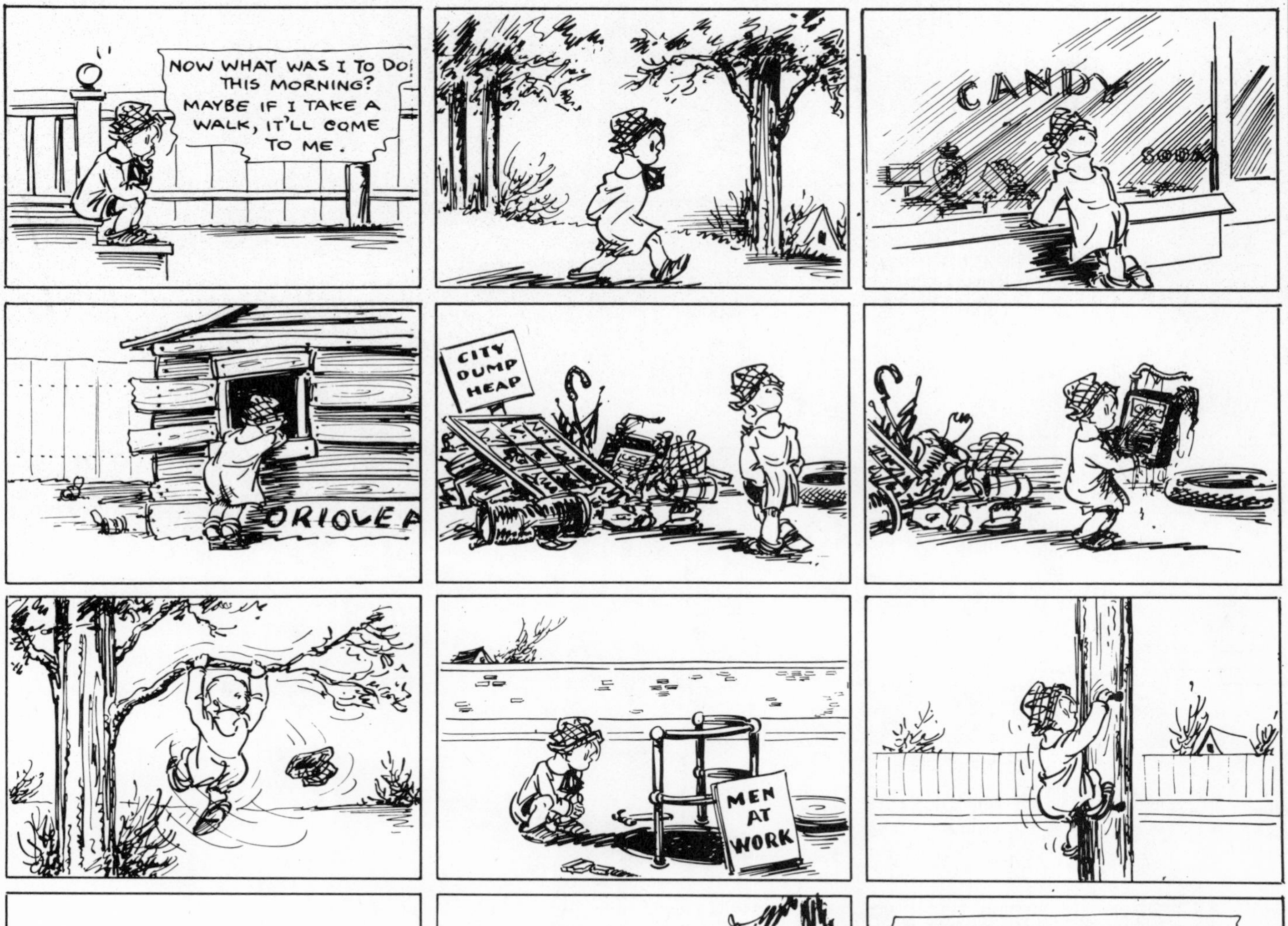
NOW WHAT WAS I TO DO THIS MORNING? MAYBE IF I TAKE A WALK, IT'LL COME TO ME.
CANDY
CITY DUMP HEAP
MEN AT WORK
WHAT DID I COME OUT HERE FOR, ANYWAY?
Percy L. Crosby, Great Britain rights © 1935, King Features Syndicate, Inc.
4-28

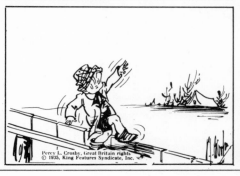

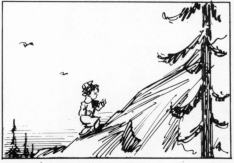

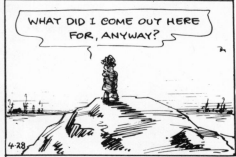

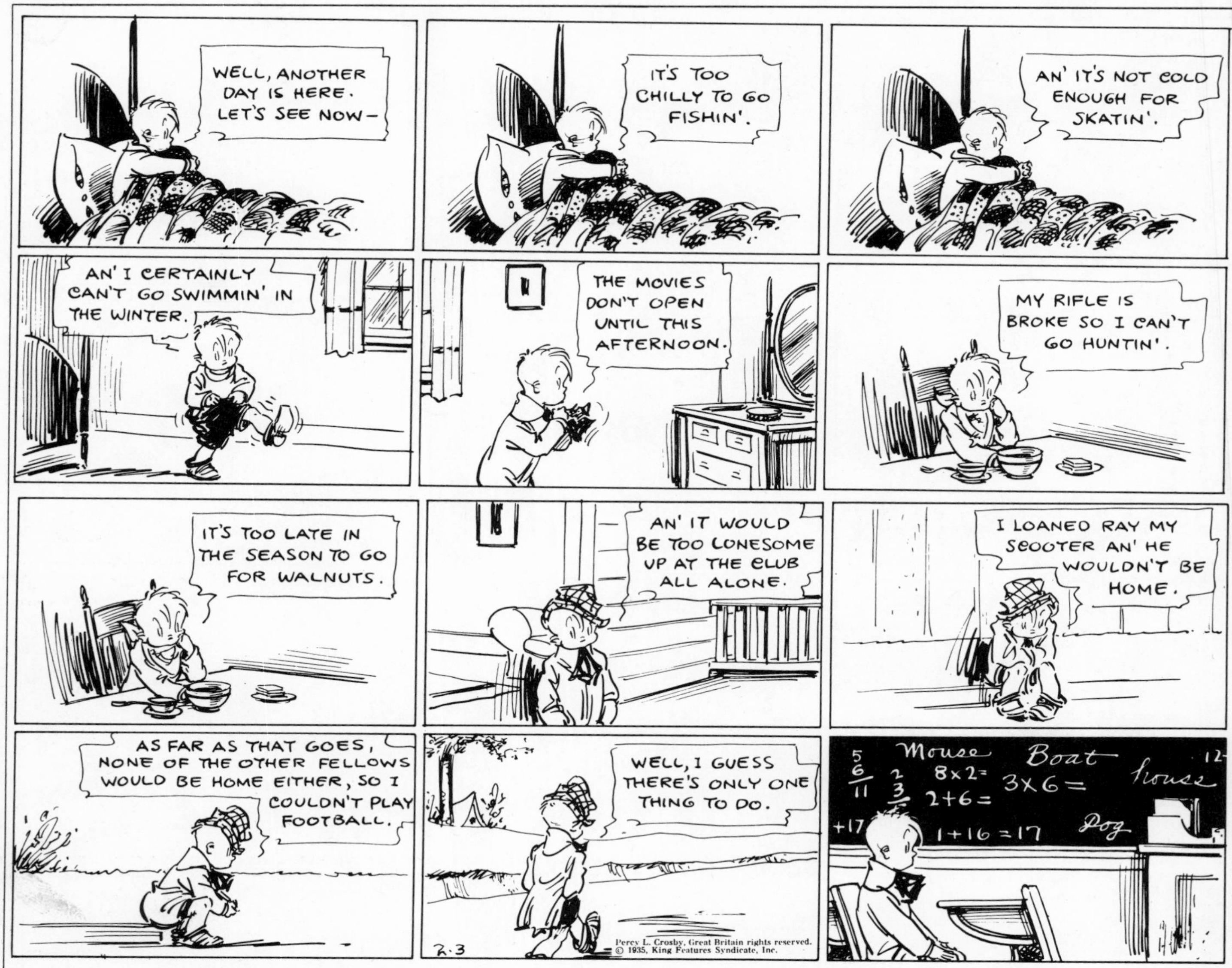
WELL, ANOTHER DAY IS HERE. LET'S SEE NOW—
IT'S TOO CHILLY TO GO FISHIN'.
AN' IT'S NOT COLD ENOUGH FOR SKATIN'.
AN' I CERTAINLY CAN'T GO SWIMMIN' IN THE WINTER.
THE MOVIES DON'T OPEN UNTIL THIS AFTERNOON.
MY RIFLE IS BROKE SO I CAN'T GO HUNTIN'.
IT'S TOO LATE IN THE SEASON TO GO FOR WALNUTS.
AN' IT WOULD BE TOO LONESOME UP AT THE CLUB ALL ALONE.
I LOANED RAY MY SCOOTER AN' HE WOULDN'T BE HOME.
AS FAR AS THAT GOES, NONE OF THE OTHER FELLOWS WOULD BE HOME EITHER, SO I COULDN'T PLAY FOOTBALL.
WELL, I GUESS THERE'S ONLY ONE THING TO DO.
2·3
Percy L. Crosby, Great Britain rights reserved.
© 1935, King Features Syndicate, Inc.
Mouse
Boat
House
Dog
8x2=
3x6=
2+6=
1+16=17

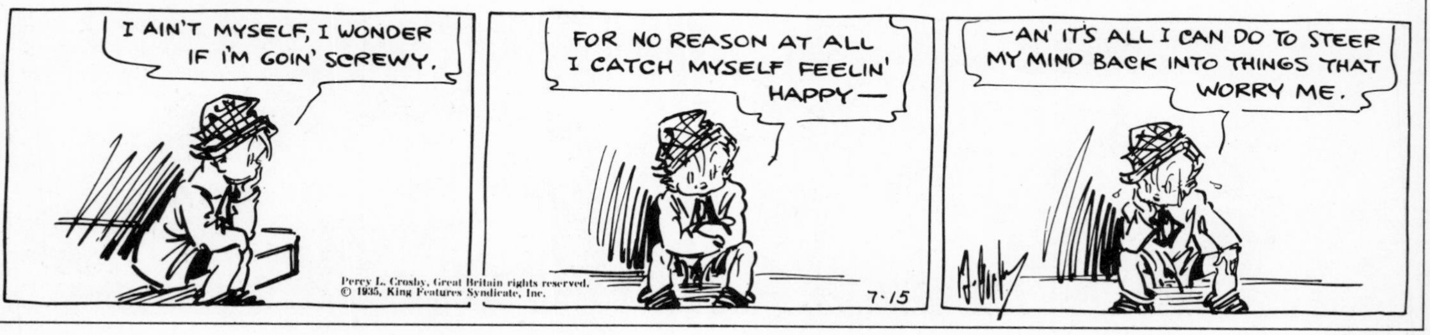
I AIN'T MYSELF, I WONDER IF I'M GOIN' SCREWY.
FOR NO REASON AT ALL I CATCH MYSELF FEELIN' HAPPY—
—AN' IT'S ALL I CAN DO TO STEER MY MIND BACK INTO THINGS THAT WORRY ME.
Percy L. Crosby, Great Britain rights reserved.
© 1935, King Features Syndicate, Inc.
7·15

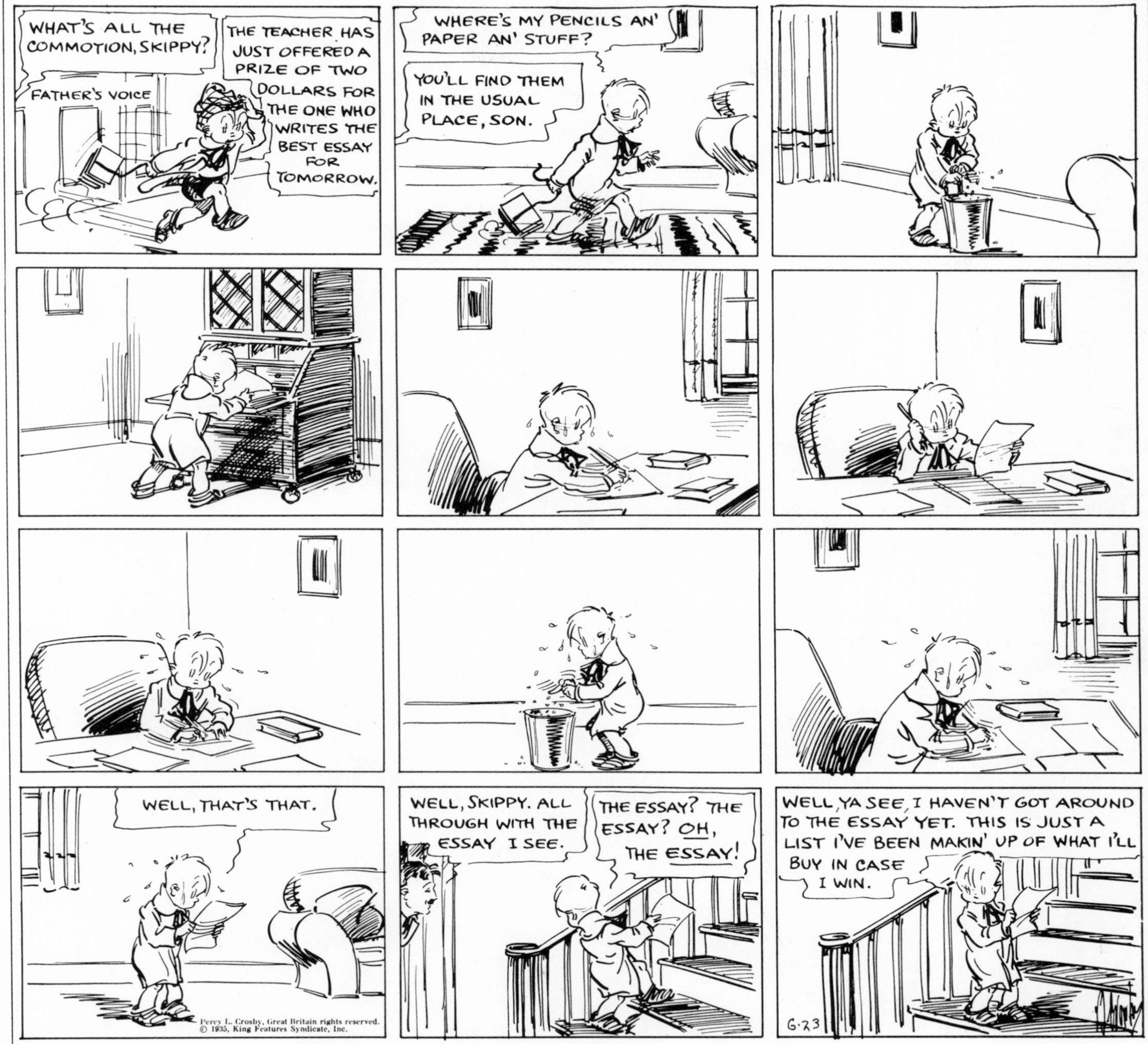
WHAT'S ALL THE COMMOTION, SKIPPY?
FATHER'S VOICE
THE TEACHER HAS JUST OFFERED A PRIZE OF TWO DOLLARS FOR THE ONE WHO WRITES THE BEST ESSAY FOR TOMORROW.
WHERE'S MY PENCILS AN' PAPER AN' STUFF?
YOU'LL FIND THEM IN THE USUAL PLACE, SON.
WELL, THAT'S THAT.
WELL, SKIPPY. ALL THROUGH WITH THE ESSAY I SEE.
THE ESSAY? THE ESSAY? OH, THE ESSAY!
WELL, YA SEE, I HAVEN'T GOT AROUND TO THE ESSAY YET. THIS IS JUST A LIST I'VE BEEN MAKIN' UP OF WHAT I'LL BUY IN CASE I WIN.
Percy L. Crosby, Great Britain rights reserved.
© 1935, King Features Syndicate, Inc.
6·23

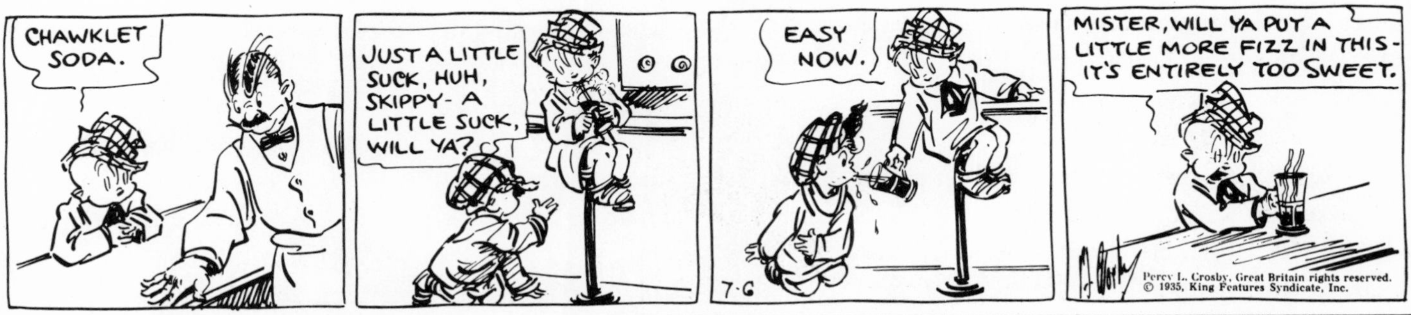
CHAWKLET SODA.
JUST A LITTLE SUCK, HUH, SKIPPY- A LITTLE SUCK, WILL YA?
EASY NOW.
7·6
MISTER, WILL YA PUT A LITTLE MORE FIZZ IN THIS- IT'S ENTIRELY TOO SWEET.
Percy L. Crosby, Great Britain rights reserved.
© 1935, King Features Syndicate, Inc.

7 / KINGS PARK

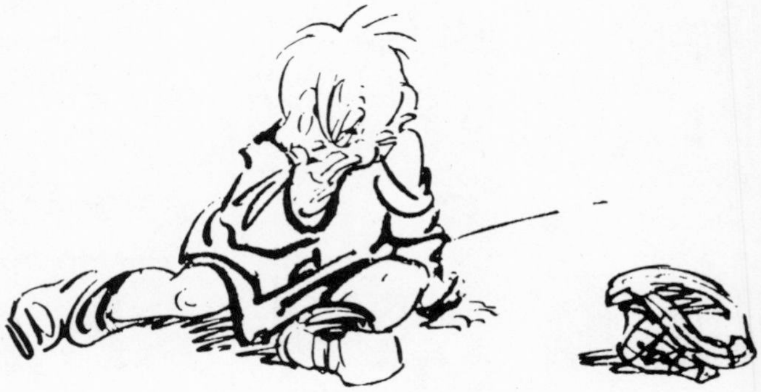

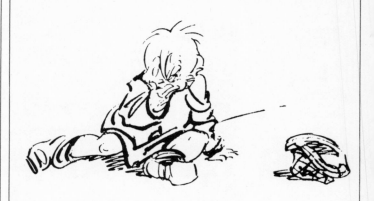

"I was all alone here on Christmas Eve in 1949—my first Christmas of confinement, and the hideous aspect of it all is too terrible to relate," Crosby wrote in a memoir. His sudden and stunning ruin left him bewildered and almost smothered his spirit. "I began to take myself apart wondering how everything had gone wrong." But within months, he was writing Carolyn of plans for the future. He was eager to resume his career, and most of all to finish several novels. He clearly anticipated a complete recovery and an early release. Soon he found to his dismay that a mental institution was much like communism: "It was easy to get into the place, but getting out was similar to running a race through a briared garden maze." This time the maze had no exit.

Percy Crosby was diagnosed "paranoid schizophrenic." A later report described him as being forever litigious and expressing delusional trends involving high government officials. Crosby's litany of persecutors included President Franklin D. Roosevelt, the Federal Bureau of Investigation and J. Edgar Hoover, the Internal Revenue Service, Al Capone and other racketeers, and Skippy peanut butter, among others. ("The steal of Skippy peanut butter," as Crosby termed it, became one of his most obsessive complaints. For years he had been in litigation with the manufacturer, claiming infringement of the Skippy trademark, registered by Crosby on March 15, 1923.) Such seemingly wild and bizarre postulations, coupled with his suicide attempt, led to the diagnosis.

Tragic questions remain unanswered about Crosby's years at Kings Park. There is reason to believe that today Crosby would either not be committed, or at the least would not be confined for sixteen years. In retrospect, there is a question about the correctness of his diagnosis. This involves, in part, a judgment as to the extent that his "delusions" correspond to reality. An investigation would have established that some of his fears—surveillance by the FBI, the IRS campaign, Skippy peanut butter—had some substance. In the light of what became known in the 1970s about actions taken by J. Edgar Hoover and the FBI in the surveillance, illegal wiretapping, violation of postal laws, and other measures directed toward what they perceived as "enemies of the state," it is not unreasonable to speculate that Crosby's "threats" in the Washington papers might have earned such attention from Hoover. Certainly, Crosby's fears would not now be so readily described as paranoia as they were then.

The vague definitions of mental illnesses and the inexact practice of clinical diagnosis at that time often led to abuse. Studies have established that, every year, thousands of sane men and women were wrongfully committed. In his autobiography, *Insanity, Inside Out*, Kenneth Donaldson, a young man in Florida who liked to send letters about foreign policy to the White House, describes being institutionalized after diagnosis as a "schizophrenic-reacting paranoid type." For years he also experienced persecutory fears that people were after him, just as Crosby did. It took Donaldson fifteen years to prove he was unjustly committed. Crosby's productivity and capacity to create works of merit, as well as reports of his generally normal demeanor, suggest that he might have been a similar victim. Today, since the Supreme Court's 1975 ruling that neither eccentricity nor public unease with a person's behavior can justify involuntary confinement, his legal redress would almost certainly be facilitated.

Artistic genius is an enigma; it cannot be understood with normal psychology. When an artist searches for creative solitude, it can be misunderstood as an "unhealthy withdrawal." Intense discipline in his work can be seen as "compulsion," tension as "anxiety depression," and detachment as "narcissism." One psychoanalyst maintains that at times the "demon" in an artist is so strong that he permanently hovers near what normal people call insanity. Also, a genius frequently has a recuperative power whereby he is able to survive crises that would crush a normal human being.

Crosby's suicide attempt precipitated his confinement. Having suffered a series of severe emotional stresses—the destruction of his marriage; the loss of his home, children, and fortune; and, perhaps most profound for his ego, the death of Skippy—the suicide attempt, rather than evidence of a long-developed psychotic structure, might have been simply an understandable reaction. Also, Crosby had been drinking heavily before his breakdown, which probably aggravated his despair.

Thrown into a world of isolation such as he had never known before, Crosby somehow found the means for survival. He began to write "to save myself from being gobbled up by that monster—loneliness." His work became his therapy. He got back to drawing some of his favorite subjects: dancers, skaters, horses. But never Skippy. Crosby's extensive writing at Kings Park was lucid and often brilliant, and is striking evidence of his ability to recover and function. He made no other suicide attempt, even though he was permitted scissors and razor blades for use in his drawing.

Crosby had to fight not only his depression and melancholia, but also the very environment which was supposed to aid his recovery. Many of the inmates and even the staff never knew that he was *Skippy*'s creator, or if they heard were disbelieving. Most referred to him as "the author." Crosby's Social Security and war compensation for his injury provided him with a small room, barely large enough for a bed and a taboret. "The meager light in the room is such that any patch of daylight has to be cherished." The television blasted from breakfast to lights-out at night, apparently for its stupefying effect on the patients, and perhaps to drown out the screams and fights that echoed through the halls. When told that "TV is a boon," Crosby answered, "Only to a loon or a goon." For one whose tolerance of background sounds to his work had been limited to his favorite symphonies, the effect of the din was shattering. "I tried to draw under such bedlam, but soon realized under such uncalled for cacophony that my brush strokes were going awry." Writing was even more difficult. In desperation, Crosby persuaded a sympathetic attendant to allow him into the mess room after curfew. There, for years, Crosby would write and draw through the night at a cafeteria table. But this privilege, too, was finally cut off with a change in the staff.

Crosby began to be viewed by personnel and patients alike as an eccentric among eccentrics. They didn't understand his work, let alone his dedication to it. He was constantly plagued by taunts—and worse. He complained of beatings by personnel and attacks by inmates. Lights were turned on and off repeatedly while he was writing or drawing. His door was slammed incessantly. Most frustrating of all, there were constant thefts: his precious books, his drawings, his art supplies. He often found hundreds of his meticulously hand-lettered manuscript pages thrown helter-skelter around the room, "and nothing could be worse to a creator—even Hell!" He finally obtained a footlocker in which to keep his treasured manuscripts, and from then on he kept its key on a string tied around his neck. Even then, the locker was rifled from time to time. He lost his last few prized possessions: an inscribed gold watch presented by the men of his platoon in World War I, and a ring with the Crosby crest which he had proudly used to wax-seal his important papers. (Appropriately for Crosby, the crest included, in addition to the symbols of knighthood and heraldry, the motto: *Indignante florebit justus invidia. The just man shall flourish, though envy be indignant.*)

Crosby began to send his manuscripts to publishers and magazines. In what must have been especially galling for the lifetime foe of censorship, he had to hand over any mail to the superintendent for screening. From his meager resource of twenty dollars a month for spending money, Crosby began to pay attendants to mail his letters and manuscripts from outside the institution. Only when he received an answer did he know whether in fact the letters had been mailed. There is evidence to believe that many were not, especially those with any criticism of the institution, and Crosby frequently expressed such feelings about the place in his poetry and prose. Many submissions evoked no response, and others only routine rejection slips. Only rarely did anyone recognize the name Percy Crosby.

Crosby began to despair of ever having his work published while he was institutionalized. He noted: "It is useless to send my stories, essays, poems, to any publisher or magazine while I have this address." He resigned himself to being an author without a reader. Nor was there anyone with whom he could converse about his work, art, and literature. So Crosby invented a reader and made him a character in many of his stories. He was Crosby's alter ego, with whom he often engaged in Socratic-like dialogue.

"With the props knocked from under you, what did you do to pass the time? How did you ever keep from going mad?"

"I sat down and started writing another book, making believe I had a reader."

At another point, he wrote, "Since I have no reader, I had to laugh at the books myself, and that's the most dangerous thing a professional humorist can do!" But even under the miserable circumstances of Kings Park, Crosby's irrepressible sense of humor didn't desert him. He created the character of Jester Jargon, a kind of comic-tragic narrator, who appears in *A Book of Terse, Light Verse: Could Anything Be Worse?*, for which Crosby did a frontispiece drawing of a crying jester. In one charming fantasy in the tradition of Palmer Cox's *Brownies*, Crosby spun out an allegory of prison life and censorship with the imposing title "The Commissioner of the Fairy Police Escorts the Officers of the Super-Surveillance Society through the Prison of Fairyland." The prison system was so good that rubber bands had to be installed on the prison walls to flip back riffraff fairies attempting to break *into* jail. Another story, a satire centered on the

The Artist Confined

Crosby continued to draw throughout his years at Kings Park. Frequently he sketched his fellow inmates—sad, lonely men with dead expressions and catatonic stares. His favorite subjects, however, remained his beloved horses, dancers, and athletes—captured in feverish swirls of movement. Occasionally in his dim prison he would adorn a manuscript with a lone gull, flying free in a long, graceful arc.

then hotly debated issue of prayers in school, resurrected the character of the teacher, Miss Larkin, from Crosby's *Skippy* novel. In an episode somewhat salacious for the rather prudish Crosby, the school's janitor inadvertently uses quick-drying glue when repainting the faculty toilet seat, and Miss Larkin finds herself embarrassingly stuck. Plumbers have to hacksaw off the entire toilet and carry the mortified Miss Larkin, still affixed to the porcelain facility (although delicately shrouded by a sheet), through the classroom. As she passes by, the principal commands the children to bow their heads and pray for Miss Larkin. Thus Crosby made the point that at certain times prayers may be needed in the school.

Crosby would often write to Carolyn, pleading to be taken home. "The doctors will be glad to release me if you sign me out and take full responsibility." Such a possibility was verified by at least one friend who visited Crosby at Kings Park, but Carolyn, a diabetic, may simply have been unable to assume the burden. Her own health was beginning to deteriorate, and she was working every day as a dietitian from 5:30 A.M. Crosby wrote to friends and acquaintances pleading for a lawyer to help him get out, but to no avail. So complete was his break with the outside world that Crosby's children did not know that he was still alive. His daughters Barbara and Joan had graduated from Vassar, Carol from the Rhode Island School of Design, and his son, Skip, a graduate of Dartmouth and Harvard, had become a geologist. In desperation, Crosby sat down one day and penned a letter to his son. The boy had been nine years old when he had last seen him, and they had not communicated since. The letter read, in part: "I did that for my father—took him out of work and supported him until his death—will you not do the same for your father? It is *imperative* that you come to see me." In a touching addenda, Crosby carefully lettered a resume of his credits—books, exhibitions, awards, and excerpts from reviews of his work. According to Crosby's second wife, Dale, it was never received. Crosby set down his bitterness: "Since this philosopher has been railroaded for 'the insanity of common sense,' I never saw my four children again, and that's twenty years—twenty long years!"

The years went by, but Crosby never lost hope for his eventual release. The uncertainty became the greatest horror. "Confined in an insane asylum, unjustly committed, is far worse than prison," Crosby wrote, "for the convicts know when they are going to be released. . . . God's 'delays' are worse than God's 'denials.'" But his faith in that God seemed to sustain him. "I'm holding on with only a shred of hope that God above will not let me down." But after long years, even that faith was questioned: "Ten long, weary years in jail and hope becomes threadbare—praise God from whom all blessings flow: *Why?* What blessings?"

Crosby was now almost completely cut off and forgotten. The infrequent visits from Carolyn ceased. Her fragile health now made the arduous trip to Long Island impossible. There were rare visits from one or two friends and his sisters—Ethel, who now lived in Florida, and Gladys, in upstate New York. What such visits can mean to someone confined like Crosby is seen in a letter to Gladys: "Tell Ethel not to feel out of place if, when she arrives, my eyes focus on her hands to see if she has a thermos bottle with coffee and jelly doughnuts to match. In a place like this (and you'd be surprised how easy it is to become a life member) the one confined never looks at the face of the visitor. Just the hands."

Rube Goldberg was one of the few cartoonists to write Crosby and one of the very few to visit him at Kings Park. They spoke of old times, and Goldberg later recalled that Percy, so appreciative of the visit, broke down and cried. Goldberg wondered, too, why Percy remained there. He seemed so perfectly normal. Edward Kuekes, a noted political cartoonist, never knew Crosby, but learning of his illness he wrote a kind and supportive letter expressing his lifelong admiration for Crosby's work. Crosby was deeply touched and wrote in reply: "It was truly the finest sporting gesture on your part to write such a heartwarming letter to me when our positions are in complete reverse, especially since you won the 1953 Pulitzer Prize accolade. My deep gratitude to you cannot be expressed in suitable words, except to say that your letter is the most benevolent event that has happened in my controlled stay here . . ."

Throughout the years, Crosby continued to work on what he referred to as his "Opus," an ambitious series of books on the arts that he now considered would be his life's major achievement. But the obstacles seemed insurmountable. At one point, he wrote in his journal: "I cannot go on with Opus for I am stopped on the Book of Art because I have to go to the Metropolitan Museum to see Rembrandt, da Vinci, Michelangelo again . . . or to the library for research. . . . *I want to complete it so much—so very much!*" If he succeeded in obtaining a reference book, it would soon be stolen, leaving him to rely on his memory. And a remarkable memory it was. For one whose formal education had ended in his sophomore year of high school, the extent of Crosby's knowledge and power of recall was extraordinary. In addition to the book of art, Crosby's "Opus" included separate books of philosophy (ranging from the Greeks to Kant and Descartes), literature (including critiques of all the major figures such as Shakespeare, Tolstoy, and Ibsen), dance, drama, poetry, and music.

At times he threatened to destroy all his work out of frustration. But he continued to write on, and his copybooks and manuscripts began to fill the battered trunk. In addition to his "Opus," there were numerous novels. Several were based on his World War I experiences. One of great length continued the life of Skippy as he grew to manhood. There were also short stories, essays, political analyses, and books of poetry. On the cover of *Songs of Hope and Comfort*, Crosby noted, "My last book of poems." They were intended for women in need of solace, those who were ill and dying, or just lonely, women with whom Crosby must now have identified.

Another anniversary of Crosby's confinement drew near. "*To those imprisoned, Christmas is a Christ-awful day!*" Crosby wrote. In his journal, one passage gave voice to Crosby's continuing agony:

It's heartbreaking to watch the iron rain coming down—ever pouring down—ever pouring down—day after day—week after week and month after month, and another year goes snail-stepping by. Then the long, weary nights, split by screams and yells, where the one confined grips the bars and sees the stars all blinking to keep back the tears. *Truly, it is like being slowly drowned in quicksand, knowing in your heart that genius is slowly but surely being smothered. Terrible as nine hours on the cross must have been, the slow, deadly torture of just going down and down can be worse. For eleven years these feet never have touched the grass.*

Many of Crosby's stories were based on his observations of the inmates at Kings Park. One story in *Jester Jargon* is a bitter account of a patient's unfaithful, scheming wife, who keeps her husband in an institution. The husband bravely keeps up the pretense of their mutual love to his fellow inmates. One visiting day, he dresses up in his best and waits patiently all day, but the wife fails to come. Unable to face the truth, he commits suicide. One of the friends muses: "All these places are just husband-shedding carnivals!" It was a common characterization by the inmates of Kings Park, and one that Crosby began to accept as the reason for his own confinement.

Carolyn Crosby died on November 8, 1959, and with her Crosby's hopes for eventual freedom. "Now sixty-eight years old," he noted in his journal, "and I'm on the toboggan to the grave." Another entry read, "If it be my fate to be buried in Potter's Field with a blanket epitaph, I can still laugh . . . I have no complaint. . . . Mozart was buried in a pauper's field, and to this day his body has never been found."

Unaccountably, Crosby was moved from his small room to an open yard of forty men. He wrote bitterly: "All drawings, paintings, and even dictionary taken. . . . Only a chair and tiny table, comb, brush and empty bed. . . . From six A.M. to eleven P.M., all one has to see are vacant stares." Amazingly, he somehow managed to continue to write and draw despite the Kafka-like world that surrounded him. There was a noticeable change in his art, however. He began to sketch anguished portraits of his fellow inmates that remind one of Daumier, or a screaming head in the manner of Munch. Several watercolors, landscapes of tortured trees and swirling skies, are eerie in their resemblance to Van Gogh. The screamers, catatonics, and schizophrenics were a reality that could fulfill a paranoid nightmare. They took over Crosby's art, and finally his writing. There now seemed to be a disintegration of his personality. Contrary to his lifelong beliefs, anti-Semitism motivated the characterization of some of those he blamed for past injustices. His health slowly failed and he developed a severe pathology of the heart. He was subject to hemorrhaging, and often drawings or pads would be soaked with blood. Even so, hope occasionally flickered: "Will help ever, ever come? I wonder. Even writing this, a brainless attendant ever pounces on me with taunts, but I'm still at the helm in a strong sea." He set down a Christmas list of things he most wanted: "Fountain pen—ink—large bond paper for drawing dancers, divers, and horses—Need books, nothing to read—mince pie—copy of paintings—pipe—drawing tissue—eraser—carbon—yellow pads—watercolor brushes—stamps—if I'm to send out more stories. . . . My whole dream has been to contact a publisher for my books." There were no articles of clothing on the list, although Crosby, once a fastidious dresser, now had a wardrobe of one pair of threadbare pants. He was now truly a knight in tatters, but with his humor intact: "If my pants don't give way, I could pass for the Beau Brummel of the Bowery."

Crosby's life at Kings Park was long years of despair, frustration, and agony. Yet, at times, he achieved a fulfillment and forged an inner peace in that crucible of bitterness. His salvation was his belief in himself and his art and his God. He came to accept his fate with spirituality, and consoled himself with the thought that if he were really the "child of destiny," as his mother had been told, then Kings Park, too, was part of the grand design. While the years were wasted, anguished, and worse, in some ways they were his most productive and heroic. For sixteen years, Crosby personally triumphed over mental and physical illness, neglect, abuse, ridicule, and loneliness. He would not give in to petty tyrannies, real or imagined. He continued to wage his private war for truth and to satisfy an unquenchable fire of creativity.

On December 8, 1964, on his seventy-third birthday, Percy Crosby died at Kings Park Hospital. He was buried in Pine Lawn Veterans' Cemetery on Long Island.

HEY, THROW US IN ONE O' THEM SPARRIN' PARTNERS!
FOR A CHAMPEEN, SKIPPY, I THINK YA' SPEND TOO MUCH TIME ON THESE REHOISALS.
JULY 24

AN' NOW WHEN THAT NEW KID WHAT'S ALWAYS BRAGGIN' COMES ALONG, I'LL SEE HOW BRAVE HE IS.
WHOOO! WHOOO!
!?!
WHOO! WHOOO!
WHOO! WHOOO!!!
© 1931 Percy L. Crosby. Great Britain rights reserved. King Features Syndicate, Inc.
5-10
IT'S A FUNNY TIME TO BE DELIVERING LAUNDRY!

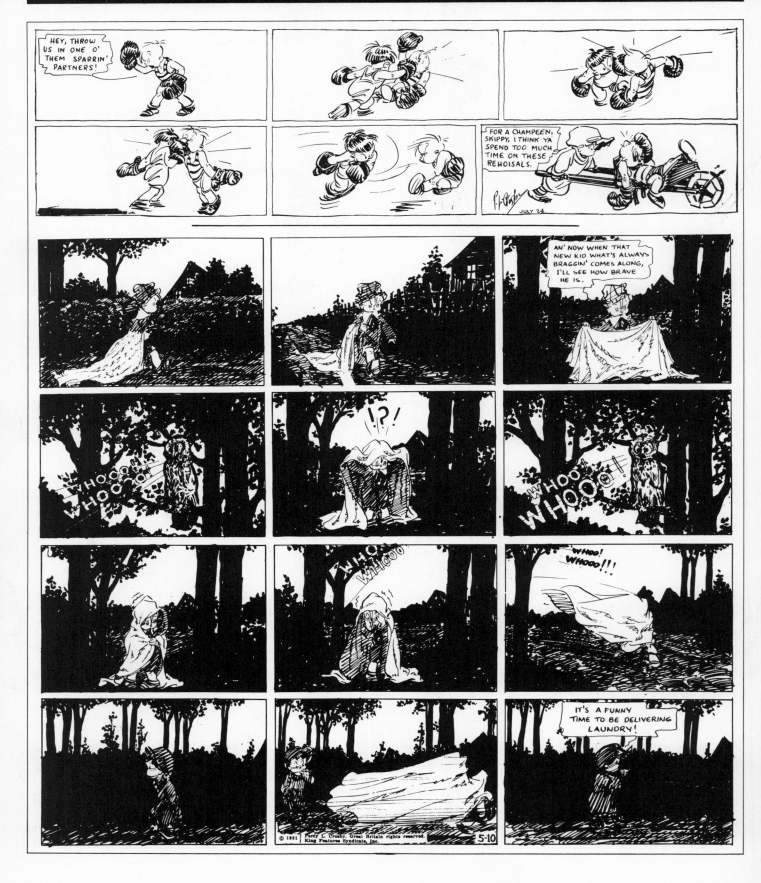

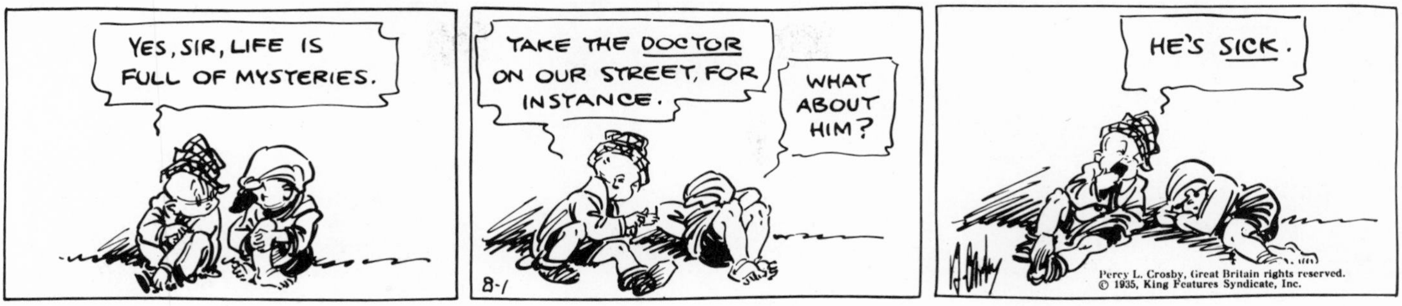
YES, SIR, LIFE IS FULL OF MYSTERIES.
TAKE THE DOCTOR ON OUR STREET, FOR INSTANCE.
WHAT ABOUT HIM?
8-1
HE'S SICK.
Percy L. Crosby, Great Britain rights reserved.
© 1935, King Features Syndicate, Inc.

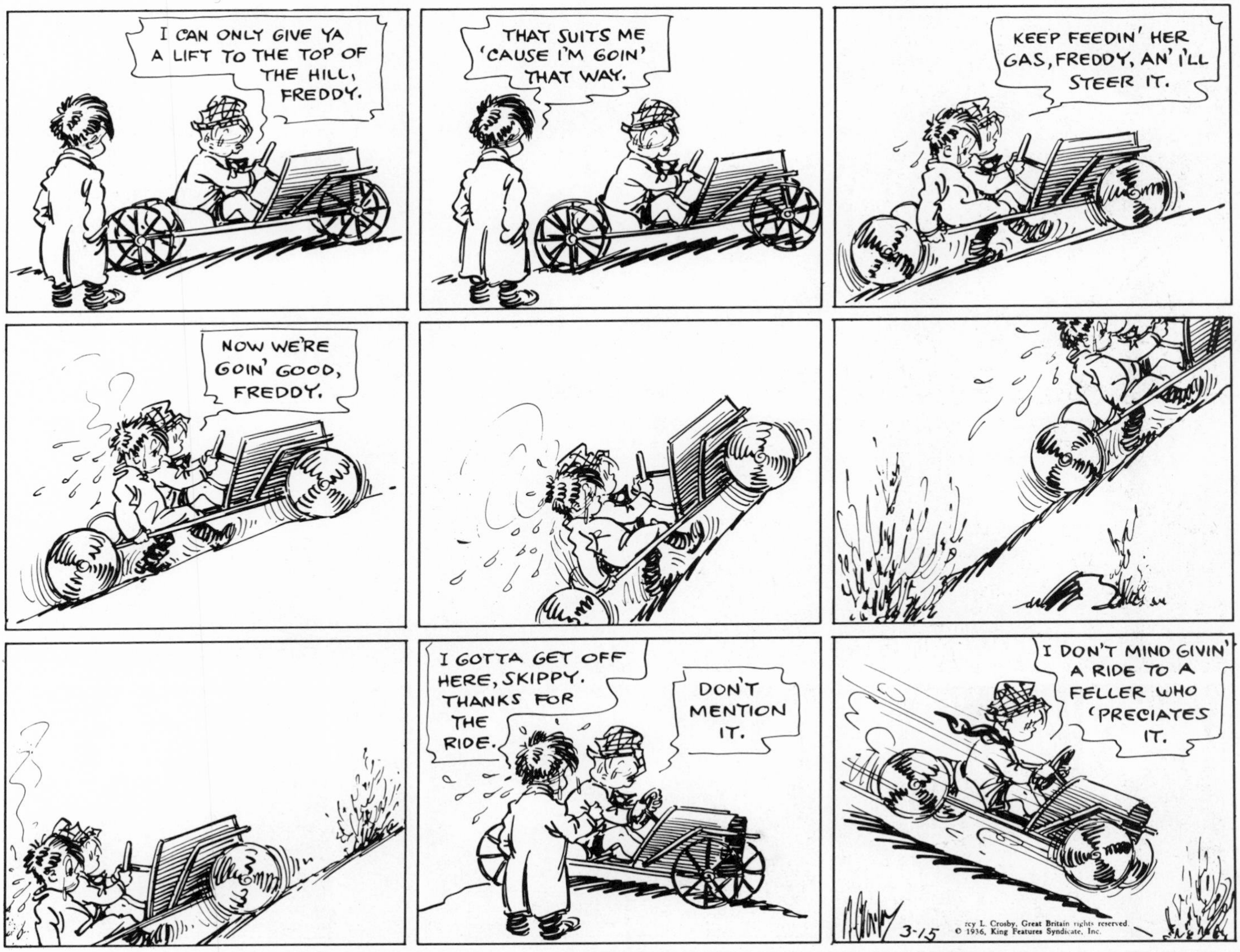
I CAN ONLY GIVE YA A LIFT TO THE TOP OF THE HILL, FREDDY.
THAT SUITS ME 'CAUSE I'M GOIN' THAT WAY.
KEEP FEEDIN' HER GAS, FREDDY, AN' I'LL STEER IT.
NOW WE'RE GOIN' GOOD, FREDDY.
I GOTTA GET OFF HERE, SKIPPY. THANKS FOR THE RIDE.
DON'T MENTION IT.
I DON'T MIND GIVIN' A RIDE TO A FELLER WHO 'PRECIATES IT.
3-15
rcy L. Crosby, Great Britain rights reserved.
© 1936, King Features Syndicate, Inc.

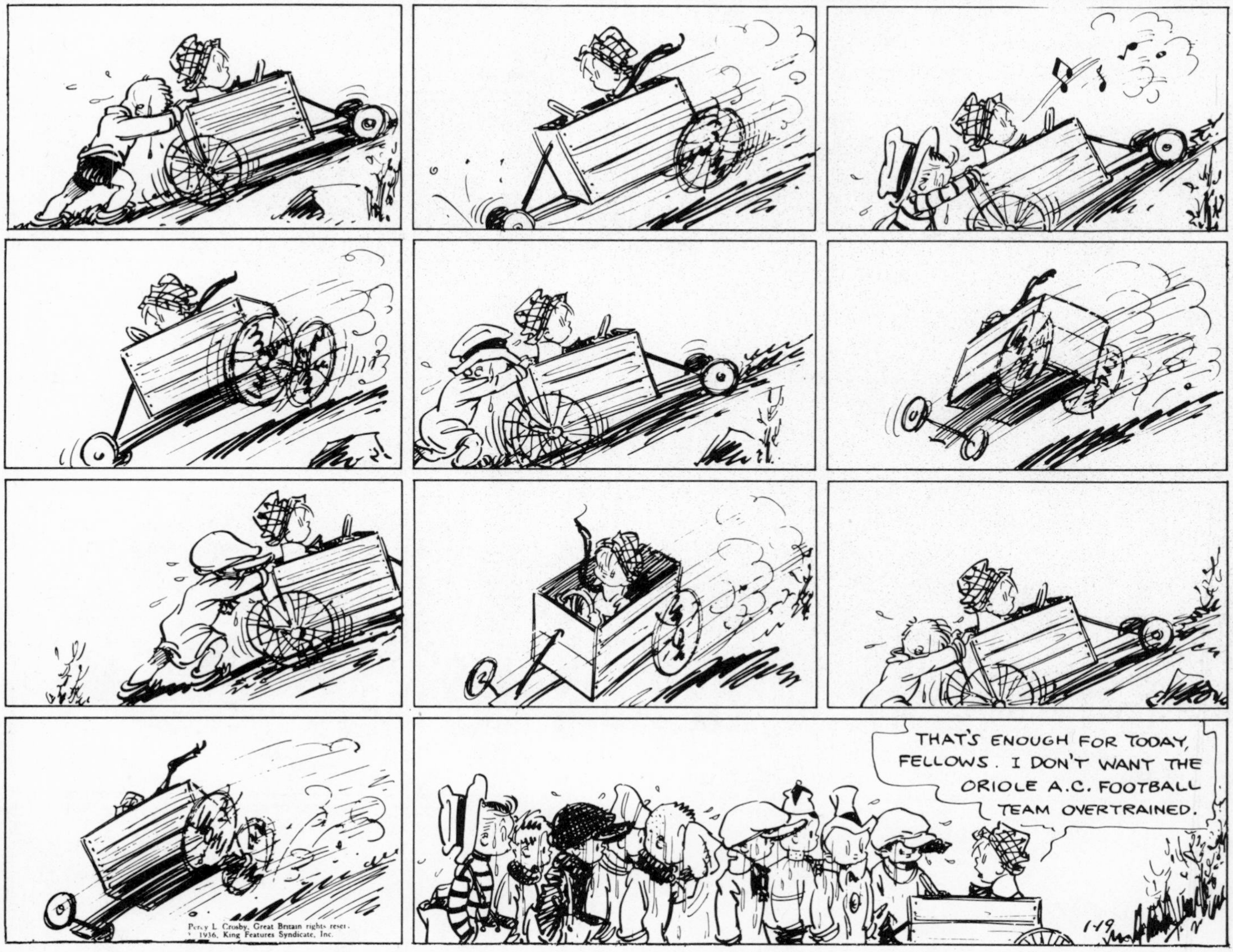
THAT'S ENOUGH FOR TODAY, FELLOWS. I DON'T WANT THE ORIOLE A.C. FOOTBALL TEAM OVERTRAINED.
Percy L. Crosby, Great Britain rights reser.
1936, King Features Syndicate, Inc.
1-19

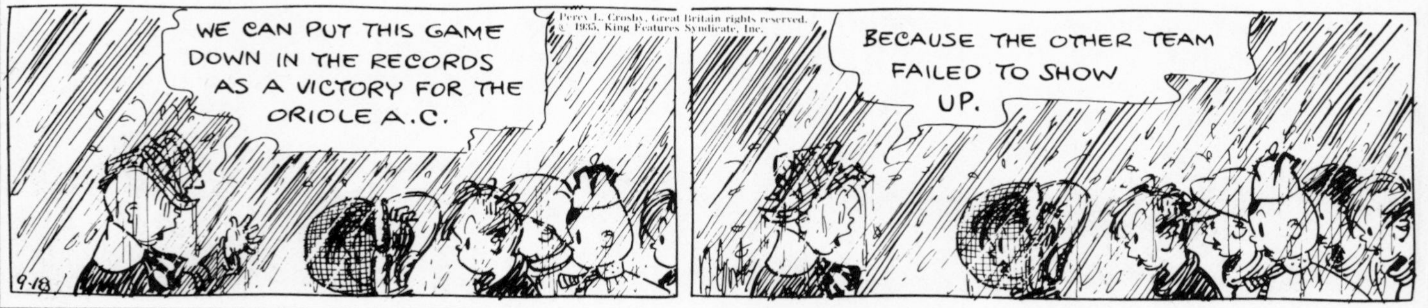
WE CAN PUT THIS GAME DOWN IN THE RECORDS AS A VICTORY FOR THE ORIOLE A.C.
Percy L. Crosby, Great Britain rights reserved.
1935, King Features Syndicate, Inc.
BECAUSE THE OTHER TEAM FAILED TO SHOW UP.
9-18

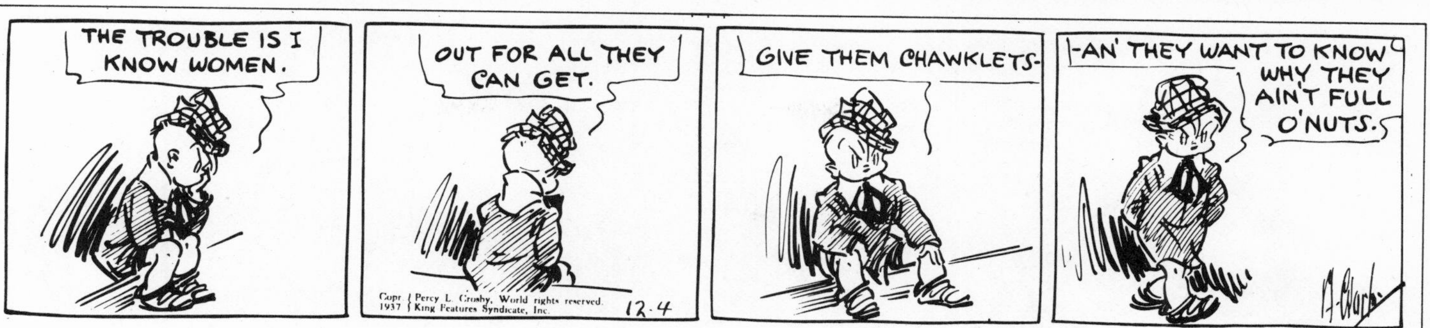
THE TROUBLE IS I KNOW WOMEN.
OUT FOR ALL THEY CAN GET.
GIVE THEM CHAWKLETS-
-AN' THEY WANT TO KNOW WHY THEY AIN'T FULL O'NUTS.
12-4

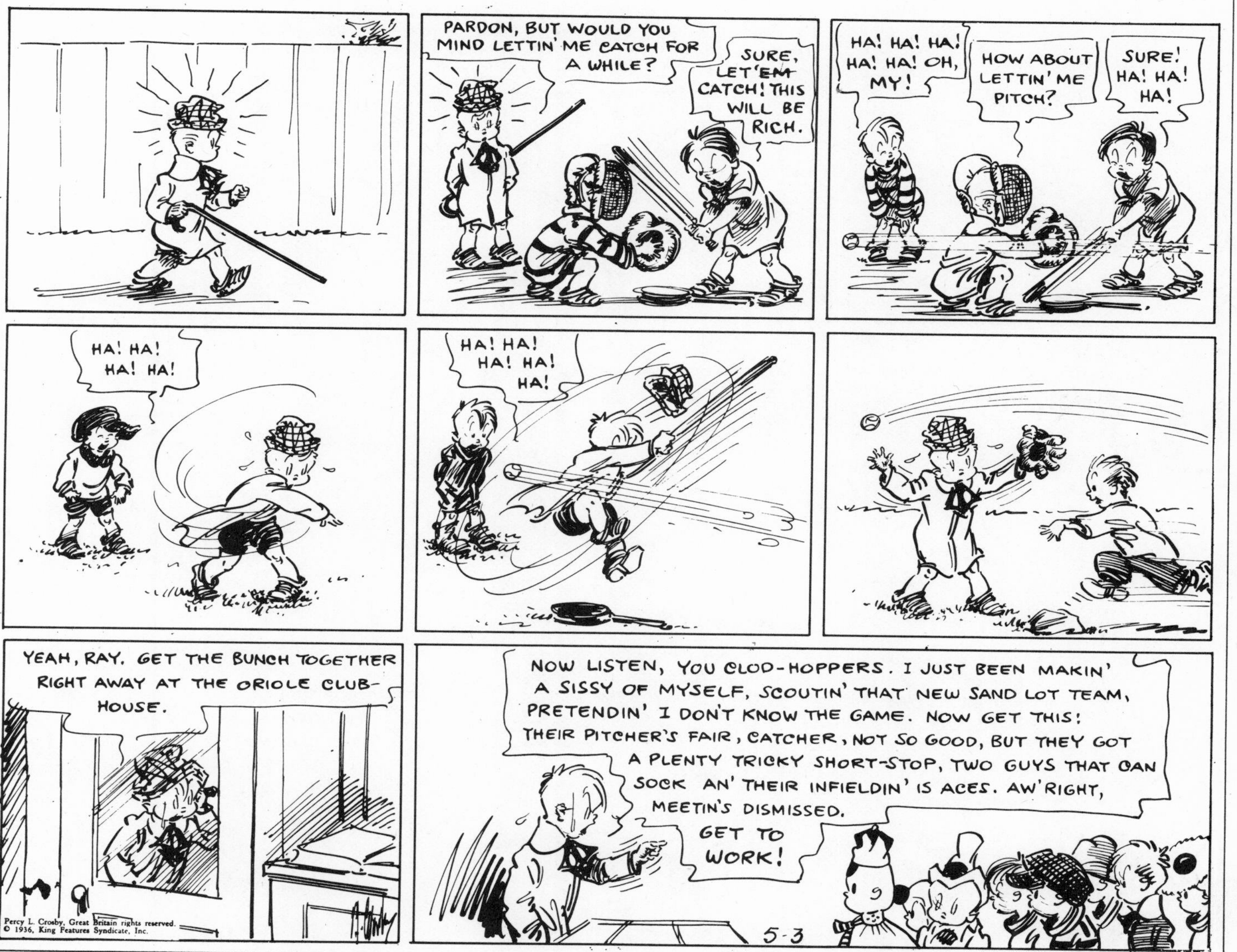
PARDON, BUT WOULD YOU MIND LETTIN' ME CATCH FOR A WHILE?
SURE, LET 'EM CATCH! THIS WILL BE RICH.
HA! HA! HA! HA! HA! OH, MY!
HOW ABOUT LETTIN' ME PITCH?
SURE! HA! HA! HA!
HA! HA! HA! HA!
HA! HA! HA! HA! HA!
YEAH, RAY. GET THE BUNCH TOGETHER RIGHT AWAY AT THE ORIOLE CLUB-HOUSE.
NOW LISTEN, YOU CLOD-HOPPERS. I JUST BEEN MAKIN' A SISSY OF MYSELF, SCOUTIN' THAT NEW SAND LOT TEAM, PRETENDIN' I DON'T KNOW THE GAME. NOW GET THIS: THEIR PITCHER'S FAIR, CATCHER, NOT SO GOOD, BUT THEY GOT A PLENTY TRICKY SHORT-STOP, TWO GUYS THAT CAN SOCK AN' THEIR INFIELDIN' IS ACES. AW'RIGHT, MEETIN'S DISMISSED.
GET TO WORK!
5-3

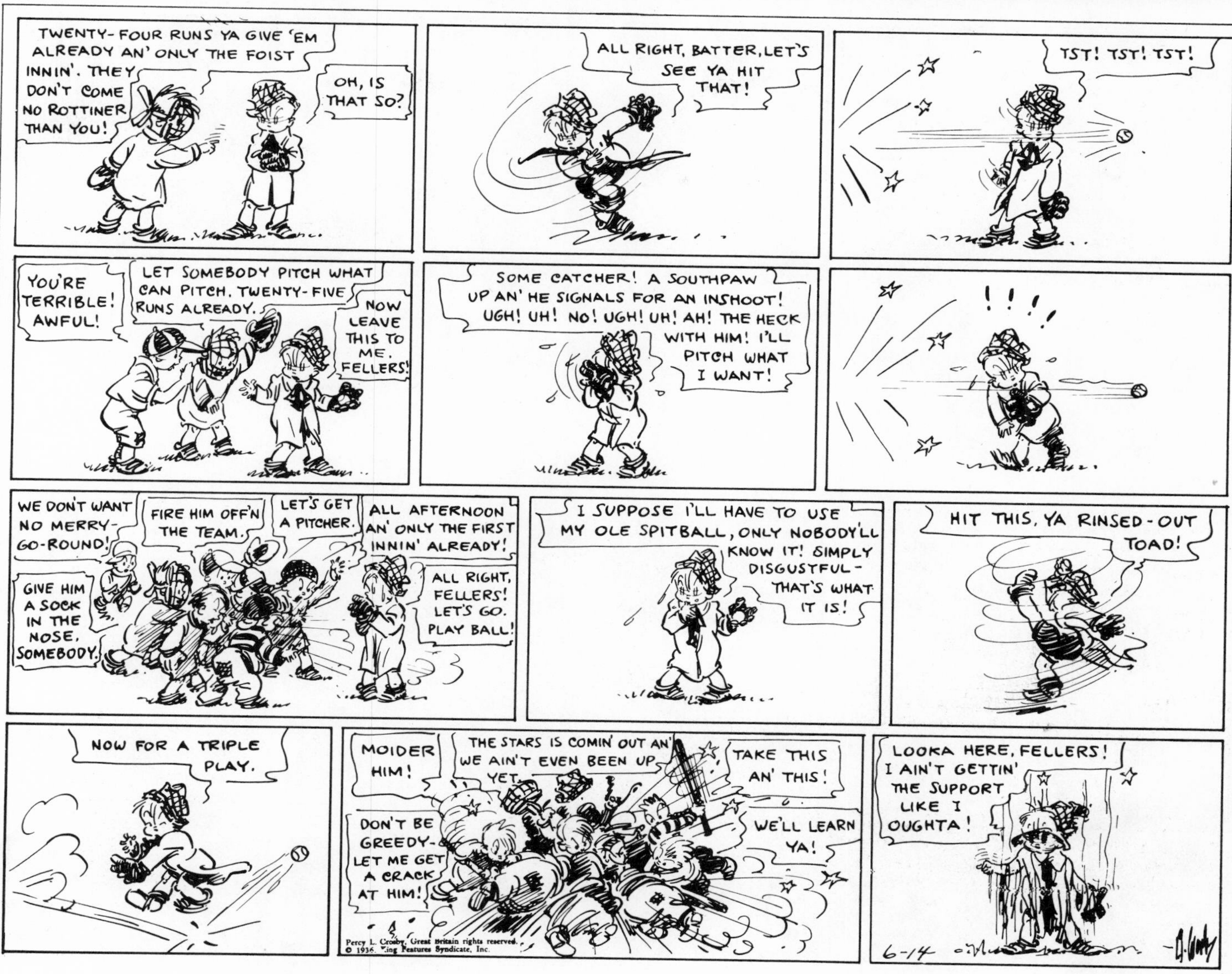
TWENTY-FOUR RUNS YA GIVE 'EM ALREADY AN' ONLY THE FOIST INNIN'. THEY DON'T COME NO ROTTINER THAN YOU!
OH, IS THAT SO?
ALL RIGHT, BATTER, LET'S SEE YA HIT THAT!
TST! TST! TST!
YOU'RE TERRIBLE! AWFUL!
LET SOMEBODY PITCH WHAT CAN PITCH. TWENTY-FIVE RUNS ALREADY.
NOW LEAVE THIS TO ME, FELLERS!
SOME CATCHER! A SOUTHPAW UP AN' HE SIGNALS FOR AN INSHOOT! UGH! UH! NO! UGH! UH! AH! THE HECK WITH HIM! I'LL PITCH WHAT I WANT!
! ! ! !
WE DON'T WANT NO MERRY-GO-ROUND!
FIRE HIM OFF'N THE TEAM.
LET'S GET A PITCHER.
ALL AFTERNOON AN' ONLY THE FIRST INNIN' ALREADY!
GIVE HIM A SOCK IN THE NOSE, SOMEBODY!
ALL RIGHT, FELLERS! LET'S GO. PLAY BALL!
I SUPPOSE I'LL HAVE TO USE MY OLE SPITBALL, ONLY NOBODY'LL KNOW IT! SIMPLY DISGUSTFUL- THAT'S WHAT IT IS!
HIT THIS, YA RINSED-OUT TOAD!
NOW FOR A TRIPLE PLAY.
MOIDER HIM!
THE STARS IS COMIN' OUT AN' WE AIN'T EVEN BEEN UP YET.
TAKE THIS AN' THIS!
DON'T BE GREEDY- LET ME GET A CRACK AT HIM!
WE'LL LEARN YA!
Percy L. Crosby, Great Britain rights reserved. © 1936 King Features Syndicate, Inc.
LOOKA HERE, FELLERS! I AIN'T GETTIN' THE SUPPORT LIKE I OUGHTA!
6-14

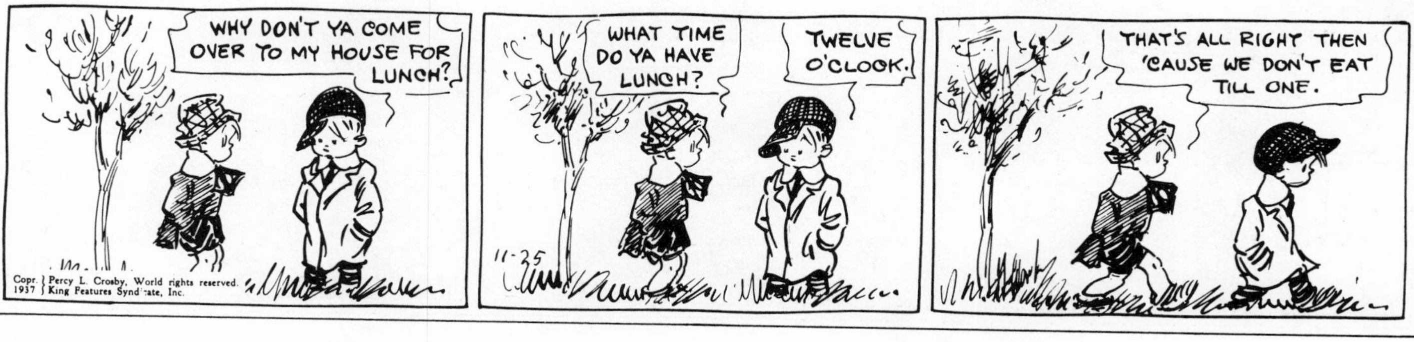
WHY DON'T YA COME OVER TO MY HOUSE FOR LUNCH?
Copr. 1937 Percy L. Crosby, World rights reserved. King Features Syndicate, Inc.
WHAT TIME DO YA HAVE LUNCH?
TWELVE O'CLOCK.
11-25
THAT'S ALL RIGHT THEN 'CAUSE WE DON'T EAT TILL ONE.

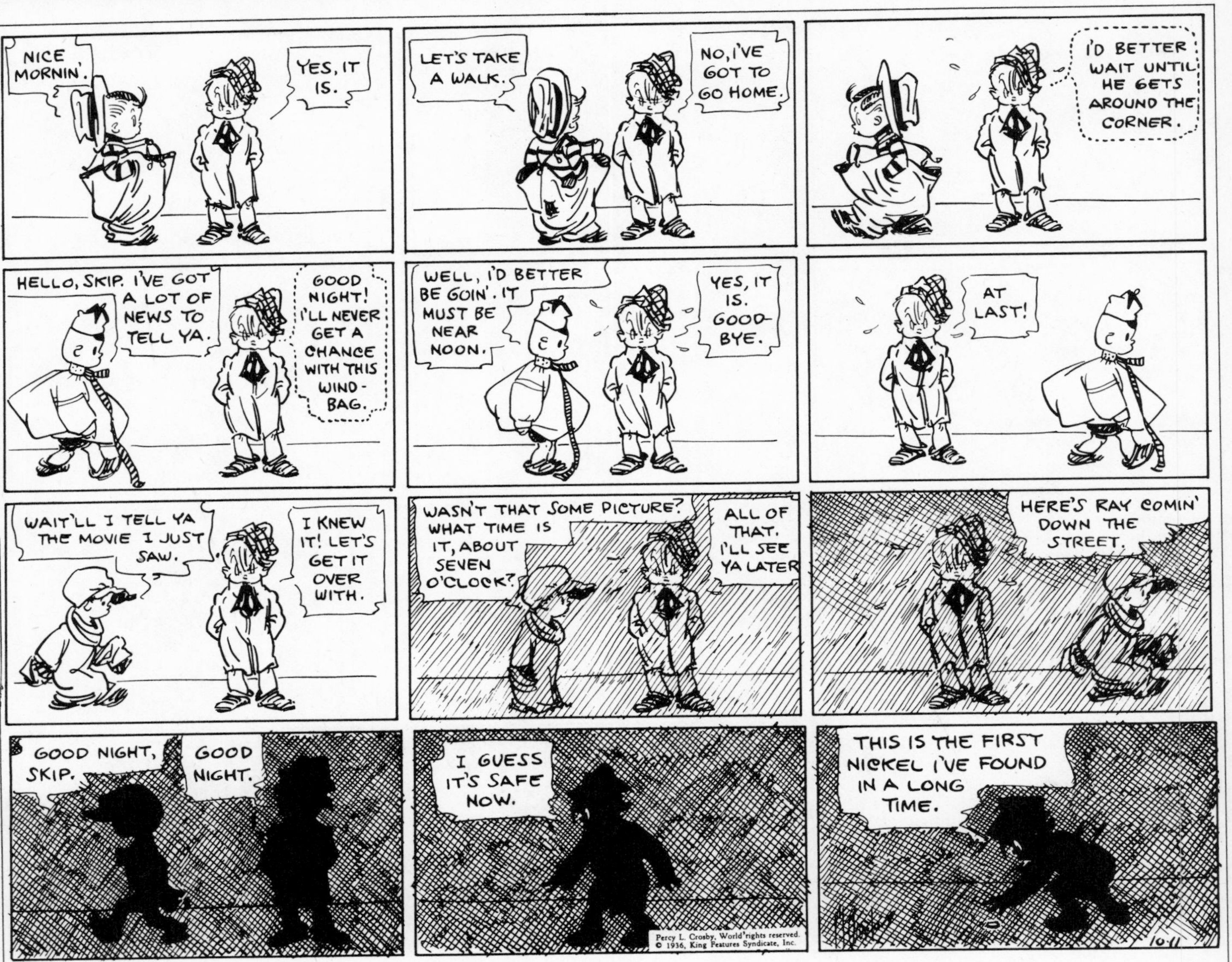
NICE MORNIN'.
YES, IT IS.
LET'S TAKE A WALK.
NO, I'VE GOT TO GO HOME.
I'D BETTER WAIT UNTIL HE GETS AROUND THE CORNER.
HELLO, SKIP. I'VE GOT A LOT OF NEWS TO TELL YA.
GOOD NIGHT! I'LL NEVER GET A CHANCE WITH THIS WIND-BAG.
WELL, I'D BETTER BE GOIN'. IT MUST BE NEAR NOON.
YES, IT IS. GOOD-BYE.
AT LAST!
WAIT'LL I TELL YA THE MOVIE I JUST SAW.
I KNEW IT! LET'S GET IT OVER WITH.
WASN'T THAT SOME PICTURE? WHAT TIME IS IT, ABOUT SEVEN O'CLOCK?
ALL OF THAT. I'LL SEE YA LATER
HERE'S RAY COMIN' DOWN THE STREET.
GOOD NIGHT, SKIP.
GOOD NIGHT.
I GUESS IT'S SAFE NOW.
Percy L. Crosby, World rights reserved. © 1936, King Features Syndicate, Inc.
THIS IS THE FIRST NICKEL I'VE FOUND IN A LONG TIME.
10-11

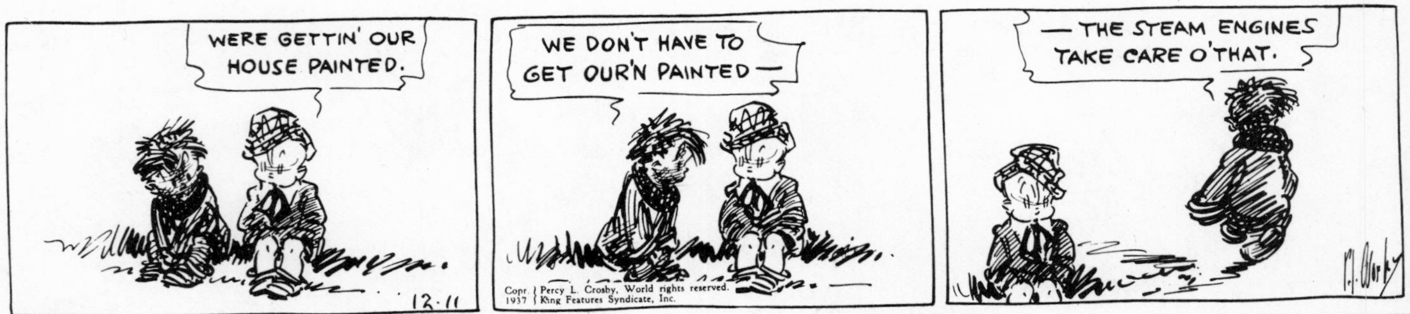
WERE GETTIN' OUR HOUSE PAINTED.
12-11
WE DON'T HAVE TO GET OUR'N PAINTED —
Copr. 1937 Percy L. Crosby, World rights reserved. King Features Syndicate, Inc.
— THE STEAM ENGINES TAKE CARE O'THAT.

I DON'T FEEL SO GOOD.
MAYBE IF YA TOOK A LITTLE WALK YOU'D FEEL BETTER.
NO, THAT DON'T DO ANY GOOD.
3-31

PAPA, CAN I GO DOWN TO THE OFFICE WITH YOU SOMETIME AN' STAY ALL DAY?
WELL, WE'LL SEE.
CAN I GO TO CUBA SOMETIME OR MAYBE MEXICO? WHY DON'T YOU TAKE ME ON A LONG TRIP OR MAYBE TO EUROPE?
WELL, WE'LL SEE.
MAYBE IN THE MEANTIME WE CAN GO OUT CAMPIN' UP IN ALASKA AN' DO SOME SHOOTIN' AN' FISHIN' OFF THE ICE-BERGS. THAT WOULD BE NICE.
WELL, WE'LL SEE.
ALL THE OTHER KIDS I KNOW HAVE BEEN SOME PLACE OR OTHER AN' I FEEL SO IGNORANT WHEN THEY TALK ABOUT EUROPE AN' ASIA AN' THE ROCKIES AN' THE GANGES. I JUST HAVE TO SIT AROUND AN' SAY NOTHIN' AN' GULP AN' THEN TRAVELS ALWAYS HELPS YOU IN GEOGRAPHY, TOO.
IT WOULD BE NICE IF WE COULD GO SOME PLACE OR OTHER. DO YOU LIKE EGYPT? THAT'D BE A NICE PLACE TO GO. WHAT DO YA SAY, POP? HOW ABOUT IT?
WELL, WE'LL SEE.
WELL, I WAS JUST THINKIN', COULD I GO TO THE MOVIES?
YES, HERE'S A QUARTER. YOU BETTER HURRY.
12-19
CAN YA GO TO THE MOVIES?
YEAH.
Copr. 1937 Percy L. Crosby, World rights reserved. King Features Syndicate, Inc.

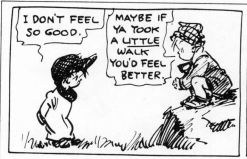

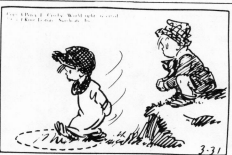

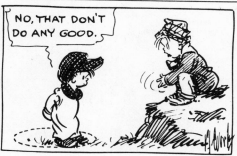

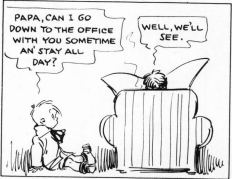

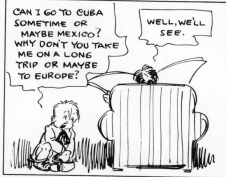

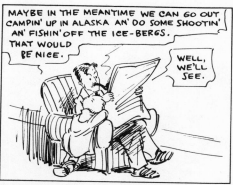

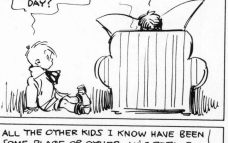

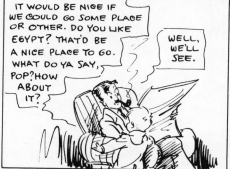

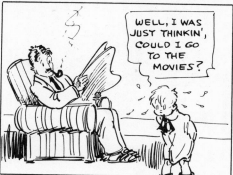

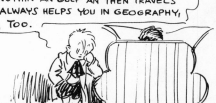

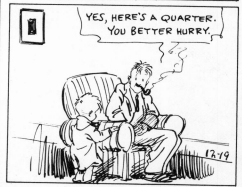

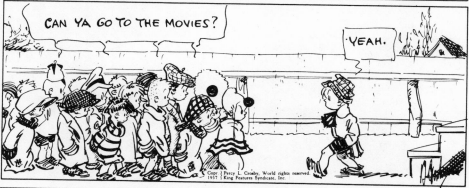

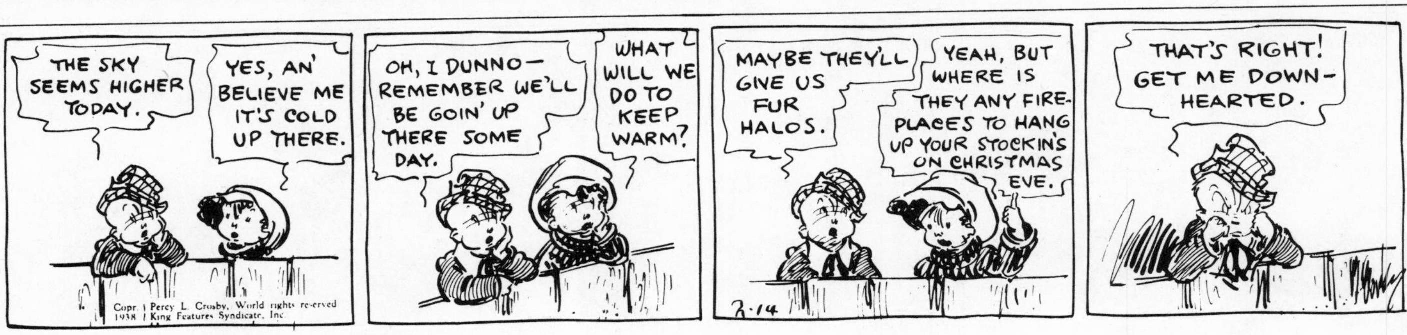
THE SKY SEEMS HIGHER TODAY.
YES, AN' BELIEVE ME IT'S COLD UP THERE.
OH, I DUNNO— REMEMBER WE'LL BE GOIN' UP THERE SOME DAY.
WHAT WILL WE DO TO KEEP WARM?
MAYBE THEY'LL GIVE US FUR HALOS.
YEAH, BUT WHERE IS THEY ANY FIRE-PLACES TO HANG UP YOUR STOCKIN'S ON CHRISTMAS EVE.
THAT'S RIGHT! GET ME DOWN-HEARTED.
Copr. 1938 Percy L. Crosby, World rights reserved King Features Syndicate, Inc
2-14

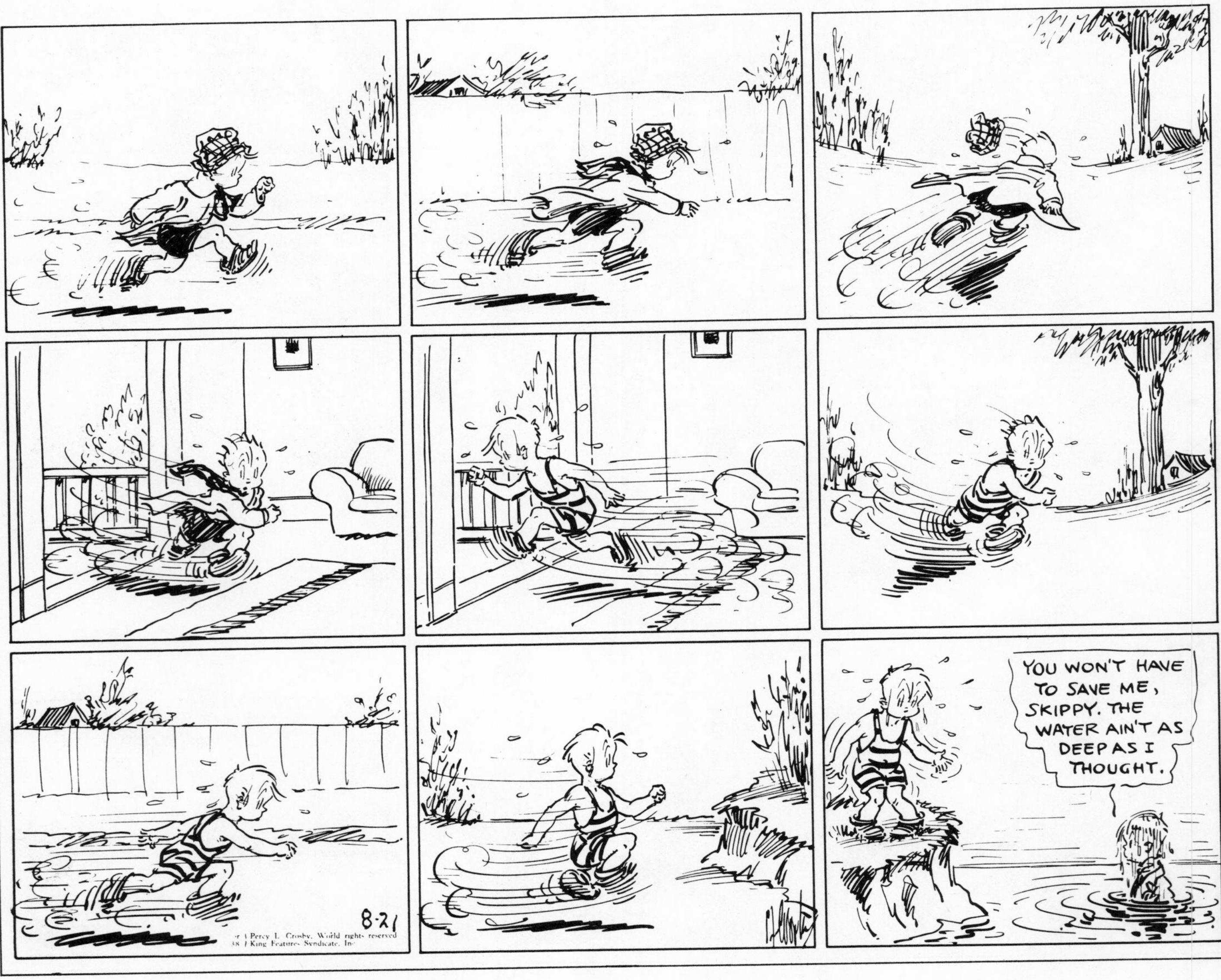
8-21
YOU WON'T HAVE TO SAVE ME, SKIPPY. THE WATER AIN'T AS DEEP AS I THOUGHT.

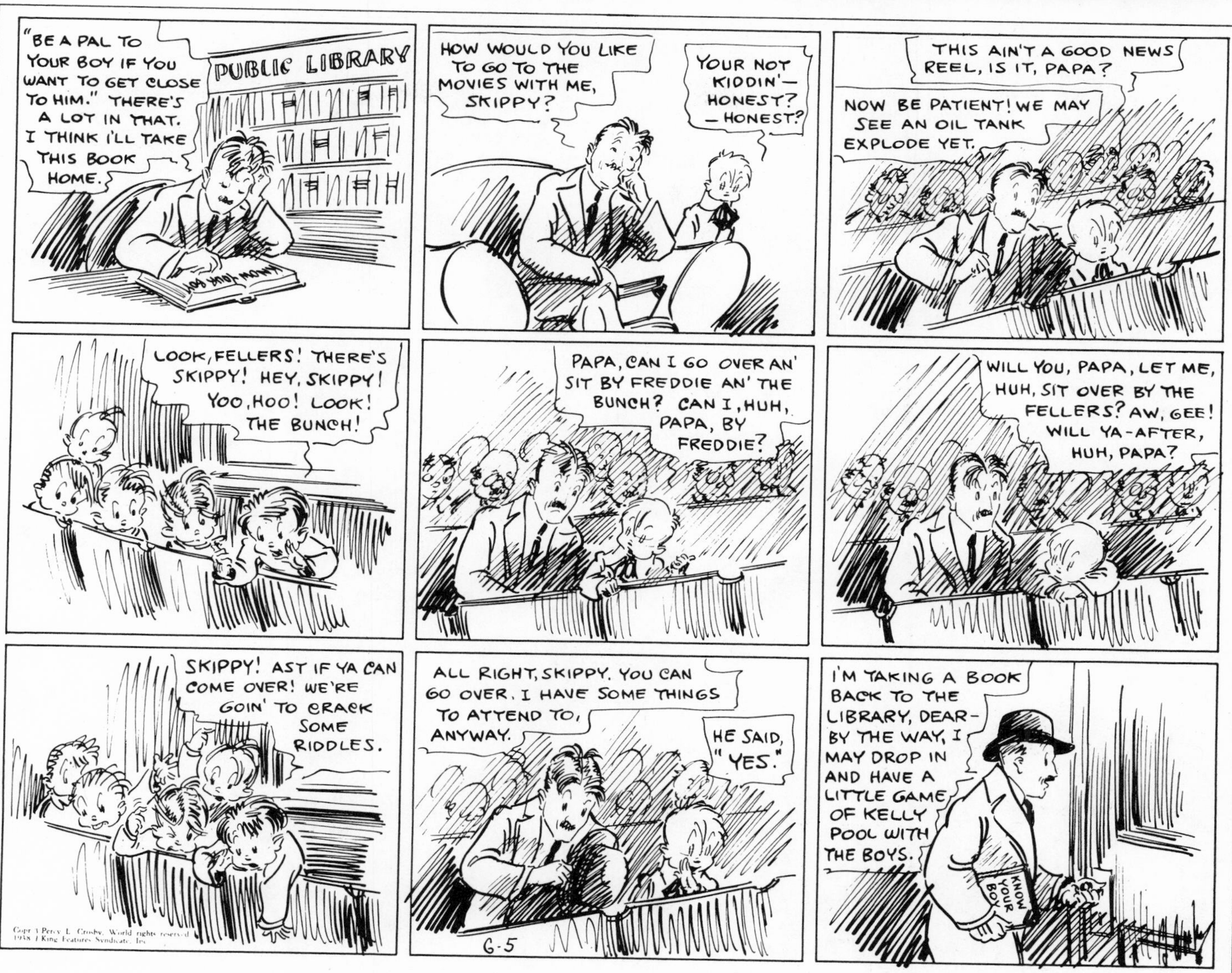
"BE A PAL TO YOUR BOY IF YOU WANT TO GET CLOSE TO HIM." THERE'S A LOT IN THAT. I THINK I'LL TAKE THIS BOOK HOME.
PUBLIC LIBRARY
HOW WOULD YOU LIKE TO GO TO THE MOVIES WITH ME, SKIPPY?
YOUR NOT KIDDIN'— HONEST? —HONEST?
THIS AIN'T A GOOD NEWS REEL, IS IT, PAPA?
NOW BE PATIENT! WE MAY SEE AN OIL TANK EXPLODE YET.
LOOK, FELLERS! THERE'S SKIPPY! HEY, SKIPPY! YOO, HOO! LOOK! THE BUNCH!
PAPA, CAN I GO OVER AN' SIT BY FREDDIE AN' THE BUNCH? CAN I, HUH, PAPA, BY FREDDIE?
WILL YOU, PAPA, LET ME, HUH, SIT OVER BY THE FELLERS? AW, GEE! WILL YA-AFTER, HUH, PAPA?
SKIPPY! AST IF YA CAN COME OVER! WE'RE GOIN' TO CRACK SOME RIDDLES.
ALL RIGHT, SKIPPY. YOU CAN GO OVER. I HAVE SOME THINGS TO ATTEND TO, ANYWAY.
HE SAID, "YES."
I'M TAKING A BOOK BACK TO THE LIBRARY, DEAR—BY THE WAY, I MAY DROP IN AND HAVE A LITTLE GAME OF KELLY POOL WITH THE BOYS.
KNOW YOUR BOY
Copr. Percy L. Crosby, World rights reserved 1938 King Features Syndicate, Inc.
6-5

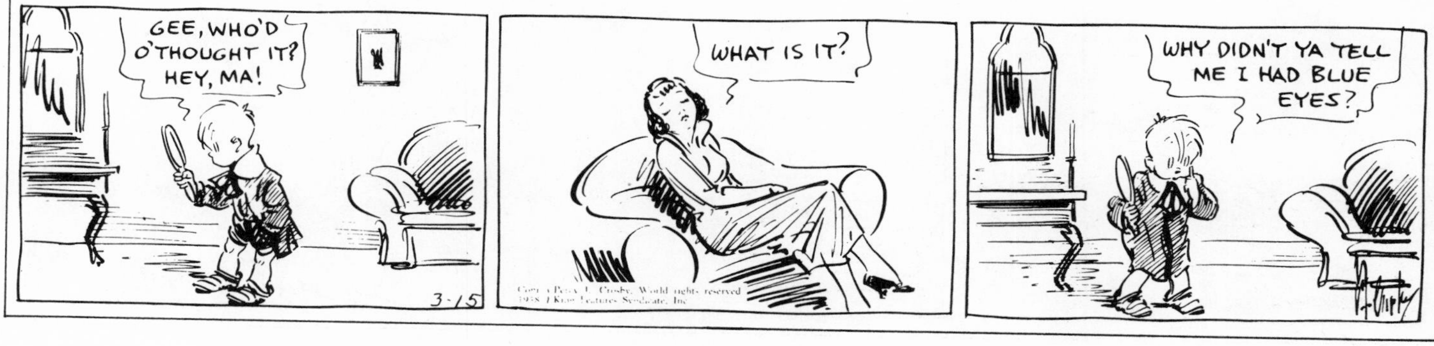
GEE, WHO'D O'THOUGHT IT? HEY, MA!
WHAT IS IT?
WHY DIDN'T YA TELL ME I HAD BLUE EYES?
Copr. Percy L. Crosby, World rights reserved 1938 King Features Syndicate, Inc.
3-15

THERE'S GIANTS AN' THERE'S DWARFS; THERE'S THIN PEOPLE AN' THERE'S FAT PEOPLE, AN' THERE'S ALL SORTS OF PEOPLE WITH DIFFERENT COLOR. THERE'S PRETTY PEOPLE AN' THERE'S UNPRETTY PEOPLE.
WHO'S THE SMARTEST OF ALL O'THEM?
THERE'S BUTTERCUPS, THERE'S ROSES. THERE'S DAISIES AN' THERE'S ORCHIDS. THERE'S NASTURTIUMS AN' THERE'S CHRYSANTHEMUMS. THERE'S TULIPS AN' GERANIUMS AN' THERE'S GARDENIAS.
WHICH FLOWER GETS THE MOST SUNSHINE?
Copr. Percy L. Crosby, World rights reserved
1978 King Features Syndicate, Inc.
5·26
LET'S GO DOWN TO DUSENBERRY'S AN' GET A CHOCOLATE SODA.

YOU SEEM KINDA HAPPY.
I AM. LET'S SIT DOWN AN' I'LL TELL YA ABOUT IT.
MAMA WANTED PAPA TO BRING HOME A CAT TONIGHT AN' I WANTED A DOG.
SO I PUT UP SUCH A HOLLER, MAMA GAVE IN AN' PAPA IS GONNA BRING HOME A DOG TONIGHT.
THAT'S VERY LOVELY.
8·19
HELLO, PAPA? BRING HOME THE CAT!

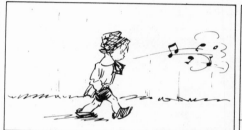

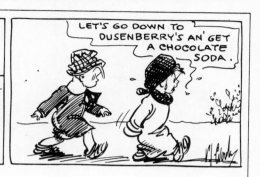

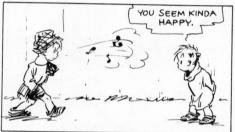

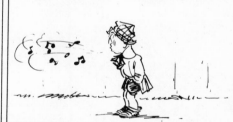

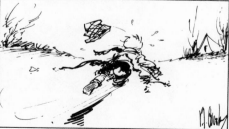

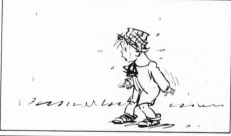

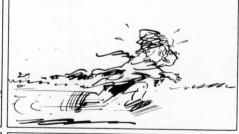

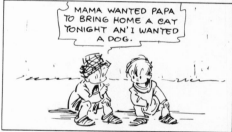

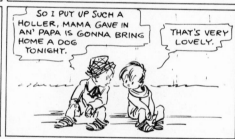

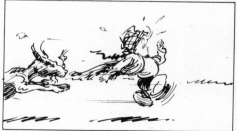

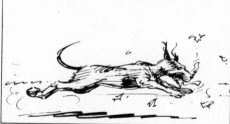

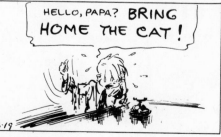

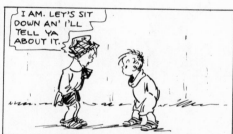

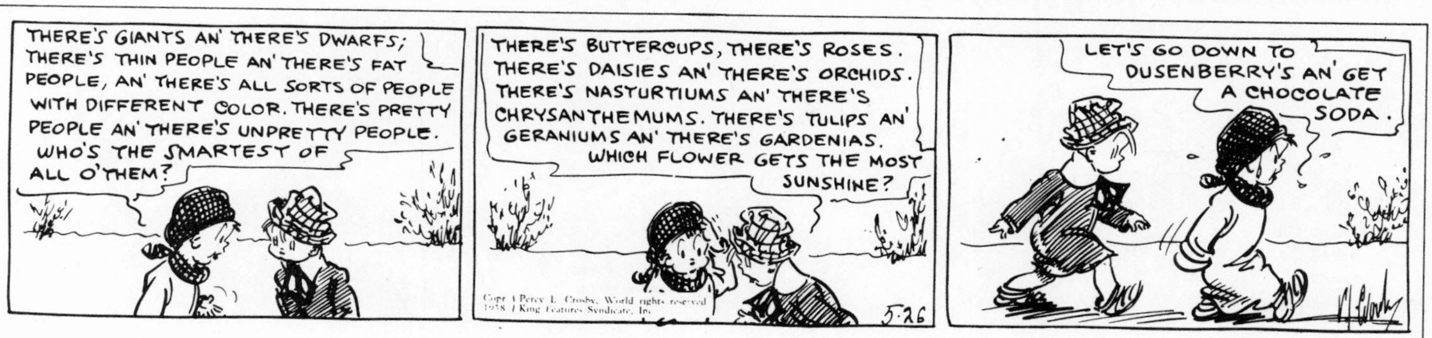

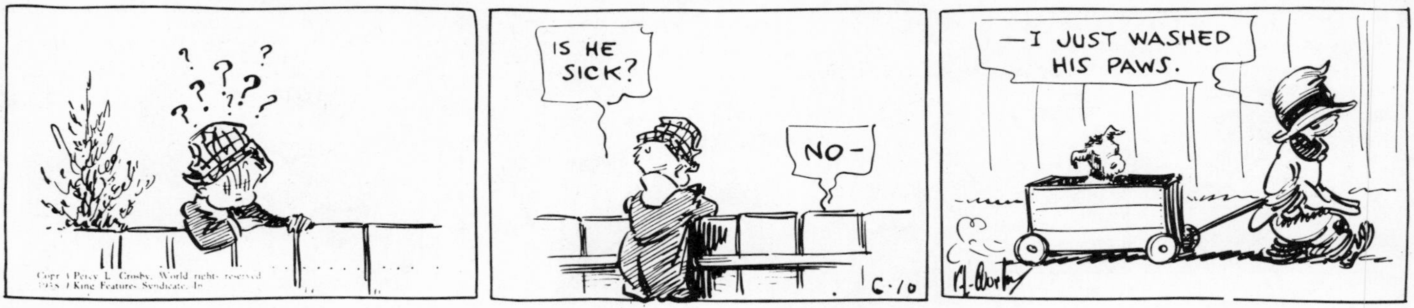
? ? ? ? ? ? ? ?
IS HE SICK?
NO-
—I JUST WASHED HIS PAWS.
6·10
Copr. by Percy L. Crosby, World rights reserved 1938 (King Features Syndicate, In

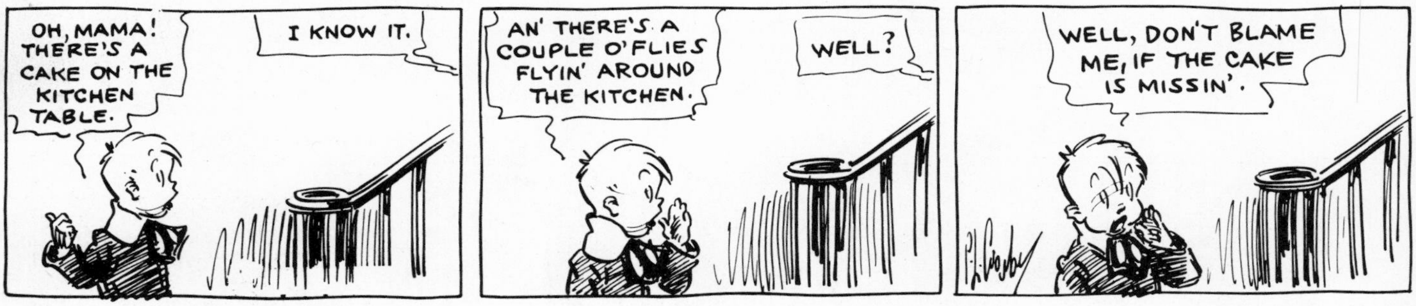
OH, MAMA! THERE'S A CAKE ON THE KITCHEN TABLE.
I KNOW IT.
AN' THERE'S A COUPLE O' FLIES FLYIN' AROUND THE KITCHEN.
WELL?
WELL, DON'T BLAME ME, IF THE CAKE IS MISSIN'.

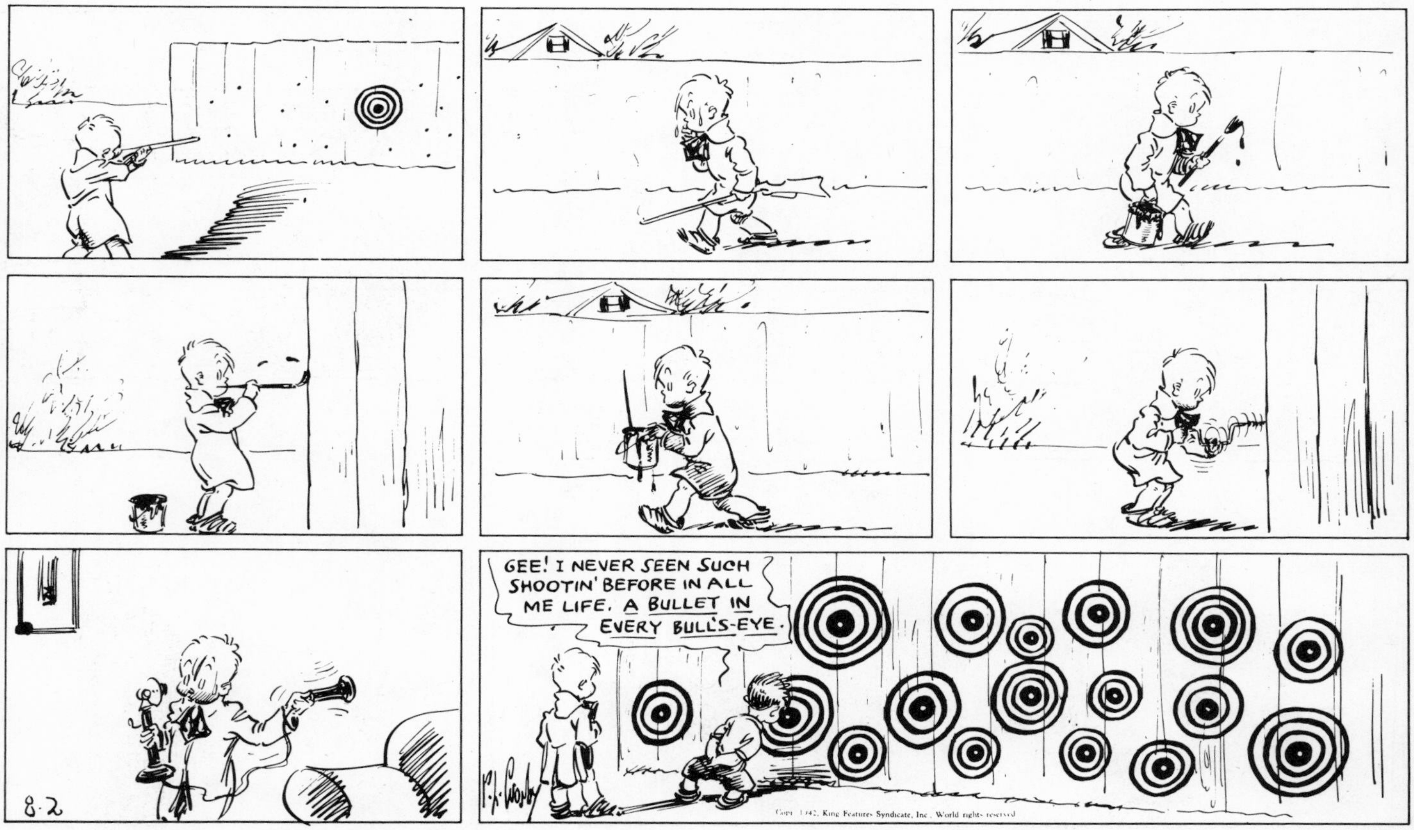
8·2
GEE! I NEVER SEEN SUCH SHOOTIN' BEFORE IN ALL ME LIFE. A BULLET IN EVERY BULL'S-EYE.
Copr. 1942, King Features Syndicate, Inc. World rights reserved

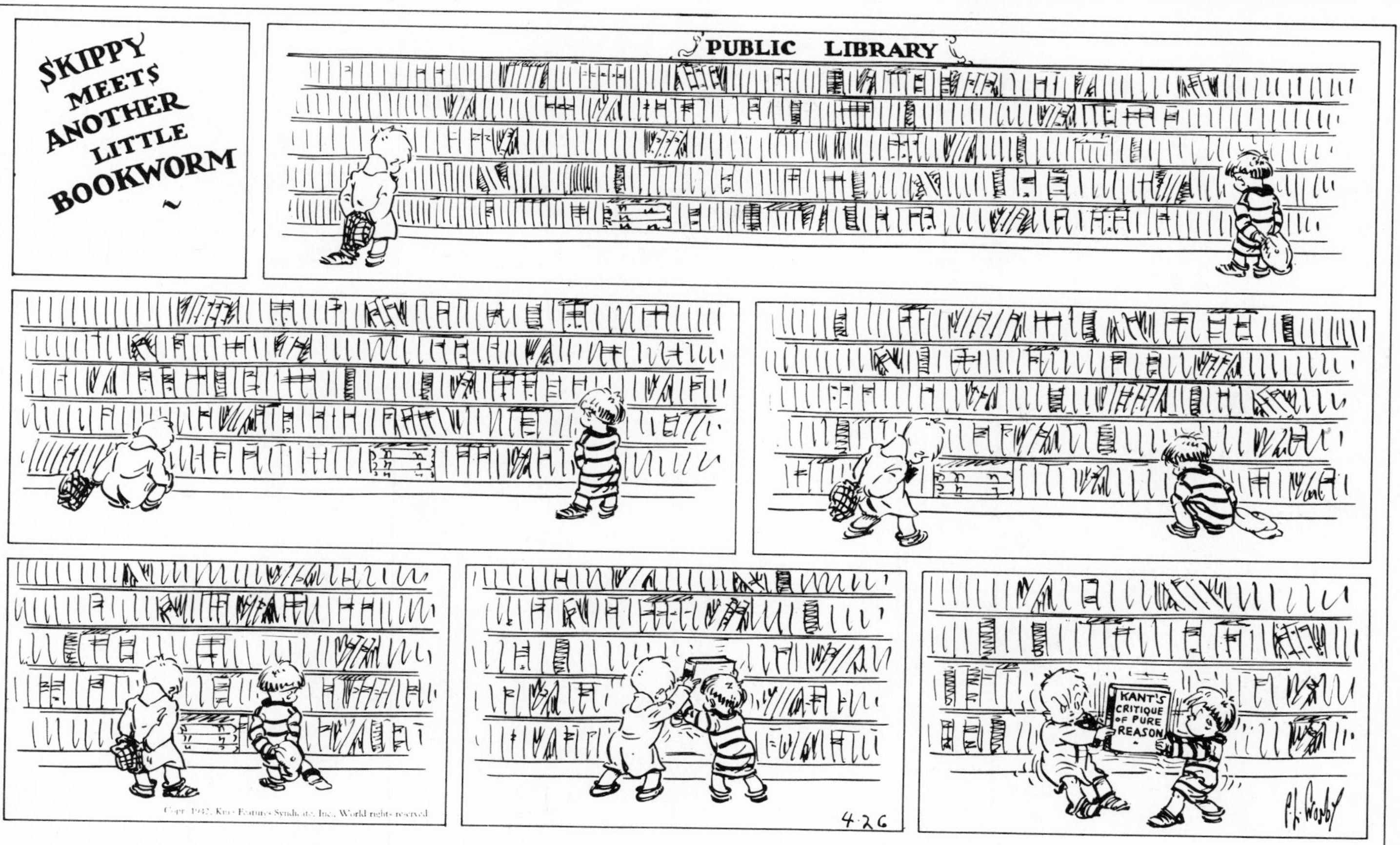
SKIPPY MEETS ANOTHER LITTLE BOOKWORM
PUBLIC LIBRARY
KANT'S CRITIQUE OF PURE REASON
4·26
P. L. Crosby

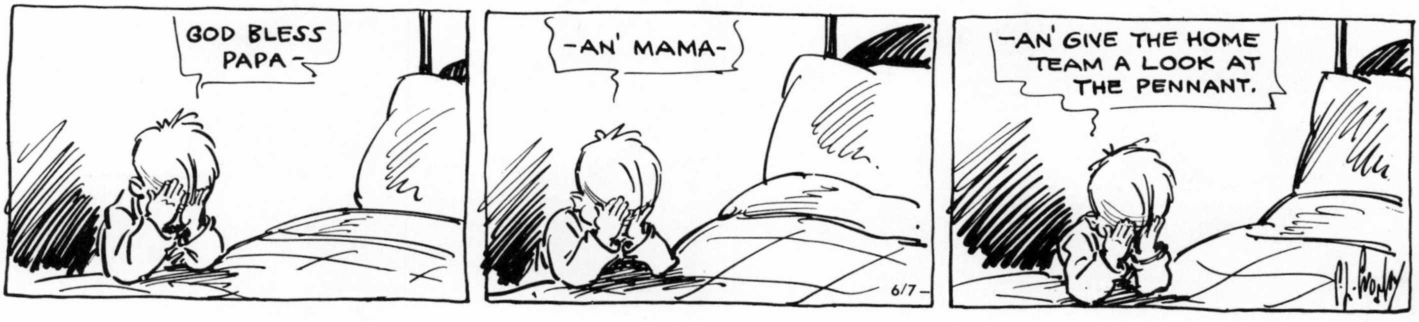
GOD BLESS PAPA–
–AN' MAMA–
–AN' GIVE THE HOME TEAM A LOOK AT THE PENNANT.
6/7–
P. L. Crosby

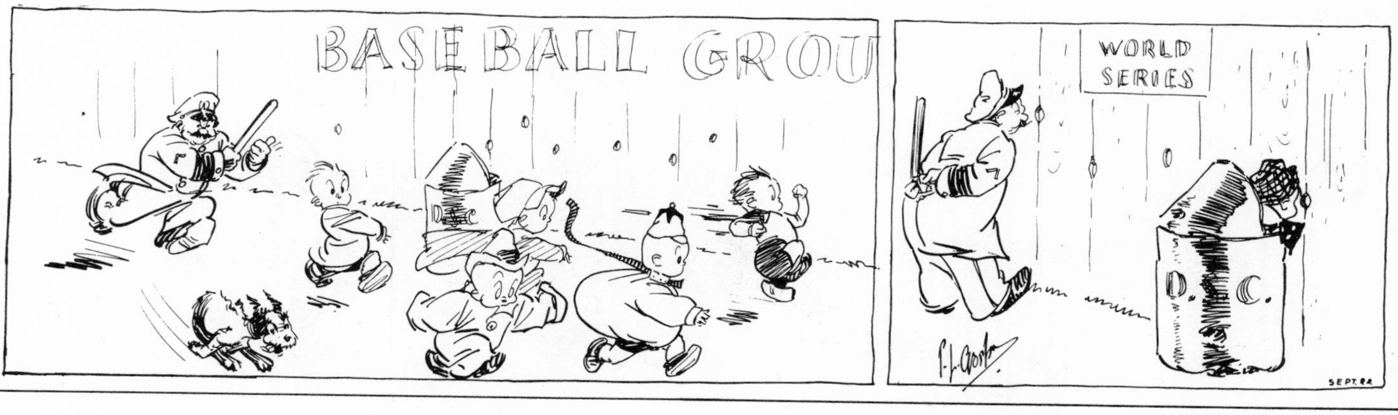
BASEBALL GROU
D.C.
WORLD SERIES
D. C.
P. L. Crosby
SEPT. 22

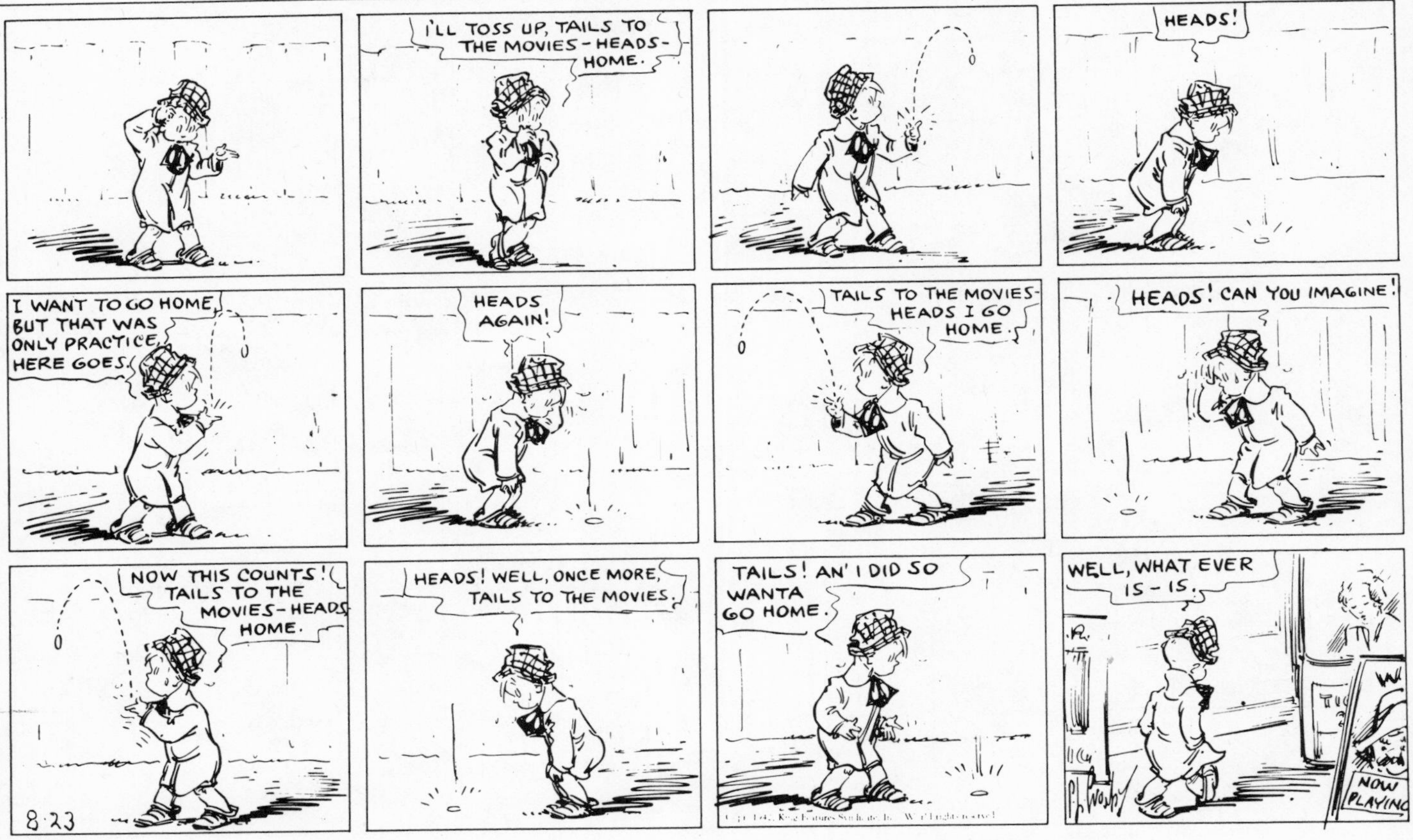
I'LL TOSS UP, TAILS TO THE MOVIES - HEADS - HOME.
HEADS!
I WANT TO GO HOME, BUT THAT WAS ONLY PRACTICE, HERE GOES.
HEADS AGAIN!
TAILS TO THE MOVIES - HEADS I GO HOME.
HEADS! CAN YOU IMAGINE!
NOW THIS COUNTS! TAILS TO THE MOVIES - HEADS - HOME.
HEADS! WELL, ONCE MORE, TAILS TO THE MOVIES.
TAILS! AN' I DID SO WANTA GO HOME.
WELL, WHAT EVER IS - IS.
NOW PLAYING
8·23

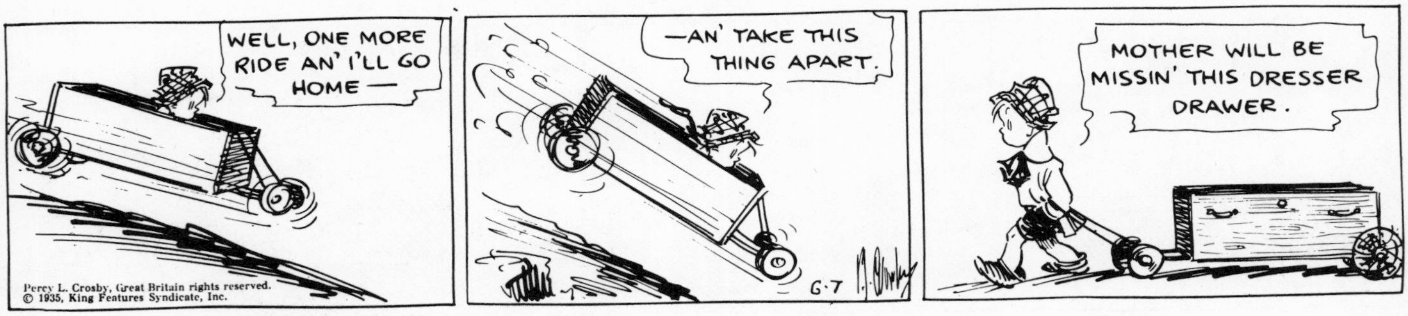
WELL, ONE MORE RIDE AN' I'LL GO HOME —
—AN' TAKE THIS THING APART.
MOTHER WILL BE MISSIN' THIS DRESSER DRAWER.
Percy L. Crosby, Great Britain rights reserved.
© 1935, King Features Syndicate, Inc.
6·7

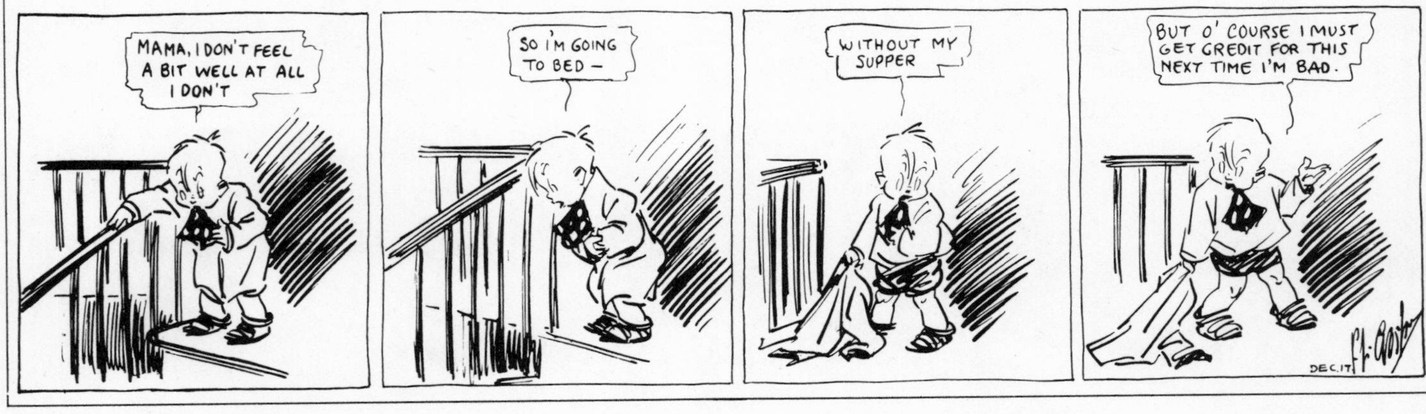
MAMA, I DON'T FEEL A BIT WELL AT ALL I DON'T
SO I'M GOING TO BED —
WITHOUT MY SUPPER
BUT O' COURSE I MUST GET CREDIT FOR THIS NEXT TIME I'M BAD.
DEC.17

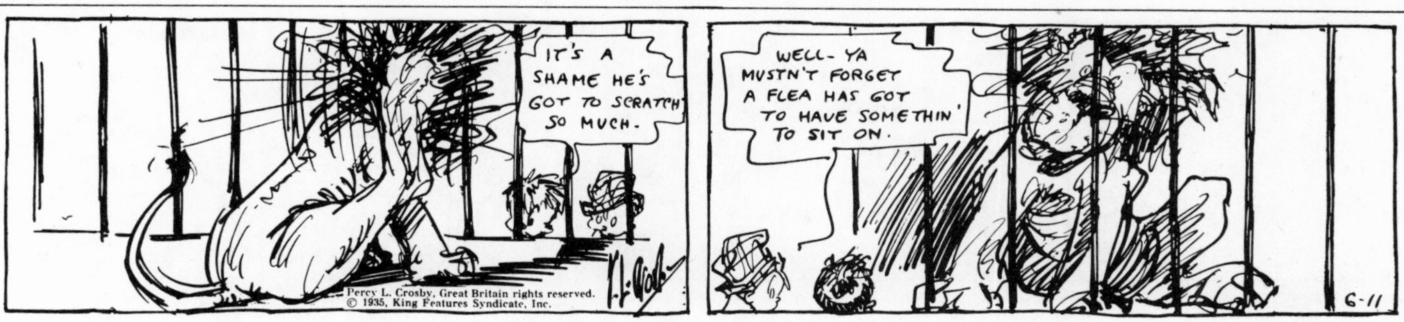
IT'S A SHAME HE'S GOT TO SCRATCH SO MUCH.
Percy L. Crosby, Great Britain rights reserved.
© 1935, King Features Syndicate, Inc.
WELL- YA MUSTN'T FORGET A FLEA HAS GOT TO HAVE SOMETHIN' TO SIT ON.
6-11

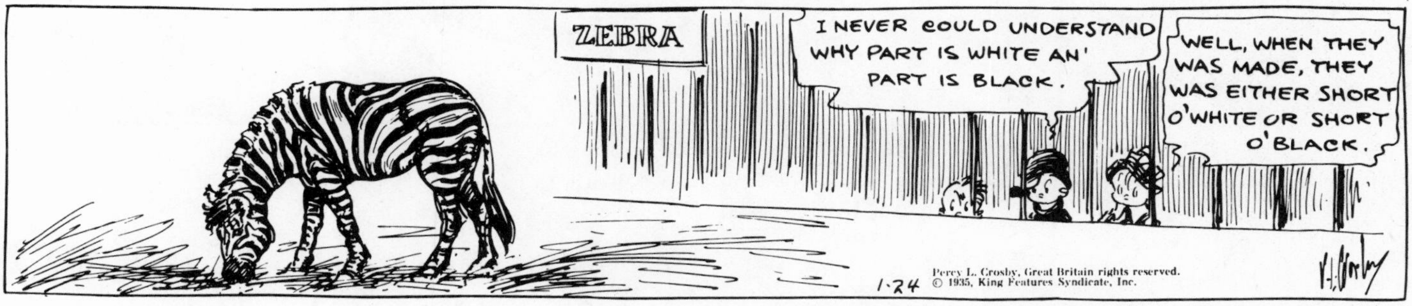
ZEBRA
I NEVER COULD UNDERSTAND WHY PART IS WHITE AN' PART IS BLACK.
WELL, WHEN THEY WAS MADE, THEY WAS EITHER SHORT O'WHITE OR SHORT O'BLACK.
1-24
Percy L. Crosby, Great Britain rights reserved.
© 1935, King Features Syndicate, Inc.

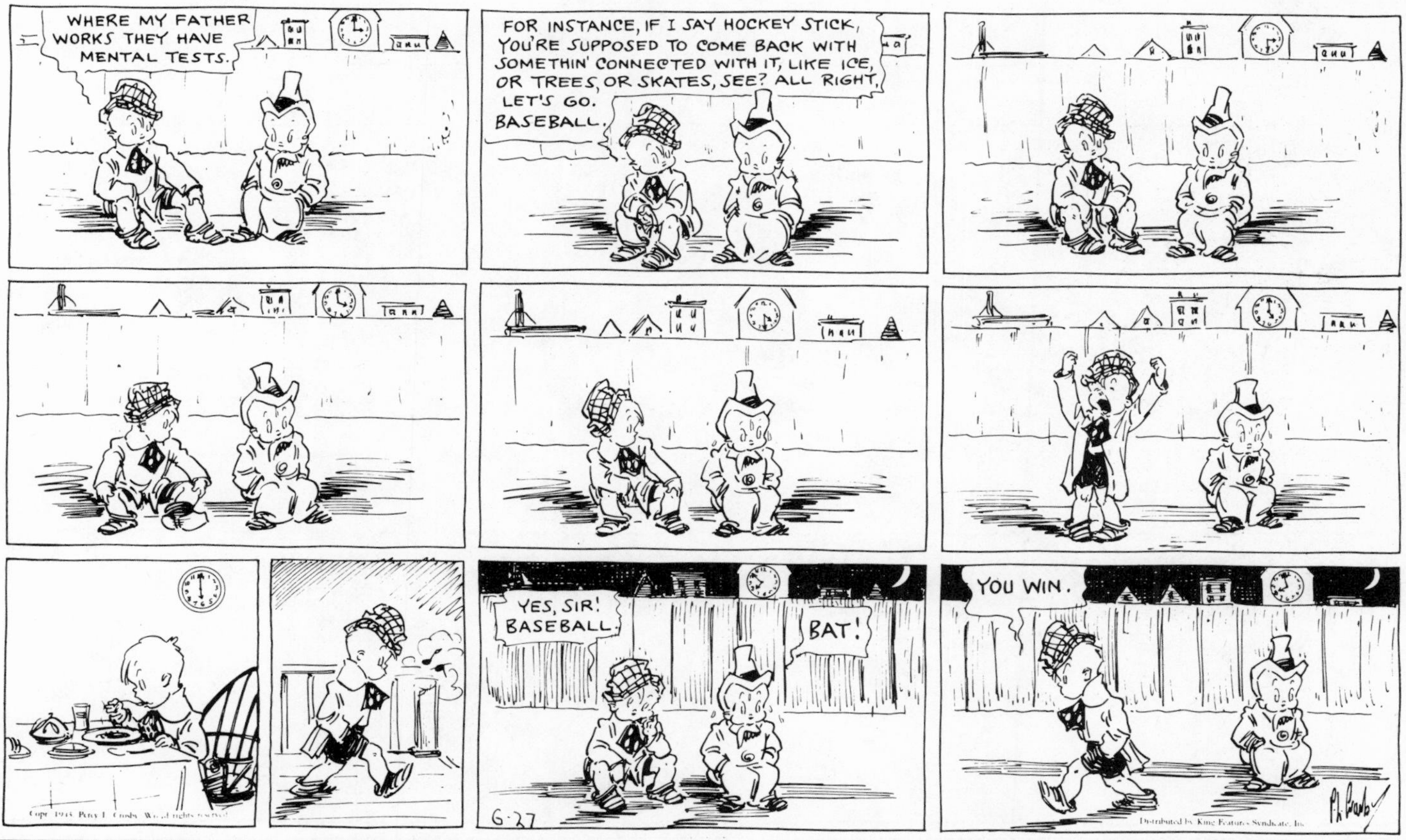
WHERE MY FATHER WORKS THEY HAVE MENTAL TESTS.
FOR INSTANCE, IF I SAY HOCKEY STICK, YOU'RE SUPPOSED TO COME BACK WITH SOMETHIN' CONNECTED WITH IT, LIKE ICE, OR TREES, OR SKATES, SEE? ALL RIGHT, LET'S GO. BASEBALL.
YES, SIR! BASEBALL.
BAT!
6-27
YOU WIN.
Distributed by King Features Syndicate, Inc.

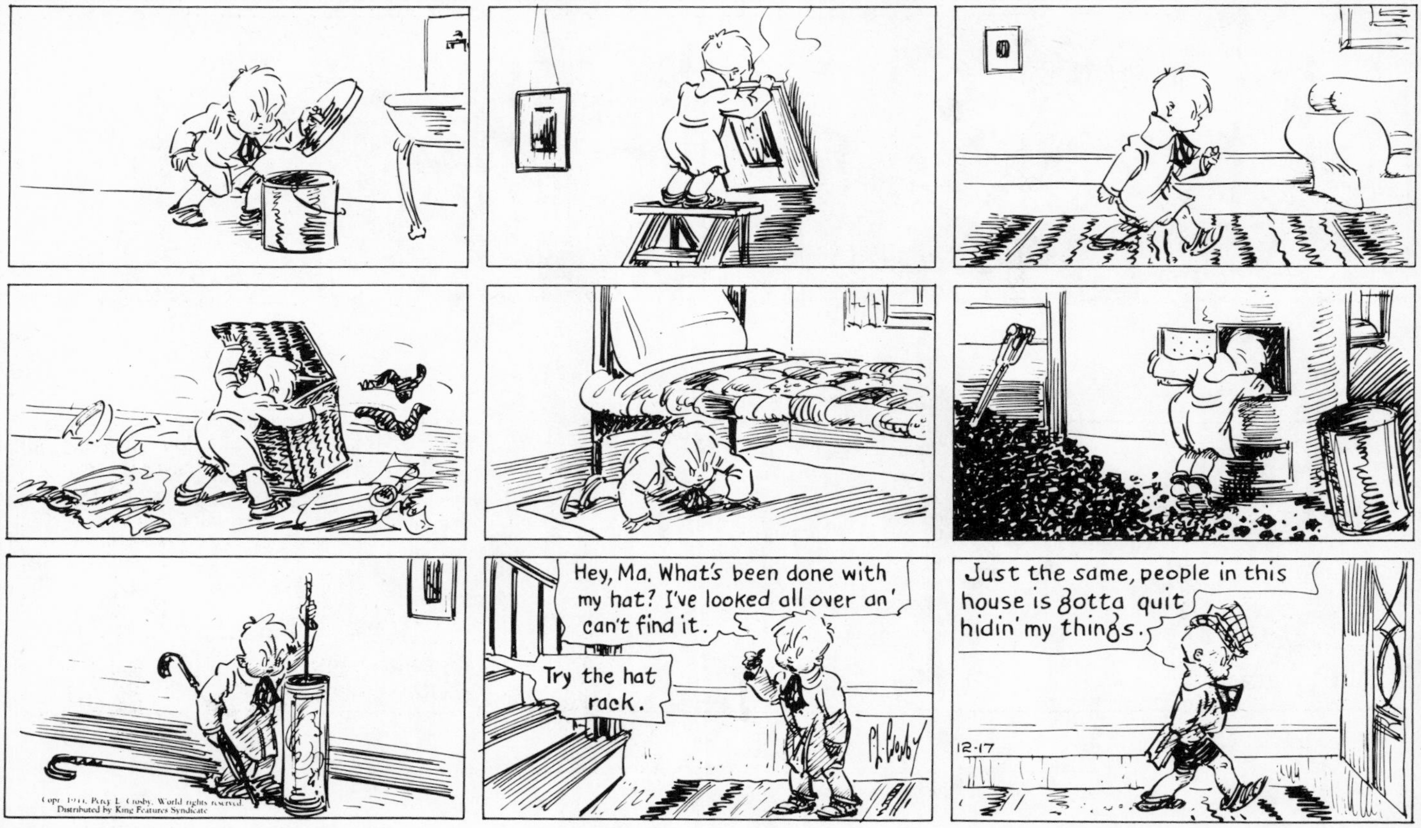
Hey, Ma. What's been done with my hat? I've looked all over an' can't find it.
Try the hat rack.
Just the same, people in this house is gotta quit hidin' my things.
12-17
Copr. Percy L. Crosby. World rights reserved.
Distributed by King Features Syndicate

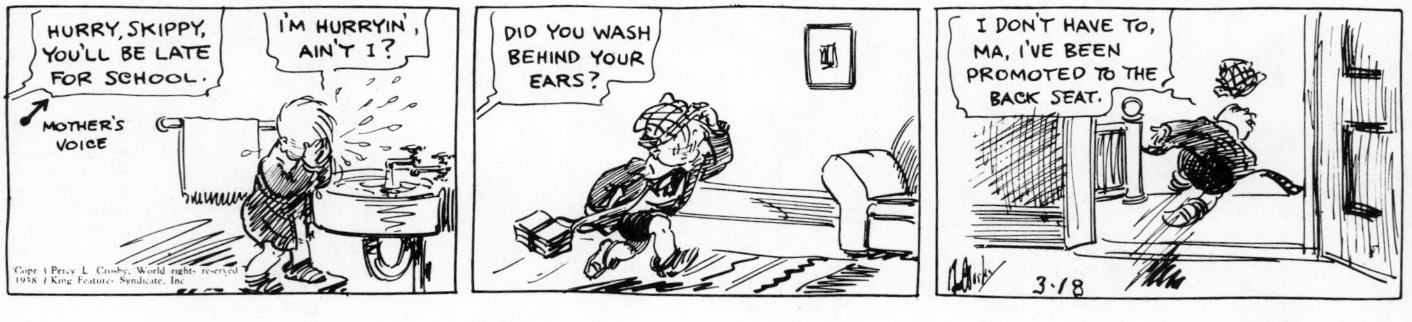
HURRY, SKIPPY, YOU'LL BE LATE FOR SCHOOL.
MOTHER'S VOICE
I'M HURRYIN', AIN'T I?
DID YOU WASH BEHIND YOUR EARS?
I DON'T HAVE TO, MA, I'VE BEEN PROMOTED TO THE BACK SEAT.
3-18
Copr. Percy L. Crosby. World rights reserved
1938 King Features Syndicate, Inc

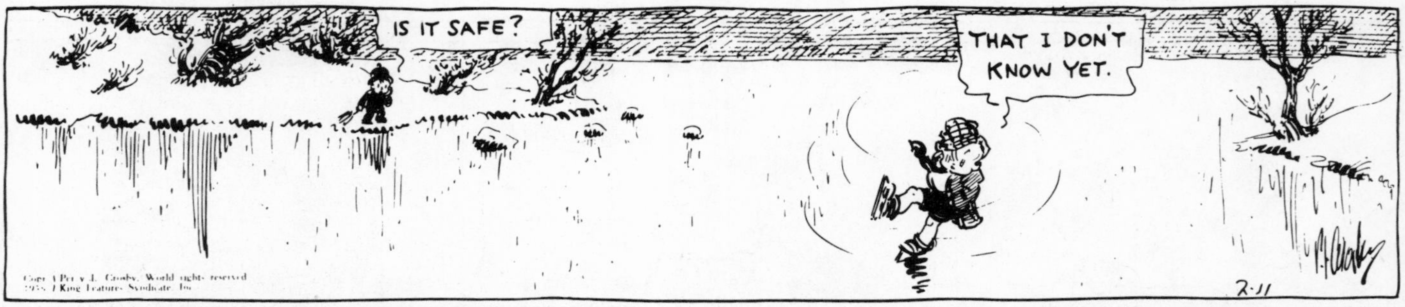
IS IT SAFE?
THAT I DON'T KNOW YET.
2-11
World rights reserved
King Features Syndicate

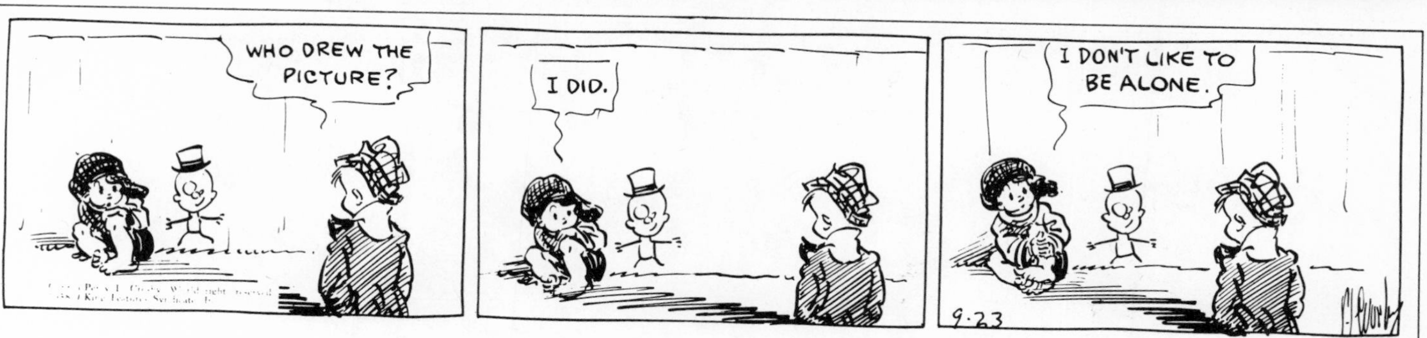
WHO DREW THE PICTURE?
I DID.
I DON'T LIKE TO BE ALONE.
9-23

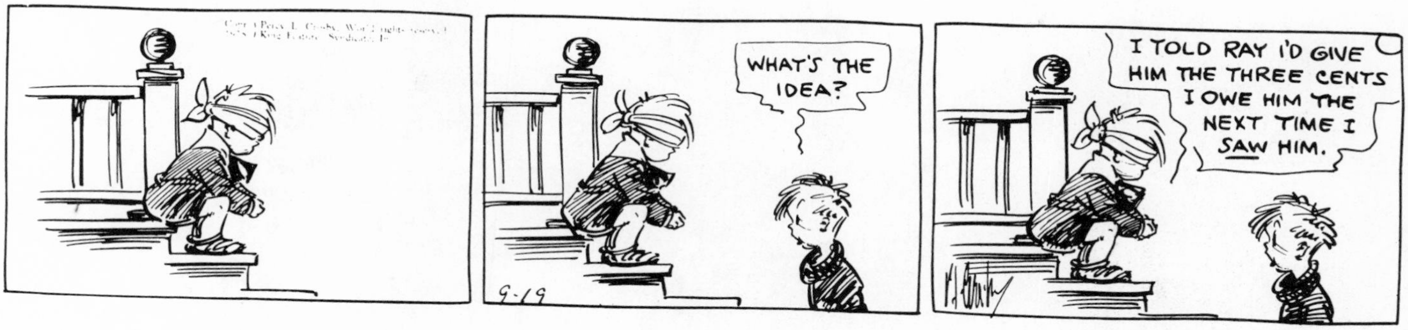
WHAT'S THE IDEA?
9-19
I TOLD RAY I'D GIVE HIM THE THREE CENTS I OWE HIM THE NEXT TIME I SAW HIM.

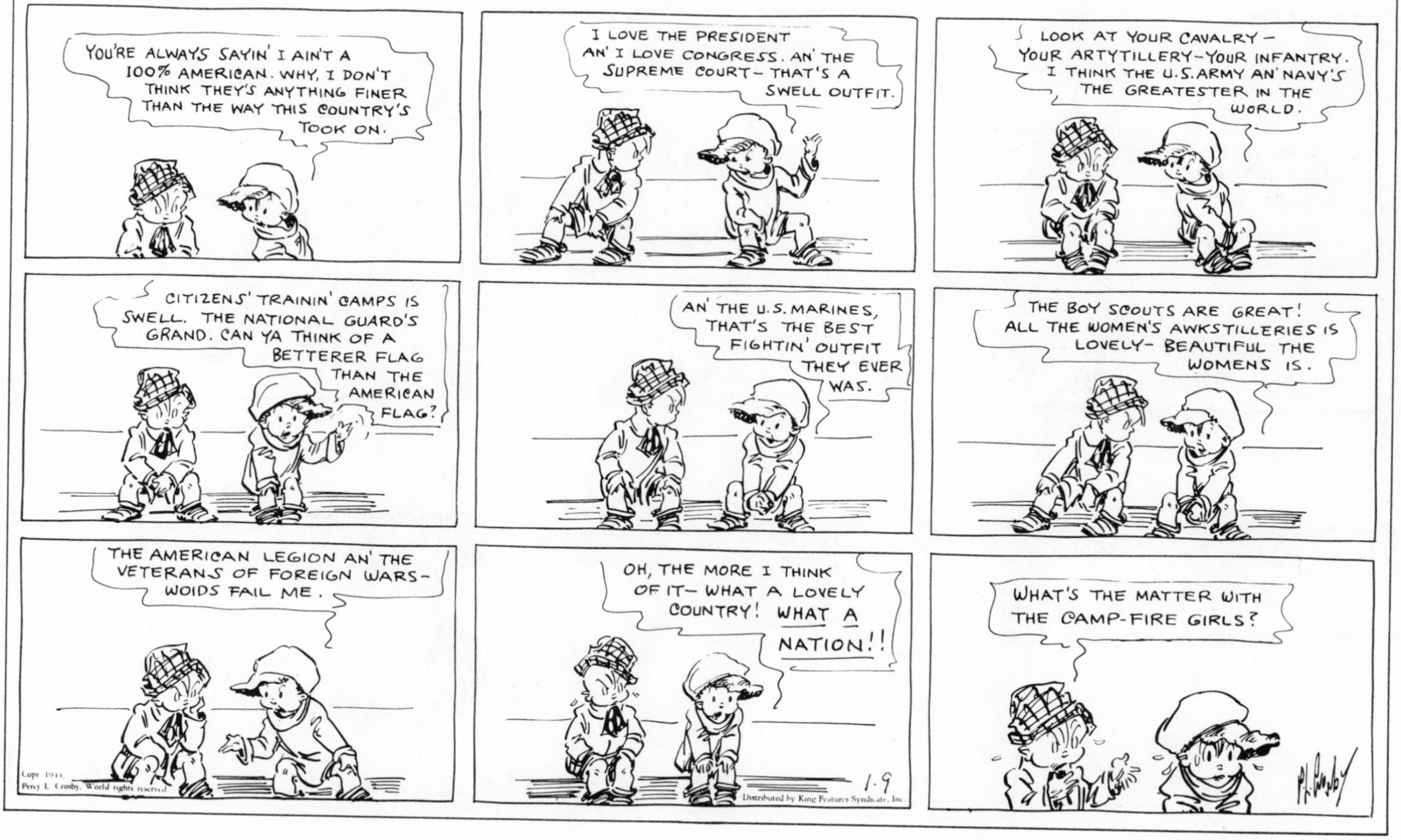
YOU'RE ALWAYS SAYIN' I AIN'T A 100% AMERICAN. WHY, I DON'T THINK THEY'S ANYTHING FINER THAN THE WAY THIS COUNTRY'S TOOK ON.
I LOVE THE PRESIDENT AN' I LOVE CONGRESS. AN' THE SUPREME COURT- THAT'S A SWELL OUTFIT.
LOOK AT YOUR CAVALRY - YOUR ARTYTILLERY- YOUR INFANTRY. I THINK THE U.S. ARMY AN' NAVY'S THE GREATESTER IN THE WORLD.
CITIZENS' TRAININ' CAMPS IS SWELL. THE NATIONAL GUARD'S GRAND. CAN YA THINK OF A BETTERER FLAG THAN THE AMERICAN FLAG?
AN' THE U.S. MARINES, THAT'S THE BEST FIGHTIN' OUTFIT THEY EVER WAS.
THE BOY SCOUTS ARE GREAT! ALL THE WOMEN'S AWKSTILLERIES IS LOVELY- BEAUTIFUL THE WOMENS IS.
THE AMERICAN LEGION AN' THE VETERANS OF FOREIGN WARS- WOIDS FAIL ME.
OH, THE MORE I THINK OF IT- WHAT A LOVELY COUNTRY! WHAT A NATION!!
WHAT'S THE MATTER WITH THE CAMP-FIRE GIRLS?
Percy L. Crosby, World rights reserved
1-9
Distributed by King Features Syndicate, Inc.

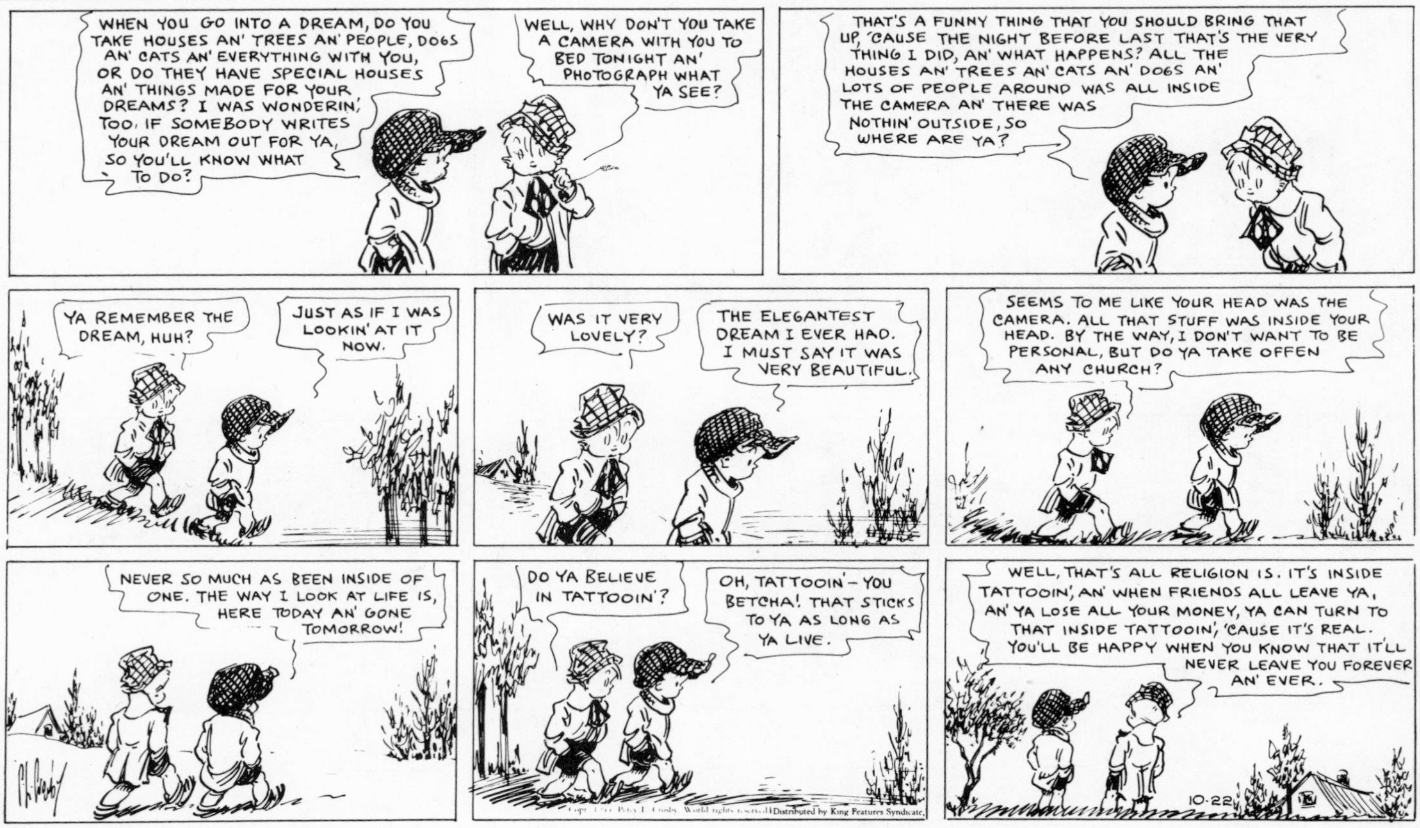
WHEN YOU GO INTO A DREAM, DO YOU TAKE HOUSES AN' TREES AN' PEOPLE, DOGS AN' CATS AN' EVERYTHING WITH YOU, OR DO THEY HAVE SPECIAL HOUSES AN' THINGS MADE FOR YOUR DREAMS? I WAS WONDERIN', TOO, IF SOMEBODY WRITES YOUR DREAM OUT FOR YA, SO YOU'LL KNOW WHAT TO DO?
WELL, WHY DON'T YOU TAKE A CAMERA WITH YOU TO BED TONIGHT AN' PHOTOGRAPH WHAT YA SEE?
THAT'S A FUNNY THING THAT YOU SHOULD BRING THAT UP, 'CAUSE THE NIGHT BEFORE LAST THAT'S THE VERY THING I DID, AN' WHAT HAPPENS? ALL THE HOUSES AN' TREES AN' CATS AN' DOGS AN' LOTS OF PEOPLE AROUND WAS ALL INSIDE THE CAMERA AN' THERE WAS NOTHIN' OUTSIDE, SO WHERE ARE YA?
YA REMEMBER THE DREAM, HUH?
JUST AS IF I WAS LOOKIN' AT IT NOW.
WAS IT VERY LOVELY?
THE ELEGANTEST DREAM I EVER HAD. I MUST SAY IT WAS VERY BEAUTIFUL.
SEEMS TO ME LIKE YOUR HEAD WAS THE CAMERA. ALL THAT STUFF WAS INSIDE YOUR HEAD. BY THE WAY, I DON'T WANT TO BE PERSONAL, BUT DO YA TAKE OFFEN ANY CHURCH?
NEVER SO MUCH AS BEEN INSIDE OF ONE. THE WAY I LOOK AT LIFE IS, HERE TODAY AN' GONE TOMORROW!
DO YA BELIEVE IN TATTOOIN'?
OH, TATTOOIN' – YOU BETCHA! THAT STICKS TO YA AS LONG AS YA LIVE.
WELL, THAT'S ALL RELIGION IS. IT'S INSIDE TATTOOIN', AN' WHEN FRIENDS ALL LEAVE YA, AN' YA LOSE ALL YOUR MONEY, YA CAN TURN TO THAT INSIDE TATTOOIN', 'CAUSE IT'S REAL. YOU'LL BE HAPPY WHEN YOU KNOW THAT IT'LL NEVER LEAVE YOU FOREVER AN' EVER.
Distributed by King Features Syndicate.
10-22

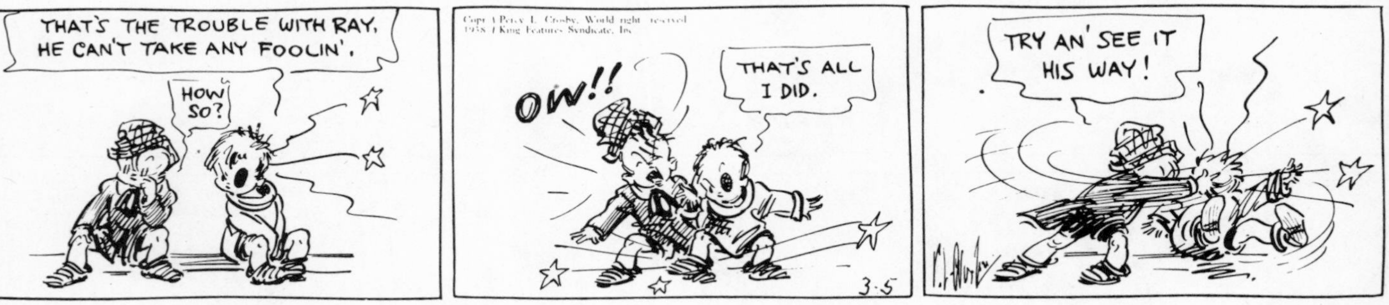
THAT'S THE TROUBLE WITH RAY, HE CAN'T TAKE ANY FOOLIN'.
HOW SO?
OW!!
THAT'S ALL I DID.
TRY AN' SEE IT HIS WAY!
3-5

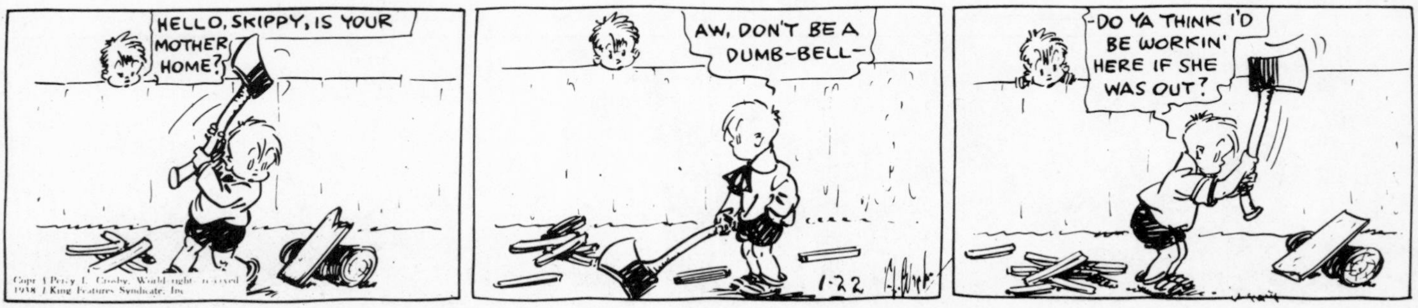
HELLO, SKIPPY, IS YOUR MOTHER HOME?
AW, DON'T BE A DUMB-BELL–
–DO YA THINK I'D BE WORKIN' HERE IF SHE WAS OUT?
1-22

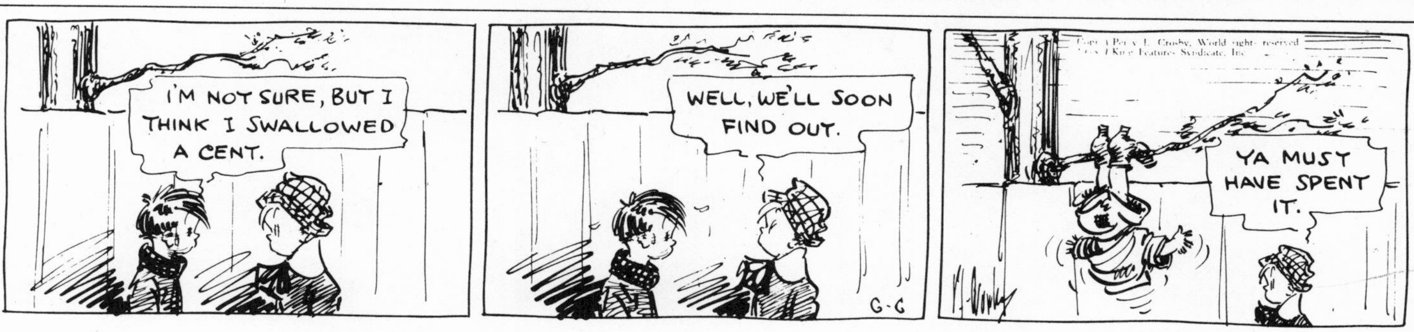
I'M NOT SURE, BUT I THINK I SWALLOWED A CENT.
WELL, WE'LL SOON FIND OUT.
6-6
YA MUST HAVE SPENT IT.

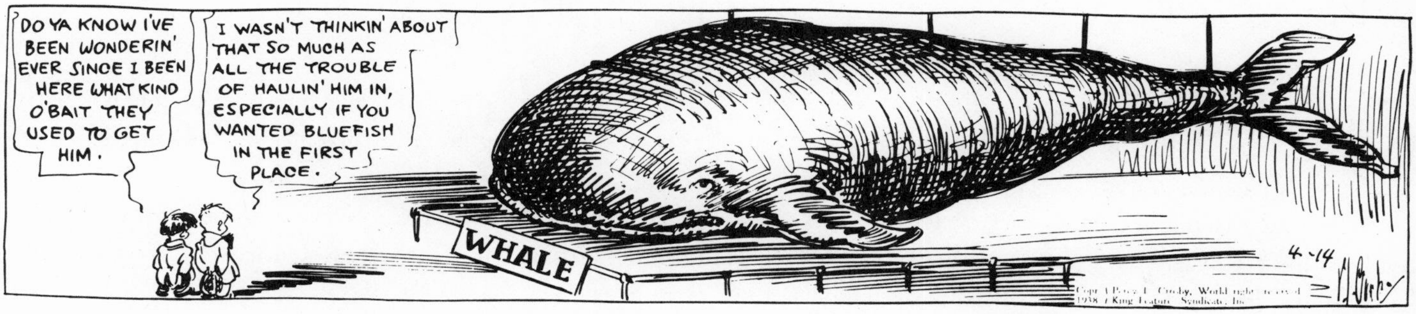
DO YA KNOW I'VE BEEN WONDERIN' EVER SINCE I BEEN HERE WHAT KIND O'BAIT THEY USED TO GET HIM.
I WASN'T THINKIN' ABOUT THAT SO MUCH AS ALL THE TROUBLE OF HAULIN' HIM IN, ESPECIALLY IF YOU WANTED BLUEFISH IN THE FIRST PLACE.
WHALE
4-14

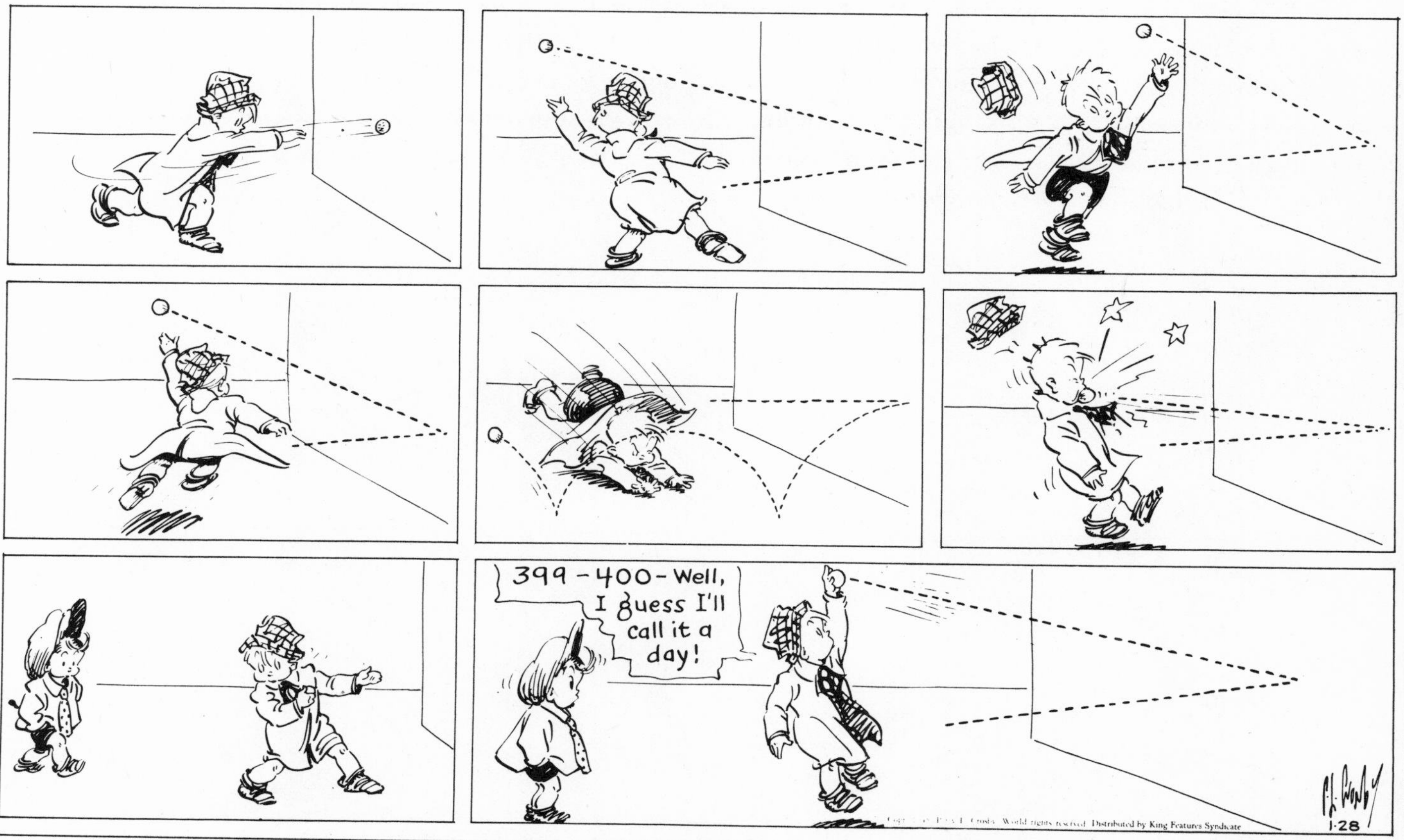
399 - 400 - Well, I guess I'll call it a day!
1-28

One of the country's leading authorities on the comics, Jerry Robinson is himself a cartoonist, as well as an artist, author, and historian whose work ranges from more than thirty adult and juvenile books to the first classic *Batman* comic books—for which he created The Joker, the comics' first supervillain. His recent books include: *The Comics: An Illustrated History of Comic Strip Art*, acclaimed as the definitive study of the genre; *The World's Greatest Comics Quiz;* and *Professor Egghead's Best Riddles*. A past president of the National Cartoonists Society and now president of the American Association of Editorial Cartoonists, he produced the first major gallery show of the cartoon arts (Graham Gallery, New York) as well as the most comprehensive exhibition of the cartoon even held in America, at the Kennedy Center, Washington. He currently lectures on "Cartoon and Comic Strip Art" at the New School for Social Research in New York. Nominated five times for the National Cartoonists Society Reuben Awards, he won the Best Syndicated Panel *(Still Life)*, the Best Special Feature *(Flubs & Fluffs)*, and the Best Comic Book Artist. He was one of three artists selected to represent the United States at the Montreal Pavilion of Humor and received the Presidente Senato Medal at the annual Salon of Humor in Bordighera, Italy. His current daily editorial cartoon of political and social satire, *Life with Robinson*, is nationally syndicated by the Cartoonists & Writers Syndicate.